A History of the United States

You are holding a reproduction of an original work that is in the public domain in the United States of America, and possibly other countries.You may freely copy and distribute this work as no entity (individual or corporate) has a copyright on the body of the work.This book may contain prior copyright references, and library stamps (as most of these works were scanned from library copies).These have been scanned and retained as part of the historical artifact.

This book may have occasional imperfections such as missing or blurred pages, poor pictures, errant marks, etc. that were either part of the original artifact, or were introduced by the scanning process. We believe this work is culturally important, and despite the imperfections, have elected to bring it back into print as part of our continuing commitment to the preservation of printed works worldwide. We appreciate your understanding of the imperfections in the preservation process, and hope you enjoy this valuable book.

A

HISTORY

OF THE

UNITED STATES,

FROM

THE DISCOVERY OF AMERICA

TO

THE RESTORATION OF THE STUARTS.

A

HISTORY

OF THE

UNITED STATES,

FROM THE DISCOVERY OF THE AMERICAN CONTINENT
TO THE PRESENT TIME.

BY GEORGE BANCROFT.

VOL. I.

BOSTON:
PUBLISHED BY CHARLES BOWEN.
LONDON:
R. J. KENNETT.
1834.

Entered, according to Act of Congress, in the year 1834,
By GEORGE BANCROFT,
in the Clerk's Office of the District Court of Massachusetts.

PREFACE.

I HAVE formed the design of writing a History of the United States from the Discovery of the American Continent to the present time. As the moment arrives for publishing a portion of the work, I am impressed more strongly than ever with a sense of the grandeur and vastness of the subject; and am ready to charge myself with presumption for venturing on so bold an enterprise. I can find for myself no excuse but in the sincerity, with which I have sought to collect truth from trust-worthy documents and testimony. I have desired to give to the work the interest of authenticity. I have applied, as I have proceeded, the principles of historical scepticism, and, not allowing myself to grow weary in comparing witnesses or consulting codes of laws, I have endeavored to impart originality to my narrative, by deriving it entirely from writings and sources, which were the contemporaries of the events that are described. Where different nations or different parties have been engaged in the same scenes, I have not failed to examine their respective reports. Such an investigation on any country would be laborious; I need not say how much the labor is increased by the extent of our republic, the differences in the origin and early government of its component parts, and the multiplicity of topics, which require to be discussed and arranged.

Much error had become incorporated with American History. Many of the early writers in Europe were only careful to explain the physical qualities of the country; and the political institutions of dependent colonies were not thought worthy of exact inquiry. The early history was often written with a carelessness, which seized on rumors and vague recollections as sufficient authority for an assertion, which satisfied prejudice by wanton perversions, and which, where materials were not at hand, substituted the inferences of the writer for authenticated facts. These early books have ever since been cited as authorities, and the errors, sometimes repeated even by considerate writers whose distrust was not excited, have almost acquired a prescriptive right to a place in the annals of America. This state of things has increased the difficulty of my undertaking, and, I believe also, its utility; and I cannot regret the labor, which has enabled me to present, under a somewhat new aspect, the early love of liberty in Virginia; the causes and nature of its loyalty; its commercial freedom; the colonial policy of Cromwell; the independent spirit of Maryland; the early institutions of Rhode-Island; and the stern independence of the New-England Puritans. On these and other points, on which I have differed from received accounts, I appeal with confidence to the judgment of those, who are critically acquainted with the sources of our early history.

I have dwelt at considerable length on this first period, because it contains the germ of our Institutions. The maturity of the nation is but a continuation of its youth. The spirit of the colonies demanded freedom from the beginning. It was in this period, that Virginia first asserted the doctrine of popular sovereignty; that the people of Maryland constituted their own government; that New-Plymouth, Connecticut, New Haven, New-Hampshire, Maine, rested their legislation on the popular will, that Massachusetts declared itself a perfect commonwealth.

In the progress of the work I have been most liberally aided by the directors of our chief public libraries; especially the library at Cambridge, on American history the richest in the world, has been opened to me as freely as if it had been my own.

The arrangement of the materials has been not the least difficult part of my labor. A few topics have been anticipated; a few, reserved for an opportunity, where they can be more successfully grouped with other incidents. To give unity to the account of New-Belgium, I reserve the subject for the next volume.

For the work which I have undertaken, will necessarily extend to four or perhaps five volumes. I aim at being concise; but also at giving a full picture of the progress of American Institutions. The first volume is now published separately, and for a double motive. The work has already occasioned long preparation, and its completion will require further years of exertion; I have been unwilling to travel so long a journey alone; and desire, as I proceed, to correct my own judgment by the criticisms of candor. I have thought that the public would recognize the sincerity of my inquiries, and that in those states, where the materials of history have as yet been less carefully collected, and less critically compared, I should make for myself friends, disposed to assist in placing within my reach the sources of information, which are essential to success.

BOSTON, JUNE 16, 1834.

CONTENTS.

INTRODUCTION, p. 1.

CHAPTER I.

EARLY VOYAGES. — FRENCH SETTLEMENTS.

Icelandic Voyages, p. 4—Columbus, 6—First Voyage of the Cabots, 8—Sebastian Cabot, 11—Portuguese Voyage, 15—French Voyages, 16—Verrazzani, 17—Cartier, 21—Roberval, 25—De la Roche, 28—Champlain, 29—French Settlements in Acadia and Canada, 31.

CHAPTER II.

SPANIARDS IN THE UNITED STATES.

Spanish love of Maratime Adventure, p. 34—Ponce de Leon, 36—Diego Miruelo. Fernandez, 39—Grijalva. Garay, 40—De Ayllon, 41—Cortes. Gomez, 43—Pamphilo de Narvaez, 44—Ferdinand de Soto, 47—Soto sails for Florida, 49—Enters Georgia, 52—Alabama, 54—Mississippi, 57—Discovery of the Mississippi River, 58—Soto enters Arkansas and Missouri, 59—Condition of the Native Tribes, 61—Death and Burial of Soto, 63—Spaniards on the Red River, 64—They leave the United States, 65—Missionaries in Florida, 66—Florida Abandoned, 67—Coligny plans a Settlement, 68—Huguenots in South-Carolina, 69—Coligny's Second Colony, 71—Attacked by the Spaniards, 74—St. Augustine, the oldest town in the United States—Massacre of the French, 79—Avenged by de Gourgues, 81—Extent of Spanish Dominions in America, 82.

CHAPTER III.

ENGLAND TAKES POSSESSION OF THE UNITED STATES.

Voyages in the reign of Henry VIII. p. 85—Rut, 86—Hore, 87—Parliament legislates on America, 88—Voyage in search of a Northeast Passage, 89—Frobisher's Three Voyages, 92—Drake in the Oregon Territory,

98—Fisheries, 99—Sir Humphrey Gilbert, 100—His First Voyage, 101—Gilbert and Walter Raleigh, 102—Gilbert perishes at sea, 104—Raleigh's Patent, 104—Voyage of Amidas and Barlow, 105—Raleigh sends a Colony to North-Carolina, 108—Native Inhabitants, 111—Ill success of the Colony, 113—Its Return, 116—Grenville, 117—City of Raleigh, 118—New Colony in North-Carolina, 119—Virginia Dare, 120—Raleigh's Assigns, 122—The Roanoke Colony is lost, 123—Character of Raleigh, 123—Gosnold, 127—Pring, 129—Weymouth, 130—Character of the Early Navigators, 131.

CHAPTER IV.

COLONIZATION OF VIRGINIA.

Condition of England favors Colonization, p. 134—The First Charter, 136—King James legislates for Virginia, 139—Colonists embark, 140—Arrive in Virginia, 141—Jamestown, 142—Distress of the Colony, 143—Energy of Smith, 144—Smith a Captive, 145—Saved by Pocahontas, 147—Smith explores the Chesapeake, 149—Smith's Administration, 150—Second Charter, 152—Lord De La Ware, 153—Character of Smith, 155—The Starving Time, 156—Arrival of Lord De La Ware, 157—Dale introduces Martial Law, 159—Sir Thomas Gates, 160—Third Charter, 162—Pocahontas and Rolfe, 163—Attack on the French, 164—Dale's Administration—Tenure of Lands, 166—Tobacco, 168—Argall, 169—Yeardley—First Colonial Assembly, 170—Virginia acquires Civil Freedom, 173.

CHAPTER V.

SLAVERY.—DISSOLUTION OF THE LONDON COMPANY.

Origin of Negro Slavery, p. 177—Negroes in Portugal and Spain, 178—Native Americans enslaved, 179—Negro Slavery in the West-Indies, 182—Opinions, 184—England and the Slave Trade, 186—New-England and the Slave Trade, 187—Servants, 188—Slavery in Virginia, 189—Wyatt's Administration, 190—The Aborigines, 192—A Massacre and a War, 195—King James contends with the London Company, 199—Commissioners in Virginia, 203—Spirit of the Virginians, 204—Dissolution of the Company, 206—Virginia retains its liberties, 207.

CHAPTER VI.

RESTRICTIONS ON COLONIAL COMMERCE.

Charles I. p. 209—Virginia retains its Liberties, 210—Death of Yeardley, 211—Harvey's Administration, 213—Sir Francis Wyatt's, 218—Sir William Berkeley's Administration, 219—Intolerance, 222—A second

Massacre and War, 223—Prosperity of Virginia, 225—Parliament asserts its supremacy, 227—Origin of the Navigation Act, 228—Commercial Policy of Cromwell, 233—Of the Stuarts, 235—The Parliament and Virginia, 239—Virginia Capitulates, 240—Virginia during the Protectorate, 242—Virginia and its inhabitants, 246.

CHAPTER VII.
COLONIZATION OF MARYLAND.

Discovery, p. 253 — Early Settlements, 254 — Sir George Calvert, 255—Charter, 259—Freedom of Conscience, 262—Opposition of Virginia, 263—First Emigration, 264—Legislative Liberty, 267—Clayborne 268—Civil Liberty, 269—Happiness, 271—An Indian War, 272—Ingle's Rebellion, 273—Religious Liberty, 275—Maryland during the Commonwealth, 278—During the Protectorate, 281—Popular Sovereignty exercised, 284.

CHAPTER VIII.
THE PILGRIMS.

Influence of Calvin, p. 286—Early voyages to New-England, 287—Colony at Sagadahoc, 288—John Smith in New-England, 290—The Council of Plymouth, 292—Its Territory, 294—The Reformation in England, 295—Luther and Calvin, 299—Reign of Edward VI., 300—Hooper, the Puritan, 301—Puritans in exile, 302—Elizabeth and the Church of England, 305—Progress of Puritanism, 306—The Independents, 309—Persecution of all Non-conformists, 311—Is ineffectual, 312—Character of King James, 314—Lord Bacon's tolerant views, 317—Conference at Hampton Court, 319—The Parliament favors the Puritans, 321—Convocation, 321—The Pilgrims, 323—They fly from England, 325—In Holland, 326—They form a Partnership, 330—Sail for America, 331—The Pilgrims at Cape Cod, 334—Landing of the Fathers, 337—The first Winter at Plymouth, 338—Famine, Oppression, 340—Intercourse with the Indians, 341—Weston, 344—Dissolution of the Partnership, 345—Progress and Character of the Old Colony, 346.

CHAPTER IX.
EXTENDED COLONIZATION OF NEW-ENGLAND.

Plymouth Monopoly opposed, p. 351—West, Gorges, Morrell, 353—Contest in Parliament, 354—New-Hampshire, 355—Maine, 358—Nova-Scotia, 359—Conquest and Restoration of Canada, 362—Maine, 363—Conant at Cape Ann, 367—Massachusetts Company purchase Lands, 368—Ob-

xii   CONTENTS.

tain a Charter, 370—First Government, 374—Higginson's Emigration, 375—Religious Independence, 377—Banishment of the Brownes, 378—The Conclusions, 380—Transfer of the Charter, 381—Winthrop's Emigration, 383—First Autumn and Winter, 386—Organization of the Government, 389—Progress of Liberty, 393—The Puritans exclusive, 395—Roger Williams, 397—His exile, 409—He plants Providence, 411—His Character, 412—Hugh Peter and Henry Vane, 414—Order of Nobility proposed, 416—Rejected, 417—Antinomian Controversy, 418—Wheelwright exiled, 424—Rhode-Island and Exeter, 425—Connecticut colonized, 426—Pequod War, 429—Constitution of Connecticut, 435—New-Haven, 436.

CHAPTER X.

THE UNITED COLONIES OF NEW-ENGLAND.

Views of the English Government, p. 438—Liberty threatened, 439—Massachusetts resists, 440—The Council for New-England surrenders its Charter, 441—A quo warranto, 442—Persecutions in England, 443—John Hamden, 445—Massachusetts threatens to declare itself independent, 446—Commotion in Scotland, 447—Condition of New-England, 449—New-Hampshire, 452—Gorton, 453—Confederacy, 454—Miantonomoh, 457—Rhode-Island, 459—Maine, 463—Massachusetts, 467—Political Parties, 469—Vassall and Childe's Disturbance, 473—Long Parliament resisted, 476—Synod, 480—Peace with New-Belgium, 482—Acadia, 482—Cromwell's favor, 483—Laws against Irreligion and Sectarianism, 484—Persecution of Quakers, 490—Free Schools, 497—Harvard College, 498—Character of Puritanism, 499—Restoration of the Stuarts, 508.

ERRATA.

The candid reader is requested to correct the following errata. Page 58, note 3, for Elliot's, read Ellicot's.—p. 59, line 1, for late, read later.—p. 127 and 128, in the margin, for 1603, read 1602.—p. 139, line 10, for charter, read check.—p. 160, note 1, line 1, for Justin, read Peter.—p. 253, line 4, for it was, read it was not.—p. 348, in the margin, for 1622, read 1662.

HISTORY

OF THE

UNITED STATES.

INTRODUCTION.

THE United States of America constitute an essential portion of a great political system, embracing all the civilized nations of the earth. At a period when the force of moral opinion is rapidly increasing, they have the precedence in the practice and the defence of the equal rights of man. The sovereignty of the people is here a conceded axiom, and the laws, established upon that basis, are cherished with faithful patriotism. While the nations of Europe aspire after change, our constitution engages the fond admiration of the people, by which it has been established. Prosperity follows the execution of even justice; invention is quickened by the freedom of competition; and labor rewarded with sure and unexampled returns. Domestic peace is maintained without the aid of a military establishment; public sentiment permits the existence of but few standing troops, and those only along the seaboard and on the frontiers. A gallant navy protects our commerce, which spreads its banners on every sea, and extends its enterprize to every clime. Our diplomatic relations connect us on terms of equality and honest friendship with the chief powers of the world; while we avoid entangling participation in their intrigues, their passions, and their wars. Our national resources are developed by an earnest culture of the arts of peace. Every man enjoys the fruits of his industry; every mind is free to publish its convictions. Our government, by its organization, is necessarily identified with the interests of the people, and relies exclusively on their attachment for its durability and support. Even the enemies of the state, if there are any among us, have liberty to express themselves undisturbed; and are safely tolerated, where reason is left free to combat their errors. Nor is the constitution a dead letter, unalterably fixed; it has the capacity for improvement, receiving into itself whatever changes time and the public will may require; and is safe from decay, so long as that will retains its energy. New states are forming in the wilderness; canals, intersecting our plains and crossing our highlands, open numerous channels to internal commerce; manufactures prosper along our watercourses; the use of steam on our rivers and railroads annihilates distance by the acceleration of speed. Our wealth and population, already giving us a place in the first rank of nations, are so rapidly cumulative, that the former is increased four-fold, and the latter is doubled, in every period of twenty-two or twenty-three years. There is no national debt; the community is opulent; the government economical; and the public treasury full. Religion, neither persecuted nor paid by the state, is sustained by the regard for public morals, and the convictions of an enlightened faith. Intelligence is diffused with unparalleled universality; a free press teems with the choicest productions of all nations and ages. There are more daily journals in the United States than in the world beside. A public document of general interest is, within a month, reproduced in at least a million of copies, and is brought within the reach of every individual in the country. An immense concourse of emigrants of the most various lineage is perpetually crowding to our shores; and the principles of liberty, uniting all interests by the operation of equal laws, blend the discordant elements into harmonious union. Other governments are convulsed by the innovations and reforms of neighboring states; our constitution, fixed in the affections of the people, from whose choice it has sprung, neutralizes the influence of foreign principles, and fearlessly opens an asylum to the virtuous, the unfortunate, and the oppressed of every nation.

And yet it is but little more than two centuries, since the oldest of our states received its first permanent colony. Before that time the whole territory was an unproductive waste. Throughout its wide extent the arts had not erected a monument. Its only inhabitants were a few scattered tribes of feeble barbarians, destitute of commerce, of political connexion, and of morals. The axe and the ploughshare were unknown. The soil, which had been gathering fertility from the repose of centuries, was lavishing its strength in magnificent but useless vegetation. In the view of civilization the immense domain was a solitude.

It is the object of the present work to explain, how the change in the condition of our land has been accomplished; and, as the fortunes of a nation are not controlled by blind destiny, to follow the steps, by which a favoring Providence, calling our institutions into being, has conducted the country to its present happiness and glory.

PART I.

COLONIAL HISTORY.

CHAPTER I.

EARLY VOYAGES. FRENCH SETTLEMENTS.

THE enterprize of Columbus, the most memorable maritime enterprize in the history of the world, formed between Europe and America the communication which will never cease. The national pride of an Icelandic historian[1] has indeed claimed for his ancestors the glory of having discovered the western hemisphere. It is said, that they passed from their own island to Greenland, and were driven by adverse winds from Greenland to the shores of Labrador; that the voyage was often repeated; that the coasts of America were extensively

CHAP. I.
1492.

1000, or 1003.

---

[1] Thormoder Thorfæus, Historia Winlandiæ Antiquæ; printed at Copenhagen, 1705. Compare Crantz's History of Greenland, b. iv. c. i. sec. 7. Robertson's History of America: Notes and Illustrations: Note xvii.
Of American authors, consult Wheaton's History of the Northmen, p. 22—28; Belknap's Am. Biography, v. i. p. 47—58; Yates and Moulton's History of the State of New-York, Part i. p. 110—125; Irving's Life of Columbus, first edition, v. iii. p. 292—300.
These writers, with the exception of Irving, favor the opinion, that the Icelanders reached America. Thorfæus has been consulted quite as often as Sturleson, the original historian, whose work contains the tradition. Franklin's opinion is given but casually in a private letter. Works, v. vi. p. 102.

explored,[1] and colonies established on the shores of Nova Scotia or Newfoundland.[2] It is even suggested, that these early adventurers anchored near the harbor of Boston;[3] or in the bays of New-Jersey.[4] But this belief rests only on a narrative,[5] traditional in its form and obscure in its meaning, although of undoubted antiquity.[6] The geographical details are so vague, that they cannot even sustain a conjecture; the accounts of the mildness of the winter and the fertility of nature in the climes which were visited, are, on any hypothesis, fictitious or exaggerated; while the remark,[7] which should define the length of the shortest winter's day, has received interpretations to suit every latitude[8] from New-York to Cape Farewell. The first discoveries in Greenland were in a high northern latitude; Vinland was but another and more southern portion of the same extensive territory.[9]

Imagination had conceived the idea, that vast inhabited regions lay unexplored in the west; and

---

[1] Moulton's New-York, p. 115.
[2] Belknap's American Biography, v. i. p. 52—56.
[3] Wheaton's History of the Northmen, p. 24.
[4] Moulton's New-York, p. 115, 116.
[5] See the original Icelandic Saga itself, collated from several manuscripts, and printed with a translation into Danish and Latin, in Gerhard Schöning's edition of Historia Regum Norvegicorum, conscripta a Snorrio Sturlæ Filio, v. i. p. 304—325. Copenhagen, 1777, in folio.
[6] On Snorre Sturleson, see Wheaton's Northmen, p.100—109.
[7] Historia Reg. Norv. v. i. p.309. Sól hafdi par eyktar stad oc dagmála stad, um skamm-degi.

[8] Schöning in Hist. Norv. v. i. p. 309, says nine hours; Thorfæus, p. 7, and in the Addenda, p. 2, suits his exposition to the latitude of Newfoundland, and allows eight hours; Pontoppidan (see Belknap's Biog. v. i. p. 52,) reduces the day to six.
[9] This opinion is forced upon me by a perusal of the Saga itself in the Latin version. I find it confirmed in a recent publication—Discovery and Adventures in the Polar Seas and Regions, by Leslie, Jameson, and Murray, p. 87 of the New-York edition of 1832. He that would learn a lesson of historical scepticism, should compare the narrative of Sturleson with the glowing and confident commentary in Moulton.

poets[1] had declared, that empires beyond the ocean would one day be revealed to the daring navigator. But Columbus deserves the undivided glory of having realized that belief. During his lifetime he met with no adequate recompense. The self-love of the Spanish monarch was offended at receiving from a foreigner in his employ benefits too vast for requital; and the contemporaries of the great navigator persecuted the merit, which they could not adequately reward. Nor had posterity been mindful to gather into a finished picture the memorials of his career, till the genius of Irving, with candor, liberality, and original research, made a record[2] of his eventful life, and in mild but enduring colors sketched his sombre inflexibility of purpose, his deep religious enthusiasm, and the disinterested magnanimity of his character.

Columbus was a native of Genoa. The commerce of the middle ages, conducted chiefly upon the Mediterranean Sea, had enriched the Italian republics, and had been chiefly engrossed by their citizens. The path for enterprize now lay across the ocean.

---

[1] By far the most remarkable passage in an early writer, predicting, with much amplification, the future career of discovery, I have seen quoted only in the History of the Reign of Ferdinand and Isabella, the Catholic, of Spain; a history not yet completed, but of which I have been favored by the author with the opportunity of consulting the manuscript. The writer necessarily includes the career of Columbus. I may well omit to dwell upon a topic, which does not directly belong to my subject, and which has been so amply and so successfully treated. The reign of Ferdinand and Isabella is, in part, an American theme, for it connects the political history of Europe and the New World.

[2] Tasso, La Gerusalemme Liberata, c. xv. st. 30—32.

Tu spiegherai, Colombo, a un nuovo polo
Lontane si le fortunate antenne,
Ch' appena seguirà con gli occhi il volo
La fama, ch' ha mille occhi e mille penne.
Canti ella Alcide e Bacco; e di te solo
Basti ai posteri tuoi, ch' alquanto accenne,
Che quel poco darà lunga memoria
Di poema degnissima e d' istoria.

CHAP. I.

1492.

8   JOHN AND SEBASTIAN CABOT.

CHAP. I.
1492.

The states which bordered upon the Atlantic, Spain, Portugal, and England, became competitors for the possession of the New World, and the control of the traffic, which its discovery was to call into being; but the nation, which, by long and successful experience, had become deservedly celebrated for its skill in navigation, continued for a season to furnish the most able maritime commanders. Italians had the glory of making the discoveries, from which Italy derived no accessions of wealth or power.

1497.
June 24.

In the new career of western adventure, the American continent was first discovered under the auspices of the English, and the coast of the United States by a native[1] of England. In the history of maritime enterprize in the New World, the achievements of John and Sebastian Cabot are, in boldness, success, and results, second only to those of Columbus.[2] The wars of the houses of York and Lancaster had ceased; tranquillity and thrifty industry had been restored by the prudent severity of Henry VII.; the spirit of commercial activity began to be successfully fostered; and the marts of England were thronged with Lombard adventurers. The fisheries of the north had long tempted the merchants of Bristol to an intercourse with Iceland;[3] and the nau-

---

[1] Sebastian Cabot declares himself a native of Bristol. The decisive authority is a marginal note of Eden, in the History of the Travayles in the East and West Indies, by R. Eden and R. Willes, 1577, fol. 267. "Sebastian Cabot tolde me, that he was borne in Brystow," &c. Compare Memoir of Cabot, p. 67—69.

[2] S. Parmenius of Buda in Hakluyt's Collection, v. iii. p. 183, edition of 1810, and in i. Mass. Hist. Coll. v. ix. p. 74.

Magnanimus nostra in regione Cabotus, Proximus a magno ostendit sua vela Colombo.

[3] Selden's Mare Clausum, lib. ii. c. 32. Et præsertim versus insulam de Islande, &c. &c.

tical skill, necessary to buffet the storms of the Atlantic, had been acquired in this branch of northern commerce. Nor is it impossible, that some uncertain traditions respecting the remote discoveries, which Icelanders had made in Greenland towards the northwest, "where the lands[1] did nearest meet," should have excited "firm and pregnant conjectures." The magnificent achievement of Columbus, revealing the wonderful truth, of which the germs may have existed in the imagination of every thoughtful mariner, won the admiration which was due to an enterprize that seemed more divine than human, and kindled in the breasts of the emulous a vehement desire to gain as signal[2] renown in the same career of daring; while the politic king of England desired to share in the large returns, which were promised by maritime adventure. It was, therefore, not difficult for John Cabot, a Venetian merchant, residing at Bristol, to engage Henry VII. in plans for discovery. He obtained from that monarch a patent,[3] empowering himself and his three sons, or either of them, their heirs, or their deputies, to sail into the eastern, western, or northern sea, with a fleet of five ships, at their own proper expense and charges; to search for islands, countries, provinces, or regions, hitherto unseen by Christian people; to affix the banners of Eng-

---

[1] Bacon's Hist. of Henry VII. in his works ed. 1824, v. v. p. 149.
[2] Conversation respecting Seb. Cabot, reported in Ramusio, Discorso sopra li Viaggi delle Spetierie, tom. i. fol. 402, ed. sec. 1554. Hak. v. iii. p. 28. Hakluyt's reference to Ramusio is wrong. The passage from Ramusio is also in Eden's Travayles, ed. 1577, fol. 267.—De Thou. Hist. l. xliv. v. ii. p. 530, ed. 1626.
[3] See the patent in Hakluyt, v. iii. p. 25, 26; Chalmer's Polit. Annals, p. 7, 8, and in Hazard's Hist. Coll. v. i. p. 9.

land on any city, island, or continent, that they might find; and, as vassals of the English crown to possess and occupy the territories that might be discovered. It was further stipulated in this "most ancient American state paper of England,"[1] that the patentees should be strictly bound in their voyages to land at the port of Bristol, and to pay to the king one fifth part of the emoluments of the navigation; while the exclusive right of frequenting all the countries that might be found, was reserved, unconditionally and without limit of time, to the family of the Cabots and their assigns. Under this patent, containing the worst features of colonial monopoly and commercial restriction, John Cabot[2] and his celebrated son Sebastian, embarked for the west. Of what tempests they encountered, what mutinies they calmed, no record has been preserved. The discovery of the American continent,[3] probably in the latitude of fifty-six degrees, far, therefore, to the north of the straits of Belle-Isle, among the polar bears, the rude savages, and the dismal cliffs of Labrador, was the fruit of the voyage.

It has been attempted to deprive the father of the glory of having accompanied the expedition. The surest documentary evidence confirms his claims. He and his son Sebastian first approached the continent,

---

[1] Chalmers, p. 7.
[2] Second patent to John Cabot, of Feb. 3, 1498, first printed in Memoir of Sebastian Cabot, p. 75. The extract from the map of Sebastian Cabot is equally explicit. Hakluyt, v. iii. p. 27.
[3] Extract from Cabot's map, in Hakluyt, v. i. p. 27. Ramusio sopra li viaggi, &c. v. i. fol. 402. The map of Ortelius, in his Theatrum Orbis Terrarum, gives the island St. John in latitude fifty-six degrees. The work of Ortelius, in the editions of 1584 and of 1592 is at Cambridge.

DISCOVERY OF THE AMERICAN CONTINENT.   11

which no European had dared to visit, or had known CHAP. I. to exist. The navigators hastened homewards to announce their success. Thus the discovery of our 1497. continent was an exploit of private mercantile adventure; and the possession of the new found "land and isles," was a right, vested by an exclusive patent in the family of a Bristol merchant. Yet the Cabots derived little benefit from the expedition, which their genius had suggested, and of which they alone had defrayed the expense. Posterity hardly remembered, that they had reached the American continent nearly fourteen months before Columbus, on his third voyage, came in sight of the main land; 1498, and almost two years before Americus Vespucci 1499. sailed west of the Canaries. But England acquired Aug. 1. through their energy such a right to North America, as this indisputable priority could confer. Henry VII. and his successors recognized the claims of Spain and Portugal, only so far as they actually occupied the territories, to which they laid pretension; and, at a later day, the English parliament and the English courts derided a title, founded, not upon occupancy, but upon a grant from the Roman Pontiff.[1]

Confidence and zeal awakened; and Henry grew 1498. circumspect in the concession of rights, which now seemed about to become of immense value. A new Feb. patent[2] was issued to John Cabot, less ample in the 3.

---

[1] Proceedings and Debates of the House of Commons, 1620 and 1621, v. i. p. 250, 251.
Seb. Cabot, p. 75. Stow's Chronicle, 1498, in Hakluyt, v. iii. p. 30, 31. Memoir of Cabot, p. 80—86.
[2] See the patent in Memoir of

CHAP. privileges which it conferred; and his son Sebastian,
I.
1498. a native of Bristol, a youthful adventurer of great
benevolence and courtesy, daring in conception and
patient in execution, a man whose active mind for
more than half a century was employed in guiding
the commercial enterprize, which the nations of the
west were developing, and whose extraordinary merits have been recently vindicated with ingenious and
successful diligence, pursued the paths of discovery,
1498. which he, with his father, had opened. A voyage was
again undertaken; purposes of traffic were connected
with it; and the frugal king was himself a partner[1]
in the expenditure. The object of this new expedition
was, in part, to explore "what manner of landes[2] those
Indies were to inhabit;" and perhaps, also, a hope
was entertained of reaching the rich empire of Cathay. Embarking in May, Sebastian Cabot, with a
company of three hundred men, sailed for Labrador,
by way of Iceland; and reached the continent in the
latitude of fifty-eight degrees. The severity of the
cold, the strangeness of the unknown land, and his
declared purpose of exploring the country, induced
him to turn to the south; and, having proceeded along
the shores of the United States to the southern boundary of Maryland,[3] or perhaps to the latitude of

[1] Memoir of Seb. Cabot, p. 85.
[2] Peter Martyr, of Anghiera, d. iii. l. vi. Also in Eden, fol. 124, 125, and in Hakluyt, v. v. p. 283, and Hakluyt, v. iii. p. 29, 30.
Gomara, Historia de las Indias, c. xxxix. The passage is quoted in Eden and Willes, fol. 228, and less perfect in Hakluyt, v. iii. p. 30. Herrera, d. i. l. vi. c. xvi, is confused.

Compare also the conversation in Ramusio, where we must suppose, that the narrator confounds this with the preceding voyage. Ramusio, v. i. fol. 403, or Eden and Willes, fol. 267. I am indebted for the use of Ramusio and of many other valuable works, to Mr. E. Everett, of Charlestown.
[3] Gomara. Hasta treinta i ocho Grados.

Albemarle Sound,[1] want of provisions induced him to return to England.

Curiosity desires to trace the further career of the great seaman, who, with his father, gave a continent to England. The maps which he sketched of his discoveries, and the accounts which he wrote of his adventures, have perished, and the history of the next years of his life is involved in obscurity. Yet it does not admit of a reasonable doubt, that, perhaps in 1517,[2] after he had been in the employment of Ferdinand of Spain, and before he received the appointment of Pilot-Major from Charles V., he sailed from England to discover the North Western passage. The testimony respecting this expedition is confused and difficult of explanation; the circumstances which attended it, are variously related; and are assigned to other and earlier voyages. A connected and probable account can be given only by comparing the evidence, and extracting the several incidents from different and contradictory narratives. Yet the main fact is indisputable; Sebastian Cabot passed through the straits and entered the bay,[3] which, after the lapse of nearly a century, took their name from Hudson. He himself wrote a "discourse of naviga-

---

[1] Peter Martyr. Ut Herculei freti latitudinis fere gradus equarit. &c.

[2] See Eden, in Mem. of Cabot, p. 102, and Thorne's letter, ib. p. 103. Compare chaps. xiii. xiv. and xv. of the Memoir.

The account in Hakluyt, v. iii. p. 591, 592, may give the date of the voyage correctly; but then there must be a gross mistake as to its destination.

Peter Martyr, d. iii. c. v. merits regard. Expectat indies, ut navigia sibi parentur, quibus arcanum hoc naturæ latens jam tandem detegatur. Martis mense anni futuri MDXVI. puto ad explorandum discessurum. Failing to sail from Spain, he went to England.

[3] Anderson was the first of the later writers to mention the fact. Anderson's History of Commerce, v. i. p. 321, under the year 1496. Ed. 1764.

tion," in which the entrance of the strait was laid down with great precision " on a card, drawn by his own hand."[1] He boldly prosecuted his design, making his way through regions, into which it was, long afterwards, esteemed an act of the most intrepid maritime adventure to penetrate, till on June the eleventh, as we are informed from a letter written by the navigator himself, he had attained the altitude of sixty-seven and a half degrees,[2] ever in the hope of finding a passage into the Indian Ocean. The sea was still open; but the cowardice of a naval officer, and the mutiny of the mariners, compelled him to return, though his own confidence in the possibility of effecting the passage remained unimpaired.

The career of Sebastian Cabot was in the issue as honorable, as it had in the opening been glorious. He conciliated universal regard by the placid mildness of his character. Unlike the stern enthusiasm of Columbus, he was distinguished by serenity and contentment. For sixty years, during a period when maritime adventure engaged the most intense public curiosity, he was reverenced for his achievements and his skill.

He had attended the congress,[3] which assembled at Badajoz to divide the islands of the Moluccas between Portugal and Spain; he subsequently sailed to South America, under the auspices of Charles V., though not with entire success.[4] On his return to his

---

[1] Ortelius, Map of America in Theatrum Orbis Terrarum. Eden and Willes, fol. 223. Sir H. Gilbert, in Hakluyt, v. iii. p. 49, 50.
[2] Discorso del Ramusio sopra il terzo volume, &c. Come mi fu scritto, gia molti anni sono, dal Signor Sabastian Gabotto.
[3] Eden's Travayles, fol. 449.
[4] Eden's Travayles, fol. 226.

native land, he advanced the commerce of England by opposing a mercantile monopoly, and was pensioned and rewarded for his merits as the Great Seaman.¹ It was he who framed the instructions for the expedition, which discovered the passage to Archangel.² He lived to an extreme old age, and loved his profession to the last; in the hour of death his wandering thoughts were upon the ocean.³ The discoverer of the territory of our country, was one of the most extraordinary men of his age; there is deep cause for regret, that time has spared so few memorials of his career. Himself incapable of jealousy, he did not escape detraction.⁴ He gave England a continent, and no one knows his burial-place.⁵

It was after long solicitations, that Columbus had obtained the opportunity of discovery. Upon the certainty of success, a throng of adventurers eagerly engaged in voyages, to explore the New World, or to plunder its inhabitants. The king of PORTUGAL, grieved at having neglected Columbus, readily favored an expedition for northern discovery. Gaspar Cortereal⁶ was appointed commander of the enterprize. He reached the shores of North America,

CHAP. I.

1549.

1553.

1500.

Herrera, d. iii. l. ix. c. iii. Compare Herrera, d. iii. l. x. c. i. near the close of the chapter. The Spaniard praises but sparingly the great navigator, who had rendered more important services to England than to Spain.
¹ Hazard's Collection, v. i. p. 23. Memoir of Cabot, p. 185.
² Hakluyt, v. i. p. 251—255. Purchas' Pilgrims, v. i. p. 915.
³ Memoir of Cabot, p. 219.
⁴ Peter Martyr, d. iii. l. vi.; in Eden, fol. 125.

⁵ Memoir of Cabot, p. 220.
⁶ See the leading document on the voyage of Cortereal, in a letter from Pietro Pasqualigo, Venetian Ambassador in Portugal, written to his brother, October 19, 1501, in Paesi novamente ritrovati et Novo Mondo da Alberico Vesputio Florentino intitulato. L. vi. c. cxxv. The original, in the edition of Milan, 1508, and the French translation, are both in the library of Harvard College.

CHAP. I.

1501.

ranged the coast for a distance of six or seven hundred miles, and carefully observed the country and its inhabitants. The most northern point[1] which he attained, was probably about the fiftieth degree. Of the country along which he sailed, he had occasion to admire the brilliant freshness of the verdure, and the density of the stately forests. The pines, well adapted for masts and yards, promised to become an object of gainful commerce. But men were already with the Portuguese an established article of traffic; the inhabitants of the American coast seemed well fitted for labor; and Cortereal freighted his ships

1501. Aug. 8.

with more than fifty Indians, whom, on his return, he sold as slaves. It was soon resolved to renew the expedition; but the adventurer never returned. His death was ascribed to a combat with the natives, whom he desired to kidnap; the name of Labrador, transferred to a more northern coast, is, probably, a memorial of his crime;[2] and is, perhaps, the only permanent trace of Portuguese adventure within the limits of North America.

The FRENCH entered without delay into the competition for the commerce and the soil of America.

1504. Within seven years of the discovery of the continent, the fisheries of Newfoundland were known to the hardy mariners of Brittany and Normandy.[3] The island

---

[1] Herrera, d. i. l. vi. c. xvi. Gomara, c. xxxvii. Also in Eden, fol. 227. Galvano, in Hakluyt, v. iv. p. 419. Purchas, v. i. p. 915, 916. Memoir of Seb. Cabot, b. ii. c. iii. and iv.

[2] Memoir of Seb. Cabot, p. 242.

Compare Navarette, Viages Menores, v. iii. p. 43, 44.

[3] Charlevoix Hist. Gen. de la Nouv. Fr. v. i. p. 3, ed. of 1744, 4to; Champlain's Voyages, v. i. p. 9; Navarette Colleccion, &c. v. iii. p. 176—180, argues against the

VOYAGE OF VERRAZZANI FOR FRANCE.

of Cape Breton acquired its name from their remembrance of home, and in France it was usual to esteem them the discoverers of the country.[1] A map of the gulf of Saint Lawrence was drawn by Denys,[2] a citizen of Honfleur; and the fishermen of the northeast of France derived wealth from the regions, which, it was reluctantly confessed, had been first visited by the Cabots.

The fisheries had for some years been successfully pursued; savages from the northeastern coast had been brought to France;[3] plans of colonization in North-America had been suggested;[4] when at length Francis I., a monarch who had invited Da Vinci and Cellini to transplant the fine arts into his kingdom, employed John Verrazzani, another Florentine, to explore the new regions, which had alike excited curiosity and hope. It was by way of the isle of Madeira, that the Italian, parting from a fleet which had pursued a gainful commerce in the ports of Spain, sailed for America,[5] with a single ship, resolute to make discovery of new countries. The Dolphin, though it had "the good hap of a fortunate name," was overtaken by as terrible a tempest, as mariners ever encountered; and fifty days elapsed, before the continent appeared in view. At length, in the latitude of

CHAP. I.

1506.

1508.
1518.

1523.

1524.
Jan. 17.

---

statement in the text. Compare Memoir of Cabot, p. 316.
[1] Verrazzani, in Hakluyt, v. iii. p. 363.
[2] Charlevoix, Nouv. France, v. i. p. 3 and 4.
[3] Charlevoix, Nouv. France, v. i. p. 4.
[4] Mémoires de l'Amérique, v. i. p. 31, in Holmes, v. i. p. 37.
[5] See Verrazzani's letter to Francis I., from Dieppe, July 8, 1524, in Hakluyt, v. iii. p. 357—364, or in N. Y. Hist. Coll. v. i. p. 45—60. It is also in Ramusio. Compare Charlevoix Hist. N. F. v. i. p. 5—8.

Wilmington,[1] Verrazzani could congratulate himself on beholding land, which had never been seen by any European. But no convenient harbor was found, though the search extended fifty leagues to the south. Returning towards the north, he cast anchor on the coast; all the shore was shoal, but free from rocks and covered with fine sand; the country was flat. It was the coast of North-Carolina. Mutual was the wonder of the inquisitive foreigners, and the mild and feeble natives. The russet color of the Indians seemed like the complexion of the Saracens; their dress was of skins; their ornaments, garlands of feathers. They welcomed with hospitality the strangers, whom they had not yet learned to fear. As the Dolphin ploughed its way to the north, the country seemed more inviting; it was thought, that imagination could not conceive of more delightful fields and forests; the groves, redolent with fragrance, spread their perfumes far from the shore, and gave promise of the spices of the East. The mania of the times raged among the crew; in their eyes the color of the earth argued an abundance of gold. The savages were more humane than their guests. A young sailor, who had nearly been drowned, was revived by the courtesy of the natives; the voyagers robbed a mother of her child, and attempted to kidnap a young woman. Such crimes can be prompted even by the feeble passion of curiosity, and the desire to gratify a vulgar wonder.

The harbor of New-York especially attracted

[1] S. Miller's Discourse in New-York Historical Coll. v. i. p. 23.

notice, for its great convenience and pleasantness; the eyes of the covetous could discern mineral wealth in the hills of New-Jersey.[1]

In the spacious haven of Newport, Verrazzani remained for fifteen days. The natives were "the goodliest people" that he had found in the whole voyage. They were liberal and friendly; yet so ignorant, that, though instruments of steel and iron were often exhibited, they did not form a conception of their use, nor learn to covet their possession.[2]

Leaving the waters of Rhode-Island, the persevering mariner sailed along the whole coast of New-England to Nova Scotia, till he approached the latitude of fifty degrees. The natives of the more northern region were hostile and jealous; it was impossible to conciliate their confidence; they were willing to traffic, for they had learned the use of iron; but in their exchanges they demanded knives and weapons of steel. Perhaps this coast had been visited for slaves; its inhabitants had become wise enough to dread the vices of Europeans.

In July, Verrazzani was once more in France. His own narrative of the voyage is the earliest original account, now extant, of the coast of the United States. He advanced the knowledge of the country; and he gave to France some claim to an extensive territory, on the pretext of discovery.[3]

---

[1] Hakluyt, v. iii. p. 360, 361. N. Y. Hist. Coll. v. i. p. 52, 53. Moulton's New-York, v. i. p. 138, 139.
[2] Hakluyt, v. iii. p. 361. Moulton's New-York, v. i. p. 147, 148.
Miller, in N. Y. Hist. Coll. v. i. p. 25. Belknap's American Biog. v. i. p. 33.
[3] Chalmers' Annals, p. 512 Harris' Voyages, v. ii. p. 348, 349.

CHAP. I.

1525.

1525.
Feb.
24.

1527.

1537.

The historians of maritime adventure agree, that Verrazzani again embarked upon an expedition, from which, it is usually added, he never returned. Did he sail once more under the auspices of France?[1] When the monarch had just lost every thing but honor in the disastrous battle of Pavia, is it probable, that the impoverished government could have sent forth another expedition? Did he relinquish the service of France for that of England? It is hardly a safe conjecture, that he was murdered in an encounter with savages, while on a voyage of discovery, which Henry VIII. had favored.[2] Hakluyt asserts, that Verrazzani was thrice on the coast of America, and that he gave a map of it to the English monarch.[3] It is the common tradition, that he perished at sea, having been engaged in an expedition of which no tidings were ever heard. Such a report might easily be spread respecting a great navigator, who had disappeared from the public view; and the rumor might be adopted by an incautious historian. It is probable, that Verrazzani had only retired from the fatigues of the life of a mariner; and, while others believed him buried in the ocean, he may have long enjoyed at Rome the friendship of men of letters, and the delights of more tranquil employment.[4] Yet such is the obscu-

---

[1] Charlevoix, Nouv. Fr. v. i. p. 7, 8.
[2] Memoir of Sebastian Cabot, p. 271—276.
[3] Hakl. Divers Voyages, 1582, quoted in Mem. of Cabot, p. 272. Of this early work of Hakluyt, there is no copy in the country.
[4] See Annibale Caro, Lettere Familiari, tom. i. let. 12, p. 14, in the edition of Bologna, 1819. The letter has this passage, "A voi, Verrazzano, come a cercatore di nuovi mondi, e delle meraviglie d'essi, non posso ancora dir cosa digna della vostra carta, perchè

rity of the accounts respecting his life, that certainty cannot be established.[1]

But the misfortunes of the French monarchy did not affect the industry of its fishermen; who, amidst the miseries of France, still resorted to Newfoundland. There exists a letter[2] to Henry VIII., from the haven of St. John, in Newfoundland, written by an English captain, in which he declares, he found in that one harbor eleven sail of Normans and one Breton, engaged in the fishery. The French king, engrossed by the passionate and unsuccessful rivalry with Charles V., could hardly respect so humble an interest. But Chabot, Admiral of France,[3] a man of bravery and influence, acquainted by his office with the fishermen, on whose vessels he levied some small exactions[4] for his private emolument, interested Francis in the design of exploring and colonizing the New World. James Cartier, a mariner of St. Malo,

non avemo passate terre, che non sieno state scoperte da voi, o da vostro fratello. This letter is sent to him, as to one of the family of Signor de' Gaddi, at Rome, October 13, 1537. But for the allusion to the brother, there would be little room for doubt. I add a passage from Tiraboschi, in the hope that it may meet the eye of some active member of the New-York Historical Society. The narrative to which it alludes, might easily be obtained, and, as it has never been printed, would be a very appropriate and valuable paper for insertion among the collections of that body.

Nella libreria strozziana in Firenze, oltre la relazione sopracennata, conservasi manoscritta una Narrazione cosmografica, assai be-ne distesi, di tutti i paesi, ch' egli avea in quel viaggio osservati, e da essa raccogliesi, ch' egli ancora avea formato il disegno di tentar per quei mari il passaggio all' Indie orientali. Tiraboschi, v. vii. p. 261, 262.

[1] Ma é tale l' oscurità intorno alle cose di Verrazzani, che nulla possiamo stabilir con certezza. Tiraboschi, v. vii. p. 263, ed. Flor. 1809.

Compare, also, Ensayo Cronologico, à la Historia de la Florida, p. 8. Año, MDXXIV.
[2] Rut's letter to Henry VIII. in Purchas, v. iii. p. 809.
[3] Charlevoix, Nouv. Fr. v. i. p. 8.
[4] Anquetil Hist. de France, v. v. p. 397.

CHAP. was selected to lead the expedition.[1] His several
I. voyages are of great moment; for they had a per-
1534. manent effect in guiding the attention of France to
April
20. the region of the St. Lawrence. It was in April,
that the mariner, with two ships, left the harbor of
May St. Malo; and prosperous weather brought him in
10. twenty days upon the coasts of Newfoundland.
Having almost circumnavigated the island, he turned
to the south, and, crossing the gulf, entered the bay,
which he called des Chaleurs, from the intense heats
July of mid-summer. Finding no passage to the west,
12. he sailed along the coast, and entered the smaller
inlet of Gaspe. There, upon a point of land, at the
entrance of the haven, a lofty cross was raised,
bearing a shield, with the lilies of France and an
appropriate inscription. Henceforth the soil was
to be esteemed a part of the dominions of the French
Aug. king. Leaving the bay of Gaspe, Cartier entered
the great river of Canada, and sailed up its channel,
till he could discern land on either side. As he was
Aug. unprepared to remain during the winter, it then be-
9. came necessary to return; the little fleet embarked
Sept. for Europe, and, in less than thirty days,[2] entered the
5. harbor of St. Malo in security. His native city and
France were filled with the tidings of his discoveries.
The voyage had been easy and successful. Even at

[1] See Cartier's account in Hakluyt, v. iii. p. 250—202. Compare Charlevoix, N. F. v. i. p. 8, 9; Purchas, v. i. p. 931; Ibid, v. iv. p. 1605; Belknap's Am. Biography, v. i. p. 161—163.
[2] Holmes' Annals, v. i. p. 65. "He returned in April." Not so.

Compare Hakluyt, v. iii. p. 261, or Belknap, v. i. p. 163. The excellent annalist rarely is in error, even in minute particulars. He merits the gratitude of every student of American history. Purchas, v. i. p. 931, edition of 1617, says:— " Francis I. sent thither James

this day, the passage to and fro is not often made more rapidly or more safely.

Could a gallant nation, which was then ready to contend for power and honor with the united force of Austria and Spain, hesitate to pursue the career of discovery, so prosperously opened? The court listened to the urgency of the friends of Cartier;[1] a new commission was issued; three well furnished ships were provided by the king; and some of the young nobility of France volunteered to join the new expedition. Solemn preparations were made for departure; religion prepared a splendid pageant, previous to the embarkation; the whole company, repairing to the cathedral, received absolution and the bishop's blessing. The adventurers were eager to cross the Atlantic; and the squadron sailed[2] for the New World, full of hopes of discoveries and plans of colonization in the territory, which now began to be known as New-France.[3]

It was after a stormy voyage, that they arrived within sight of Newfoundland. Passing to the west of that island, on the day of St. Lawrence, they gave the name of that martyr to a portion of the noble gulf which opened before them; a name which has gradually extended to the whole gulf, and to the river. Sailing to the north of Anticosti, they ascended the stream in September, as far as a pleasant harbor in the isle, since

---

Breton." This person can be no other than James Cartier, a Breton.
[1] Charlevoix, N. F. v. i. p. 9.
[2] See the original account of the voyage in Hakluyt, v. iii. p. 262—285. Compare Charlevoix, N. F. v. i. p. 8—15; Belknap's American Biog. v. i. p. 164—178. Purchas is less copious.
[3] Hakluyt, v. iii. p. 285.

CHAP. I.

1535.

called Orleans. The natives received them with unsuspecting hospitality. Leaving his ships safely moored, Cartier, in a boat, sailed up the majestic stream to the chief Indian settlement on the island of Hochelaga. The town lay at the foot of a hill, which he climbed. As he reached the summit, he was moved to admiration by the prospect before him of woods, and waters and mountains. Imagination presented it as the future emporium of inland commerce, and the metropolis of a prosperous province; filled with bright anticipations, he called the hill Mont-Real,[1] and time, that has transferred the name to the island, is realizing his visions. Cartier also gathered of the Indians some indistinct account of the countries, now contained in the north of Vermont and New-York. Rejoining his ships, the winter, rendered frightful by the ravages of the scurvy, was passed, where they were anchored. At the approach of spring, a cross was solemnly erected upon land, and on it a shield was suspended, which bore the arms of France, and an inscription, declaring Francis to be the rightful king of these new found regions. Having thus claimed possession of the territory,

1536. July 6.

the Breton mariner returned to Europe, and once more entered St. Malo in security.

1536, to 1540.

The description which Cartier gave of the country, bordering on the St. Lawrence, furnished arguments[2] against attempting a colony. The intense severity of the climate terrified even the inhabitants of the north of France; and no mines of silver and gold,

[1] Hakluyt, v. iii. p. 272.   [2] Charlevoix, N. F. v. i. p. 20.

no veins, abounding in diamonds and precious stones, had been promised by the faithful narrative of the voyage. Three or four years, therefore, elapsed, before plans of colonization were renewed. Yet imagination did not fail to anticipate the establishment of a state upon the fertile banks of a river, which surpassed all the streams of Europe in grandeur, and flowed through a country, situated between nearly the same parallels as France. Soon after a short peace had terminated the third desperate struggle between Francis I. and Charles V., attention to America was again awakened; there were not wanting men at court, who deemed it unworthy a gallant nation to abandon the enterprize; and a nobleman of Picardy, Francis de la Roque, Lord of Roberval, a man of considerable provincial distinction, sought and obtained[1] a commission. It was easy to confer provinces and plant colonies upon parchment; Roberval could congratulate himself on being the acknowledged lord of the unknown Norimbega, and viceroy, with full regal authority over the immense territories and islands, which lie near the gulf or along the river St. Lawrence. But the ambitious nobleman could not dispense with the services of the former naval commander, who possessed the confidence of the king; and Cartier also received a commission.[2] Its terms merit consideration. He was appointed captain general and chief pilot of the

---

[1] Charlevoix, N. F. v. i. p. 20, 21. The accounts which Charlevoix gives of this expedition, are too full of errors, to require special criticism. We follow the documents and the original accounts in Lescarbot and Hakluyt.
[2] Hazard's Coll. v. i. p. 19—21.

CHAP. I.
1540.

expedition; he was directed to take with him persons of every trade and art; to repair to the newly discovered territory; and to dwell there with the natives.[1] But where were the honest tradesmen and industrious mechanics to be found, who would repair to this New World? The commission gave Cartier full authority to ransack the prisons; to rescue the unfortunate and the criminal; and to make up the complement of his men from their number.[2] Thieves or homicides, the spendthrift or the fraudulent bankrupt, the debtors to justice or its victims, prisoners rightfully or wrongfully detained, excepting only those arrested for treason or counterfeiting money, these were the people, by whom the colony was, in part, to be established.

1541.

May 23.

The division of authority between Cartier and Roberval of itself defeated the enterprize.[3] Roberval was ambitious of power; and Cartier desired the exclusive honor of discovery.[4] They neither embarked in company, nor acted in concert. Cartier sailed[5] from St. Malo the next spring after the date of his commission; he arrived at the scene of his former adventures, ascended the St. Lawrence, and,

---

[1] Converser avec les peuples d'iceux, et avec eux habiter (si besoin est.) Hazard, v. i. p. 20.
[2] Hazard, v. i. p. 20, 21.
[3] See the accounts in Hakluyt, v. iii. p. 286—297. Compare Belknap's American Biography, v. i. p. 178—182.
[4] Hakluyt, v. iii. p. 295.
[5] Holmes, in Annals, v. i. p. 70, 71, places the departure of Cartier May 23, 1540. He follows, undoubtedly, the date in Hak. v. iii. p. 286; which is, however, a misprint, or an error. For, first, the patent of Cartier was not issued till October, 1640; next, the annalist can find no occupation for Cartier in Canada for one whole year; and further, it is undisputed, that Roberval did not sail till April, 1542, and it is expressly said in the account of Roberval's voyage, Hak. v. iii. p. 295, that "Jaques Cartier and his company" were "sent with five sayles the yeere before." Belknap makes a similar mistake. American Biography, v. i. p. 178.

near the site of Quebec, built a fort for the security of his party;[1] but no considerable advances in geographical knowledge appear to have been made. The winter passed in sullenness and gloom. In June of the following year, he and his ships stole away and returned to France, just as Roberval arrived with a considerable reinforcement. Unsustained by Cartier, Roberval accomplished no more than a verification of previous discoveries. Remaining about a year in America, he abandoned his immense viceroyalty. Estates in Picardy were better than titles in Norimbega. His subjects must have been a sad company; during the winter, one was hanged for theft; several were put in irons; and "divers persons, as well women as men," were whipped. By these means quiet was preserved.[2] Perhaps the expedition on its return entered the bay of Massachusetts;[3] the French diplomatists always contended, that Boston was built within the original limits of New-France.

CHAP. I.

1541.

1542.

The commission of Roberval was followed by no permanent results. It is confidently said,[4] that, at a later date, he again embarked for his viceroyalty, accompanied by a numerous train of adventurers; and, as he was never more heard of, he may have perished at sea.

1549.

Can it be a matter of surprise, that, for the next fifty years, no further discoveries were attempted by

1550. to 1600

---

[1] Chalmers places this event in 1545, entirely without reason. Chalmers, p. 82.
[2] Hakluyt, v. iii. p. 296.
[3] See the narrative of the Pilot, in Hakluyt, v. iii. p. 294. "I have been at a bay as farre as 42 degrees between Norumbega and Florida."
[4] Charlevoix, N. F. v. i. p. 22.

VOYAGE OF DE LA ROCHE.

the government of a nation, which had become a prey to the fury of civil wars and the fiercest contests of vindictive fanaticism? There was, indeed, a plan matured among the protestants of France for a colony in what was then called Florida. The melancholy results of this effort of private enterprize will presently be recorded; a government, which could devise the massacre of St. Bartholomew, was neither worthy nor able to lay the foundation of new states.

At length, under the mild and tolerant reign of Henry IV., the star of France emerged from the clouds of blood, treachery and civil war, which had so long eclipsed her glory. The number and importance of the fishing stages had increased;[1] in 1578 there were one hundred and fifty French vessels at Newfoundland, and even regular trading voyages[2] for the purpose of traffic with the natives, now began to be successfully made. At a later period, a French mariner is spoken of, who, before 1609, had made more than forty voyages to the fisheries on the American coast.[3] The purpose of founding a permanent French empire in America was now vigorously renewed. A commission,[4] not less ample than that which had been conceded to Roberval, was issued to the Marquis de la Roche, a nobleman of Brittany. Yet his enterprize entirely failed. He swept the prisons of France in search of emigrants;

---

[1] Hakluyt, v. iii. p. 171. A letter from Parkhurst, in 1578.
[2] Hakluyt, v. iii. p. 233.
[3] Purchas, v. iv. p. 1605; Lescarbot, in Purchas, v. iv. p. 1640.
[4] Charlevoix, N. F. v. i. p. 107. Haliburton's Hist. of N. Scotia, v. i. p. 10, 11. Purchas, v. iv. p. 1807.

those miserable men he established on the isle of Sable; and the wretched exiles, terrified at their solitude and the barrenness of the soil, sighed for their dungeons. After some years, a few, who survived, were once more brought within the influence of civilized life. The miserable men were pardoned for their former crimes. A temporary exile to America was deemed a sufficient commutation for a long imprisonment.

The prospect of gain prompted the next enterprize. A monopoly of the fur-trade, with an ample patent, was obtained by Chauvin;[1] and Pontgravé, a merchant of St. Malo, shared the traffic. The voyage was repeated, for it was lucrative. The death of Chauvin prevented his settling a colony.

A firmer hope of success was entertained, when a company of merchants of Rouen was formed by the governor of Dieppe; and Samuel Champlain,[2] of Brouage, an officer of bravery, experience and skill, was appointed to direct the expedition. For Champlain by his natural disposition "delighted marvellously in these enterprizes," and became the father of the French settlements in Canada. He possessed a clear and penetrating understanding with a spirit of cautious inquiry; untiring perseverance with great mobility; indefatigable activity with the most fearless courage. The account of his first expedition[3] gives proof of sound judgment and accurate observation. It is full of careful remarks on the

---
[1] Charlevoix, N. F. v. i. p. 110, 111.
[2] Charlevoix, N. F. v. i. p. 111.
[3] Purchas' Pilgrims, v. iv. p. 1605—1619. Compare Belknap's American Biog. v. i. p. 322, 323.

manners and character of the savage tribes, not less than of exact details on the geography of the country; and the position of Quebec, an Indian word which signifies a strait, was already selected as the appropriate site for a fort.

Champlain returned to France just before an exclusive patent[1] had been issued to De Monts. The sovereignty of Acadia, the country from the fortieth to the forty-sixth degree of latitude, that is, from Philadelphia to beyond Montreal, the special monopoly of the lucrative fur-trade,[2] the exclusive right of granting the soil, admitting emigrants, controlling trade, and appropriating domains, were some of the privileges, which the charter conceded. The vagabonds,[3] idlers, and men without a profession, as well in the towns as in the villages of France, and all banished men, were doomed to lend him aid. The certain profits of a lucrative monopoly were added to the honors of territorial jurisdiction. Wealth and glory were alike expected.

An expedition[4] was prepared without delay, and left the shores of France, not to return, till a permanent French settlement should be made in America. All New-France was now contained in two ships;[5] which followed the well-known path to Nova Scotia.

---

[1] See the patent, in Purchas, v. iv. p. 1619, 1620, much abridged. It is entire in Hazard, v. i. p. 45—48. Lescarbot, t. ii. p. 432—446.

[2] Charlevoix, N. F. v. i. p. 111.

[3] Prevaloir des vagabonds, personnes oiseuses et sans aveu, &c. Hazard, v. i. p. 47.

[4] On this expedition the materials are ample. Lescarbot, l. iv. in Purchas, v. iv. p. 1620—1641. Compare Charlevoix, N. Fr. v. i. p. 111, and ff. Of American authors, Belknap's Am. Biog. v. i. p. 323, and ff.; Haliburton's Nova Scotia, v. i. p. 12, and ff.; Holmes' Annals, v. i. p. 121, 122; and Williamson's elaborate History of Maine, v. i. p. 188.

[5] Les. in Purchas, v. iv. p. 1620.

FRENCH SETTLEMENT AT PORT ROYAL.

The summer glided away, while the emigrants trafficked with the natives and explored the coasts. The harbor, called Annapolis after the conquest of Acadia by Queen Ann, an excellent harbor, though difficult of access, possessing a small but navigable river, which abounded in fish and is bordered by beautiful meadows, so pleased the imagination of Poutrincourt,[1] a leader in the enterprize, that he sued for a grant of it from De Monts, and, naming it Port Royal, determined to reside there with his family. The company of De Monts made their first attempt at a settlement on the island of St. Croix,[2] at the mouth of the river of the same name. That river subsequently was adopted as the boundary of the United States; and when a question was raised, which stream was the true St. Croix, the remains of the fortification[3] of De Monts assisted to decide the question. Yet the island was so ill suited to the purposes of the colony, that, in the following spring, it was abandoned, and the whole company removed to Port Royal.[4]

The judgment of De Monts clearly saw, that, for an agricultural colony, a situation in a milder climate was more desirable; and, in the view of making a settlement at the south, he explored and claimed for France, the rivers, the coasts and the bays of New-

CHAP. I.

1604.

1604.

1605.

1605.

---

[1] Lescarbot, in Purchas, v. iv. p. 1621. Compare Haliburton's Nova Scotia, v. i. p. 15.
[2] Lescarbot, in Purchas, v. iv. p. 1622; Charlevoix, N. F. v. i. p. 115, 116.
[3] Webber's remark, in note in Holmes' Annals, v. i. p. 122. Compare Belknap's Am. Biog. v. i. p. 326—330; Williamson's Hist. of Maine, v. i. p. 189—191.
[4] Lescarbot, in Purchas, v. iv. p. 1622, and more particularly p. 1626; Chalmers' Annals, p. 82; Charlevoix, N. F. v. i. p. 116; Purchas, v. i. p. 934, 935.

England, as far, at least, as Cape Cod.[1] The numbers and hostility of the savages led him to delay a removal, since his colonists were so few. Yet the purpose remained. Thrice in the spring of the following year did Dupont,[2] his lieutenant, attempt to complete the discovery. Twice he was driven back by adverse winds; and at the third attempt, his vessel was wrecked. Poutrincourt, who had visited France and was now returned with supplies, himself renewed the design;[3] but meeting with disasters among the shoals of Cape Cod, he, too, returned to Port Royal. The soil of New-England was reserved for other emigrants; it was at Port Royal, that a French settlement, on the American continent, was first permanently made; two years before James river was discovered, and three years before a cabin had been raised in Canada.

For it was not till after the remonstrances of the French merchants had effected the revocation of the monopoly of De Monts, and even procured the cancelling of his commission, that a company of merchants of Dieppe and St. Malo, founded Quebec.[4] The design was executed by Champlain, who acted not as a merchant, but as a citizen,[5] aiming not at the profits of trade, but at the glory of founding a state. The city of Quebec was begun; that is to

---

[1] Lescarbot, in Purchas, v. iv. p. 1625, 1626; Belknap's American Biog. v. i. p. 328, 329; Haliburton's Nova Scotia, v. i. p. 19, &c. &c.

[2] Lescarbot, in Purchas, v. iv. p. 1627; Belknap's Am. Biog. v. i. p. 331.

[3] Lescarbot, in Purchas, v. iv. p. 1631—1635; Belknap's American Biog. v. i. p. 332.

[4] Lescarbot, in Purchas, v. iv. p. 1641; Voltaire, Esprit des Mœurs, &c. &c. c. cli.

[5] Charlevoix, Nouv. Fr. v. i. p. 121.

say, rude cottages were framed; a few fields were cleared, and one or two gardens planted. The next year, that singularly bold adventurer, attended but by two Europeans, joined a party of savages in an expedition[1] against the Iroquois. He ascended the Sorel, and explored the lake which lies within our republic, and which, bearing his name, will perpetuate his memory. It was Champlain, who successfully established the authority of the French on the banks of the St. Lawrence, in the territory, then called New-France. Thus the humble industry of the fishermen of Normandy and Brittany promised their country the acquisition of an empire.

CHAP. I.

1609.

[1] Additions to Nova Francia, in Purchas, v. iv. p. 1642, 1643.

CHAPTER II.

SPANIARDS IN THE UNITED STATES.

I HAVE traced the progress of events, which, for a season, gave to France the uncertain possession of Acadia and Canada. The same nation laid claim to large and undefined regions at the southern extremity of our republic. The expedition of Francis I. discovered the continent in a latitude, south of the coast which Cabot had explored; but Verrazzani had yet been anticipated. The claim to Florida, on the ground of discovery, belonged to the Spanish; and was successfully asserted.

Extraordinary success had kindled in the Spanish nation an equally extraordinary enthusiasm. No sooner had the New World revealed itself to their enterprize, than the valiant men, who had won laurels under Ferdinand among the mountains of Andalusia, sought a new career of glory in more remote adventures. The weapons that had been tried in the battles with the Moors, and the military skill that had been acquired in the romantic conquest of Grenada,[1] were now turned against the feeble occupants of America. The passions of avarice and

---

[1] In no work of Irving's is his peculiar genius more beautifully displayed than in the Conquest of Grenada.

religious zeal were strangely blended; and the heroes of Spain sailed to the west, as if they had been bound on a new crusade, where infinite wealth was to reward their piety. The Spanish nation had become infatuated with a fondness for novelties; the "chivalry of the ocean" despised the range of Europe, as too narrow and offering to their extravagant ambition nothing beyond mediocrity. America was the region of romance, where the heated imagination could indulge in the boldest delusions; where the simple natives ignorantly wore the most precious ornaments; and, by the side of the clear runs of water, the sands sparkled with gold. What way soever, says the historian of the ocean, the Spaniards are called, with a beck only, or a whispering voice, to any thing rising above water, they speedily prepare themselves to fly, and forsake certainties under the hope of more brilliant success. To carve out provinces with the sword, to divide the spoils of empires, to plunder the accumulated treasures of some ancient Indian dynasty, to return from a roving expedition with a crowd of enslaved captives and a profusion of spoils, soon became the ordinary dreams, in which the excited minds of the Spaniards delighted to indulge. Ease, fortune, life, all were squandered in the pursuit of a game, where, if the issue was uncertain, success was sometimes obtained, greater than the boldest imagination had dared to anticipate. Is it strange, that these adventurers were often superstitious? The New World and its wealth were in themselves so wonderful, that why should credit be withheld from the wildest fictions? Why should not the hope be indulged, that the laws of nature themselves would yield to the desires of men so fortunate and so brave?

1512. Juan Ponce de Leon was the discoverer of Florida. His youth had been passed in military service in Spain; and, during the wars in Grenada, he had shared in the wild exploits of predatory valor. No sooner had the return of the first voyage across the Atlantic given an assurance of a New World, than he hastened to participate in the dangers and the spoils of adventure in America. He was a fellow 1493. voyager of Columbus in his second expedition. In the wars of Hispaniola he had been a gallant soldier; and Ovando had rewarded him with the government of the eastern province of that island. From the hills in his jurisdiction, he could behold, across the clear waters of a placid sea, the magnificent vegetation of Porto Rico, which distance rendered still more admirable, as it was seen through the transpa- 1508. rent atmosphere of the tropics. A visit to the island stimulated the cupidity of avarice; and Ponce as- 1509. pired to the government. He obtained the station; inured to sanguinary war, he was inexorably severe in his administration; he oppressed the natives; he amassed wealth. But his commission as governor of Porto Rico conflicted with the claims of the family of Columbus; and policy, as well as justice, required his removal. Ponce was displaced.

Yet, in the midst of an archipelago and in the vicinity of a continent, what need was there for a brave soldier to pine at the loss of power over a wild though fertile island? Age had not tempered the love of enterprize; he longed to advance his fortunes by the conquest of a kingdom, and to retrieve a reputation, which was not without a blemish.[1] Besides; the veteran soldier, whose cheeks had been furrowed by hard service, as well as by years, had heard, and had believed the tale, of a fountain, which possessed virtues to renovate the life of those who should bathe in its stream, or give a perpetuity of youth to the happy man who should drink of its ever-flowing waters. So universal was this tradition, that it was credited in Spain, not by all the people and the court only, but by those, who were distinguished for virtue and intelligence.[2] Nature was to discover the secrets, for which alchymy had toiled in vain; and the elixir of life was to flow from a perpetual fountain of the New World, in the midst of a country glittering with gems and gold.

Ponce embarked at Porto Rico, with a squadron of three ships, fitted out at his own expense, for his voyage to fairy land. He touched at Guanahani; he sailed among the Bahamas; but the laws of nature remained inexorable. On Easter Sunday, which the Spaniards call Pascua Florida, land was seen. It was supposed to be an island, and received the name of Florida, from the day on which it was discovered, and from the aspect of the forests, which were then brilliant with a profusion of blossoms, and

---

[1] Peter Martyr, d. iii. l. x. Hakluyt, v. v. p. 307.
[2] Peter Martyr, d. vii. l. vii. in Hakluyt, v. v. p. 422, and d. ii. c. x. p. 251, 252.

gay with the fresh verdure of early spring. Bad weather would not allow the squadron to approach land; at length the aged soldier was able to go on shore, in the latitude of thirty degrees and eight minutes; some miles, therefore, to the north of St. Augustine. The territory was claimed for Spain. Ponce remained for many weeks to investigate the coast which he had discovered; though the currents of the gulf stream, and the islands, between which the channel was yet unknown, threatened shipwreck. He doubled Cape Florida; he sailed among the group, which he named Tortugas; and, despairing of entire success, he returned to Porto Rico, leaving a trusty follower to continue the research. The Indians had every where displayed determined hostility. Ponce de Leon remained an old man; but Spanish commerce acquired a new channel through the gulf of Florida, and Spain a new province, which imagination could esteem immeasurably rich, since its interior was unknown.

The government of Florida was the reward, which Ponce received from the king of Spain; but the dignity was accompanied with the onerous condition, that he should colonize the country, which he was appointed to rule. Preparations in Spain and an expedition against the Carribbee Indians, delayed his return to Florida. When, after a long interval, he proceeded with two ships to take possession of his province and select a site for a colony, his company was attacked by the Indians with implacable fury. Many Spaniards were killed; the survivors were forced to hurry to their ships; Ponce de Leon himself, mortally wounded by an arrow, returned to Cuba to die. So ended the adventurer, who had coveted immeasurable wealth, and had hoped for perpetual youth. The discoverer of Florida had desired immortality on earth, and gained its shadow.[1]

Meantime, commerce may have discovered a path to Florida; and Diego Miruelo, a careless sea captain, sailing from Havana, is said to have approached the coast, and trafficked with the natives. He could not tell distinctly in what harbor he had anchored; he brought home specimens of gold, obtained in exchange for toys; and his report swelled the rumors, already credited, of the wealth of the country. Florida had at once obtained a governor; it now constituted a part of a bishoprick.[2] 1516.

The expedition of Francisco Fernandez, of Cordova, leaving the port of Havana, and sailing west by south, discovered the province of Yucatan and the bay of Campeachy. He turned his prow to the north; but, whatever may be asserted by careless historians, he was, by no means, able to trace the coast to any harbor which Ponce de Leon had visited.[3] At a place, where he had landed for supplies 1517.

---

[1] On Ponce de Leon, I have used Herrera, d. i. l. ix. c. x. xi. and xii., and d. i. l. x. c. xvi. Peter Martyr, d. iv. l. v., and d. v. l. i. and d. vii. l. iv. In Hakluyt, v. v. p. 320, 333, and 416. Gomara, Hist. Gen. de las Ind. c. xlv. Garcilaso de la Vega, Hist. de la Florida, l. i. c. iii, and l. vi. c. xxii. p. 2, 3, and 266 of the folio edition of 1723. Cardenas z Cano, Ensayo Cronologico para la Hist. Gen. de la Florida, d. i. p. 1, 2 and 5. Edition of 1723, in folio. The author's true name is Andres Gonzalez de Barcia. Navarette, Colleccion, v. iii. p. 50—53. Compare, also, Eden and Willes, fol. 228, 229. Purchas, v. i. p. 957.

[2] Florida del Inca, Vega, l. i. c. ii. Ensayo Cronologico, d. i. Año. MDXVI.

[3] The Ensayo Cronologico para la Historia General de la Flori-

CHAP. of water, his company was suddenly assailed, and
II.
he himself mortally wounded.

1518. The pilot whom Fernandez had employed, soon conducted another squadron to the same shores. The knowledge already acquired, was extended, and under happier auspices; and Grijalva, the commander of the fleet, explored the coast from Yucatan towards Panuco. The masses of gold which he collected, the rumors of the empire of Montezuma, its magnificence and its extent, heedlessly confirmed by the costly presents of the unsuspecting natives, were sufficient to inflame the coldest imagination; and excited the enterprize of Cortes. The voyage did not reach the shores of Florida.[1]

1518. But while Grijalva was opening the way to the conquest of Mexico, the line of the American coast, from the Tortugas to Panuco, is said to have been examined, yet not with care, by an expedition, which was planned, if not conducted, by Francisco Garay, the governor of Jamaica. The general outline of the gulf of Mexico, now became known.[2] Garay encountered the determined hostility of the natives; a danger which eventually proved less disastrous to him, than the rivalry of his own countrymen. The adventurers in New-Spain would endure no independent neighbor; the governor of Jamaica became

---

da is not sufficiently discriminating. The error asserted with confidence in d. i. Año. MDXVII, p. 3, may be corrected from Bern. Diaz. l. i. c. i. and iii. Gomara, c. lii. Ant. de Solis, l. i. c. vi. Peter Martyr, d. iv. l. i. and ii. Herrera, d. ii. l. ii. c. xvii. and xviii.

[1] Peter Martyr, d. iv. l. iii. and iv., in Hakluyt, v. v. p. 315—319. Herrera, d. ii. l. iii. c. ix. Bern. Diaz. l. i. c. ix—xiv. Ant. de Solis, l. i. c. vii., viii., ix. Gomara, c. xlix.

[2] Peter Martyr, d. v. l. i. Gomara, c. xlvi.

SOUTH-CAROLINA—VAZQUEZ DE AYLLON.

involved in a career, which, as it ultimately tempted him to dispute the possession of a province with Cortes, led him to the loss of fortune and an inglorious death. The progress of discovery along the southern boundary of the United States, was but little advanced by the expedition, of which the circumstances have been variously related.[1]

A voyage for slaves brought the Spaniards still further upon the northern coast. A company of seven, of whom the most distinguished was Lucas Vazquez de Ayllon, fitted out two slave ships from St. Domingo, in quest of laborers for their plantations and mines. From the Bahama islands, they passed to the coast of South-Carolina, a country which was called Chicora. The Combahee[2] river received the name of the Jordan; the name of St. Helena, given to a cape, now belongs to the sound. The natives of this region had not yet had cause to fear Europeans; their natural fastnesses had not yet been invaded; and if they fled at the approach of men from the slave ships, it was rather from timid wonder, than from a sense of peril. Gifts were interchanged; a liberal hospitality was offered to the strangers; confidence was established. At length the natives were invited to visit the ships; they came in cheerful throngs; the decks were covered. Immediately the ships weighed anchor; the sails were unfurled, and the prows turned towards St. Domingo. Husbands were torn from their wives

1520.

---

[1] Peter Matyr, d. v. l. i. Gomara, c. xlvii. Ensayo Cronologico, p. 3, 4. Herrera, d. ii. l. iii. c. vii. T. Southey's History of the West Indies, v. i. p. 135. [2] Holmes' Annals, v. i. p. 47.

CHAP. and children from their parents. Thus the seeds of
II.
war were lavishly scattered, where peace only had
1520. prevailed, and enmity was spread through the regions, where friendship had been cherished. The crime was unprofitable, and was finally avenged. One of the returning ships foundered at sea, and the guilty and guiltless perished; many of the captives in the other sickened and died.

The events that followed, mark the character of the times. Vazquez, repairing to Spain, boasted of his expedition, as if it entitled him to reward, and the emperor, Charles V., acknowledged his claim. In those days, the Spanish monarch conferred a kind of appointment, which, however strange its character may appear, still has its parallel in history. Not only were provinces granted; countries were distributed to be subdued; and Lucas Vazquez de Ayllon begged to be appointed to the conquest of Chicora. After long entreaty he obtained his suit.

1524. The issue of the new and bolder enterprize was disastrous to the undertaker. He wasted his fortune
1525. in preparations; his largest ship was stranded in the river Jordan; many of his men were killed by the natives, whom wrongs had quickened to active resistance; he himself escaped only to suffer from wounded pride; and, conscious of having done nothing worthy of being remembered, the sense of humiliation is said to have hastened his death.[1]

[1] Peter Martyr, d. vii. c. ii. Gomara, c. xlii. Herrera, d. iii. l. viii. c. viii. Herrera's West Indies, in Purchas, v. iv. p. 869. Galvano, in Hakluyt, v. iv. p. 429. Ensayo Cronologico, p. 4, 5, 6. 8, 9, and 160. Roberts' Florida, p. 27, 28. Virginia richly valued, &c. &c., the Portuguese Relation, chapter xiv. Hakluyt, v. v. p. 503.

The love of adventure did not wholly extinguish the desire for maritime discovery. When Cortes was able to pause from his success in Mexico, and devise further schemes for ingratiating himself with the Spanish monarch, he proposed to solve the problem of a northwest passage; the secret which has so long baffled the enterprize of the most courageous and persevering navigators. He deemed the existence of the passage unquestionable, and by simultaneous voyages along the American coast, on the Pacific and on the Atlantic, he hoped to complete the discovery, to which Sebastian Cabot had pointed the way.[1]

The design of Cortes remained but the offer of loyalty. A voyage to the northwest was really undertaken by Stephen Gomez, an experienced naval officer, who had been with Magellan in the first memorable passage into the Pacific Ocean. The expedition was decreed by the council for the Indies, in the hope of discovering the northern route to India, which, notwithstanding it had been sought for in vain, was yet universally believed to exist. His ship entered the bays of New-York and New-England; on old Spanish maps, that portion of our territory is marked as the land of Gomez. Failing to discover a passage, and fearful to return without success and without a freight, he filled his vessel with robust Indians, to be sold as slaves. Brilliant expectations had been raised; and the conclusion

[1] Quarta Carta, o Relacion de Don Fernando Cortes. S. xix. in Barcia's Historiadores Primitivos, tom. i. p. 151, 152. The same may be found in the Italian of Ramusio, v. iii. fol. 294, ed. 1665.

was esteemed despicably ludicrous. The Spaniards scorned to repeat their voyages to the cold and frozen north; in the south, and in the south only, they looked for "great and exceeding riches."[1] The adventure of Gomez had no political results. It had been furthered by the enemies of Cabot, who was, at that time, in the service of Spain; and it established the reputation of the Bristol mariner.[2]

But neither the fondness of the Spanish monarch for extensive domains, nor the desire of the nobility for new governments, nor the passion of adventurers for undiscovered wealth, would permit the abandonment of the conquest of Florida. Permission to invade that territory was next sought for and obtained by Pamphilo de Narvaez, a man of no great virtue or reputation. This is the same person, who had been sent by the jealous governor of Cuba to take Cortes prisoner, and who, after having declared him an outlaw, was himself easily defeated. He lost an eye in the affray, and his own troops deserted him. When brought into the presence of the man, whom he had promised to arrest, he said to him, "Esteem it great good fortune, that you have taken me captive." Cortes replied, and with truth, "It is the least of the things I have done in Mexico."[3]

The territory, placed at the mercy of Narvaez, extended to the river of Palms; further, therefore, to the west, than the territory which was after-

---

[1] Peter Martyr, d. viii. l. x.
[2] Peter Martyr, d. vi. l. x., and d. viii. l. x. Gomara, c. xl. Herrera, d. iii. l. viii. c. viii.
[3] Cortes, Carta de Relacion, c. i. s. xxxv—xxxvii. in Barcia, v. i. p. 36—44. Gomara, Cronica de la Nueva España, c. xcvi—ci.

wards included in Louisiana. His expedition was as unsuccessful as his attempt against Cortes, but it was memorable for its disasters. Of three hundred men, of whom eighty were mounted, but four or five returned. The valor of the natives, thirst, famine and pestilence, the want of concert between the ships and the men set on shore, the errors of judgment in the commanders, rapidly melted away the unsuccessful company. It is not possible to ascertain, with exactness, the point where Narvaez first landed in Florida; probably it was at a bay, a little east of the meridian of Cape St. Antony, in Cuba; it may have been, therefore, not far from the bay now called Appalachee. The party soon struck into the interior; they knew not where they were, nor whither they were going; and followed the directions of the natives. These, with a sagacity, careful to save themselves from danger, described the distant territory as full of gold; and freed themselves from the presence of troublesome guests, by exciting a hope that covetousness could elsewhere be gratified. The town of Appalachee, which was thought to contain immense accumulations of wealth, proved to be an inconsiderable collection of wigwams. It was probably in the region of the bay of Pensacola, that the remnant of the party, after a ramble of eight hundred miles, finally came again upon the sea, in a condition of extreme penury. Here they manufactured rude boats, in which none but desperate men would have embarked; and Narvaez and most of his companions, after having passed nearly six months in Florida,

CHAP. II.

1528.

April.

June.

Sept. 22.

perished in a storm near the mouth of the Mississippi.[1] One ship's company was wrecked upon an island; most of those who were saved, died of famine. The four who ultimately reached Mexico by land, succeeded only after years of hardships. The simple narrative of their wanderings, their wretchedness, and their courageous enterprize, could not but have been full of marvels; the story, which one of them published, and of which the truth was affirmed, on oath, before a magistrate, is disfigured by bold exaggerations and the wildest fictions.[2] The knowledge of the bays and rivers of Florida on the gulf of Mexico, was not essentially increased; the strange tales of miraculous cures, of natural prodigies and of the resuscitation of the dead, were harmless falsehoods; the wanderers, on their return, persevered in the far more fatal assertion, that Florida was the richest country in the world.[3]

The assertion was readily believed, even by those, to whom the wealth of Mexico and Peru was familiarly known. To no one was credulity more disas-

---

[1] Prince, p. 86, is a safe interpreter.

[2] On Narvaez, the original work is, Naufragios de Alvar Nuñez Cabeça de Vaca, en la Florida; in Barcia, t. ii. p. 1—43. There is an Italian version in Ramusio, v. iii. fol. 310—330. The English version in Purchas, v. iv. p. 1499—1528, is from the Italian. Compare Gomara, c. xlvi.; Herrera, d. iv. l. iv. c. iv—vii., and d. iv. l. v. c. v.; Purchas, v. i. p. 957, 958—962. Examen Apologetico, in Barcia, v. i. at the end, does not confer authority on Nuñez. The scepticism of Benzo, in Calveto's Novæ Novi Orbis Historiæ, l. ii. c. xiii. p. 206, is praiseworthy. Compare, also, Roberts' Florida, p. 28—32, and a note in Holmes' Annals, v. i. p. 59; Ensayo Cronologico, p. 10; Vega, l. ii. p. ii. c. vi. Hints may also be found scattered through Vega's Historia de la Florida, and in the Portuguese account in Hakluyt, v. v.

[3] Virginia Valued; The Portuguese Account; Dedication in Hakluyt, v. v. p. 479; Herrera, d. iii. l. viii. c. viii.; Hakluyt, v. v. p. 484.; Vega, l. i. c. v.

trous than to Ferdinand de Soto, a native of Xeres, and now an ambitious courtier. He had himself gained fame and fortune by military service in the New World. He had been the favorite companion of Pizarro in the conquest of Peru, where he had distinguished himself for conduct and valor. At the storming of Cusco, he had surpassed his companions in arms. He assisted in arresting the unhappy Atahualpa; and he shared in the immense ransom, with which the credulous Inca purchased the promise of freedom. Perceiving the angry divisions, which were threatened by the jealousy of the Spaniards in Peru, Soto had seasonably withdrawn, with his share of the spoils; and now appeared in Spain to enjoy his reputation, to display his opulence, and to solicit advancement. His reception was triumphant; success of all kinds awaited him. The daughter of the distinguished nobleman, under whom he had first served as a poor adventurer, became his wife;[1] and the special favor of Charles V. invited his ambition to prefer a large request. It had ever been believed, that the depths of the continent at the north concealed cities as magnificent and temples as richly endowed, as any which had yet been plundered within the limits of the tropics. Soto desired to rival Cortes in glory and surpass Pizarro in wealth. Blinded by avarice and the love of power, he repaired to Valladolid and demanded permission to conquer Florida at his own cost; and Charles V. readily conceded to so renowned a commander the govern-

---

[1] Portuguese Relation, c. i.; in Hakluyt, v. v. p. 483.

ment of the isle of Cuba, with absolute power over the immense territory, to which the name of Florida was still vaguely applied.[1]

No sooner was the design of the new expedition published in Spain, than the wildest hopes were indulged. How brilliant must be the prospect, since even the conqueror of Peru was willing to hazard his fortune and the greatness of his name? Adventurers assembled as volunteers; many of them, people of noble birth and good estates. Houses and vineyards, lands for tillage, and rows of olive trees in the Ajarrafe of Seville, were sold, as in the times of the crusades, to obtain the means of military equipments. The port of San Lucar of Barrameda was crowded with those, who hastened to solicit permission to share in the enterprize. Even soldiers of Portugal desired to be enrolled for the service. A muster was held; the Portuguese appeared in the glittering array of burnished armor; and the Castilians, brilliant with hopes, were "very gallant with silk upon silk." Soto gave directions as to the armament; from the numerous aspirants, he selected for his companions six hundred men in the bloom of life, the flower of the peninsula; many persons of good account, who had sold estates for their equipments, were obliged to remain behind.[2]

---

[1] Portuguese Relation, c. i. p. 483.; Vega, l. i. c. i.; Herrera, d. iv. l. i. c. iii.

[2] Port. Rel. c. ii. and iii.; Vega, l. i. c. v. and vi. When the authorities vary, I follow that, which is least highly colored, and give the smaller number. Vega says there were a thousand men, and he strenuously vindicates his own integrity and love of truth. He wrote from the accounts of eye-witnesses, whom he examined; he was not himself an eye-witness.

SOTO EMBARKS FOR CUBA AND FLORIDA.

The fleet sailed as gaily as if it had been but a holiday excursion of a bridal party. In Cuba the precaution was used to send vessels to Florida to explore a harbor; and two Indians, brought as captives to Havana, invented such falsehoods, as they perceived would be acceptable. They conversed by signs; and the signs were interpreted as affirming, that Florida abounded in gold. The news spread great contentment; Soto and his troops were restless with longing for the hour of their departure to the conquest of "the richest country which had yet been discovered."[1] The infection spread in Cuba; and Vasco Porcallo, an aged and a wealthy man, lavished his fortune in magnificent preparations.[2]

Soto had been welcomed in Cuba by long and brilliant festivals and rejoicings. At length, all preparations were completed; leaving his wife to govern the island, he and his company, full of unbounded expectations, embarked for Florida; and, in about a fortnight, his fleet anchored in the bay of Spiritu Santo.[3] The soldiers went on shore; the horses, between two and three hundred in number, were disembarked; and the men of the expedition stood upon the soil which they had so eagerly desired to tread. Soto would listen to no augury but that of success; and, like Cortes, he refused to retain his ships, lest they should afford a temptation to retreat. Most of them were sent to Havana.[4]

CHAP. II.

1538.

1539. May.

[1] Portuguese Relation, c. i. 489; Vega, l. i. part i. c. i. p. 23.
[2] Vega, l. i. c. xii. [4] Portuguese Relation, c. x. p.
[3] Portuguese Relation, c. vii. p. 493.

The aged Porcallo, a leading man in the enterprize, soon grew alarmed, and began to remember his establishments in Cuba. It had been a principal object with him to obtain slaves for his estates and mines; despairing of success, and terrified with the marshes and thick forests, he also sailed for the island, where he could enjoy his wealth in security. Soto was indignant at the desertion; but concealed his anger.[1]

And now began the nomadic march of the adventurers; a numerous body of horsemen, besides infantry, completely armed; a force, exceeding in numbers and equipments, the famous expeditions against the empires of Mexico and Peru. Every thing was provided, that experience in former invasions and the cruelty of avarice could suggest; chains[2] for captives, and the instruments of a forge; arms of all kinds then in use, and bloodhounds as auxiliaries against the feeble natives;[3] ample stores of food, and, as a last resort, a drove of hogs, which would soon swarm in the favoring climate, where the forests and the Indian maize furnished abundant sustenance. It was a roving expedition of gallant freebooters in quest of fortune. It was a romantic stroll of men, whom avarice rendered ferocious, through unexplored regions, over unknown paths; wherever rumor might point to the residence of some chieftain with more than Peruvian wealth, or the ill-interpreted signs of the ignorant natives might seem to promise

---

[1] Portuguese Relation, c. x. p. 493; Vega, l. ii. part i. c. xi. and xii. p. 39, 40.
[2] Port. Rel. c. xi. and xii. p. 496.
[3] Portuguese Relation, c. xi. p. 494, 495, and elsewhere.

a harvest of gold. Religious zeal was also united with avarice; there were not only cavalry and foot-soldiers, with all that belongs to warlike array; twelve priests, besides other ecclesiastics, accompanied the expedition. Florida was to become catholic, during the scenes of robbery and carnage that were to follow. Ornaments, such as are used at the service of mass,[1] were carefully provided; every festival was to be kept; every religious practice to be observed. As the troop marched through the wilderness, each solemn procession, which the usages of the church enjoined, was scrupulously instituted.[2]

The wanderings of the first season brought the company from the bay of Spiritu Santo to the country of the Appalachians, east of the Flint river, and not far from the head of the bay of Appalachee.[3] The names of the intermediate places cannot be identified. The march was tedious and full of dangers. The Indians were always hostile; two captives of the former expedition escaped; a Spaniard, who had been kept in slavery from the time of Narvaez, could give no accounts of any country where there was silver or gold.[4] The guides would purposely lead the Castilians astray, and involve them in morasses; even though death, under the fangs of the bloodhounds, was the certain punishment. The whole company grew dispirited, and desired the

---

[1] Portuguese Relation, c. xix. p. 512.
[2] Portuguese Relation, c. xx, p. 514, and in various places speaks of the Friars and Priests. Vega. l. i. c. vi. p. 9; L iv. c. vi. p. 179, 180, and elsewhere. Herrera in many places confirms the statement.
[3] Portuguese Relation, c. xii.; Vega, l. ii. part ii. c. iv.; McCulloh's Researches, p. 524.
[4] Port. Relation, c. ix. p. 492.

CHAP. II.
1539.

governor to return, since the country opened no brilliant prospects. "I will not turn back," said Soto, "till I have seen the poverty of the country with my own eyes."¹ The hostile Indians, who were taken prisoners, were in part put to death, in part enslaved. These were led in chains, with iron collars about their necks; their service was, to grind the maize and to carry the baggage. An exploring party discovered Ochus,² the harbor of Pensacola; and a message was sent to Cuba, desiring that in the ensuing year supplies for the expedition might be sent to that place.³

1540.
Mar. 3.

Early in the spring of the following year, the Spaniards renewed their march, with an Indian guide, who promised to lead the way to a country, governed by a woman, and where gold so abounded, that the art of melting and refining it was understood. He seemed to describe the process so well, that the credulous Spaniards took heart, and exclaimed, "He must have seen it, or the devil has taught him." They, therefore, eagerly hastened to the northeast; they passed the Alatamaha; they admired the fertile valleys of Georgia, rich, productive, and full of good rivers. They passed a northern tributary of the Alatamaha, and a southern branch of the Ogechee; and, at length, came upon the Ogechee

April itself, which, in April, flowed with a full channel and a strong current. Much of the time, the Spaniards were in wild solitudes; they suffered for want of

¹ Portuguese Relation, c. xi. p. 495.
² Ibid, c. xii. p. 498.
³ Compare Portuguese Relation, c. vii—xii. and Vega, l. ii. part i. and ii. p. 23—106.

salt and of meat. Their Indian guide would have been torn in pieces by the dogs, if he had not still been needed to assist the interpreter. Of four Indian captives, whom they questioned, one bluntly answered, he knew no country such as they described; and the governor ordered him to be burnt, for what was esteemed his falsehood. The sight of the execution quickened the invention of his companions; and the Spaniards made their way to the small Indian settlement of Cutifa-Chiqui. A dagger and a rosary were found here; the story of the Indians traced them to the expedition of Vazquez de Ayllon; and a two days' journey would reach, it was believed, the harbor of St. Helena. The soldiers thought of home; and desired, either to make a settlement on the fruitful soil around them, or to return. The governor was "a stern man, and of few words." Willingly hearing the opinions of others, he was inflexible, when he had once declared his own mind; and all his followers, "condescending to his will," continued to indulge delusive hopes.[1]

The direction of the march was now to the north; to the comparatively sterile country of the Cherokees,[2] and in part through a district, in which gold is now found. The inhabitants were poor but gentle; they liberally offered such presents, as their habits of life permitted, deer skins and wild hens. Soto could hardly have crossed the mountains, so as to

[1] Portuguese Relation, c. xiii. and xiv. p. 498—504; Vega, l. iii. c. ii.—xvii. Compare Belknap's American Biography, v. i. p. 188. I cannot follow McCulloh, p. 524.
[2] Nuttall's Arkansas, p. 124; McCulloh's Researches, p. 524.

enter the basin of the Tennessee river;[1] it seems, rather, that he passed from the head-waters of the Savannah, or the Chattahouchee, to the head-waters of the Coosa. The name of Canasauga, a village, at which he halted, is still given to a branch of the latter stream. For several months, the Spaniards were in the valleys, which send their waters to the bay of Mobile; Chiaha was an island, distant about a hundred miles from Canasauga. An exploring party, which was sent to the north, were appalled by the aspect of the Apalachian chain, and pronounced the mountains impassable. They had looked for mines of copper and gold; and their only plunder was a buffalo robe.[2]

In the latter part of July, the Spaniards were at Coosa. In the course of the season, they had occasion to praise the wild grape of the country, the same probably which has since been thought worthy of culture. A southerly direction led the train to Tuscaloosa; nor was it long before the wanderers reached a considerable town on the Alabama, above the junction of the Tombecbee; and about one hundred miles, or six days' journey, from Pensacola. The town was called Mavilla, or Mobile, a name, which is still preserved, and applied, not to the bay only, but to the river, after the union of its numerous tributaries. The Spaniards, tired of lodging in the fields, desired to occupy the town; the Indians rose to resist the invaders, whom they distrusted and

---

[1] Martin's Louisiana, v. i. p. 11. 504—506; Vega, l. iii. c. xvii.—
[2] Portuguese Relation, c. xv. p. xxii. p. 134—141.

feared. A battle ensued; the terrors of their cavalry gave the victory to the Spaniards. I know not if a more bloody Indian fight ever occurred on the soil of the United States; the town was set on fire; and two thousand five hundred Indians are said to have been slain, suffocated, or burned. They had fought with desperate courage; and, but for the flames, which consumed their light and dense settlements, they would have effectually repulsed the invaders. "Of the Christians, eighteen died;" one hundred and fifty were wounded with arrows; twelve horses were slain and seventy hurt. The flames had not spared the baggage of the Spaniards; it was within the town, and was entirely consumed.[1]

Meanwhile, ships from Cuba had arrived at Ochus, now Pensacola. Soto was too proud to confess his failure. He had made no important discoveries; he had gathered no stores of silver and gold, which he might send to tempt new adventurers; the fires of Mobile had consumed the curious collections which he had made. It marks the resolute cupidity and stubborn pride, with which the expedition was conducted that he determined to send no news of himself, until, like Cortes, he had found some rich country.[2]

But the region above the mouth of the Mobile was populous and hostile; and yet too poor to promise plunder. Soto retreated towards the north; his troops already reduced, by sickness and warfare,

---

[1] Port. Rel. c. xvii.—xix. p. 508 —512. Vega is very extravagant in his account of the battle. L. iii. c. xxvii.—xxxi. On localities, compare Belknap, v. i. p. 189, 190, and McCulloh, p. 525.
[2] Portuguese Relation, c. xix. p. 512, 513.

CHAP. II.

Dec. 17.

1541.

Mar.

to five hundred men. A month passed away, before he reached winter quarters at Chicaça, a small town in the country of the Chickasaws, in the upper part of the state of Mississippi; probably on the western bank of the Yazoo. The weather was severe, and snow fell; but maize was yet standing in the open fields. The Spaniards were able to gather a supply of food, and the deserted town, with such rude cabins as they added, afforded them shelter through the winter. Yet no mines of Peru were discovered; no ornaments of gold adorned the rude savages; their wealth was the harvest of corn, and wigwams were their only palaces; they were poor and independent; they were hardy and loved freedom. When spring[1] opened, Soto, as he had usually done with other tribes, demanded of the chieftain of the Chickasaws two hundred men to carry the burdens of his company. The Indians hesitated. Human nature is the same in every age and in every climate. Like the inhabitants of Athens in the days of Themistocles, or those of Moscow of a recent day, the Chickasaws, unwilling to see strangers and enemies occupy their homes, in the dead of night, deceiving the sentinels, set fire to their own village, in which the Castilians were encamped.[2] On a sudden, half the houses were in flames; and the loudest notes of the war-whoop rung through the air. The Indians, could they have acted with calm bravery, might have gained an easy and entire victory; but they trembled

[1] Vega says January. L. iii. c. xxxvi. p. 166.
[2] Vega, l. iii. c. xxxvi., xxxvii. and xxxviii. Port. Account, c. xx. xxi.

at their own success; and feared the unequal battle against weapons of steel. Many of the horses had broken loose; these, terrified and without riders, roamed through the forest, of which the burning village illuminated the shades, and seemed to the ignorant natives the gathering of hostile squadrons. Others of the horses perished in the stables; most of the swine were consumed; eleven of the Christians were burned, or lost their lives in the tumult. The clothes which had been saved from the fires of Mobile, were destroyed, and the Spaniards, now as naked as the natives, suffered from the cold. Weapons and equipments were consumed or spoiled. Had the Indians made a resolute onset on this night or the next, the Spaniards would have been unable to resist. But in a respite of a week, forges were erected, swords newly tempered, and good ashen lances were made, equal to the best of Biscay. When the Indians attacked the camp, they found "the Christians" prepared.

CHAP. II.

1541.

Mar. 15.

All the disasters which had been encountered, far from diminishing the boldness of the governor, served only to confirm his obstinacy by wounding his pride. Should he, who had promised greater booty than Mexico or Peru had yielded, now return as a defeated fugitive, so naked, that his troops were clad only in skins and mats of ivy? The search for some wealthy region was renewed; the caravan marched still further to the west. For seven days, it struggled through a wilderness of forests and marshes; and, at length, came to Indian settlements in the

April 25.

CHAP. vicinity of the Mississippi. Soto was himself the
II.
first of Europeans to behold the magnificent river,
1541. which rolled its immense current of waters through
the splendid vegetation of a wide, alluvial soil. The
lapse of nearly three centuries has not changed the
character of the stream; it was then described as
more than a mile broad; flowing with a strong
current, and forcing, by the weight of its waters, a
channel of great depth. The water was always
muddy; trees and timber were continually floating
down the stream.[1]

The Spaniards were guided to the Mississippi by
natives; and were directed to one of the usual
crossing places, probably at the lowest Chickasaw
bluff,[2] not far from the thirty-fifth parallel of latitude.[3] The Indians from the opposite shore brought
gifts of fish, and loaves, made of the fruit of the
persimmon. They showed a desire to offer resistance; but soon becoming convinced of the superior
power of the strangers, the feeble nations acknowledged their weakness, and, ceasing to defy an enemy,
who could not be resisted, they suffered injury without attempting open retaliation. The canoes of the

[1] Portuguese Account, c. xxii. Vega, l. iv. c. iii. I never rely on Vega alone.
[2] Portuguese Account, c. xxxii. and xxxiii. taken in connexion with the more diffuse account of Vega, l. iv. c. v.
[3] Belknap's Am. Biog. v. i. p. 192, "Within the thirty-fourth degree." Andrew Elliot's Journal, p. 125. "Thirty-four degrees and ten minutes." Martin's Louisiana, v. i. p. 12. "A little below the lowest Chickasaw bluff." Nuttall's Travels in Arkansas, p. 248. "The lowest Chickasaw bluff." McCulloh's Researches, p. 526. "Twenty or thirty miles below the mouth of the Arkansas river." Mr. Nuttall, p. 248, and elsewhere, gives to Vega, the praise which is due to the more accurate account of the Portuguese gentleman. The two are by no means identical. Vega deserves to have excited scepticism.

natives were too weak to transport horses; almost a month expired, before boats, large enough to hold three horsemen each, were constructed for crossing the river. At length the Spaniards embarked upon the Mississippi; and Europeans were borne to its western bank.

The Kaskaskias Indians, at that time, occupied a province southwest of the Missouri;[1] Soto had heard its praises; he believed in its vicinity to mineral wealth; and he determined to visit its towns. In ascending the Mississippi, the party was often obliged to wade through morasses; at length, they came, as it would seem, upon the district of Little Prairie, and the dry and elevated lands, which extend towards New-Madrid. The wild fruits of that region were abundant; the pecan nut, the mulberry, and the two kinds of wild plums, furnished the natives with articles of food. At Pacaha, the northernmost point, which Soto reached near the Mississippi, he remained forty days. The spot cannot be identified; but the accounts of the amusements of the Spaniards contain ample confirmation of the truth of the narrative. Fish were taken, such as are now found in the fresh waters of that region; one of them, the spade fish,[2] the strangest and most whimsical production of the muddy streams of the west, so rare, that, even now, it is hardly to be found in any museum, is accurately described by the best historian of the expedition.[3]

---

[1] Charlevoix, Journal Historique, let. xxviii. Nuttal's Arkansas, p. 82, 250 and 251. McCulloh disagrees; p. 526—528.

[2] Platirostra Edentula.

[3] Portuguese Relation, c. xxiv. "There was another fish, called a peele fish; it had a snout of a

60   SPANIARDS IN MISSOURI AND ARKANSAS.

CHAP. II.
1541.
Aug.

An exploring party, which was sent to examine the regions to the north, reported that it was almost a desert. The country, still nearer the Missouri, was said by the Indians to be thinly inhabited; the bison abounded there so much, that no maize could be cultivated; and the few inhabitants were hunters. Soto turned, therefore, to the west and northwest; and plunged still more deeply into the interior of the continent. The highlands of White river, more than two hundred miles from the Mississippi, were probably the limit of his ramble in this direction. The mountains offered neither gems nor gold; and the disappointed adventurers marched to the south.[1] They passed through a succession of towns, of which the position cannot be fixed; till, at length, we find them among the Tunicas,[2] near the hot springs and saline tributaries of the Washita.[3] It was at Autiamque, a town on the same river,[4] that they passed the winter; they had arrived at the settlement through the country of the Kappaws.

The native tribes, every where on the route, were found in a state of civilization beyond that of nomadic tribes. They had fixed places of abode; and subsisted upon the produce of the fields, more than upon the chase. Ignorant of the arts of life,

cubit long, and at the end of the upper lip, it was made like a peele. It had no scales." Compare Flint's Geography of the Mississippi Valley, v. i. p. 85, second edition. Journal of Philadelphia Academy of Nat. Science, v. i. part ii. p. 227—229. Nuttall's Arkansas, p. 254.
[1] Portuguese Relation, c. xxv.—xxvii. p. 522—527.

[2] Charlevoix, Journal Historique, let. xxxi.
[3] Portuguese Narrative, c. xxvi. Nuttall's Arkansas, p. 215, 216, and 257.
[4] The river of Autiamque, Cayas, the saline regions, and afterwards of Nilco, was the same. Portuguese Relation, c. xxviii. p. 528.

they could offer no resistance to their unwelcome visiters; the bow and arrow were the most effective weapons, with which they were acquainted. They seem not to have been turbulent or quarrelsome; but as the population was moderate, and the earth fruitful, the tribes were not accustomed to contend with each other for the possession of territories. They were an agricultural people. Their dress was, in part, mats, wrought of ivy and bulrushes, of the bark and lint of trees; in cold weather, they wore mantles, woven of feathers. The settlements were by tribes; each tribe occupied what the Spaniards called a province; their villages were generally near together; but were composed of few habitations. The Spaniards treated them with no other forbearance, than their own selfishness demanded, and enslaved such as offended, employing them as porters and guides. On a slight suspicion, they would cut off the hands of numbers of the natives, for punishment or intimidation.[1] The guide, who was unsuccessful, or who purposely led them away from the settlements of his tribe, would be seized and thrown to the hounds. Sometimes a native was condemned to the flames. Any trifling

---

[1] Inter alia sævitiæ exempla ab eo edita hoc unum insigne est. Quindecim Cacicos captos jam in potestate habebat; nisi locum unde aurum sumerent, indicarent, minatur se omnes crematurum: miseri illi metu mortis oblato consternati, securi de facilitate credentis, nec quid dicerent satis scientes, promittunt se intra octiduum in eum locum deducturos unde aurum magna copia sumeret. Jam duodecim dierum iter peregerant, nec ullum auri vestigium aut indicium exstabat. Itaque elusus Gubernator et multum indignatus, truncatos manibus dimittit.

Calveto from Benzo, Hist. Novi Orbis Nov. l. ii. c. xiii. in de Bry, part iv. p. 47. Something similar to this may have occurred, but I have not ventured to insert the story. De Bry illustrates the action, real or imaginary, with a picture.

SPANIARDS IN ARKANSAS AND LOUISIANA.

CHAP. II.

1541.

consideration of safety would induce the governor to set fire to a hamlet. He did not delight in cruelty; but the happiness, the life, and the rights of the Indians, were held of no account. The approach of the Spaniards was heard with dismay; and their departure hastened by the suggestion of wealthier lands at a great distance.

1542. Mar. 6.

In the spring of the following year, Soto determined to descend the Washita to its junction, and to get tidings of the sea. As he advanced, he was soon lost amidst the bayous and marshes, which are found along the Red river and its tributaries. Near the Mississippi, he came upon the country of Nilco, which was well peopled. The river was there larger than the Gaudalquiver at Seville. At last, he arrived

April 17.

at the province, where the Washita, already united with the Red river, enters the Mississippi.[1] The province was called Guachoya. Soto anxiously inquired the distance to the sea; the chieftain of Guachoya could not tell. Were there settlements extending along the river to its mouth? It was answered, that its lower banks were an uninhabited waste. Unwilling to believe so disheartening a tale, Soto sent one of his men with eight horsemen, to descend the banks of the Mississippi, and explore the country. They travelled eight days, and were able to advance not much more than thirty miles; they were so delayed by the frequent bayous, the impassa-

[1] McCulloh places Guachoya near the Arkansas river. He does not make sufficient allowance for an exaggeration of distances, and for the delays on the Mississippi during the night-time; p. 529—531. I do not think there is room for a doubt. Nuttall, Martin, and many others, agree with the statement, which is given in the text.

ble cane-brakes, and the dense woods.¹ The governor received the intelligence with concern; he suffered from anxiety and gloom. His horses and men were dying around him. A tribe of Indians near Natchez sent him a defiance; and he was no longer able to punish their temerity. His stubborn pride was changed by long disappointments into a wasting melancholy; and his health sunk rapidly and entirely under a conflict of emotions. A mortal sickness ensued, during which he had little comfort, and was neither visited nor attended as he should have been. Believing his death near at hand, he yielded to the wishes of his companions, and named a successor. On the next day he died. Thus perished the governor of Cuba, and the successful associate of Pizarro. His miserable end was the more observed, from the greatness of his former prosperity. His soldiers pronounced his eulogy, by grieving for their loss; the priests chanted over his body the first requiems that were ever heard on the waters of the Mississippi. To conceal his death, his body was wrapped in a mantle, and, in the stillness of midnight, was silently sunk in the middle of the stream. The discoverer of the Mississippi slept beneath its waters. He had crossed a large part of the continent in search of gold, and found nothing so remarkable as his burial-place.²

No longer guided by the energy and pride of Soto, the company resolved on reaching New-Spain with-

CHAP. II.

1542.

May 21.

June.

[1] Portuguese Account, c. xxix. c. vii. and viii. Vega embellishes as usual. Herrera, d. vii. l. p. 531, 532. Vega, l. v. part i. vii. c. iii.
[2] Portuguese Relation, c. xxx.

out delay. Should they embark in such miserable boats, as they could construct, and descend the river? Or should they seek a path to Mexico through the forests? They were unanimous in the opinion, that it was less dangerous to go by land; the hope was still cherished, that some wealthy state, some opulent city, might yet be discovered, and all fatigues be forgotten in the midst of victory and spoils. Again they penetrated the western wilderness; in July, they found themselves in the country of the Natchitoches;[1] but the Red river was so swollen, that it was impossible for them to pass. They soon became bewildered, and knew not where they were; the Indian guides purposely led them astray; "they went up and down through very great woods," without making any progress. The wilderness, into which they had wandered, was sterile and thinly inhabited; the few inhabitants were migratory tribes, subsisting by the chase. The Spaniards, at last, believed themselves to be three hundred miles or more, west of the Mississippi. Desperate as the resolution seemed, it was determined to return once more to its banks, and follow its current to the sea. There were not wanting men, whose hopes and whose courage were not yet exhausted; but Moscoso, the new governor, had long "desired to see himself in a place where he might sleep his full sleep."[2]

They came upon the Mississippi at Minoya, a few leagues above the mouth of Red river; often wading

---

[1] Vega introduces the Natchitoches too soon. L. v. part i. c. i. See Portuguese Account, c. xxxii. and xxxiii. p. 534, 535. Compare Nuttall's Arkansas, p. 264.
[2] Portuguese Relation, c. xxxiv.

SPANIARDS DESERT THE UNITED STATES. 65

through deep waters; and grateful to God if, at night, they could find a dry resting-place. The Indians, whom they had enslaved, died in great numbers; in Minoya, many Christians died; and most of them were attacked by a dangerous epidemic.[1]

CHAP. II.

1542.

Nor was the labor yet at an end; it was no easy task for men in their condition to build brigantines. Erecting a forge, they struck off the fetters from the slaves; and, gathering every scrap of iron in the camp, they wrought it into nails. Timber was sawed by hand with a large saw, which they had always carried with them. They caulked their vessels with a weed like hemp; barrels, capable of holding water, were with difficulty made; to obtain supplies of provision, all the hogs and even the horses were killed, and their flesh preserved by drying; and the neighboring townships of Indians were so plundered of their food, that the miserable inhabitants would come about the Spaniards begging for a few kernels of their own maize, and often died from weakness and want of food. The rising of the Mississippi assisted the launching of the seven brigantines; they were frail barks, which had no decks; and, as from the want of iron the nails were of necessity short, they were constructed of very thin planks, so that the least shock would have broken them in pieces. Thus provided, in seventeen days the fugitives reached the gulf of Mexico; the distance seemed to them two hundred and fifty leagues, and was not much less than

1543.
Jan.
to
July.

July
2—18

[1] Portuguese Relation, c. xxxv.

CHAP. II.
1543.
Sept. 10.

five hundred miles. They were the first to observe, that for some distance from the mouth of the Mississippi the sea is not salt, so great is the volume of fresh water which the river discharges. Following, for the most part, the coast, it was more than fifty days before the men, who finally escaped, now no more than three hundred and eleven in number, entered the river Panuco.[1]

Such is the history of the first visit of Europeans to the Mississippi; the honor of the discovery belongs, without a doubt, to the Spaniards. There

1544. were not wanting adventurers, who desired to make one more attempt to possess the country by force of arms; their request was refused.[2] Religious zeal

[1] On Soto's expedition, by far the best account is that of the Portuguese Eye-witness, first published in 1557, and by Hakluyt, in English, in 1609. It may be found in Hakluyt, v. v. p. 477—550. There is an imperfect abridgement of it in Purchas, v. iv. p. 1528—1556; and a still more imperfect one in Roberts' Florida, p. 33—79. This narrative is remarkably good, and contains internal evidence of its credibility. Nuttall erroneously attributes it to Vega. The work of Vega is an extravagant romance, yet founded upon facts. Numbers and distances are magnified; and every thing embellished with great boldness. His history is not without its value, but must be consulted with extreme caution. Herrera, d. vi. l. vii. c. ix.—xii., and d. vii. l. vii. c. i.—xi. is not an original authority, and his statements furnish merely cumulative evidence. The Ensayo Cronologico contains nothing of moment on the subject. Lescarbot, N. Fr. tom. i. p. 36, and Charlevoix, N. Fr. tom. i. p. 24, and v. iii. p. 408, offer no new views. Du Pratz is unnecessarily sceptical. The French translator of Vega has not a word of valuable criticism. Of English authors, neither Purchas nor Harris have furnished any useful illustrations. Of books, published in America, Belknap, in Am. Biog. v. i. p. 185—195, comments with his usual care. McCulloh, in his Researches, Appendix, iii. p. 523—531, makes an earnest attempt to trace the route of Soto. So Nuttall, in his Travels in Arkansas, Appendix, p. 247—267. Nuttall had himself roved through the same regions, and his opinions are justly entitled to much deference. Flint only glances at the subject. Stoddard, in his Sketches, p. 4, is vague and without detail. I have compared all these authors; the account in Hakluyt, with good modern maps, can lead to firm conclusions.

[2] Ensayo Cronologico, Año, MDXLIV.

was more persevering; Louis Cancello, a missionary of the Dominican order, gained, through Philip, then heir apparent in Spain, permission to visit Florida, and attempt the peaceful conversion of the natives. Christianity was to conquer the land, against which so many expeditions had failed. The Spanish governors were directed to favor the design; all slaves, that had been taken from the northern shore of the gulf of Mexico, were to be manumitted and restored to their country. The ship was fitted out with much solemnity; but the priests, who sought the first interview with the natives, were feared as enemies, and, being immediately attacked, Louis and two others fell martyrs to their zeal.[1]

Florida was abandoned. It seemed as if death guarded the avenues to the country.[2] While the Castilians were every where else victorious, Florida was wet with the blood of the invaders, who had still been unable to possess themselves of her soil. The coast of our republic on the gulf of Mexico was not, at this time, disputed by any other nation with Spain; while that power claimed, under the name of Florida, the whole seacoast as far as Newfoundland,[3] and even to the remotest north. In Spanish geography, Canada was a part of Florida.[4] Yet within

---

[1] Ensayo Cronologico, p. 25, 26.; Vega, l. vi. c. xxii. p. 267.; Gomara, c. xlv.; Urbani Calvetonis de Gallorum in Floridam expeditione Brevis Historia, c. i., annexed to Nov. Nov. Orbis Hist. p. 432, 433; Eden and Willes, fol. 229; De Bry's introduction and parergon to his Brevis Narratio eorum quæ in Florida Gallis acciderunt. Thuani Hist. l. xliv.

[2] Gom. c. xlv.; Vega, l. vi. c. xxii.

[3] Herrera's Description of the West Indies, c. viii. in Purchas, v. iv. p. 868.

[4] Bolvio á la Florida Champlain; entrò en Quebec, &c Ensayo Cronologico, p. 179.

COLIGNY PLANS A COLONY OF HUGUENOTS.

CHAP. II.

1549. that whole extent, not a Spanish fort was erected, not a harbor was occupied; not one settlement was planned. The first permanent establishment of the Spaniards in Florida was the result of jealous bigotry.

1562. For France had begun to settle the region with a colony of protestants; and Calvinism, which, with the special co-operation of Calvin himself, had, for a

1555. short season, occupied the coasts of Brazil and the harbor of Rio Janeiro,[1] was now to be planted on the borders of Florida. Coligny had long desired to establish a refuge for the Huguenots and a protestant French empire in America. Disappointed in his first effort by the apostacy and faithlessness of his agent, Villegagnon, he still persevered; moved alike by religious zeal and by a passion for the honor of

1562. France. The expedition which he now planned, was entrusted to the command of John Ribault of Dieppe, a brave man of maritime experience and a firm protestant, and was attended by some of the best of the young French nobility, as well as by veteran troops. The feeble Charles IX. conceded

Feb. 18. an ample commission, and the squadron set sail for the shores of North-America. Desiring to establish their plantation in a genial clime, land was first made in the latitude of St. Augustine; the fine river, which we call the St. Johns,[2] was discovered and

May. named the river of May. It is the St. Matheo[3] of

[1] De Thou's Hist. l. xvi. Lery, Hist. Nav. in Bras. An abridgement of the description, but not of the personal narrative, appears in Purchas, v. iv. p. 1325—1347. Lescarbot, N. F. l. ii. t. i. p. 143—214; Southey's Brazil, part i. c. ix.; True Declaration of the State of Virginia, 1610, p. 12, 13.
[2] Compare the criticism of Holmes' Annals, v. i. p. 567. Holmes surpasses Charlevoix in accuracy.
[3] Ensayo Cronologico, p. 43.

the Spaniards. The forests of mulberries were admired, and caterpillars readily mistaken for silk worms. The cape received a French name; as the ships sailed along the coast, the numerous streams were called after the rivers of France; and America, for a while, had its Seine, its Loire, and its Garonne. In searching for the Jordan or Combahee, they came upon Port Royal entrance,[1] which seemed the outlet of a magnificent river. The greatest ships of France and the argosies of Venice could ride securely in the deep water of the harbor. The site for a first settlement is apt to be injudiciously selected; the local advantages, which favor the growth of large cities, are discovered only by time. It was on Lemon Island, that a monumental stone, engraved with the arms of France, was proudly raised;[2] and as the company looked round upon the immense oaks, which were venerable from the growth of centuries, the profusion of wild fowls, the groves of pine, the flowers so fragrant, that the whole air was perfumed, they already regarded the country as a province of their native land. Ribault determined to leave a colony; twenty-six composed the whole party, which was to keep possession of the continent. Fort Charles, the Carolina,[3] so called in honor of Charles

CHAP. II.

1562.

---

[1] Laudonniere, in Hakluyt, v. iii. p. 373. The description is sufficiently minute and accurate; removing all doubt. Before the geography of the country was well known, there was room for the error of Charlevoix, Nouv. Fr. v. i. p. 25, who places the settlement at the mouth of the Edisto, an error, which is followed by Chalmers, p. 513. It is no reproach to Charlevoix, that his geography of the coast of Florida is confused and inaccurate. Compare Johnson's Life of Greene, v. i. p. 477.

[2] The stone is supposed to have been seen in 1832; though the sea has gradually encroached upon the island.

[3] Munitionem Carolinam, de re-

HUGUENOTS NEAR BEAUFORT, SOUTH-CAROLINA.

CHAP. IX. of France, first gave a name to the country, a century before it was colonized by the English.

1562.
July 20.
Ribault[1] and the ships arrived safely in France. But the fires of civil war had been kindled in all the provinces of the kingdom; and the promised reinforcements for Carolina were never levied. The situation of the French became precarious. The natives were friendly; but the soldiers themselves were insubordinate; and dissensions prevailed. The commandant at Carolina repressed the turbulent spirit with arbitrary cruelty; and lost his life in a mutiny, which his ungovernable passion had provoked. The new commander succeeded in restoring order. But the love of his native land is a passion easily revived in the breast of a Frenchman; and the company resolved to embark in such a brigantine,

1563. as they could themselves construct. Intoxicated with joy at the thought of returning home, they neglected to provide sufficient stores; and they were overtaken by famine at sea, with its attendant crimes. A small English bark at length boarded their vessel, and, setting the most feeble on shore upon the coast of France, carried the rest to the queen of England. Thus fell the first attempt of France in French Florida, near the southern confines of South-Carolina. The country was still a desert.[2]

gis nomine dictum. De Thou, l. xliv. p. 531, edition of 1626.

[1] Ribault immediately made a report, which was translated and printed in England, in 1563, republished by Hakluyt, in 1582, and omitted in the future editions of Hakluyt, for the more full account of Laudonniere, who was likewise engaged in the voyage. Of Ribault's short tract, there is no copy within my reach. It belongs to South-Carolina to reprint it. See Memoir of Sebastian Cabot, p. 37, 38, 39.

[2] Laudonniere, in Hakluyt, v.

SECOND COLONY OF COLIGNY.

After the treacherous peace between Charles IX. and the Huguenots, Coligny renewed his solicitations for the colonization of Florida. The king gave consent; three ships were conceded for the service; and Laudonniere, who, in the former voyage, had been upon the American coast, a man of great intelligence, though a seaman rather than a soldier, was appointed to lead forth the colony. Emigrants readily appeared; for the climate of Florida was so celebrated, that, according to rumor, the duration of human life was doubled under its genial influences;[1] and men still dreamed of rich mines of gold in the interior. Coligny was desirous of obtaining accurate descriptions of the country; and James Le Moyne, called de Morgues, an ingenious painter, was commissioned to execute colored drawings of the objects, which might engage his curiosity. A voyage of sixty days brought the fleet, by the way of the Canaries and the Antilles, to the shores of Florida. The harbor of Port Royal, rendered gloomy by recollections of misery, was avoided; and after searching the coast and discovering places, which were so full of amenity, that melancholy itself could not but change its humor, as it gazed, the followers of Calvin planted themselves on the banks of the river May. They sung a psalm of thanksgiving, and gathered courage from acts of devotion. The fort, now erected, was also named Carolina. The result of

CHAP. II.

1564.

April 22 to June 22.

iii. p. 371—384. Compare De Thou, a contemporary, l. xliv. p. 530, 531. Charlevoix, N. Fr. v. i. p. 24—35; Ensayo Cronologico, p. 42—45; Lescarbot, Nouv. Fr. l. i. c. v.—vii. t. i. p. 41—62.
 [1] De Thou. l. xliv. p. 532.; Hakluyt, v. iv. p. 389.

CHAP. II.
1564.

this attempt to procure for France immense dominions at the south of our republic, through the agency of a Huguenot colony, has been very frequently narrated;[1] in the history of human nature it forms a dark picture of vindictive bigotry.

The French were hospitably welcomed by the natives; a monument, bearing the arms of France, was crowned with laurels and its base encircled with baskets of corn. What need is there of minutely relating the simple manners of the natives; the dissensions of rival tribes; the largesses, offered to the strangers to secure their protection or their alliance; the improvident prodigality with which careless soldiers wasted the supplies of food; the certain approach of scarcity; the gifts and the tribute, levied from the Indians by entreaty, menace, or force? By degrees, the confidence of the natives was exhausted; they had welcomed powerful guests, who promised to become their benefactors, and who now robbed their humble granaries.

[1] There are four original accounts by eye-witnesses. Laudonniere, in Hakluyt, v. iii. p. 384—419. Le Moyne, in de Bry, part ii., together with the Epistola Supplicatoria, from the widows and orphans of the sufferers, to Charles IX.; also in de Bry, part ii. Challus, or Challusius of Dieppe, whose account I have found annexed to Calveto's Nov. Nov. Orb. Hist. under the title, De Gallorum Expeditione in Floridam, p. 433—469. And the Spanish account by Solis de las Meras, the brother-in-law and apologist of Melendez, in Ensayo Cronologico, p. 85—90. On Solis, compare Crisis del Ensayo, p. 22, 23. I have drawn my narrative from a comparison of these four accounts; consulting also the admirable De Thou, a genuine worshipper at the shrine of truth, l. xliv.; the diffuse Barcia's Ensayo Cronologico, p. 42—94; the elaborate and circumstantial narrative of Charlevoix, N. Fr. t. i. p. 24—106; and the account of Lescarbot, t. i. c. viii.—xviii. t. i. p. 62—129. The accounts do not essentially vary. Voltaire and many others have repeated the tale. Purchas, v. i. p. 358, and v. iv. p. 1604; Roberts' Florida, p. 81—85; Hewitt's Carolina and Georgia, v. i. p. 18—20; Williamson's North-Carolina, v. i. p. 17—34.; Chalmers, p. 513. These have given no new ideas.

But the worst evil in the new settlement was the character of the emigrants. Though patriotism and religious enthusiasm had prompted the expedition, the inferior class of the colonists was a motley group of dissolute men. Mutinies were frequent. The men were mad with the passion for sudden wealth; and a party, under the pretence of desiring to escape from famine, compelled Laudonniere to sign an order, permitting their embarkation for New-Spain. No sooner were they possessed of this apparent sanction of the chief, than they equipped two vessels, and began a career of piracy against the Spanish. Thus the French were the aggressors in the first act of hostility in the New World; an act of crime and temerity, which was soon avenged. The pirate vessel was taken; and most of the men disposed of as prisoners or slaves. A few escaped in a boat; these could find no shelter but at fort Carolina, where Laudonniere sentenced the ring-leaders to death.

CHAP II.

1564.

1564. Dec. 8.

Meantime, the scarcity became extreme; and the friendship of the natives was entirely forfeited by unprofitable severity. March was gone, and there were no supplies from France; April passed away, and the expected recruits had not arrived; May came, but it brought nothing to sustain the hopes of the exiles. It was resolved to return to Europe in such miserable brigantines, as despair could construct. Just then, Sir John Hawkins,[1] the slave-merchant, arrived from the West Indies. He came

1565.

Aug. 3.

[1] Hawkins, in Hakluyt, v. iii. p. 615, 616.

fresh from the sale of a cargo of Africans, whom he had kidnapped with signal ruthlessness; and he now displayed the most generous sympathy, not only providing a liberal supply of provisions, but relinquishing a vessel from his own fleet. Preparations were continued; the colony was on the point of embarking, when sails were descried. Ribault had arrived to assume the command; bringing with him supplies of every kind, emigrants with their families, garden seeds, implements of husbandry, and the various kinds of domestic animals. The French, now wild with joy, seemed about to acquire a home, and Calvinism to become fixed in the inviting regions of Florida.

But Spain had never relinquished her claim to that territory; where, if she had not planted colonies, she had buried many hundreds of her bravest sons. Should the proud Philip II. abandon a part of his dominions to France? Should he suffer his commercial monopoly to be endangered by a rival settlement in the vicinity of the West Indies? Should the bigotted Romanist permit the heresy of Calvinism to be planted in the neighborhood of his Catholic provinces? There had appeared at the Spanish court a bold commander, well fitted for acts of reckless hostility. Pedro Melendez de Avilès had, in a long career of military service, become accustomed to scenes of blood; and his natural ferocity had been confirmed by his course of life. The wars against the Protestants of Holland had nourished his bigotry; and, as a naval commander, often encoun-

MELENDEZ APPOINTED GOVERNOR OF FLORIDA.   75

tering pirates, whom the laws of nations exclude CHAP.
from mercy, he had become inured to acts of prompt II.
and unsparing vengeance. He had acquired wealth 1565.
in Spanish America, which was no school of benevolence; and his conduct there had provoked an inquiry,
which, after a long arrest, ended in his conviction.
The nature of his offences is not apparent; the justice of the sentence is confirmed, for the king, who
knew him well, esteemed his bravery and received
him again into his service, remitted only a moiety of
his fine. The heir of Melendez had been shipwrecked among the Bermudas; the father desired
to return and search among the islands for tidings of
his only son. Philip II. suggested the conquest and Mar.
colonization of Florida; and a compact was soon   20.
framed and confirmed, by which Melendez, who
desired an opportunity to retrieve his honor, was
constituted the hereditary governor of a territory of
almost unlimited extent.[1]

The terms of the compact[2] are curious. Melendez, on his part, promised, at his own cost, in the
following May, to invade Florida with at least five
hundred men; to complete its conquest within three
years; to explore its currents and channels, the dangers of its coasts, and the depth of its havens; to
establish a colony of at least five hundred persons,
of whom one hundred should be married men; to
introduce at least twelve ecclesiastics, besides four
jesuits. It was further stipulated, that he should
transport to his province all kinds of domestic

[1] Ensayo Cronolog. p. 57—65.   [2] Ibid, p. 66.

animals. The bigotted Philip II. had no scruples respecting slavery; Melendez contracted to import into Florida five hundred negro slaves. The sugar cane was to become a staple of the country.

The king, in return, promised the adventurer various commercial immunities; the office of governor for life, with the right of naming his son-in-law as his successor; an estate of twenty-five square leagues in the immediate vicinity of the settlement; a salary of two thousand ducats, chargeable on the revenues of the province; and a fifteenth part of all royal perquisites.

Meantime, news arrived, as the French writers assert, through the treachery of the court of France, that the Huguenots had made a plantation in Florida, and that Ribault was preparing to set sail with reinforcements. The cry was raised, that the heretics must be extirpated; the enthusiasm of fanaticism was kindled, and Melendez readily obtained all the forces, which he required. More than twenty-five hundred persons, soldiers, sailors, priests, jesuits, married men with their families, laborers and mechanics, and, with the exception of three hundred soldiers, all at the cost of Melendez, engaged in the invasion. After delays, occasioned by a storm, the expedition set sail; and the trade winds soon bore them rapidly across the Atlantic. A tempest scattered the fleet on its passage; it was with only one third part of his forces, that Melendez arrived at the harbor of St. John in Porto Rico. But he esteemed celerity the secret of success; and, refusing to await

the arrival of the rest of his squadron, he sailed for
Florida. It had ever been his design to explore the
coast; to select a favorable site for a fort or a settlement; and, after the construction of fortifications, to
attack the French. It was on the day which the
customs of Rome have consecrated to the memory
of one of the most eloquent sons of Africa and one
of the most venerated of the fathers of the church,
that he came in sight of Florida.[1] For four days,
he sailed along the coast, uncertain where the French
were established; on the fifth day, he landed and
gathered from the Indians accounts of the Huguenots. At the same time, he discovered a fine haven
and beautiful river; and, remembering the saint, on
whose day he came upon the coast, he gave to the
harbor and to the stream the name of St. Augustine.[2]
Sailing, then, to the north, he discovered a portion
of the French fleet, and observed the nature of the
road, where they were anchored. The French
demanded his name and objects. "I am Melendez
of Spain," replied he; "sent with strict orders from
my king to gibbet and behead all the protestants in
these regions. The Frenchman, who is a catholic,
I will spare; every heretic shall die."[3] The French
fleet, unprepared for action, cut its cables; the
Spaniards, for some time, continued an ineffectual
chase.

It was at the hour of vespers, on the evening preceding the festival of the nativity of Mary, that

CHAP.
II.

1565.

Aug.
28.

Sept.
2

Sept.
4

Sept.
7.

---

[1] Ensayo Cronolog. p. 68—70. [2] Ensayo Cronologico, p. 75, 76. It
[2] Ensayo Cronolog. p. 71.   is the account of the apologist and
[3] El que fuere herege, morirá. admirer of Melendez.

FORT CAROLINA ATTACKED BY MELENDEZ.

CHAP. II.

1565.
Sept.
8.

the Spaniards returned to the harbor of St. Augustine. At noonday of the festival itself, the governor went on shore, to take possession of the continent in the name of his king. The bigotted Philip II. was proclaimed monarch of all North America. The solemn mass of our lady was performed, and the foundation of St. Augustine was immediately laid.[1] It is by more than forty years the oldest town in the United States. Houses in it are yet standing, which are said to have been built many years before Virginia was colonized.[2]

By the French it was debated, whether they should improve their fortifications and await the approach of the Spaniards, or proceed to sea and attack their enemy? Against the advice of his officers, Ribault resolved upon the latter course. Hardly

Sept.
10.

had he left the harbor for the open sea, before there arose a fearful storm, which continued till October, and wrecked every ship of the French fleet on the Florida coast. The vessels were dashed against the rocks about fifty leagues south of fort Carolina; most of the men escaped with their lives.

The Spanish ships also suffered, but not so severely; and the troops at St. Augustine were entirely safe. They knew that the French settlement was left in a defenceless state; with a fanatical indifference to toil, Melendez led his men through the lakes, and marshes, and forests, that divided the

[1] Laudonniere. "They put their soldiers, victual, and munition, on land." Hakluyt, v. iii. p. 433. Ensayo Cronologico, p. 76, 77. Prince Murat, in American Quarterly Review, v. ii. p. 216. De Thou, l. xliv.
[2] Stoddard's Sketches, p. 120.

St. Augustine from the St. Johns; and, with a furious onset, surprised the weak garrison, who had looked only towards the sea for the approach of danger. After a short contest, the Spaniards were masters of the fort. A scene of carnage ensued; soldiers, women, children, the aged, the sick, were alike massacred. The Spanish account asserts, that Melendez ordered women and young children to be spared; yet not till after the havoc had long been raging.

Nearly two hundred persons were killed. A few escaped into the woods, among them Laudonniere, Challus and Le Moyne, who have related the horrors of the scene. But whither should they fly? Death met them in the woods; and the heavens, the earth, the sea, and men, all seemed conspired against them. Should they surrender, appealing to the sympathy of their conquerors? "Let us," said Challus, "trust in the mercy of God, rather than of these men." A few gave themselves up, and were immediately murdered. The others, after the severest sufferings, found their way to the sea-side, and were received on board two small French vessels, which had remained in the harbor. The Spaniards, angry that any should have escaped, insulted the corpses of the dead with wanton barbarity.

The victory had been gained on the festival of St. Matthew; and hence the Spanish name of the river May. After the carnage was completed, mass was said; a cross was raised; and the site for a church selected, on ground still smoking with the blood of a peaceful colony. So easily is the human mind the dupe of its own prejudices; so easily can fanaticism connect acts of savage ferocity with the rites of a merciful religion.

The shipwrecked men were, in their turn, soon discovered. They were in a state of helpless weakness, wasted by their fatigues at sea, half famished, destitute of water and of food. Should they surrender to the Spaniards? Melendez invited them to rely on his compassion;[1] the French capitulated, and were received among the Spaniards in such successive divisions, as a boat could at once ferry across the river, which separated the parties. As the captives stepped upon the bank which their enemies occupied, their hands were tied behind them, and in this way they were marched towards St. Augustine, like a flock of sheep, driven to the slaughter-house. As they approached the fort, a signal was given; and, amidst the sound of trumpets and drums, the Spaniards fell upon the unhappy men, who had confided in their humanity, and who could offer no resistance. A few catholics were spared; some mechanics were reserved as slaves; the rest were massacred, "not as Frenchmen, but as protestants." The whole number of the victims of bigotry, here and at the fort, is said, by the French, to have been about nine hundred;[2] the Spanish accounts diminish the number of the slain, but not the atrocity of the

---

[1] So says his apologist; si ellos quieren entregarle las Vanderas, è las armas, è ponerse en su misericordia, lo pueden hacer, para que èl haga de ellos lo que Dios le diere de gracia. Is not this an implied promise of mercy?

[2] Epistola Supplicatoria, &c. in de Bry, part ii. Ceciderunt plures quam noningenti.

deed. Melendez returned to Spain, impoverished but triumphant. The French government heard of the outrage with apathy; and made not even a remonstrance on the ruin of a colony, which, if it had been protected, would have given to its country a flourishing empire in the south, before England had planted a single spot on the new continent. History has been more faithful; and has assisted humanity by giving to the crime of Melendez an infamous notoriety.[1] The first town in the United States sprung from the unrelenting bigotry of the Spanish king. We admire the rapid growth of our larger cities; the sudden transformation of portions of the wilderness into blooming states. St. Augustine presents a stronger contrast in its transition from the bigotted policy of Philip II. to the American principles of religious liberty. Its origin should be carefully remembered, for it is a fixed point, from which to measure the liberal influence of time; the progress of modern civilization; the victories of the American mind, in its contests for the interests of humanity.

The Huguenots and the French nation did not share in the apathy of the court. Dominic de Gourgues,—a bold soldier of Gascony, whose life had been a series of adventures, now employed in the army against Spain, now a prisoner and a galley-slave among the Spaniards, taken by the Turks with the vessel in which he rowed, and redeemed by the

1567.

---

[1] Apud suos infamis. Grotius. Holmes unnecessarily makes Melendez a suicide. See Ensayo Cronologico, p. 150, 151.

commander of the knights of Malta,—burned with a desire to avenge his own wrongs and the honor of his country. The sale of his property and the contributions of his friends, furnished the means of equipping three ships, in which with one hundred and fifty men he embarked for Florida. His strength was not sufficient to occupy the country permanently; he desired only to destroy and revenge. He was able to surprise two forts near the mouth of the St. Matheo; and, as terror magnified the number of his followers, the consternation of the Spaniards enabled him to gain possession of the larger fort near the spot, which the French colony had fortified. But he was not strong enough to maintain his position; he, therefore, hastily retreated and sailed to Europe, having first hanged his prisoners upon the trees, and placed over them the inscription: "I do not this as unto Spaniards or mariners, but as unto traitors, robbers and murderers."[1] The natives, who had been ill-treated both by the Spaniards and the French, enjoyed the savage consolation of seeing their enemies butcher one another.

The attack of the fiery Gascon was but a passing storm. France disavowed the expedition and relinquished all pretension to Florida. Spain grasped at it, as a portion of her dominions, and, if discovery could confer a right, her claim was founded in justice. Cuba now formed the centre of her West Indian possessions, and every thing around it was

[1] Hakluyt, v. iii. p. 426—432; Lescarbot, l. ii. c. xix. t. i. p. 129 De Bry, part ii.; De Thou, l. xliv.; —141; Charlevoix, t. i. p. 95, Ensayo Cronologico, p. 135—138; &c.

included within her empire. Sovereignty was asserted, not only over the archipelagos within the tropics, but over the whole continent round the inner seas. From the remotest southeastern cape of the Caribbean along the whole shore to the cape of Florida and beyond it, all was hers. The gulf of Mexico lay embosomed within her territories.

CHAPTER III.

ENGLAND TAKES POSSESSION OF THE UNITED STATES.

CHAP. III.

1569, to 1575.

The attempts of the French to colonize Florida, though unprotected and unsuccessful, were not without an important influence on succeeding events. About the time of the return of de Gourgues, Walter Raleigh,[1] a young Englishman, had abruptly left the university of Oxford to take part in the civil contests between the Huguenots and the Catholics in France, and, with the prince of Navarre, afterwards Henry IV., was learning the art of war under the veteran Coligny. The protestant party was, at that time, strongly excited with indignation at the massacre, which de Gourgues had avenged; and Raleigh could not but gather from his associates and his commander intelligence respecting Florida and the navigation to those regions. Some of the miserable men, who escaped from the first expedition, had been conducted to Elizabeth,[2] and had kindled in the public mind in England a desire for the possession of the southern coast of our republic; the reports of Hawkins,[3] who had been the benefactor of the French on the river May, increased the national excitement; and

---

[1] Oldys' Raleigh, p. 16, 17; Tytler's Raleigh, p. 19—23.
[2] Hakluyt, v. iii. p. 384.
[3] Ibid, v. iii. p. 612—617.

de Morgues,[1] the painter, who had sketched in Florida the most remarkable appearances of nature, ultimately found the opportunity of finishing his designs, through the munificence of Raleigh.

The progress of English maritime enterprize had prepared the way for vigorous efforts at colonization. The second expedition of the Cabots was, as we have seen, connected with plans for settlements. Other commissions, for the same object, were issued by Henry VII. In the patent, which an American historian has recently published,[2] the design of establishing emigrants in the New World is distinctly proposed, and encouraged by the concession of a limited monopoly of the colonial trade and of commercial privileges. It is probable, that at least one voyage was made under the authority of this commission; for in the year after it was granted, natives of North America, in their wild attire, were exhibited to the public wonder of England and the English court.[3]

Yet if a voyage was actually made, its success was inconsiderable. A new patent,[4] with larger concessions, was issued, in part to the same patentees; and there is reason to believe, that the king now favored by gratuities[5] the expedition, which no longer appeared to promise any considerable returns. Where no profits followed adventure, navigation soon

1498.

1501.
Mar.
19.

1502.

1502.
Dec.
9.

---

[1] Hakluyt, v. iii. p. 364. Compare a marginal note to v. iii. p. 425.
[2] Memoir of S. Cabot, p. 306—314. The author, Richard Biddle of Pittsburgh, has done honor to himself, his subject and his country. His volume is a model of fidelity in historic research.
[3] Stow's Annals, 1502, p. 483, 484.
[4] Rymer's Fœdera, v. xiii. p. 37—42; Bacon's Henry VII.
[5] Mem. of S. Cab. p. 226. Note.

CHAP. III.

languished. Yet the connexion between England and the New Found Land was never abandoned. Documentary evidence exists of voyages[1] favored by the English, till the time, when the Normans, the Biscayans and the Bretons, began to frequent the fisheries on the American coast. Is it probable, that English mariners ever wholly resigned to a rival nation the benefits arising from their own discoveries?

1509, to 1547.

Nor was the reign of Henry VIII. unfavorable to the mercantile interests of his kingdom; and that monarch, while his life was still unstained by profligacy, and his passions not yet hardened into the stubborn selfishness of despotism, considered the discovery of the north as his "charge and duty," and made such experiments, as the favorable situation of England appeared to demand.[2] An account has

1517. already been given of the last voyage of discovery, in which Sebastian Cabot was personally engaged for his native land. Is it not probable, that other expeditions were made, with the favor of king Henry and of Wolsey, although no distinct account of

1527. them has been preserved? Of one such voyage for the discovery of a northwest passage, there exists a relation,[3] written by Rut, the commander of one of the ships, and forwarded from the haven of St. John in Newfoundland. This implies a direct and established intercourse between England and the American coast. Some part of the country was explored;

---

[1] Note in Memoir of Sebastian Cabot, p. 229, 230.
[2] Thorne's letter, in 1527, to Henry VIII. in Hakluyt, v. i. p. 236.
[3] Purchas, v. iii. p. 809; Hakluyt, v. iii. p. 167, 168; Memoir of Sebastian Cabot, part ii. c. ix.

for the English never abandoned the hope of planting a colony on the continent which Cabot had discovered.

CHAP.
III.
1527.

The jealousy of the Spanish nation was excited, and already began to fear English rivalry in the New World.[1] Henry VIII. was vigorous in his attempts to check piracy; and the navigation of his subjects was extended under the security of his protection. The banner of St. George was often displayed in the harbors of Northern Africa and in the Levant;[2] and when commerce, emancipated from the confinement of the inner seas, went boldly forth to make the ocean its chief highway, England became more emulous to engage in a competition, in which her position gave her a pledge of success. When voyages for traffic were already made by English merchants between the coasts of Africa and Brazil, it may be safely believed, that the nearer shores of North America were not neglected.

1530.

An account exists of one expedition, which was "assisted by the good countenance of Henry VIII." But the incidents, as they were related to the inquisitive Hakluyt by "the only man then alive, that had been in the discovery," are embellished with improbable aggravations of distress. Memory, at all periods of life, is easily deceived by the imagination; and men, who relate marvellous tales of personal adventure, are the first to become the dupes of their own inventions. The old sailor, perhaps, believed his

[1] Herrera, d. ii. l. v. c. iii. Compare Oviedo, l. xix. c. xiii. in Ramusio, v. iii. fol. 204.
[2] Hill's Naval History, p. 267.

story, in which frequent repetition may have gradually deepened the shades of horror. Cannibalism is the crime of famine at sea; men do not often devour one another on shore, least of all, on a coast, abounding in wild fowl and fish. The English may have suffered from want; and as a French ship, "well furnished with vittails," approached Newfoundland, they obtained possession of it by a stroke of "policie," which, if dishonest, seems not to have been regarded as disgraceful, and set sail for England. The French followed in the English ship, and complained of the exchange. It shows the favor of Henry VIII. to maritime enterprize, that he pardoned his subjects the wrong, and of his own private purse "made full and royal recompense to the French."[1]

1541. The statute books of England soon gave proof, that the "new land" of America had engaged the attention of parliament;[2] and, after the accession of Edward, the fisheries of Newfoundland obtained 1548. the protection of a special act.[3] The preamble to this latter statute, declares the navigation to have been burdened for years by exactions from the officers of the admiralty; and its enactments forbid the continuance of the oppression. An active commerce must have long existed, since exactions, levied upon it, had almost become prescriptive.

But India was still esteemed the great region of wealth; and England, then having no anticipation of one day becoming the sovereign of Hindostan, hoped

---

[1] Hakluyt, v. iii. p. 168—170.
[2] 33 Henry VIII., c. ii.; Ruffhead, v. ii. p. 304.
[3] 2 Edward VI., in Ruffhead, v. ii. p. 412; Hakluyt, v. iii. p. 170; Hazard, v. i. p. 22, 23.

VOYAGE IN SEARCH OF A NORTHEAST PASSAGE.

for a peaceful intercourse only by the discovery of a new and nearer passage to Southern Asia. Thrice at least, perhaps thrice by Cabot alone, the attempt at a northwestern passage had been made; and always in vain. A northeast passage was now proposed; the fleet of Willoughby and Chancellor was to reach the rich lands of Cathay by doubling the northern promontory of Lapland. The ships parted company. The fate of Willoughby was as tragical, as the issue of the voyage of Chancellor was successful. The admiral with one of the ships was driven, by the severity of the polar autumn, to seek shelter in a Lapland harbor, which afforded protection against storms, but not against the rigors of the season. When search was made for him in the following spring, Willoughby himself was found dead in his cabin; and his journal, detailing his sufferings from the polar winter, was complete probably to the day, when his senses were suspended by the intolerable cold. His ship's company lay dead in various parts of the vessel, some alone, some in groups. The other ship reached the harbor of Archangel. This was "the discovery of Russia," and the commencement of maritime commerce with that empire. A Spanish writer calls the result of the voyage, "a discovery of new Indies."[1] The Russian nation, one of the oldest and least mixed in Europe, now awakening from a long lethargy, emerged into political distinction. We have seen

CHAP. III.

1553.

1554.

[1] Hakluyt, v. i. p. 251—284; —301; Purchas, v. iii. p. 462, Turner's England, v. iii. p. 296 463.

CHAP. III.

that, about eleven years from this time, the first town in the United States' territory was permanently built. So rapid are the changes on the theatre of nations! One of the leading powers of the age but about two and a half centuries ago became known to Western Europe; another had not then one white man within its limits.

The principle of joint-stock companies, so favorable to every enterprize of uncertain result, by dividing the risks, and by nourishing a spirit of emulous zeal in behalf of an inviting scheme, was applied to the purposes of navigation; and a compa-

1555. ny of merchant adventurers was incorporated for the discovery of unknown lands.[1]

1553, For even the intolerance of Queen Mary could
to
1558. not check the passion for maritime adventure. The sea was becoming the element on which English valor was to display its greatest boldness; English sailors neither feared the sultry heats and consuming fevers of the tropics, nor the intense severity of northern cold. The trade to Russia, now that the port of Archangel had been discovered, gradually increased and became very lucrative; and a regular

1553. and as yet an innocent commerce was carried on with
1554. Africa.[2] The marriage of Mary with the king of
July
25. Spain, tended to excite the emulation, which it was designed to check. The enthusiasm, awakened by the brilliant pageantry, with which king Philip was introduced into London, excited Richard Eden[3] to

---

[1] Hakluyt, v. i. p. 298—304.
[2] The Viage to Guinea in 1553, in Eden and Willes, fol. 336, 337-353.
[3] Eden's Decades, first published in 1555.

ELIZABETH FAVORS ENGLISH COMMERCE.

gather into a volume the history of the most memorable maritime expeditions. Religious restraints, the thirst for rapid wealth, the desire of strange adventure, had driven the boldest spirits of Spain to the New World; their deeds had been commemorated by the copious and accurate details of the Spanish historians; and the English, through the alliance of their sovereign made familiar with the Spanish language and literature, became emulous of Spanish success beyond the ocean.

The firmness of Elizabeth seconded the enterprize of her subjects. They were rendered the more proud and intractable for the short and unsuccessful effort to make England an appendage to Spain; and the triumph of protestantism, quickening the spirit of nationality, gave a new impulse to the people. England, no longer the ally, but the antagonist of Philip, claimed the glory of being the mistress of the northern seas, and prepared to extend its commerce to every clime. The queen strengthened her navy; filled her arsenals; and encouraged the building of ships in England; she animated the adventurers to Russia and to Africa by her special protection; and while her subjects were endeavoring to penetrate into Persia by land, and enlarge their commerce with the east[1] by combining the use of ships and caravans, the harbors of Spanish America were at the same time visited by their privateers in pursuit of the rich galleons of

1558.

1561, to 1568.

---
[1] Eden and Willes. The voyages of Persia, travelled by the merchantes of London, &c. in 1561, 1567, 1568, fol. 321, and ff.

CHAP. III.
1574-8

Spain, and at least from thirty to fifty English ships came annually to the bays and banks of Newfoundland.[1]

The possibility of effecting a northwest passage had ever been maintained by Cabot. The study of geography had now become an interesting pursuit; the press teemed with books of travels, maps and descriptions of the earth; and Sir Humphrey Gilbert, reposing from the toils of war, engaged deeply in the science of cosmography. A judicious and well written argument[2] in favor of the possibility of a northwestern passage was the fruit of his literary industry.

1576.

The same views were entertained by one of the boldest men, who ever ventured upon the ocean. For fifteen years, Martin Frobisher, an Englishman, well versed in various navigation, had revolved the design of accomplishing the discovery of the northwestern passage; esteeming it "the only thing of the world, that was yet left undone, by which a notable minde might be made famous and fortunate."[3] Too poor himself to provide a ship, it was in vain, that he conferred with friends; in vain he offered his services to merchants. After years of desire, his representations found a hearing at court; and Dudley, earl of Warwick, liberally promoted his design.[4] Two small barks of twenty-five and of twenty tuns, with a pinnace of ten tuns burden,

[1] Parkhurst, in Hakluyt, v. iii. p. 171.
[2] Hakluyt, v. iii. p. 32—47.
[3] Best, in Hakluyt, v. iii. p. 86.
[4] Willes' Essay for M. Frobisher's voyage, in Eden and Willes, fol. 230, and ff.; in Hakluyt, v. iii. p. 47—52.

composed the whole fleet, which was to enter gulfs, that none but Cabot had visited. As they dropped down the Thames, Queen Elizabeth waved her hand in token of favor, and, by an honorable message, transmitted her approbation of an adventure, which her own treasures had not contributed to advance. During a storm on the voyage, the pinnace was swallowed up by the sea; the mariners in the Michael became terrified and turned their prow homewards; but Frobisher, in a vessel, not surpassing in tunnage the barge of a man-of-war, made his way, fearless and unattended, to the shores of Labrador, and to a passage or inlet, north of the entrance of Hudson's bay. A strange perversion has transferred the scene of his discoveries to the eastern coast of Greenland;[1] it was among a group of American islands, in the latitude of sixty-three degrees and eight minutes, that he entered what seemed to be a strait. Hope suggested that his object was obtained, that the land on the south was America, on the north was the continent of Asia; and that the strait opened into the immense Pacific. Great praise is due to Frobisher, even though he penetrated less deeply than Cabot into the bays and among the islands of this Meta Incognita, this unknown goal of discovery. Yet his voyage was a failure. To land upon an island, and, perhaps, on the main, to gather up stones and rubbish, in token of having taken possession of the country for Elizabeth, to seize one of

[1] Forster's Northern Voyages, p. 274—284; Hist. des Voyages, t. xv. p. 94—100.

CHAP. III.

the natives of the north for exhibition to the gaze of Europe, these were all the results which he accomplished.

1577. What followed marks the insane passions of the age. America and mines were always thought of together. A stone, which had been brought from the frozen regions, was pronounced by the refiners of London, to contain gold. The news excited the wakeful avarice of the city; there were not wanting those, who endeavored to purchase of Elizabeth a lease of the new lands, of which the loose minerals were so full of the precious metal. A fleet was immediately fitted out, to procure more of the gold, rather than to make any further research for the passage into the Pacific; and the queen, who had contributed nothing to the voyage of discovery, sent a large ship of her own to join the expedition, which was now to conduct to infinite opulence. More men than could be employed, volunteered their services; those who were discharged, resigned their brilliant hopes with reluctance. The mariners,

May 27. having received the communion, embarked for the arctic El Dorado, "and with a merrie wind" soon

June 7. arrived at the Orkneys. As they reached the northeastern coast of America, the dangers of the polar seas became imminent; mountains of ice encompassed them on every side; but as the icebergs were brilliant in the high latitude with the light of an almost perpetual summer's day, the worst perils were avoided. Yet the mariners were alternately agitated with fears of shipwreck and joy at escape.

At one moment they expected death; and at the next, they looked for gold. The fleet made no discoveries; it did not advance so far as Frobisher alone had done.[1] But it found an abundance of earth, which, even to the incredulous, seemed plainly to contain the coveted wealth; besides, spiders abounded; and "spiders were" affirmed to be "true signs of great store of gold."[2] In freighting the ships, the admiral himself toiled like a painful laborer. How strange, in human affairs, is the mixture of sublime courage and ludicrous folly! What bolder maritime enterprize, than, in that day, a voyage to lands lying north of Hudson's straits! What folly more egregious, than to have gone there for a lading of useless earth!

But credulity is apt to be self-willed. What is there which the passion for gold will not prompt? It defies danger and laughs at obstacles; it resists loss and anticipates treasures; unrelenting in its pursuit, it is deaf to the voice of mercy, and blind to the cautions of judgment; it can penetrate the prairies of Arkansas, and covet the moss-grown barrens of the Esquimaux. I have now to relate the first attempt of the English, under the patronage of Elizabeth, to plant an establishment in America.[3]

It was believed, that the rich mines of the polar regions would countervail the charges of a costly adventure; the hope of a passage to Cathay increased; and for the security of the newly discovered

---

[1] Best, in Hakluyt, v. iii. p. 95. How rich then the alcoves of a library!
[2] Settle, in Hakluyt, v. iii. p. 63.   [3] Hakluyt, v. iii. p. 71—73.

CHAP. III.
1578.

lands, soldiers and discreet men were selected to become their inhabitants. A magnificent fleet of fifteen sail was collected, in part, at the expense of Elizabeth; the sons of the English gentry embarked as volunteers; one hundred persons were selected to form the colony, which was to secure to England a country more desirable than Peru, a country, too inhospitable to produce a tree or a shrub, yet where gold lay, not charily concealed in mines, but glistening in heaps upon the surface. Twelve vessels were to return immediately with cargoes of the ore; three were ordered to remain and aid the settlement. The northwest passage was now become of less consideration; Asia itself could not vie with this hyperborean archipelago.

1578.
May 31, to Sept. 28.

But the entrance to these wealthy islands was rendered difficult by frost; and the fleet of Frobisher, as it now approached the American coast, was bewildered among the immense icebergs, which were so vast, that, as they melted, torrents poured from them in sparkling waterfalls. One vessel was crushed and sunk; though the men on board were saved. In the mists and dangers, the ships lost their course and came into the straits, which have since been called Hudson's; and which lie south of the imagined gold regions. The admiral believed himself able to pass through to the South Sea, and resolve the doubt respecting the passage. But his duty as a mercantile agent controlled his desire of glory as a navigator. He struggled to regain the harbor, where his vessels were to be laden; and, after encountering peril of every kind; "getting in at one gap and out at another;" escaping only by miracle from hidden rocks and unknown currents, ice and a lee shore, which was, at one time, avoided only by a prosperous breath of wind in the very moment of extreme danger, he at last arrived at the haven in the countess of Warwick's sound. The zeal of the volunteer colonists had moderated; and the disheartened sailors were ready to mutiny. One ship, laden with provisions for the colony, deserted and returned; and an island was discovered with enough of the black ore "to suffice all the gold-gluttons of the world." The plan of the settlement was abandoned. It only remained to freight the home-bound ships with a store of minerals. They, who engage in a foolish project, combine, in case of failure, to conceal their loss; for a confession of the truth would be an impeachment of their judgment; so that unfortunate speculations are promptly consigned to oblivion. The adventurers and the historians of the voyages are all silent about the disposition which was made of the cargo of their fleet. The knowledge of the seas was not extended by the voyage; the credulity of avarice met with a rebuke; and the belief in regions of gold among the Esquimaux was dissipated; but there remained a firm conviction, that a passage to the Pacific ocean might yet be threaded among the icebergs and northern islands of America.[1]

[1] On Frobisher, consult the original accounts of Hall, Settle, Ellis and Best, with R. Hakluyt's instructions, in Hak. v. iii. p. 52-129.

98   DRAKE IN THE OREGON TERRITORY.

CHAP.
III.

While Frobisher was thus attempting to obtain wealth and fame on the northeast coast of America, the western limits of the territory of the United States became known. Embarking on a voyage in 1577, quest of fortune, Francis Drake acquired immense to 1580. treasures as a freebooter in the Spanish harbors on the Pacific; and, having laden his ship with spoils, gained for himself enduring glory by circumnavigating the globe. But before following in the path, which the ship of Magellan had thus far alone dared to pursue, Drake determined to explore the northwestern coast of America, in the hope of discovering the strait which connects the oceans. With this view, he crossed the equator, sailed beyond the peninsula of California, and followed the continent to the latitude of forty-three degrees, corresponding to the latitude of the southern borders of New-1579. Hampshire.[1] Here the cold seemed intolerable to June. men, who had just left the tropics. Despairing of success, he retired to a harbor in a milder latitude, within the limits of Mexico; and, having repaired his ship, and named the country New-Albion, he sailed for England, through the seas of Asia. Thus was the southern part of the Oregon territory first visited by Englishmen; yet not till after a voyage of 1542. the Spanish from Acapulco, commanded by Cabrillo, a Portuguese, had traced the American continent to within two and a half degrees of the mouth of Co-1593. lumbia river;[2] while, thirteen years after the voyage

[1] Course of Sir Francis Drake, in Hakluyt, v. iii. p. 524; Johnson's Life of Drake.
[2] Forster's Northern Voyages, b. iii. c. iv. s. ii.

of Drake, John de Fuca, a mariner from the isle of Greece, then in the employ of the viceroy of Mexico, sailed into the bay, which is now known as the gulf of Georgia, and, having for twenty days steered through its intricate windings and numerous islands, returned with a belief, that the entrance to the long desired passage into the Atlantic had been found.[1]

The lustre of the name of Drake is borrowed from his success. In itself, this part of his career was but a splendid piracy against a nation, with which his sovereign and his country professed to be at peace. Oxenham, a subordinate officer, who had ventured to imitate his master, was taken by the Spaniards and hanged; nor was his punishment either unexpected or censured in England as severe. The exploits of Drake, except so far as they nourished a love for maritime affairs, were injurious to commerce; the minds of the sailors were debauched by a passion for sudden acquisitions; and to receive regular wages seemed base and unmanly, when at the easy peril of life, there was hope of boundless plunder. Commerce and colonization rest on regular industry; the humble labor of the English fishermen, who now frequented the Grand Bank, bred mariners for the navy of their country, and prepared the way for its settlements in the New World. Already four hundred vessels came annually from the harbors of Portugal and Spain, of France and England, to the shores of Newfoundland. The English

[1] Purchas, v. iv. p. 849—852. iv. Belknap's American Biogra-
Forster is sceptical; b. iii. c. iv. s. phy, v. i. p. 224—230.

were not there in such numbers as other nations, for they still frequented the fisheries of Iceland; but yet they "were commonly lords in the harbors," and, in the arrogance of naval supremacy, exacted payment for protection.[1] It is an incident, honorable to the humanity of the early voyagers, that, on one of the American islands, not far from the fishing stations, hogs and horned cattle were purposely left, that they might multiply and become a resource to some future generation of colonists.[2]

While the queen and her adventurers were dazzled by the glittering prospects of mines of gold in the frozen regions of the remote north, Sir Humphrey Gilbert, with a sounder judgment and a better knowledge, watched the progress of the fisheries and formed healthy plans for colonization. He had been a soldier and a member of parliament. He was a judicious writer on navigation;[3] and though censured for his ignorance of the principles of liberty,[4] he was esteemed for the sincerity of his piety. He was one of those, who alike despise fickleness and fear; danger never turned him aside from the pursuit of honor or the service of his sovereign; for he knew that death is inevitable and the fame of virtue immortal.[5] It was not difficult for Gilbert to obtain a liberal patent,[6] formed according to the tenor of a previous precedent; and to be of perpet-

---

[1] See the letter of Ant. Parkhurst, who had himself been for four years engaged in the Newfoundland trade, in Hakluyt, v. iii. p. 170—174.
[2] Hakluyt, v. iii. p. 197.
[3] Ibid, v. iii. p. 32—47.
[4] D'Ewes' Journal, p. 168 and 175.
[5] Gilbert, in Hakluyt, v. iii. p. 47.
[6] The patent may be found in Hakluyt, v. iii. p. 174—176; Stith's Virginia, p. 4, 5, 6; Hazard, v. i. p. 24—28.

ual efficacy, if a plantation should be established within six years. To the people, who might belong to his colony, the rights of Englishmen were promised; to Gilbert, the possession for himself or his assigns of the soil which he might discover; and the sole jurisdiction, both civil and criminal, of the territory within two hundred leagues of his settlement, with supreme executive and legislative authority. Thus the attempts at colonization, in which Cabot and Frobisher had failed, were renewed under a patent which conferred every immunity on the leader of the enterprize, and abandoned the colonists themselves to the mercy of an absolute proprietary.

Under this patent, Gilbert began to collect a company of volunteer adventurers, contributing largely from his own fortune to the preparation. Jarrings and divisions ensued, before the voyage was begun; many abandoned what they had inconsiderately undertaken; the general and a few of his assured friends, among them, perhaps, his step-brother, Walter Raleigh, put to sea; one of his ships was lost; and misfortune compelled the remainder to return.[1] The vagueness of the accounts of this expedition is ascribed to a conflict with a Spanish fleet, of which the issue was unfavorable to the little squadron of emigrants.[2] Gilbert attempted to keep his patent alive by making grants of lands. None of his assigns succeeded in establishing a colony; and he was himself too much impoverished to renew his efforts.

[1] Hayes' Report, in Hakluyt, v. 28, 29, edition of 1829.; Tytler's Life of Raleigh, p. 26, 27. iii. p. 186.
[2] Oldys' Life of Raleigh, p.

But the pupil of Coligny was possessed of an active genius, which delighted in hazardous adventure. To prosecute discoveries in the New World, lay the foundation of states, and acquire immense domains, appeared to the daring enterprize of Raleigh as easy designs, which would not interfere with the pursuit of favor and the career of glory in England. Before the limit of the charter had expired, Gilbert, assisted by his brother, equipped a new squadron. The fleet embarked under happy omens; the commander, on the eve of his departure, received from Elizabeth a golden anchor guided by a lady, a token of the queen's regard; a man of letters from Hungary accompanied the expedition; and some part of the United States would have then been colonized, had not the unhappy projector of the design been overwhelmed by a succession of disasters. Two days after leaving Plymouth, the largest ship in the fleet, which had been furnished by Raleigh, who himself remained in England, deserted under a pretence of infectious disease, and returned into harbor. Gilbert was incensed, but not intimidated. He sailed for Newfoundland; and, entering St. Johns, he summoned the Spaniards and Portuguese, and other strangers, to witness the feudal ceremonies, by which he took possession of the country for his sovereign. A pillar, on which the arms of England were infixed, was raised as a monument; and lands were granted to the fishermen in fee, on condition of the payment of a quit-rent. The "mineral-man" of the expedition, an honest and religious Saxon, was especially diligent; it was generally agreed, that "the mountains made a show of mineral substance;" the Saxon protested on his life that silver ore abounded; he was charged to keep the discovery a profound secret; and, as there were so many foreign vessels in the vicinity, the precious ore was carried on board the larger ship with such mystery, that the dull Portuguese and Spaniards suspected nothing of the matter.

It was not easy for Gilbert to preserve order in the little fleet. Many of the mariners, infected with the vices, which at that time degraded their profession, were no better than pirates; and were perpetually bent upon pillaging whatever ships fell in their way. At length, having abandoned one of their barks, the English, now in three vessels only, sailed on further discoveries, intending to visit the coast of the United States. But they had not proceeded farther to the south, than the latitude of Wiscasset, when the largest ship, from the carelessness of the crew, struck and was wrecked. Nearly a hundred men perished; the "mineral-man" and the ore were all lost; nor was it possible to rescue Parmenius, the Hungarian scholar, who should have been the historian of the expedition.

It now seemed necessary to hasten to England; Gilbert had sailed in the Squirrel, a bark of ten tuns only; and therefore convenient for entering harbors and approaching the coast. On the homeward voyage, the brave admiral would not forsake his little company, with whom he had passed so many storms and perils. A desperate resolution! The weather was extremely rough; the oldest mariner had never seen "more outrageous seas." The little frigate, not more than twice as large as the long-boat of a merchantman, "too small a bark to pass through the ocean sea at that season of the year," was nearly wrecked. The general, sitting abaft with a book in his hand, cried out to those in the Hind; "We are as neere to heaven by sea as by land." That same night, about twelve o'clock, the lights of the Squirrel suddenly disappeared, and neither the vessel nor any of its crew was ever again seen. The Hind reached Falmouth in safety.[1]

The bold spirit of Raleigh was not disheartened by the sad fate of his step-brother; but his mind revolved a settlement in a milder climate; and he was determined to secure to England those delightful countries, from which the protestants of France had been expelled. Having presented a memorial, he readily obtained from Elizabeth a patent,[2] as ample as that which had been conferred on Gilbert. It was drawn according to the principles of feudal law; Raleigh was constituted a lord proprietary, with almost unlimited powers; holding his territories by homage and an inconsiderable rent, and possessing jurisdiction over an extensive region, of which he had power to make grants according to his pleasure.

---

[1] On Gilbert, see Hayes, in Hakluyt, v. iii. p. 184—203; Parmenius to Hakluyt, v. iii. p. 203—205; Clark's Relation, ibid, p. 206—208; Gilbert to Peckham, in Purchas, v. iii. p. 808; Raleigh to Gilbert, in Tytler's Raleigh, p. 45. Compare the Lives of Raleigh by Oldys, Caylus, Thomson, Tytler.

[2] Hakluyt, v. iii. p. 297—301; Hazard, v. i. p. 33—38.

Expectations rose high, since the balmy regions of the south were now to be colonized; and the terrors of icy seas were forgotten in the hope of gaining a province in a clime of perpetual fertility, where winter hardly intruded to check the productiveness of nature. Two vessels, well laden with men and provisions, under the command of Philip Amidas and Arthur Barlow, buoyant with hope, set sail for the New World. They pursued the circuitous route by the Canaries and the islands of the West Indies; after a short stay in those islands, they sailed for the north, and were soon opposite the shores of Carolina. As they drew near land, the fragrance was, "as if they had been in the midst of some delicate garden, abounding with all kinds of odoriferous flowers." They ranged the coast for a distance of one hundred and twenty miles, in search of a convenient harbor; they entered the first haven which offered, and, after thanks to God for their safe arrival, they landed to take possession of the country for the queen of England.

CHAP. III.

1584.

April 27.

July 2.

July 13.

The spot on which this ceremony was performed, was in the island of Wocoken, the southernmost of the islands forming Ocracock inlet. These shores, at some periods of the year, cannot safely be approached by a fleet, from the hurricanes, which sweep the air in those regions, and against which the formation of the coast offers no secure roadsteads and harbors. But in the month of July, the sea was tranquil; the skies were clear; no storms were gathering; the air was agitated by none but the gentlest breezes; and the English commanders were in raptures with the beauty of the ocean, seen in the magnificence of repose, gemmed with islands, and expanding in the clearest transparency from cape to cape. The vegetation of that southern latitude struck the beholders with admiration; the forest trees had not their paragons in the world; the luxuriant vines, as they clambered up the loftiest cedars, formed graceful festoons; grapes were so plenty upon every little shrub, that the surge of the ocean, as it lazily rolled in upon the shore with the quiet winds of summer, dashed its spray upon the clusters; and natural arbors were formed of such impervious shade, that not a ray of the suns of July could penetrate their recesses. The forests were filled with birds; and, at the discharge of an arquebus, whole flocks would arise, uttering a cry, which the many echoes redoubled, till it seemed as if an army of men had shouted together.

The gentleness of the native inhabitants appeared in harmony with the loveliness of the scene. The desire of traffic overcame the timidity of the natives, and the English received a friendly welcome. On the island of Roanoke, they were entertained by the wife of Granganimeo, father of Wingina, the king, with the refinements of Arcadian hospitality. "The people were most gentle, loving and faithful, void of all guile and treason, and such as lived after the manner of the golden age." They had no cares but to guard against the moderate cold of a short winter; and to gather such food, as the earth almost spontaneously produced. And yet it was added, with singular want of comparison, that the wars of these guileless men were cruel and bloody; that domestic dissensions had almost exterminated whole tribes; that they employed the basest stratagems against their enemies; and that the practice of inviting men to a feast, that they might be murdered in the hour of confidence, was not merely a device of European bigots, but was known to the natives of Secotan. The English, too, were solicited to engage in a similar enterprize, under promise of lucrative booty.

The adventurers were satisfied with observing the general aspect of the country; no extensive examination of the coast was undertaken; Pamlico and Albemarle sound and Roanoke island were explored; and some information gathered by inquiries from the Indians; the commanders had not the courage or the enterprize to survey the country with exactness. Having made but a short stay in America, they arrived in September in the west of England, accompanied by Manteo and Wanchese, two natives of the country; and the returning voyagers gave such glowing descriptions of their discoveries, as might be expected from men who had done no more than sail over the smooth waters of a summer's sea, among "the hundred islands" of North-Carolina.[1]

[1] Amidas and Barlow's account, in Hakluyt, v. iii. p. 301—307. I have compared on this and the following voyages, Smith's Virginia, v. i. p. 80—85;. Stith's Virginia, p. 8—12; Belknap's Am. Biog. v. i. p. 206—212; Tytler's Raleigh, p. 47—54; Oldys, p. 55; Birch, p. 580, 581; Caylus, v. i. p. 33—46; Thomson, p. 32; Williamson's inaccurate History of North-Carolina, v. i. p. 28—37; and the very

CHAP. Elizabeth, as she heard their reports, esteemed her
III.
reign signalized by the discovery of the enchanting
1584. regions, and named them Virginia, as a memorial of
her state of life.

Nor was it long before Raleigh, elected to represent in parliament the county of Devon, obtained a
Dec. bill confirming his patent of discovery;[1] and while
18.
he received the honor of knighthood, as the reward of his valor, he also acquired a lucrative monopoly of wines, which enabled him to continue with vigor his schemes of colonization.[2] The prospect of becoming the proprietary of a delightful territory, with a numerous tenantry, who should yield him their fealty, inflamed his ambition; and, as the English nation listened with credulity to the descriptions of Amidas and Barlow, it was not difficult to gather a numerous company of emigrants. While a new patent[3] was issued to his friend, for the discovery of the northwestern passage, and the well-known voyages of Davis, sustained, in part, by the contributions of Raleigh himself, were increasing the acquaintance of Europe with the Arctic sea, the plan of colonizing Virginia was earnestly and steadily pursued.

1585. The new expedition was composed of seven vessels and carried one hundred and eight colonists to the shores of Carolina. Ralph Lane, a man of con-

meagre work of Martin, History of North-Carolina, v. i. p. 9—12. I have followed exclusively the contemporaneous account, deriving, in the comparison of localities, much benefit from a MS. in my possession, by J. S. Jones, of Shocco, North-Carolina, who has, with minute fidelity, explored the portion of his native state, so distinguished in early American history.
[1] D'Ewes' Journal, p. 339. 341.
[2] Tytler's Life of Raleigh, p. 54, 55; Oldys' Raleigh, p. 58, 59.
[3] Hakluyt, v. iii. p. 129—157.

siderable distinction, and so much esteemed for his services as a soldier, that he was afterwards knighted by Queen Elizabeth, was willing to act for Raleigh as governor of the colony. Sir Richard Grenville, the most able and celebrated of Raleigh's associates, distinguished for bravery among the gallant spirits of a gallant age, assumed the command of the fleet. It sailed from Plymouth, accompanied by several men of merit, whom the world remembers; by Cavendish, who soon after circumnavigated the globe; Hariot, the inventor of the system of notation in modern algebra,[1] the historian of the expedition; and With, an ingenious painter, whose sketches[2] of the natives, their habits and modes of life, were taken with beauty and exactness, and were the means of encouraging an interest in Virginia, by diffusing a knowledge of its productions.

To sail by the Canaries and the West Indies, to conduct a gainful commerce with the Spanish ports by intimidation; to capture Spanish vessels;—these were but the expected preliminaries of a voyage to Virginia. At length the fleet fell in with the main land of Florida; it was in great danger of being wrecked on the cape, which was then first called the cape of Fear; and two days after it came to anchor at Wocoken. The perils of the navigation on the shoals of that coast became too evident; the largest ship of the squadron, as it entered the harbor,

---

[1] Tyler's Life of Raleigh, p. 66. Stith's Virginia, p. 20.
[2] See the sketches, in De Bry, part ii. They are also imitated in Beverly's Virginia. Both are before me.

struck, but was not lost. It was through Ocracock inlet, that the fleet made its way to Roanoke.

But the fate of this colony was destined to be influenced by the character of the natives. Manteo, the friend of the English, and who returned with the fleet from a visit to England, was sent to the main to announce their arrival. Grenville, accompanied by Lane, Hariot, Cavendish and others, in an excursion of eight days, explored the coast as far as Secotan; and, as they relate, were well entertained of the savages. At one of the Indian towns, a silver cup had been stolen; its restoration was delayed; with hasty cruelty, Grenville ordered the village to be burnt and the standing corn to be destroyed. Not long after this action of inconsiderate revenge, the ships, having landed the colony, sailed for England; a rich Spanish prize, made by Grenville on the return voyage, secured him a courteous welcome as he entered the harbor of Plymouth. The transport ships of the colony were at the same time privateers.[1]

The employments of Lane and his colonists, after the departure of Sir Richard Grenville, could be none other than to explore the country; and in a letter, which he wrote, while his impressions were yet fresh, he expressed himself in language of enthusiastic admiration. "It is the goodliest soil under the cope of heaven; the most pleasing territory of the world; the continent is of a huge and

[1] The Voyage, in Hakluyt, v. iii. p. 307—310.

unknown greatness, and very well peopled and towned, though savagely. The climate is so wholesome, that we have not one sick, since we touched the land. If Virginia had but horses and kine, and were inhabited with English, no realm in christendom were comparable to it."¹

The keenest observer was Hariot; and he was often employed in dealing with "the natural inhabitants." He carefully observed the productions of the country, those which would furnish commodities for commerce, and those which were in use among the natives. He observed the culture of tobacco; accustomed himself to its use, and was a firm believer in its healing virtues. The culture of maize, and the extraordinary productiveness of that grain especially attracted his admiration; and the tuberous roots of the potato, when boiled, were found to be very good food. The inhabitants are described as too feeble to inspire terror; clothed in mantles and aprons of deer-skins; having no weapons but wooden swords and bows of witch-hazle with arrows of reeds; no armor but targets of bark and sticks wickered together with thread. Their towns were but small; the largest contained but thirty dwellings. The walls of the houses were made of bark, fastened to stakes; and sometimes consisted of poles fixed upright and close one by another; and at the top bent over and fastened; as arbors are sometimes made in gardens. But the great peculiarity of the Indians consisted in the want of political

[1] Lane, in Hakluyt, v. iii. p. 311.

connexion. A single town often constituted a government; a collection of ten or twenty wigwams was an independent state. The greatest chief in the whole country could not muster more than seven or eight hundred fighting men. In the interior of Europe at the present day, it is not uncommon to find adjacent villages so little connected, that their language becomes respectively tinged with local peculiarities; to Hariot, the dialect of each government seemed different from any other. The wars among themselves rarely led them to the open battle-field; they were accustomed rather to sudden surprises at daybreak or by moonlight, to ambushes and the subtle devices of cunning falsehood. Destitute of the arts, they yet displayed excellency of wit in all which they attempted. Nor were they entirely ignorant of religion; but to the credulity of polytheism, they joined a confused belief in the existence of one supreme power. It is natural to the human mind to desire immortality; the natives of Carolina believed in continued existence after death and in retributive justice. The mathematical instruments, the burning-glass, guns, clocks, and the use of letters, seemed the works of gods, rather than of men; and the English were reverenced as the pupils and favorites of heaven. In every town which Hariot entered, he displayed the bible and explained its truths; the Indians revered the volume rather than its doctrines; and with a fond superstition, they embraced the book, kissed it, and held it to their breasts and heads, as if it had been an amulet. As the colonists enjoyed uniform health and had no women with them, there were some among the Indians, who imagined the English were not born of woman, and therefore not mortal; that they were men of an old generation, risen to immortality. The terrors of fire-arms the natives could neither comprehend nor resist; every sickness, which now prevailed among them, was attributed to wounds from invisible bullets, discharged by unseen agents, with whom the air was supposed to be peopled. They prophecied, that "there were more of the English generation yet to come, to kill theirs and take their places;" and some believed, that the purpose of extermination was already matured and its execution begun.[1]

CHAP. III.

1585.

Was it strange, then, that the natives desired to be delivered from the presence of guests, by whom they feared to be supplanted? The colonists were mad with the passion for gold; and a wily savage invented, respecting the river Roanoke[2] and its banks, extravagant tales, which nothing but cupidity could have credited. The river, it was said, gushed forth from a rock, so near the Pacific ocean, that the surge of the sea sometimes dashed into its fountain; its banks were inhabited by a nation, skilled in the arts of refining the rich ore, in which the country abounded. Lane was so credulous, that he attempted to ascend the rapid current of the Roanoke; and his followers, infatuated with greedy avarice, would

1586.

Mar.

[1] Hariot, in Hakluyt, v. iii. p. 324—340.   [2] Then called Moratuck.

not return, till their stores of provisions were exhausted and they had killed and eaten the very dogs which bore them company. On this attempt to explore the interior, the English hardly advanced higher up the river than some point near the present village of Williamstown.

April. The Indians had hoped to destroy the English by thus dividing them; but the prompt return of Lane prevented open hostilities. They next conceived the plan of leaving their lands unplanted; and they were willing to abandon their fields, if famine would in consequence compel the departure of their too powerful guests. The conspiracy was defeated by the moderation of one of their aged chiefs; but the feeling of enmity could not be

May. restrained. The English believed that a general conspiracy was preparing; that fear of a foreign enemy was now teaching the natives the necessity of union; and that a grand alliance was forming, of which the object would be the destruction of the strangers by a general massacre. Perhaps the English, whom avarice had certainly rendered credulous, were now precipitate in giving faith to the suggestions of jealousy; it is certain, that in the contest of dissimulation, they proved themselves the more successful adepts. Desiring an audience of Wingina, the most active among the native chiefs, Lane and

June 1. his attendants were quickly admitted to his presence. No hostile intentions were displayed by the Indians; their reception of the English was proof of their confidence. Immediately a preconcerted watchword

ILL SUCCESS OF THE ENGLISH COLONY. 115

was given; and the Christians, falling upon the unhappy king and his principal followers, put them without mercy to death.

CHAP.
III.

1586.

It was evident that Lane did not possess the qualities suited to his station. He had not the sagacity, which could rightly interpret the stories or the designs of the natives; and the courage, like the eye, of a soldier, differs from that of a traveller. His discoveries were inconsiderable; to the south they had extended only to Secotan, in the present county of Carteret, between the Pamlico and the Neuse; to the north they reached no farther than the small river Elizabeth, which joins the Chesapeake bay below Norfolk; in the interior, the Chowan had been examined beyond the junction of the Meherrin and the Nottaway; and we have seen, that the hope of gold attracted Lane to make a short excursion up the Roanoke. Yet some general results of importance were obtained. The climate was found to be salubrious; during the year but four men had died, and of these, three brought the seeds of their disease from Europe.[1] The hope of finding better harbors at the north was confirmed; and the bay of Chesapeake was already regarded as the fit theatre for early colonization. But in the island of Roanoke the men began to despond; they looked in vain towards the ocean for supplies from England; they were sighing for the luxuries of the cities in their native land; when of a sudden it was rumored, that the sea was white with the sails of three and twenty

June 8.

[1] Hariot, in Hakluyt, v. iii. p. 340; True Declaration of Virginia, p. 32.

ships; and within three days Sir Francis Drake had anchored his fleet outside of Roanoke inlet, in "the road of their bad harbor."

He had come, on his way from the West Indies to England, to visit the colony of his friend. With the celerity of genius, he discovered the measures, which the exigency of the case required; and supplied the wants of Lane to the uttermost; giving him a bark of seventy tons, with pinnaces and small boats. Above all, he induced two experienced sea-captains to remain in the colony and employ themselves in the action of discovery. Every thing was furnished to complete the surveys along the coast and the rivers; and, in the last resort, if suffering became extreme, to transport the colony to England.

At this time an unwonted storm suddenly arose and had nearly wrecked the fleet, which lay in a most dangerous position. The bark, that had been laden with provisions for the colony, was driven out to sea; the fleet had no security but in weighing anchor and standing away from the shore; and when the tempest was over, nothing could be found of the boats and the bark, which had been set apart for the colony. The humanity of Drake was not weary; he instantly devised measures for supplying the colony with the means of continuing their discoveries; but Lane shared the despondency of his men; and Drake yielded to their unanimous desire of permission to embark in his ships for England. Thus ended the first actual settlement of the English in America. The exiles of a year had grown familiar with the favorite amusement of the lethargic Indians; and they introduced into England the general use of tobacco.[1]

CHAP. III.
1586.

The return of Lane was a precipitate desertion; a little delay would have furnished the colony with ample supplies. A few days after its departure a ship arrived, laden with all stores, needed by the infant settlement. It had been despatched by Raleigh; but finding "the paradise of the world" deserted, it could only return to England.[2] Another fortnight had hardly elapsed, when Sir Richard Grenville appeared off the coast with three well furnished ships, and renewed the vain search for the English colony. Unwilling that the English should lose possession of the country, he left fifteen men on the island of Roanoke, to be the guardians of English rights.[3]

Raleigh was not dismayed by ill success, nor borne down by losses. The enthusiasm of the people of England was diminished by the reports of the unsuccessful company of Lane; but the decisive testimony of Hariot to the excellence of the country, still rendered it easy to collect a new colony for America. The wisdom of Raleigh was particularly displayed in the policy, which he now adopted. He deter-

1587.

---

[1] On the settlement, see Lane's Particularities, &c. in Hakluyt, v. iii. p. 311—322, the original account. The reader may compare Camden, p. 286; Stith, p. 12—21; Smith, v. i. p. 86—99; Belknap, v. i. p. 213—216; Williamson, v. i. p. 37—51; Martin, v. i. p. 12—24; Tytler's Raleigh, p. 56—68; Thomson's Raleigh, c. i. and ii. and Appendix B.; Oldys, c. 65—71; Caylus, v. i. p. 46—81; Birch, p. 582—584, edition of 1829.
[2] Hakluyt, v. iii. p. 323.
[3] Hakluyt, v. iii. p. 323. Stith, p. 22, and Belknap, v. i. p. 217, say fifty men; erroneously. Smith, v. i. p. 99, began the error.

CHAP. mined to plant an agricultural state; to send emi-
III.
grants with wives and families, who should at once
1587. make their homes in the New World; and, that life
Jan.
7. and property might be secured, he granted a charter
of incorporation for the settlement, and established
a municipal government for "the city of Raleigh."
John White was appointed its governor; and to him,
with eleven assistants, the administration of the
colony was entrusted. A fleet of transport ships
was prepared at the expense of the proprietary;
"Queen Elizabeth, the godmother of Virginia,"
declined contributing "to its education." The com-
April pany, as it embarked, was cheered by the presence
26.
of women; and an ample provision of the implements of husbandry gave a pledge for successful
industry. In July, they arrived on the coast of
North-Carolina; they were saved from the dangers
of Cape Fear; and, passing Cape Hatteras, they
hastened to the isle of Roanoke, to search for the
handful of men, whom Grenville had left there as a
garrison. They found the tenements deserted and
overgrown with weeds; human bones lay scattered
on the field; wild deer were reposing in the untenanted houses; and were feeding on the productions,
which a rank vegetation still forced from the gardens.
The fort was in ruins. No vestige of surviving life
appeared. The miserable men, whom Grenville had
left, had been murdered by the Indians.

The instructions of Raleigh had designated the
place for the new settlement on the bay of the Chesapeake. It marks but little union, that Fernando,

the naval officer, eager to renew a profitable traffic in the West Indies, refused his assistance in exploring the coast, and White was compelled to remain on Roanoke. The fort of Governor Lane, "with sundry decent dwelling-houses," had been built at the northern extremity of the island; it was there, that the foundations of the city of Raleigh were laid. The island of Roanoke is now almost uninhabited; commerce has selected securer harbors for its pursuits; the intrepid pilot and the hardy "wrecker," rendered adventurously daring by their familiarity with the dangers of the coast, and in their natures wild as the storms to which their skill bids defiance, unconscious of the associations by which they are surrounded, are the only tenants of the spot, where the inquisitive stranger may yet discern the ruins of the fort, round which the cottages of the new settlement were erected.

But disasters thickened. A tribe of savages displayed implacable jealousy and murdered one of the assistants. The mother and the kindred of Manteo welcomed the English to the island of Croatan; and a mutual friendship was continued. But even this alliance was not unclouded. A detachment of the English, discovering a company of the natives whom they esteemed their enemies, fell upon them by night, as the harmless men were sitting fearlessly by their fires; and the havoc was begun, before it was perceived that these were friendly Indians.

The vanities of the world were not forgotten in Roanoke; and Manteo, the faithful Indian chief, "by the commandment of Sir Walter Raleigh," was christened on Roanoke, and invested with the title[1] of a feudal baron. It was the first peerage, erected by the English in America; and remained a solitary dignity, till Locke and Shaftesbury suggested the establishment of palatinates in Carolina, and Manteo shared his honors with the greatest philospher of his age.

As the time for the departure of the ship for England drew near, the emigrants became gloomy with apprehensions; they were conscious of their dependence on Europe; and they, with one voice, women as well as men, urged the governor to return and use his vigorous intercession for the prompt despatch of reinforcements and supplies. It was in vain that he pleaded a sense of honor, which called upon him to remain and share in person the perils of the colony, which he was appointed to govern. He was forced to yield to the general importunity.

Yet previous to his departure, his daughter, Eleanor Dare, the wife of one of the assistants, gave birth to a female child, the first offspring of English parents on the soil of the United States. The child was named from the place of its birth. The colony, now composed of eighty-nine men, seventeen women and two children, whose names are all preserved, might reasonably hope for the speedy return of the governor, who, as he sailed for England, left with them, as hostages, his daughter and his grandchild, VIRGINIA DARE.

[1] Lord of Roanoke and Dasamonguepeuk.

And yet even those ties were insufficient. The colony received no seasonable relief; and the further history of this neglected plantation is involved in gloomy uncertainty. The inhabitants of "the city of Raleigh," the emigrants from England and the first-born of America, failed, like their predecessors, in establishing an enduring settlement; but, unlike their predecessors, they awaited death in the land of their adoption. If America had no English town, it soon had English graves.[1]

For when White reached England, he found its whole attention absorbed by the threats of an invasion from Spain; and Grenville, Raleigh and Lane, not less than Frobisher, Drake and Hawkins, were engaged in planning measures of resistance. Yet Raleigh, whose patriotism did not diminish his generosity, found means to despatch White with supplies in two vessels. But the company, desiring a gainful voyage rather than a safe one, ran in chase of prizes; till at last, one of them fell in with men-of-war from Rochelle, and, after a bloody fight, was boarded and rifled. Both ships were compelled to return immediately to England, to the ruin of the colony and the displeasure of its author.[2] The delay was fatal; the independence of the English kingdom and the security of the protestant reformation were in danger; nor could the poor colonists of Roanoke be

---

[1] The original account of White, in Hakluyt, v. iii. p. 340—348. The story is repeated by Smith, Stith, Keith, Burk, Belknap, Williamson, Martin, Thomson, Tytler, and others.

[2] Hakluyt, edition 1589, p. 771; quoted in Oldys, p. 98, 99; Caylus, v. i. p. 106, 107. Tytler, p. 75; Thomson, p. 40; Belknap's American Biography, v. i. p. 219 Stith's Virginia, p. 25.

again remembered, till after the discomfiture of the invincible Armada.

1588. Even when complete success against the Spanish fleet, had crowned the arms of England, Sir Walter Raleigh found himself unable to continue the attempts at colonizing Virginia; for he had already incurred a fruitless expense of forty thousand pounds. Yet he did not despair of ultimate success; he admired the invincible constancy, which would bury the remembrance of past dangers in the glory of annexing fertile provinces to his country; and as his fortune did not permit him to renew his exertions, he used the privilege of his patent to form a company of merchants and adventurers, who were endowed by his liberality with large concessions, and who, it was hoped, would replenish Virginia with settlers. Among the men, who thus obtained an assignment of the proprietary's rights in Virginia, is found the name of Richard Hakluyt; it is the connecting link between the first efforts of England in North-Carolina and the final colonization of Virginia. The colonists at Roanoke had emigrated with a
1589. charter; the new instrument[1] was not an assignMar. 7. ment of Raleigh's patent; but extended a grant, already held under its sanction, by increasing the number to whom the rights of that charter belonged.

Yet the enterprize of the adventurers languished, for it was no longer encouraged by the profuse liber1590. ality of Raleigh. More than another year elapsed,

[1] Hazard, v. i. p. 42—45.

THE ROANOKE COLONY IS LOST. 123

before White[1] could return to search for his colony and his daughter; and then the island of Roanoke was a desert. An inscription on the bark of a tree pointed to Croatan; but the season of the year and the dangers from storms were pleaded as an excuse for an immediate return. Had the emigrants already perished? Or had they escaped with their lives to Croatan, and, through the friendship of Manteo, become familiar with the Indians? The conjecture has been hazarded,[2] that the deserted colony, neglected by their own countrymen, were hospitably adopted into the tribe of Hatteras Indians, and became amalgamated with the sons of the forest. This was the tradition of the natives at a later day, and was thought to be confirmed by the physical character of the tribe, in which the English and the Indian race seemed to have been blended. Raleigh long cherished the hope of discovering some vestiges of their existence; and though he had abandoned the design of colonizing Virginia, he yet sent at his own charge, and, it is said, at five several times,[3] to search for his liege-men. But it was all in vain; imagination received no help in its attempts to trace the fate of the colony of Roanoke.

CHAP. III.

1590.

The name of Raleigh stands highest among the statesmen of England, who advanced the colonization of the United States; and his fame belongs to American history. No Englishman of his age possessed so various or so extraordinary qualities. Cour-

---

[1] White, in Hakluyt, v. iii. p. 348, 349, and 350—357.
[2] Lawson's N. Carolina, p. 62.
[3] Purchas, v. iv. p. 1653.

age, which was never daunted, mild self-possession and fertility of invention, ensured him glory in his profession of arms, and his services in the conquest of Cadiz, or the capture of Fayal, were alone sufficient to establish his fame as a gallant and successful commander. In every danger his life was distinguished by valor, and his death was ennobled by true magnanimity.

He was not only admirable in active life as a soldier; he was an accomplished scholar. No statesman in retirement ever expressed the charms of tranquil leisure more beautifully than Raleigh; and it was not entirely with the language of grateful friendship, that Spenser described his "sweet verse, as sprinkled with nectar," and rivalling the melodies of "the summer's nightingale."[1] When an unjust verdict, contrary to probability and the evidence, "against law and against equity,"[2] on a charge, which seems to have been a pure invention, left him to languish for years in prison, with the sentence of death suspended over his head, his active genius plunged into the depths of erudition; and he, who had been a soldier, a courtier, and a seaman, now became the elaborate author of a learned history of the world.

His career as a statesman was honorable to the pupil of Coligny and the contemporary of L' Hopital. In his public policy he was thoroughly an English

---

[1] Sonnet prefixed to Faery Queen. Faery Queen, b. iii. Int. st. iv. Compare, also, Spenser's Colin Clout's come home again, verses 68—75, and Faery Queen, b. iii. c. vii. st. 36—41.

[2] The words are from Hume, an enemy to Raleigh's fame.

patriot; jealous of the honor, the prosperity, and the advancement of his country; the inexorable antagonist of the pretensions of Spain. In parliament he defended the freedom of domestic industry. When, by the operation of unequal laws, taxation was a burden upon industry rather than wealth, he argued for a change;[1] himself possessed of a lucrative monopoly, he gave his vote for the repeal of all monopolies;[2] and, while he pertinaciously used his influence with his sovereign, to mitigate the severity of the judgments against the non-conformists,[3] as a legislator he resisted the sweeping enactment of persecuting laws.[4]

In the career of discovery, his perseverance was never baffled by losses. He joined in the risks of Gilbert's expedition; contributed to the discoveries of Davis in the northwest; and himself personally explored "the insular regions and broken world" of Guiana. The sincerity of his belief in the wealth of the latter country has been unreasonably questioned. If Elizabeth had hoped for a hyperborean Peru in the arctic seas of America, why might not Raleigh expect to find the city of gold on the banks of the Oronoco? His lavish efforts in colonizing the soil of our republic, his sagacity which enjoined a settlement within the Chesapeake bay, the publications of Hariot and Hakluyt which he countenanced, if followed by losses to himself, diffused over England a knowledge of America, and an inter-

[1] Tytler, p. 238, 239.
[2] D'Ewes, p. 646; Tytler, p. 239.
[3] Oldys, p. 137—139.
[4] Thomson, p. 55; Oldys, p. 165, 166; D'Ewes, p. 517; Tytler, p. 122.

est in its destinies, and sowed the seeds, of which the fruits were to ripen during his lifetime, though not for him.

Raleigh had suffered from palsy[1] before his last expedition. He returned broken-hearted by the defeat of his hopes, by the decay of his health, and by the death of his eldest son. What shall be said of King James, who would open to an aged paralytic no other hope of liberty but through success in the discovery of mines in Guiana? What shall be said of a monarch, who could at that time, under a sentence which was originally unjust,[2] and which had slumbered for fifteen years, order the execution of the decrepid man, whose genius and valor shone brilliantly through the ravages of physical decay, and whose English heart, within a palsied frame, still beat with an undying love for his country?

The judgments of the tribunals of the Old World are often reversed at the bar of public opinion in the New. The family of the chief author of early colonization in the United States was reduced to beggary by the government of England, and he himself was beheaded. After a lapse of nearly two centuries, the state of North-Carolina, by a solemn act of legislation, revived in its capital, "THE CITY OF RALEIGH,"[3] and thus expressed its confidence in the

---

[1] Thomson's Appendix, note U. The original document.

[2] Hume, Rapin, Lingard are less favorable to Raleigh. Even Hallam, v. i. p. 482—484, vindicates him with wavering boldness. A careful comparison of the accounts of these historians, the trial, and the biographies of Raleigh, proves him to have been, on his trial, a victim of jealousy, and entirely innocent of crime. No doubt he despised King James. See Tytler, p. 285—290.

[3] Laws of North-Carolina, session of 1792, c. xiv.

GOSNOLD'S VOYAGE TO NEW-ENGLAND. 127

integrity and a grateful respect for the memory of CHAP. III.
the extraordinary man, whose name is indissolubly
connected with the early period of its history.

Some traffic with Virginia may perhaps have been
continued. But at the north, the connexion of the
English merchants was become so intimate, that, in
1593, Sir Walter Raleigh, in the house of commons, 1593.
declared the fishing of Newfoundland to be the stay
of the west countries.[1] These voyages and the previous exertions of Raleigh had trained men for the
career of discovery; and Bartholomew Gosnold,
who, perhaps, had already sailed to Virginia,[2] in the
usual route, by the Canaries and West Indies, now
conceived the idea of a direct voyage to America;
and had well nigh secured to New-England the
honor of the first permanent English colony. Sail- 1603.
ing in a small bark, directly across the Atlantic, in Mar. 26.
seven weeks he reached the continent of America in May 14.
the bay of Massachusetts, not far to the north of
Nahant.[3] He failed to observe a good harbor, and,
standing for the south, discovered the promontory,
which he called Cape Cod; a name, which would
not yield to that of the next monarch of England.
Here, he and four of his men landed; Cape Cod
was the first spot in New-England ever trod by
Englishmen.[4] Doubling the cape, and passing Nan-

---

[1] D'Ewes' Journal, p. 509.
[2] Beverley's Virginia, p. 10, second edition; Oldmixon, v. i. p. 218; Belknap's Biog. v. i. p. 101; Baylies, part iv. p. 153, 154.
[3] Belknap's Biog. v. ii. p. 103; Williamson's Maine, v. i. p. 184, 185.
[4] Grahame, in his United States, v. i. p. 38, in a note, is led into error by Oldmixon, v. i. p. 25, first edition. Sir Francis Drake was in New-Albion, on the Pacific, in June, 1579, but not in New-England. From Virginia he sailed directly homewards.

tucket, they again landed on a little island, now called No Man's Land, and afterwards passed round the promontory of Gay Head, naming it Dover Cliff. At length they entered Buzzard's Bay, a stately sound, which they called Gosnold's Hope. The westernmost of the islands was named Elizabeth, from the queen, a name, which has been transferred to the whole group. Here they beheld the rank vegetation of a virgin soil; the noble forests; the wild fruits and the flowers, bursting from the earth; the eglantine, the thorn, and the honeysuckle, the wild pea, the tansy, and young sassafras; strawberries, raspberries, grape-vines, all in profusion. There is on the island a pond, and within it lies a rocky islet; this was the position, which the adventurers selected for their residence. Here they built their storehouse and their fort; and here the foundations of the first New-England colony were to be laid. The natural features remain unchanged; the island, the pond, the islet, are all yet visible; the forests are gone; the shrubs are as luxuriant as of old; but it requires a believing eye to discern the ruins of the fort.[1]

A traffic with the natives on the main land, soon enabled Gosnold to complete his freight, which consisted chiefly of sassafras root, then greatly esteemed in pharmacy, as a sovereign panacea. The little band, which was to have nestled on the Elizabeth islands, finding their friends about to embark for Europe, despaired of obtaining seasonable supplies of

[1] I write advisedly, notwithstanding the statement in Belknap's American Biography, v. ii. p. 110.

food, and determined not to remain. Fear of an assault from the Indians, who had ceased to be friendly, the want of provisions, and jealousy respecting the distribution of the risks and profits, defeated the design. The whole party soon set sail and bore for England. The return voyage lasted but five weeks; and the expedition was completed in less than four months, during which entire health had prevailed.[1]

Gosnold and his companions spread the most favorable reports of the regions, which he had visited. Could it be, that the voyage was so safe, the climate so pleasant, the country so inviting? The merchants of Bristol, with the ready assent of Raleigh,[2] and at the instance of Richard Hakluyt, the enlightened friend and able documentary historian of these commercial enterprizes, a man, whose fame should be vindicated and asserted in the land which he helped to colonize, determined to pursue the career of investigation. The Speedwell, a small ship of fifty tuns and thirty men, the Discoverer, a bark of twenty-six tuns and thirteen men, under the command of Martin Pring, set sail for America, a few days after the death of the queen. It was a private undertaking, and therefore not retarded by that event. The ship was well provided with trinkets and merchandize, suited to a traffic with the natives;

CHAP. III.
1602.
June 18.
1603. April 10.

---

[1] On the voyage, see the original accounts in Purchas. Gosnold's letter to his father, in Purchas, v. iv. p. 1646; Archer's Relation, ibid, v. iv. p. 1647—1651; Rosier's Notes, ibid, v. iv. p. 1651—1653; Brierton's Relation, in Smith, v. i. p. 105—108. Compare, particularly, Belknap's Life of Gosnold, in American Biography, v. ii. p. 100—123

[2] Purchas, v. iv. p. 1614.

and this voyage also was successful. It reached the American coast among the islands, which skirt the harbors of Maine. The mouth of the Penobscot offered good anchorage and fishing. Pring made a discovery of the eastern rivers and harbors; the Saco, the Kennebunk, and the York; and the channel of the Piscataqua was examined for three or four leagues. Meeting no sassafras, he steered for the south; doubled Cape Ann; and went on shore in Massachusetts; but, being still unsuccessful, he again pursued a southerly track, and finally anchored in Old Town harbor, on Martha's Vineyard. The whole absence lasted about six months, and was

1606. completed without disaster or danger.[1] Pring, a few years later, repeated his voyage, and made a more accurate survey of Maine.

Enterprizes for discovery were now continuous. Bartholomew Gilbert,[2] returning from the West Indies, made an unavailing search for the colony of Raleigh. It was the last attempt to trace the remains of those unfortunate men. But as the testimony of Pring had confirmed the reports of Gosnold, the career of navigation was vigorously pursued.

1605. An expedition, promoted by the earl of Southampton and Lord Arundel, of Wardour, and commanded by George Weymouth, who, in attempting a northwest passage, had already explored the coast of Labrador, now discovered the Penobscot river. Weymouth left England in March; and, in about six weeks,

[1] See the original account, in Purchas, v. iv. p. 1654—1656. Compare Belknap's American Biography, v. ii. p. 123—133; Williamson's Maine, v. i. p. 185—187.
[2] Purchas, v. iv. p. 1656—1658.

INTREPIDITY OF THE EARLY NAVIGATORS.

came in sight of the American continent near Cape Cod. Turning to the north, he approached the coast of Maine, and ascended the western branch of the Penobscot beyond Belfast bay; where the deep channel of the broad stream, the abundance of its spacious harbors, the neighboring springs and copious rivulets, compelled the experienced mariner to admire the noble river, which is just now beginning to have upon its banks and in its ports the flourishing settlements and active commerce, that it is by nature so well adapted to sustain. Five natives were decoyed on board the ship, and Weymouth, returning to England, gave three of them to Sir Ferdinand Gorges, a friend of Raleigh, and governor of Plymouth.[1]

Such were the voyages, which led the way to the colonization of the United States. The daring and skill of these earliest adventurers upon the ocean deserve the highest admiration. The difficulties of crossing the Atlantic were new, and it required the greater courage to encounter hazards, which ignorance exaggerated. The character of the prevalent winds and currents was unknown. The possibility of making a direct passage was but gradually discovered. The imagined dangers were infinite; the real dangers, exceedingly great. The ships, at first employed for discovery, were generally of less than one hundred tons burthen; Frobisher sailed in a

---

[1] On the voyage, see Rosier's Virginian Voyage, &c. in Purchas, v. iv. p. 1659—1667; Sir Ferdinand Gorges' Brief Narration, c. ii. p. 3. Compare Belknap's American Biography, v. ii. p. 134—150; Williamson's Maine, v. i. p. 191—195. It is strange with what reckless confidence Oldmixon, v. i. p. 219, 220, can blunder.

vessel of but twenty-five tons; two of those of Columbus were without a deck; and so perilous were the voyages deemed, that the sailors were accustomed, before embarking, to perform solemn acts of devotion, as if to prepare for eternity. The anticipation of disasters was not visionary; Columbus was shipwrecked twice, and once remained for eight months on an island, without any communication with the civilized world; Hudson was turned adrift in a small boat, by a crew, whom suffering had rendered mutinous; Willoughby perished with cold; Roberval, Parmenius, Gilbert, — and how many others? — went down at sea; and such was the state of the art of navigation, that intrepidity and skill were unavailing against the elements without the favor of Heaven.

CHAPTER IV.

COLONIZATION OF VIRGINIA.

THE period of success in planting colonies in Virginia had arrived; yet not till changes had occurred, affecting the character of European politics and society, and moulding the forms of colonization. The reformation had interrupted the uniformity of religious opinion in the west of Europe; and differences in the church began to constitute the basis of political parties. Commercial intercourse equally sustained a revolution. It had been conducted on the narrow seas and by land; it now launched out upon the broadest waters; and, after the East Indies had been reached by doubling the southern promontory of Africa, the great commerce of the world was performed upon the ocean. The art of printing had become known; and the press diffused intelligence and multiplied the facilities of instruction. The feudal forms of society, which had been preserved from the middle ages, began to yield. Productive industry had, on the one side, built up the fortunes and extended the influence of the active classes; while habits of indolence and of expense had impaired the estates and diminished the power of the nobility. These changes also

CHAP. IV.
1606.

produced corresponding results in the institutions, which were to rise in America.

A revolution had equally occurred in the purposes for which voyages were undertaken. The hope of Columbus, as he sailed to the west, had been the discovery of a new passage to the East Indies. The passion for rapidly amassing gold soon became the prevailing motive. Next, the islands and countries near the equator were made the tropical gardens of the Europeans for the culture of such luxuries, as the warmest regions only can produce. At last, the higher design was matured, not to plunder, nor to destroy, nor to enslave; but to found states, to plant permanent Christian colonies, to establish for the oppressed and the enterprizing, places of refuge and abode, with all the elements of independent national existence.

The condition of England favored adventure in America. A redundant population had existed even before the peace with Spain;[1] and the timid character of King James, throwing out of employment the gallant men, who had served under Elizabeth by sea and land, left to them no option, but to engage as mercenaries in the quarrels of strangers, or to incur the hazards of emigration to a new world.[2] The minds of many persons of intelligence, rank and enterprize, were directed to Virginia. Gosnold, a brave soldier and very ingenious man, who had himself witnessed the fertility of the western soil, long

[1] Lord Bacon on Queen Elizabeth.
[2] Gorges' Brief Narration, c. ii. p. 3.

solicited the concurrence of his friends for the establishment of a colony;[1] and at last prevailed with Wingfield, a merchant of the west of England, Hunt, a clergyman, and Smith, the adventurer of rare genius and undying fame, to consent to risk their own lives and their hope of fortune in an expedition.[2] For more than a year, this little company revolved the project of a plantation. At the same time, Sir Ferdinand Gorges was gathering information of the native Americans, whom he had received from Weymouth, and whose descriptions of the country, joined to the favorable views, which he had already imbibed, filled him with the strongest desire to become a proprietary of domains beyond the Atlantic. Gorges was a man of wealth, of rank, and of influence; he readily persuaded Sir John Popham, lord chief justice of England, to share his intentions.[3] Nor had the assigns of Raleigh become indifferent to "western planting;" the most distinguished of them all, Richard Hakluyt, the historian of maritime enterprize, still favored the establishment of a colony by his personal exertions and the firm enthusiasm of his character. Possessed of whatever information could be derived from foreign sources and a correspondence with the eminent navigators of his times, and anxiously watching the progress of the attempts of Englishmen in the west, his extensive knowledge made him a counsellor in

[1] Edmund Howes' Continuation of Stowe, p. 1018. A prime authority on Virginia. See Stith, p. 229.

[2] Smith, v. i. p. 149, or Purchas, v. iv. p. 1705; Stith, p. 35. Compare Belknap, v. i. p. 239 and 252.

[3] Gorges, c. ii.—v.

CHAP. IV.
1606.

April 10.

the enterprizes which were attempted, and sustained in him and his associates the confidence, which repeated disappointments did not exhaust.[1] Thus the cause of colonization obtained in England zealous and able defenders, who, independent of any party in religion or politics, believed that a prosperous state could be established by Englishmen in the temperate regions of North America.

The king of England, too timid to be active, yet too vain to be indifferent, favored the design of enlarging his dominions. He had attempted in Scotland the introduction of the arts of life among the Highlanders and the western isles, by the establishment of colonies;[2] and the English plantations, which he formed in the northern counties of Ireland, are said to have contributed to the affluence and the security of that island.[3] When, therefore, a company of men of business and men of rank, formed by the experience of Gosnold, the enthusiasm of Smith, the perseverance of Hakluyt, the hopes of profit and the extensive influence of Popham and Gorges,[4] applied to James I. for leave "to deduce a colony into Virginia," the monarch promoted the noble work, by readily issuing an ample patent.

The first colonial charter,[5] under which the English

---

[1] Hakluyt, v. iii. passim; v. v. Dedication of Virginia Valued. The first Virginia charter contains his name.

[2] Roberfson's Scotland, b. viii.

[3] Leland's History of Ireland, v. ii. p. 204—213; Lord Bacon's speech as Chancellor to the Speaker, Works, v. iii. p. 405.

[4] Gorges, c. v. and vi.

[5] See the Charter, in Hazard, v. i. p. 51—58; Stith's Appendix, p. 1—8; Hening's Statutes of Virginia at large, v. i. p. 57—66. In referring to this collection, I cannot but add, that no other state in the Union possesses so excellent a work on its legislative history.

were planted in America, deserves careful consideration. A belt of twelve degrees on the American coast, embracing the soil from Cape Fear to Halifax, excepting perhaps the little spot in Acadia, then actually possessed by the French, was set apart to be colonized by two rival companies. Of these, the first was composed of noblemen, gentlemen, and merchants in and about London, the second, of knights, gentlemen, and merchants in the west. The London adventurers, who alone succeeded, had an exclusive right to occupy the regions from thirty-four to thirty-eight degrees of north latitude, that is, from Cape Fear to the southern limit of Maryland; the western men had equally an exclusive right to plant between forty-one and forty-five degrees. The intermediate district, from thirty-eight to forty-one degrees, was open to the competition of both companies. Yet collision was not possible; for each was to possess the soil, extending fifty miles north and south of its first settlement; so that neither could plant within one hundred miles of a colony of its rival. The conditions of tenure were homage and rent; the rent was no other than one fifth of the net produce of gold and silver, and one fifteenth of copper. The right of coining money was conceded, perhaps to facilitate commerce with the natives, who, it was hoped, would receive Christianity and the arts of civilized life. The superintendence of the whole colonial system was confided to a council in England; the local administration of each colony was entrusted to a council residing

CHAP. IV.
1606.

within its limits. The members of the superior council in England were appointed exclusively by the king, and the tenure of their office was his good pleasure. Over the colonial councils the king likewise preserved a control, for the members of them were from time to time to be ordained, made and removed according to royal instructions. Supreme legislative authority over the colonies, extending alike to their general condition and the most minute regulations, was likewise expressly reserved to the monarch. A hope was also cherished of an ultimate revenue to be derived from Virginia; a duty, to be levied on vessels trading to its harbors, was, for one and twenty years, to be wholly employed for the benefit of the plantation; at the end of that time, was to be taken for the king. To the emigrants it was promised, that they and their children should continue to be Englishmen; a concession, which secured them rights on returning to England, but offered no barrier against colonial injustice. Lands were to be held by the most favorable tenure.

Thus the first written charter of a permanent American colony, which was to be the chosen abode of liberty, gave to the mercantile corporation nothing but a desert territory, with the right of peopling and defending it; and reserved to the monarch absolute legislative authority, the control of all appointments, and a hope of an ultimate revenue. To the emigrants themselves it conceded not one elective franchise, not one of the rights of self-government. They were subjected to the ordinances of a commercial corporation, of which they could not be members, to the dominion of a domestic council, in appointing which they had no voice, to the control of a superior council in England, which had no sympathies with their rights, and finally, to the arbitrary legislation of the sovereign. Yet, bad as was this system, the reservation of power to the king, a result of his vanity, rather than of his ambition, had, at least, the advantage of mitigating the action of the commercial corporation. The charter would have been complete, had the powers of appointment and legislation been given to the people of Virginia.[1]

The summer was spent by the patentees in preparations for planting a colony, for which the vain glory of the king found a grateful occupation in framing a code of laws;[2] an exercise of royal legislation, which has been pronounced in itself illegal.[3] The superior council in England was permitted to name the colonial council; which was constituted a pure aristocracy, entirely independent of the emigrants whom they were to govern; having power to elect or remove its president, to remove any of its members, and to supply its own vacancies. Not an element of popular liberty was introduced into the form of government. Religion was specially enjoined to be established according to the doctrine and rites of the church of England; and no emigrant might withdraw his allegiance from king James, or

---

[1] Compare Chalmers, p. 13—15; Story on the Constitution, v. i. p. 22—24. v. i. p. 67—75. Compare, also, Stith's Virginia, p. 37—41; Burk's Virginia, v. i. p. 86—92.
[2] See the Instrument, in Hening,
[3] Chalmers, p. 15.

avow dissent from the royal creed. Lands were to descend according to the common law. Not only murder, manslaughter and adultery, but dangerous tumults and seditions were punishable by death; so that the security of life depended on the discretion of the magistrate, restricted only by the necessity of a trial by jury. All civil causes, requiring corporal punishment, fine or imprisonment, might be summarily determined by the president and council; who also possessed full legislative authority in cases not affecting life or limb. Kindness to the savages was enjoined. It was further, and most unwisely, though probably at the request of the corporation, ordered, that the industry and commerce of the respective colonies should for five years, at least, be conducted in a joint stock. The king also reserved to himself the right of future legislation.

Thus were the political forms of the colony established, when, on the nineteenth day of December, in the year of our Lord one thousand six hundred and six, one hundred and nine years after the discovery of the American continent by Cabot, forty-one years from the settlement of Florida, the little squadron of three vessels, the largest not exceeding one hundred tuns burthen,[1] bearing one hundred and five men, destined to remain, set sail for a harbor in Virginia.

The voyage began under inauspicious omens. Of the one hundred and five, on the list of emigrants, there were but twelve laborers and very few mechan-

[1] Smith's Virginia, v. i. p. 150.

ics.[1] They were going to a wilderness, in which, as yet, not a house was standing; and there were forty-eight gentlemen to four carpenters. Neither were there any men with families. It was evident, a commercial and not a colonial establishment was designed by the projectors. Dissensions sprung up during the voyage; as the names and instructions of the council had, by the folly of James, been carefully concealed in a box, which was not to be opened till after the arrival in Virginia, no competent authority existed to check the progress of envy and disorder.[2] The genius of Smith excited jealousy; and hope, the only power which can still the clamors and allay the feuds of the selfish, early deserted the colonists.

CHAP. IV.

1607.

Newport, who commanded the ships, was acquainted with the old passage, and, consuming the whole of the early spring in a navigation which should have been completed in February, sailed by way of the Canaries and the West India Islands. As he turned to the north, a severe storm carried his fleet beyond the settlement of Raleigh, into the magnificent bay of the Chesapeake.[3] The head lands received and retain the names of Cape Henry and Cape Charles, from the sons of King James; and within those capes a country opened, which appeared to the emigrants to "claim the prerogative over the most pleasant places in the world." Hope revived for a season, as they advanced. "Heaven

April 26.

---

[1] See the names in Smith's Virginia, v. i. p. 153, and in Purchas, v. iv. p. 1706.
[2] Smith, v. i. p. 150; Chalmers, p. 17.
[3] Smith, v. i. p. 150; Stith, p. 44.

and earth seemed never to have agreed better to frame a place for man's commodious and delightful habitation."[1] A noble river was soon entered, which was named from the monarch; and, after a search of seventeen days, the peninsula of Jamestown, about fifty miles above the mouth of the stream, was selected for the site of the colony.

Thus admirable was the country. The emigrants themselves were weakened by divisions and degraded by jealousy. So soon as the members of the council were duly constituted, they proceeded to choose Wingfield president; and then, as by their instructions they had power to do, they excluded Smith from their body, on a charge of sedition. But as his only offence consisted in the possession of enviable qualities, the attempt at his trial was abandoned,[2] and the man, without whose aid the vices of the colony would have caused its immediate ruin, was soon restored to his station.[3]

While the men were busy in felling timber and providing freight for the ships, Newport and Smith and twenty others ascended the James river to the falls. They visited the native chieftain, Powhattan, who has been styled "the emperor of the country," at his principal seat, just below the present site of Richmond. The imperial residence was a village of twelve wigwams! The savages murmured at the intrusion of strangers into the country; but Powhattan disguised his fear, and would only say,

---

[1] Smith, in Purchas, v. iv. p. 1691, or v. i. p. 114, Richmond edition; Stith's Virginia, p. 45.
[2] Smith, v. i. p. 151; Stith, p. 45.
[3] Stith, p. 47; Smith, v. i. p. 152, 153.

"They hurt you not; they take but a little waste land."[1]

About the middle of June, Newport set sail for England. What condition could be more pitiable, than that of the English whom he had left in Virginia? The proud hopes, which the beauty of the country had excited, soon vanished; and as the delusion passed away, they awoke and beheld, that they were in the wilderness. Weak in numbers, and still weaker from want of habits of industry, they were surrounded by natives, whose hostility and distrust had already been displayed; the summer heats were intolerable to their laborers; the moisture of the climate generated disease; and the fertility of the soil, covered with a rank luxuriance of forest, increased the toil of culture. Their scanty provisions had become spoiled on the long voyage. "Our drink," say they, "was unwholesome water; our lodgings, castles in the air; had we been as free from all sins as from gluttony and drunkenness, we might have been canonized for saints." Despair of mind ensued; so that, in less than a fortnight after the departure of the fleet, "hardly ten of them were able to stand;" the labor of completing some simple fortifications was exhausting; and no regular crops could be planted. During the summer, there were not, on any occasion, five able men to guard the bulwarks; the fort was filled in every corner with the groans of the sick, whose outcries, night and day, for six weeks, rent the hearts of those, who could

[1] Percy, in Purchas, v. iv. p. 1689.

minister no relief. Many times, three or four died in a night; in the morning, their bodies were trailed out of the cabins, like dogs, to be buried. Fifty men, one half of the colony, perished before autumn; among them Bartholomew Gosnold, the projector of the settlement, a man of rare merits, worthy of a perpetual memory in the plantation,[1] and whose influence had alone thus far preserved some degree of harmony in the council.[2]

Disunion completed the scene of misery. It became necessary to depose the president, who was charged with embezzling the public stores, and who was on the point of abandoning the colony and escaping to the West Indies. Ratcliffe, the new president, possessed neither judgment nor industry; so that the management of affairs fell into the hands of Smith, whose deliberate enterprize and cheerful courage alone diffused light amidst the general gloom. He was more wakeful to gather provisions, than the covetous to find gold; and strove to keep the country, more than the faint-hearted to abandon it. As autumn approached, the Indians, from the superfluity of their harvest, made a voluntary offering; and supplies were also collected by expeditions into the interior. But the conspiracies, that were still formed, to desert the settlement, could be defeated only after a skirmish, in which one of the leaders was killed; and the danger of a precipitate abandonment of Virginia continued to be imminent, till

---

[1] Edmund Howes, p. 1018. Purchas, v. iv. p. 1690. Smith and Percy were both eye-witnesses.
[2] Smith, v. i. p. 154; Percy, in

the approach of winter, when not only the navigation became more perilous, but the fear of famine was removed by the abundance of wild fowl and game.[1] Nothing then remained but to examine the country.

CHAP. IV.
1607.

The South Sea was considered the ocean path to every kind of wealth. The coast of America on the Pacific had been explored by the Spaniards and had been visited by Drake; the collections of Hakluyt had communicated to the English the results of their voyages; and the maps of that day exhibited a tolerably accurate delineation of the continent of North America. With singular ignorance of the progress of geographical knowledge, it had been expressly enjoined on the colonists, to seek a communication with the South Sea by ascending some stream which flowed from the northwest.[2] The Chickahominy was such a stream. Smith, though he did not share the ignorance of his employers, was ever willing to engage in discoveries. Leaving the colonists to enjoy the abundance, which winter had brought, he not only ascended the river, as far as he could advance in boats, but struck into the interior. His companions disobeyed his instructions, and, being surprised by the Indians, were put to death. Smith preserved his own life by the calmness of self-possession. Displaying a pocket compass, he amused the savages by an explanation of its powers, and increased their admiration of his superior genius by imparting to them some vague conceptions of the

[1] Smith, v. i. p. 154, 155; Purchas, v. iv. p. 1690; Stith, p. 48.
[2] Stith's History of Virginia, p. 43.

form of the earth and the nature of the planetary system. To the Indians, who retained him as their prisoner, his captivity was a more strange event, than any thing, of which the traditions of their tribes preserved the memory. He was allowed to send a letter to the fort at Jamestown; and the savage wonder was increased, for he seemed, by some magic, to endow the paper with the gift of intelligence. The curiosity of all the clans of the neighborhood was awakened by the prisoner; he was conducted in triumph from the settlements on the Chickahominy to the Indian villages on the Rappahannock and the Potomac; and thence, through other towns to the residence of Opechancanough, at Pamunkey. There, for the space of three days, they practised invocations and ceremonies in the hope of obtaining some insight into the mystery of his character and his designs. It was evident, that he was a being of a higher order; was his nature beneficent, or was he to be dreaded as a dangerous enemy? Their minds were bewildered, as they beheld his calm fearlessness; and they sedulously observed towards him the utmost reverence and hospitality, as if to propitiate his power, should he be rescued from their hands. The decision of his fate was referred to Powhatan; who was then residing in what is now Gloucester county on York river, at a village, to which Smith was conducted through the regions, now so celebrated, where the youthful La Fayette hovered upon the skirts of Cornwallis, and the arms of France and the Confederacy were united to achieve the crowning victory of American independence. The passion of vanity rules in forests as well as in cities; the grim warriors, as they met in council, displayed their gayest apparel before the Englishman, whose doom they had assembled to pronounce. The fears of the feeble aborigines were about to prevail, and his immediate death, already repeatedly threatened and repeatedly delayed, would have been inevitable, but for the timely intercession of Pocahontas, a girl of twelve years old, the daughter of Powhatan, whose confiding fondness Smith had easily won, and who firmly clung to his neck, as his head was bowed down to receive the strokes of the tomahawks. Her fearlessness and her entreaties persuaded the council to spare the agreeable stranger, who could make hatchets for her father, and rattles and strings of beads for herself, the favorite child. The barbarians, whose decision had long been held in suspense by the mysterious awe, which Smith had inspired, now resolved to receive him as a friend and to make him a partner of their councils. They tempted him to join their bands, and lend assistance in an attack upon the white men at Jamestown; and when his decision of character succeeded in changing the current of their thoughts, they dismissed him with mutual promises of friendship and benevolence. Thus the captivity of Smith did itself become a benefit to the colony; for he had not only observed with care the country between the James and the Potomac, and had gained some knowledge of the language and manners of the natives, but he now

ARRIVAL OF NEW EMIGRANTS.

CHAP. IV.
1608.

established a peaceful intercourse between the English and the tribes of Powhatan.[1]

Returning to Jamestown, Smith found the colony reduced to forty men, and of these, the strongest were again preparing to escape with the pinnace. This new attempt at desertion he repressed at the hazard of his life.[2] Thus passed the few first months of colonial existence in discord and misery; despair relieved and ruin prevented, by the fortitude of one man.

Meantime, the council in England, having received an increase of its numbers and its powers, determined to send out new recruits and supplies; and Newport had hardly returned from his first voyage, before he was again despatched with one hundred and twenty emigrants. Yet the joy in Virginia on their arrival was of short continuance; for the new comers were chiefly vagabond gentlemen and goldsmiths, who, in spite of the remonstrances of Smith, gave a wrong direction to the industry of the colony. They believed they had discovered grains of gold in a glittering earth, which abounded near Jamestown; and "there was now no talk, no hope, no work, but dig gold, wash gold, refine gold, load gold." The refiners were enamoured of their skill; Martin, one of the council, promised himself honors in England as the discoverer of a mine; and Newport having made an unnecessary stay of fourteen weeks,

---

[1] Smith, v. i. p. 158—162, and v. ii. p. 29—33. The story is repeated by Stith, Burk and others; and minutely by Drake, in his Indian Biography, b. iv. c. i.
[2] Smith, v. i. p. 163, 164.

and having, in defiance of the assurances of Powhatan, expected to find the Pacific just beyond the falls in James river, believed himself immeasurably rich, as he embarked for England with a freight of worthless earth.[1]

Disgusted at the follies, which he had vainly opposed, Smith undertook the perilous and honorable office of exploring the vast bay of the Chesapeake, and the numerous rivers, which are its tributaries. Two voyages, made in an open boat, with a few companions, over whom his superior courage, rather than his station as a magistrate, gave him authority, occupied him about three months of the summer, and embraced a navigation of nearly three thousand miles.[2] The slenderness of his means has been contrasted with the dignity and utility of his discoveries, and his name has been placed in the highest rank with the distinguished men, who have enlarged the bounds of geographical knowledge, and opened the way by their investigations for colonies and commerce.[3] He surveyed the bay of the Chesapeake to the Susquehannah, and left only the borders of that remote river, to remain for some years longer the fabled dwelling-place of a giant progeny.[4] The Patapsco was discovered and explored, and Smith probably entered the harbor of Baltimore.[5] The majestic Potomac, which at its mouth is seven miles broad, especially invited curiosity; and passing beyond the heights of Vernon and the city of Wash-

---

[1] Smith, v. i. p. 165—172.
[2] Smith, v. i. p. 173—192, and v. ii. p. 100; Burk, v. i. p. 125.
[3] Chalmers, p. 22.
[4] Burk's Virginia, v. i. p. 123.
[5] Stith, p. 64.

150   SMITH BECOMES PRESIDENT OF THE COUNCIL.

CHAP. IV.
1608.

ington, he ascended to the falls above Georgetown.[1] Nor did he merely explore the rivers and inlets. He penetrated the territories, established friendly relations with the native tribes, and laid the foundation for future beneficial intercourse. The map[2] which he prepared and sent to the company in London,[3] is still extant, and delineates correctly the great outlines of nature. The expedition was worthy the romantic age of American history.

Sept. 10.

Three days after his return, Smith was made president of the council. Order and industry began to be diffused by his energetic administration, when Newport, with a second supply, entered the river. About seventy new emigrants arrived; two of them, it merits notice, were females. The angry covetousness of a greedy but disappointed corporation was now fully displayed. As if their command could transmute minerals, narrow the continent, and awaken the dead, they demanded a lump of gold, or a certain passage to the South Sea; or, a feigned humanity added, one of the lost company, sent by Sir Walter Raleigh.[4] The charge of the voyage was two thousand pounds; unless the ships should return full freighted with commodities, corresponding in value to the costs of the adventure, the colonists were threatened, that "they should be left in Virginia as banished men."[5] Neither had experience

[1] Compare Smith, v. i. p. 177, with Stith, p. 65, and Smith's map.
[2] In the Richmond edition, opposite page 149. In Purchas, v. iv. opposite page 1691.
[3] Smith's letter, in Hist. v. i. p. 202.
[4] Smith's Virginia, v. i. p. 192, 193.
[5] Smith's letter, in his History, v. i. p. 200, 201; also, Smith's advertisements for the unexperienced, in iii. Mass. Hist. Coll. v. iii. p. 10.

taught the company to engage suitable persons for Virginia. "When you send again," Smith was obliged to write, "I entreat you rather send but thirty carpenters, husbandmen, gardeners, fishermen, blacksmiths, masons, and diggers up of trees' roots, well provided, than a thousand of such as we have."[1]

After the departure of the ships, Smith employed his authority to enforce industry. Six hours in the day were spent in work; the rest might be given to pastime.[2] The gentlemen had been taught the use of the axe, and had become accomplished woodcutters. It was now proclaimed as a law, that "he who will not work, shall not eat;" and Jamestown began to assume the appearance of a regular place of abode. Yet so little land had been cultivated, not more than thirty or forty acres in all, that it was still necessary for Englishmen to solicit food from the Indians, whose indolence was proverbial; and Europeans, to preserve themselves from starving, were billeted among the sons of the forest. Thus the season passed away; and of two hundred in the colony, not more than seven died.[3]

The golden anticipations of the London company had not been realized. But the cause of failure appeared in the policy, which had grasped at sudden emoluments;[4] the enthusiasm of the English seemed exalted by the train of misfortunes; and more vast and honorable plans[5] were conceived, which were to

[1] Smith, v. i. p. 202.
[2] Ibid, v. i. p. 222.
[3] Ibid, v. i. p. 222—229.
[4] Smith, in iii. Massachusetts Historical Collection, v. iii. p. 10—12.
[5] Hakluyt's Dedication of Virginia richly valued, v. v.

152   THE SECOND CHARTER OF VIRGINIA.

CHAP. IV.
1609.

be effected by more numerous and opulent associates. Not only were the limits of the colony extended, the company was enlarged by the subscriptions of many of the nobility and gentry of England, and of the tradesmen of London; and the name of the powerful Cecil, the inveterate enemy and successful rival of Raleigh, appears at the head of those,[1] who were to carry into execution the vast design, to which Raleigh, now a close prisoner in the tower, had first awakened the attention of his countrymen. At the request of the corporation which was become a very powerful body, without any regard to the rights or wishes of those who had already emigrated under the sanction of existing laws, the constitution of Virginia was radically changed.

May 23.

The new charter[2] transferred to the company the powers, which had before been reserved to the king. The supreme council in England was now to be chosen by the stockholders themselves; and, in the exercise of the powers of legislation and government, was independent of the monarch. The governor in Virginia might rule the colonists with uncontrolled authority, according to the tenor of the instructions and laws, established by the council, or, in want of them, according to his own good discretion, even in cases capital and criminal, not less than civil; and, in the event of mutiny or rebellion, he might declare martial law, being himself the judge of the necessity of the measure, and

[1] Hening, v. i. p. 81—88.   Appendix, number ii. p. 8—22.
[2] Ibid, v. i. p. 80—98; Stith, Hazard, v. i. p. 58—72.

NEW EMIGRATION FROM ENGLAND.

CHAP. IV.
1609.

the executive officer in its administration. Thus the lives, liberty and fortune of the colonists were placed at the arbitrary will of a governor, who was to be appointed by a commercial corporation. As yet not one valuable civil privilege was conceded to the emigrants.[1]

Splendid as were the auspices of the new charter, unlimited as were the powers of the patentees, the next events in the colony were still more disastrous. Lord De La Ware,[2] distinguished for his virtues, as well as rank, received the appointment of governor and captain-general for life; an avarice, which would listen to no possibility of defeat, and which already dreamed of a flourishing empire in America, surrounded him with stately officers, suited by their titles and nominal charges to the dignity of an opulent kingdom.[3] The condition of the public mind favored colonization; swarms of people desired to be transported; and the adventurers, with cheerful alacrity, contributed free-will offerings.[4] The widely diffused enthusiasm soon enabled the company to despatch a fleet of nine vessels, containing more than five hundred emigrants. The admiral of the fleet was Newport, who, with Sir Thomas Gates and Sir George Somers, was authorized to administer the affairs of the colony till the arrival of Lord Delaware.[5]

[1] Chalmers, p. 25.
[2] Walpole's Royal and Noble Authors, enlarged by Th. Park, 1806, v. ii. p. 180—183.
[3] Smith, in iii. Mass. Hist. Coll. v. iii. p. 11, and Smith, v. ii. p. 106.
[4] True Declaration of Virginia, published by the Council of Virginia, in 1610, p. 59. A leading authority.
[5] Smith, v. i. p. 233, 234; or Purchas, v. iv. p. 1729.

CHAP. IV.
1609.

The three commissioners had embarked on board the same ship.[1] When near the coast of Virginia, a hurricane[2] separated the admiral from the rest of his fleet; and his vessel was stranded on the rocks of the Bermudas. A small ketch perished; and[3] seven ships only arrived in Virginia.

A new dilemma ensued. The old charter was abrogated; and, as there was in the settlement no one, who had any authority from the new patentees, anarchy seemed at hand. The emigrants of the last arrival were dissolute gallants, packed off to escape worse destinies at home,[4] broken tradesmen, gentlemen impoverished in spirit and fortune; rakes and libertines, men more fitted to corrupt than to found a commonwealth.[5] It was not the will of God, that the new state should be formed of these materials; that such men should be the fathers of a progeny, born on the American soil, who were one day to assert American liberty by their eloquence and defend it by their valor. Hopeless as the determination appeared, Smith resolutely maintained his authority over the unruly herd; and devised new expeditions and new settlements, to furnish them occupation and support. At last, an accidental explosion of gunpowder disabled him, by inflicting wounds, which the surgical skill of Virginia could not relieve.[6] Delegating his authority to Percy, he embarked for England. Extreme suffering from his

[1] True Declaration, p. 19 and 21.
[2] Archer's letter, in Purchas, v. iv. p. 1733, 1734; Secretary Strachy's account, in Purchas, v. iv. p. 1735—1738; True Declaration of Virginia, p. 21—26.
[3] Smith, v. i. p. 234.
[4] Ibid, v. i. p. 235.
[5] Stith, p. 103.
[6] Smith, v. i. p. 239.

wounds and the ingratitude of his employers were the fruits of his services. He received for his sacrifices and his perilous exertions, not one foot of land, not the house he himself had built, not the field his own hands had planted, nor any reward but the applause of his conscience and the world.[1] He merits to be called the father of the settlement, which he had repeatedly rescued from destruction. His judgment had ever been clear in the midst of general despondency. He united the highest spirit of adventure with consummate powers of action. His courage and self-possession accomplished what others esteemed desperate. Fruitful in expedients, he was prompt in execution. Though he had been harassed by the persecutions of malignant envy, he never revived the memory of the faults of his enemies. He was accustomed to lead, not to send his men to danger; would suffer want rather than borrow, and starve sooner than not pay.[2] He had nothing counterfeit in his nature; but was open, honest and sincere. He clearly discerned, that it was the true interest of England not to seek in Virginia for gold and sudden wealth, but to enforce regular industry. "Nothing," said he, "is to be expected thence, but by labor."[3]

The colonists, no longer controlled by an acknowledged authority, were soon abandoned to improvident idleness. Their ample stock of provisions was rapidly consumed; and further supplies were refused

---

[1] Smith, v. ii. p. 102; Virginia's Verger, in Purchas, v. iv. p. 1815.
[2] Smith, v. i. p. 241. It is hardly necessary to add, that much of Smith's Generall Historie is a compilation of the works of others. Compare Belknap, v. i. p. 303, 304.
[3] Answer to the Commissioners' questions, in Smith, v. ii. p. 106.

156 THE STARVING TIME.

CHAP. IV. by the Indians, whose friendship had been due to the personal influence of Smith, and who now regarded the English with a fatal contempt. Stragglers from the town were cut off; parties, which begged food in the Indian cabins, were deliberately murdered; and plans were laid to starve and destroy the whole company. The horrors of famine ensued; while a band of about thirty, seizing on a ship, escaped to become pirates, and to plead their desperate necessity as an excuse for their crimes.[1] Smith, at his departure, had left more than four hundred and ninety persons in the colony;[2] in six months, indolence, vice and famine reduced the number to sixty; and these were so feeble and dejected, that, if relief had been delayed but ten days longer, they also must have utterly perished.[3]

1610. Sir Thomas Gates and the passengers, whose ship had been wrecked on the rocks of the Bermudas, had reached the shore without the loss of a life. The liberal fertility of the uninhabited island, teeming with natural products, for nine months sustained them in affluence. From the cedars which they felled, and the wrecks of their old ship, they, with admirable perseverance, constructed two vessels, in which they now embarked for Virginia,[4] in the hope of a happy welcome to the abundance of a prosperous colony. How great then was their horror, as they came among the scenes of death and misery,

May 24.

---

[1] True Declaration, p. 35—39. Compare Stith, p. 116, 117, or Smith, v. ii. p. 2.
[2] Smith, v. i. p. 240.
[3] Purchas, v. iv. p. 1732 and 1766; Stith, p. 117. True Declaration, p. 47; or Smith, v. ii. p. 4, says four days.
[4] True Declaration of Virginia, p. 23—26.

JAMESTOWN DESERTED. 157

of which the gloom was increased by the prospect of continued scarcity. Four pinnaces remained in the river, nor could the extremity of distress listen to any other course, than to sail for Newfoundland, and seek safety by dispersing the company among the ships of English fishermen.[1] The colonists, such is human nature, desired to burn the town in which they had been so wretched, and the exercise of their infantile vengeance was prevented only by the energy of Gates,[2] who was himself the last to desert the settlement. They fell down the stream with the tide; and, the next morning, as they drew near the mouth of the river, they encountered the long-boat of Lord Delaware; who had arrived on the coast with emigrants and supplies. The fugitives bore up the helm, and, favored by the wind, were that night once more at the fort in Jamestown.[3]

It was on the tenth day of June, that the restauration of the colony was solemnly begun by supplications to God. A deep sense of the infinite mercies of his providence overawed the colonists who had been spared by famine, the emigrants who had been shipwrecked and yet preserved, and the new comers who found wretchedness and want, where they had expected the contentment of abundance. The firmness of their resolution repelled despair; "It is," said they, "the arm of the Lord of Hosts, who would have his people pass the red sea and the wil-

CHAP. IV.

1610.

June 7.

June 8.

---

[1] True Declaration, p. 43, 44. [3] True Declaration, p. 45, 46.
[2] Ibid, p. 45; Smith, v. ii. p. 3.

158   LORD DELAWARE RESTORES VIRGINIA.

CHAP. derness, and then possess the land of Canaan."[1]
IV.
⁓⁓ After the solemn exercises of religion, Lord Dela-
1610. ware caused his commission to be read; a consultation was immediately held on the good of the colony;
and its government was organized with mildness but
decision. The evils of faction were healed by the
unity of the administration, and the dignity and virtues of the governor; and the colonists, excited by
mutual emulation, performed their tasks with alacrity. At the beginning of the day, they assembled
in the little church, which was kept neatly trimmed
with the wild flowers of the country;[2] next, they
returned to their houses to receive their allowance
of food. The settled hours of labor were from six
in the morning till ten, and from two in the after-
noon till four.[3] The houses were warm and secure,
covered above with strong boards and matted on the
inside after the fashion of the Indian wigwams.[4]
Security and affluence were returning. But the
health of Lord Delaware sunk under the cares of
his situation and the diseases of the climate; and,
after a lingering sickness, he was compelled to leave
the administration with Percy, and return to England.[5] The colony, at this time, consisted of about

[1] True Declaration, p. 48. Compare, also, the New Life of Virginia, published in 1612, and Smith, v. ii. p. 4, 5.
[2] Purchas, v. iv. p. 1753.
[3] True Declaration of Virginia, p. 48—50.
[4] Ibid, p. 50; p. 51; Smith, v. ii. 5; Purchas, v. iv. p. 1753.
[5] The New Life of Virginia, 1612. This tract is republished in the ii. Mass. Hist. Coll. v. viii. p. 199—223. The Relation of Lord De la Warre, printed in 1611, is before me. This and many other rare tracts on early Virginia history are in the Cambridge Library. Extracts from Lord Delaware's Discourses, in Smith, v. ii. p. 8 and 9; in Purchas, v. iv. p. 1762—1764. Lord Delaware dealt harshly with the Indians. I hope the account in Harris' Voyages, v. ii. p. 226, or

DALE INTRODUCES MARTIAL LAW.

two hundred men; but the departure of the governor was a disastrous event, which produced not only despondency at Jamestown, but "a damp of coldness" in the hearts of the London company; and a great reaction in the popular mind in England. In the age when the theatre was the chief place of public amusement and resort, Virginia was introduced by the stage-poets as a theme of scorn and derision.[1]

Fortunately, the adventurers, before the ill success of Lord Delaware was known, had despatched Sir Thomas Dale with liberal supplies. He arrived safely in the colony; and assumed the government, which he soon afterwards administered upon the basis of martial law. The code, written in blood, and printed and sent to Virginia by the treasurer, Sir Thomas Smith, on his own authority, and without the order or assent of the company, was chiefly a translation from the rules of war of the United Provinces. The introduction of this arbitrary system excited no indignation in the colonists, who had never obtained any franchises, and no surprise in the adventurers in England, who regarded the Virginians as the garrison of a distant citadel, more than as citizens and freemen. Historians have unnecessarily attempted to find remote causes to account for its introduction. The charter of the London company[2] had invested the governor with full authority, in cases of rebellion and mutiny, to exercise martial

---

Drake's Indian Biography, b. iv. p. 16, is incorrect.
[1] Epistle Dedicatorie to the New Life of Virginia.

[2] See the Charter, sec. xxiv. Compare Smith, v. ii. p. 10, 11; Stith, p. 122, 123, and 233. Purchas, v. iv. p. 1767.

CHAP. IV.
1611.

law, and, in the condition of the settlement, this seemed a sufficient warrant for making it the law of the land.

The letters of Dale to the council confessed the small number and weakness of the colonists; but he kindled hope in the hearts of those constant adventurers, who, in the greatest disasters, had never fainted. "If any thing otherwise than well betide me," said he, "let me commend unto your carefulness the pursuit and dignity of this business, than which your purses and endeavors will never open nor travel in a more meritorious enterprize. Take four of the best kingdoms in Christendom, and put them all together, they may no way compare with this country, either for commodities or goodness of soil."[1] Lord Delaware and Sir Thomas Gates earnestly confirmed what Dale had written, and without any delay, Gates, who has the honor, to all posterity, of being the first named in the original patent for Virginia, conducted to the New World six ships, with three hundred emigrants. A wise liberality sent also a hundred kine, as well as suitable provisions. It was the most fortunate step, which had been taken; and proved the wisdom of Cecil, Mansell, and others, whose firmness had prevailed.[2]

Aug.

The promptness of this relief merits admiration. In May, Dale had written from Virginia, and the last of August, the new recruits, under Gates, were already at Jamestown. So unlooked for was this

[1] New Life of Virginia, ii. Mass. Hist. Coll. v. viii. p. 207. [2] New Life of Virginia.

ADMINISTRATION OF GATES.

supply, that, at their approach, they were regarded with fear as a hostile fleet. Who can describe the joy which ensued, when they were found to be friends?[1] Gates assumed the government amidst the thanksgivings of the colony; and at once endeavored to employ the sentiment of religious gratitude as a foundation of order and of laws. "Good," said they, "are the beginnings, wherein God thus leads." The colony now numbered seven hundred men; and Dale, with the consent of Gates, went far up the river to found the new plantation, which, in honor of Prince Henry, a general favorite with the English people, was named Henrico.[2] But the greatest change in the condition of the colonists resulted from the establishment of private property. To each man a few acres of ground were assigned for his orchard and garden, to plant at his pleasure and for his own use.[3] So long as industry had been without its special reward, labor had been reluctantly performed, and want had as necessarily ensued. A week was wasted in doing the work of a day, and thirty men, laboring for the colony, had accomplished less, than three were now able to perform for themselves.[4] It became, henceforward, the policy of the company to encourage the settlers in gathering riches; and the sanctity of private property was recognized as the surest guarantee of obedience. Yet the rights of the Indians were little respected; nor

CHAP. IV.

1611.

---

[1] New Life of Virginia.
[2] Ibid; Smith, v. ii. p. 11, 12; Stith, p. 123, 124; Burk, v. i. p. 166, 167; Beverley, p. 25.
[3] New Life of Virginia, printed in 1612; Secretary Hamor, in Purchas, v. iv. p. 1766.
[4] Purchas, v. iv. p. 1766.

did the English disdain to appropriate, by conquest, the soil, the cabins, and the granaries of the tribe of the Appomattocks.[1]

While the colony was advancing in security, industry, and extent of subject territory, the adventurers in England desired and obtained an enlargement of their grants from the easy munificence of King James. The Bermudas and all islands within three hundred leagues of the Virginia shore, were included within the limits of their third patent;[2] a concession of no ultimate importance in American history, since the new acquisitions were soon transferred to a separate company, and were never connected with Virginia.[3] But the most remarkable change, now effected in the charter, a change, which contained within itself the germ of another revolution, consisted in giving to the corporation a democratic form. Hitherto all power had resided in the council; which, it is true, was to have its vacancies supplied by the majority of the corporation. But now it was ordered, that weekly, or even more frequent, meetings of the whole company might be convened, for the transaction of affairs of less weight; while all questions respecting government, commerce, and the disposition of lands, should be reserved for the four great and general courts; at which all officers were to be elected, and all laws established. The political rights of the colonists themselves remained unimproved; the character of the corporation was

---

[1] Hamor, in Purchas, v. iv. p. 1766 and 1768; Stith, p. 124, 125.
[2] See the Patent, in Hening, v.
i. p. 98—110. It is also in Stith and in Hazard.
[3] Stith, p. 127.

entirely changed. Power was transferred from the council to the company; and its sessions became the theatre of bold and independent discussion. A perverse financial privilege was at the same time conceded; and lotteries, though unusual in England,[1] were authorized for the benefit of the colony.[2] The lotteries produced to the company twenty-nine thousand pounds; but as they were esteemed a grievance by the nation, so they were, after a few years, noticed by parliament as a public evil, and, in consequence of the complaint of the commons, were suspended by an order of council.[3]

1621. Mar.

If the new charter enlarged the powers of the company, the progress of the colony confirmed its stability. Tribes even of the Indians submitted to the English, and, by a formal treaty, declared themselves the tributaries of King James. A marriage was the immediate cause of this change of relations.

1612.

A foraging party of the colonists, headed by Argall, had stolen away the daughter of Powhatan, and now demanded of her father a ransom. The indignant chief prepared rather for hostilities. But John Rolfe, a young Englishman, winning the favor of Pocahontas, desired her in marriage; and with the favor of Sir Thomas Dale, and to the express delight of the savage chieftain, the nuptials were solemnized according to the rites of the English church.[4] Every historian of Virginia commemorates them with approbation; distinguished families trace

[1] Chalmers, p. 32; New Life of Virginia.
[2] Hening, v. i. p. 108—109.
[3] Chalmers, p. 33.
[4] Stith's History of Virginia, p. 127—130.

their descent from this union; the Indian wife, instructed in the English language, and bearing an English name, sailed with her husband for England, and was caressed at court, and respectfully admired in the city. The immediate fruits of the marriage to the colony were a confirmed peace, not with Powhatan alone, but also with the powerful Chickahominies, who sought the friendship of the English, and demanded to be called Englishmen.[1] It might have seemed, that the European and the native races were about to become blended. Yet no such result ensued. The history of Pocahontas is full of singular incidents; from her first intercession for Smith, her regard for the English was uniform; as a wife and a mother her conduct was exemplary; her manners were those of wild simplicity and pure and ingenuous feeling. Yet strange as is her history, nothing is more singular than her marriage. The English and the Indian races remained disunited; and the weakest gradually became extinct.

The colony was now deemed to be firmly established; and the officers undertook to assert for the English king the sole right of colonizing the North American coast to the latitude of forty-five degrees. We have seen, that the French had nestled at Port Royal. It was a time of peace between France and England; the bleak climate of Acadia could hardly tempt the possessors of Virginia; in a hemisphere so wide and as yet so little occupied, the settlement of a new colony might rather seem to

[1] Stith, p. 130.

promise comfort, protection and useful intercourse. Nothing can better mark the spirit of the times, than the events which transpired. Argall, an ingenious and active young sea-captain, of coarse passions and arbitrary temper, invaded the French, whose few cabins could with difficulty be found on so extensive a coast. It was easy to surprise those, who had no reason to expect an attack; and thus the oldest Christian settlement in America, north of Florida, was pillaged and destroyed. England had vindicated her claim to Acadia; the London company had avenged the invasion of its monopolies.[1] This first contest between France and England for colonial possessions in America was, in dignity, not superior to the acts of marauders and pirates; the struggle was destined to increase, till at last, after the lapse of almost a century and a half, the strife for acres, which neither nation could cultivate, kindled a war, that spread throughout the globe.

It is said, that on his return from Acadia, Argall entered the port of New-York, but there is no room to suppose he ascended the Hudson.[2] Holland had already opened a traffic through the channel, which Hudson had discovered. Appearing among the handful of men, who were stationed on the island of Manhattan, he asserted the sovereignty of England; and, as he had the largest force, he seems to have

---

[1] Charlevoix, Nouv. France, l. iii. at the close of the book; Edmund Howes, in Stowe, p. 1018; Smith, v. ii. p. 18; Purchas, v. iv. p. 1808. Compare Purchas, p. 1765. Gorges' Description, p. 19. Compare Prince's Chronology, for June, 1613, p. 130, and Belknap's American Biography, v. ii. p. 51. Stith erroneously refers the transaction to 1614. Heylin, in his Cosmography, l. iv. p. 96, says 1613.

[2] Belknap, Am. Biography, v. ii. p. 55, thought otherwise.

CHAP.
IV.
been acknowledged, for the time, as lord of the harbor. He withdrew to boast of having reduced the settlement of Holland to subjection; and the Dutch, upon his absence, quietly pursued their profitable traffic.[1]

1614.
Mar.
Sir Thomas Gates, returning to England,[2] left the government with Dale; and employed himself successfully in England in preserving the spirit of the London company. But it was neither to English lotteries, nor to English privileged companies, that the new state was to owe its prosperity. Private industry, directed to the culture of a valuable staple, was more productive, than the patronage of England; and tobacco enriched Virginia.

1613,
to
1616.
The condition of private property in lands among the colonists, depended, in some measure, on the circumstances, under which they had emigrated. Some had been sent and maintained at the exclusive cost of the company; and were its servants. One month of their time and three acres of land were set apart for them, besides a small allowance of two bushels of corn from the public store; the rest of their labor belonged to their employers.[3] This number gradually decreased; and, in 1617, there were of them all, men, women and children, but fifty-four.[4] Others, especially the favorite settlement near the mouth of the Appomattox, were tenants, paying two and a half barrels of corn, as a yearly tribute to the

[1] Stith, p. 133; Smith's New-Jersey, p. 26.
[2] Smith, v. ii. p. 22; Stith, p. 132.
[3] Smith, v. ii. p. 17, 18; Stith, p. 132; Chalmers, p. 34.
[4] Smith, v. ii. p. 34; Stith, p. 147.

store, and giving to the public service one month's labor, which was to be required neither at seed-time nor harvest.[1] This more favorable condition was probably owing to some peculiarities in the manner, in which their expenses in emigrating had been defrayed. He, who came himself, or had sent others at his own expense, had been entitled to a hundred acres of land for each person; now that the colony was well established, the bounty on emigration was fixed at fifty acres, of which the actual occupation and culture gave a further right to as many more, to be assigned at leisure. Besides this, lands were granted as rewards of merit; yet not more than two thousand acres could be so appropriated to one person. Every adventurer, who had paid into the company's treasury twelve pounds and ten shillings, likewise obtained a title to a hundred acres of land, any where in Virginia, not yet granted or possessed, with a reserved claim to as much more.[2] Such were the earliest land laws of Virginia; imperfect and unequal as they were, they at least gave the cultivator the means of becoming a proprietor of the soil. These valuable changes were introduced by Sir Thomas Dale; a magistrate, who, notwithstanding the introduction of martial law, has gained praise for his vigor and industry, his judgment and conduct. Having remained five years in America, and now desiring to visit England and his family, he appointed George Yeardley deputy-governor, and embarked for his native country.[3]

1616.

[1] Smith, v. ii. p. 22; Stith, p. 132. 1620, p. 9, 10; Stith, p. 139, 140.
[2] State of Virginia, printed in
[3] Stith, p. 138.

CHAP. IV.

The labor of the colony had long been misdirected; in the manufacture of ashes and soap, of glass and tar, the colonists could not sustain the competition with the nations on the Baltic. Much fruitless cost had been incurred in planting vineyards. It
1615. was found, that tobacco might be profitably cultivated. The sect of gold-finders had become extinct; and now the fields, the gardens, the public squares, and even the streets of Jamestown, were planted with tobacco;[1] and the colonists dispersed, unmindful of security in their eagerness for gain. Tobacco, as it gave animation to Virginian industry, eventually became not only the staple, but the currency of the colony.

1617. With the success of industry and the security of property, the emigrants needed the possession of political rights. It is an evil, incident to a corporate body, that its officers separate their interests as managers from their interests as partial proprietors. This was found to be none the less true, where an extensive territory was the estate to be managed; and embittered parties contended for the posts of emolument and honor. It was under the influence of a faction, which rarely obtained a majority, that the office of deputy-governor was entrusted to Argall. Martial law was at that time the common law of the country; that the despotism of the new deputy, who was both self-willed and avaricious, might be complete, he was further invested with the place of admiral of the country and the adjoining seas.[2]

[1] Smith, v. ii. p. 33.   [2] Stith, p. 145.

ARGALL'S DESPOTIC ADMINISTRATION.

The return of Lord Delaware to America might have restored tranquillity; the health of that nobleman was not equal to the voyage; he embarked with many emigrants, but did not live to reach Virginia.[1] The tyranny of Argall was, therefore, left unrestrained; but his indiscriminate rapacity and vices were destined to defeat themselves, and procure for the colony an inestimable benefit; for they led him to defraud the company, as well as to oppress the colonists. The condition of Virginia became intolerable; the labor of the settlers was perverted to the benefit of the governor; servitude, for a limited period, became a common penalty, annexed to trifling offences; and, in a colony where martial law still continued in force, life itself was insecure against his capricious passions. The first appeal, ever made from America to England, directed, not to the king, but to the company, was in behalf of one whom Argall had wantonly condemned to death, and whom he had with great difficulty been prevailed upon to spare.[2] The colony was fast falling into disrepute, and the report of the tyranny established beyond the Atlantic, checked emigration. A reformation was demanded, and was conceded with guarantees for the future; because the interests of the colonists and the company coincided in requiring a redress of their common wrongs. After a strenuous contest on the part of rival factions for the

CHAP. IV.

1617.

1618

---

[1] Stith, p. 148. In Royal and Noble Authors, v. ii. p. 180—183, Lord Delaware is said to have died at Wherwell, Hants, June 7, 1618. The writers on Virginia uniformly relate, that he died at sea. Smith, v. ii. p. 34.
[2] Stith, p. 150—153.

control of the company, the influence of Sir Edwin Sandys prevailed; Argall was displaced, and the mild and popular Yeardley was now appointed captain-general of the colony.[1] But before the new chief magistrate could arrive in Virginia, Argall had withdrawn, having previously, by fraudulent devices, preserved for himself and his partners the fruits of his extortions.[2] The London company suffered the usual plagues of corporations, faithless agents and fruitless law-suits.[3]

The administration of Yeardley began with acts of benevolence. The ancient planters were fully released from all further service to the colony, and were confirmed in the possession of their estates, both personal and real, as amply as the subjects of England. The burdens imposed by his predecessor were removed,[4] and martial law gradually disappeared.[5] But these were not the only benefits, conferred through Yeardley; his administration marks an era in the progress of American liberty.

By the direction of the London company,[6] the authority of the governor was limited by a council, which had power to redress such wrongs as he should commit; and the colonists themselves were admitted to a share in legislation. In June, 1619, the first colonial assembly that ever met in Virginia,[7] was convened at Jamestown. The governor, the newly

---

[1] Stith, p. 154.
[2] Ibid, p. 157.
[3] The company's Chief Root of the Differences and Discontents, in Burk, v. i. p. 317—322; the leading authority, written in 1623.
[4] Stith, p. 158.
[5] Ibid, p. 161; Chalmers, p. 44.
[6] State of Virginia, 1620, p. 6, 7. A rare tract of the highest authority. It is in the Cambridge Library.
[7] Hening, v. i. p. 118.

appointed council, and the representatives of the boroughs, hence called burgesses,[1] constituted the first popular representative body, ever convened in the western hemisphere. All matters were debated, which were thought expedient for the good of the colony.[2] The legislative enactments of these earliest American law-givers, now no longer extant, could not be of force, till they were ratified by the company in England. It does not appear, that the ratification took place; yet they were acknowledged to have been "in their greatest part very well and judiciously carried."[3] The gratitude of the Virginians was expressed with cheerful alacrity; former griefs were buried in oblivion; and the representatives of the colony expressed their "greatest possible thanks" for the care of the company in settling the plantation.[4]

This was the happy dawn of legislative liberty in America. They, who had been dependent on the will of a governor, now claimed the privileges of Englishmen, and demanded a code based upon the English laws. They were now willing to regard Virginia as their country and their home; and, since English jurisprudence was established and legislative liberty permitted, they resolved to perpetuate the colony.

The patriot party in England, now possessed of the control of the London company, engaged with

[1] Stith, p. 160.
[2] Smith, v. ii. p. 39.
[3] Ancient Records, in Hening, v. i. p. 121, 122.
[4] State of Virginia, 1620, p. 7; Purchas, v. iv. p. 1775, 1776. Chalmers, p. 44, perversely attributes to the colonial assembly the language employed by the London company.

CHAP. IV.
1619.

earnestness in schemes to advance the population and establish the liberties of Virginia; and Sir Edwin Sandys, the new treasurer, was a man of such judgment and firmness, that no intimidations, not even threats of blood, could deter him from investigating and reforming the abuses, by which the progress of the colony had been retarded.[1] At his accession to office, after twelve years' labor and an expenditure of eighty thousand pounds by the company, there were in the colony no more than six hundred persons, men, women and children; and now, in one year, he provided a passage to Virginia for twelve hundred and sixty-one persons.[2] Nor must the character of the emigration be overlooked. "The people of Virginia had not been settled in their minds," and, as, before the recent changes, they had gone there with the design of ultimately returning to England, it was necessary to multiply attachments to the soil. Few women had as yet dared to cross the Atlantic; but now the promise of prosperity induced ninety[3] agreeable persons, young and incorrupt,[4] to listen to the wishes of the company and the benevolent advice of Sandys, and to embark for the colony, where they were assured of a welcome. They were transported at the expense of the corporation; and were married to the tenants of the company; or to men, who were well able to support them, and who willingly defrayed the costs

[1] Chief Root of the Differences, in Burk, v. i. p. 323; Stith, p. 159.
[2] A Note of the Shipping, Men and Provisions sent to Virginia in 1619, p. 1, 2 and 3.
[3] Ibid, p. 3.
[4] Stith, p. 165.

of their passage, which were rigorously demanded.[1] The adventure succeeded so well, that it was designed to send the next year another consignment of one hundred;[2] but before these could be collected, the company found itself so poor, that its design could be accomplished only by a subscription. After some delays, sixty were actually despatched, maids of virtuous education, young, handsome, and well recommended. The price rose from one hundred and twenty to one hundred and fifty pounds of tobacco, or even more; so that all the original charges might be repaid. The debt for a wife was a debt of honor, and took precedence of any other; and the company, in conferring employments, gave a preference to the married men. Domestic ties were formed; virtuous sentiments and habits of thrift ensued; the tide of emigration swelled; within three years fifty patents for land were granted, and three thousand five hundred persons found their way to Virginia.[3]

The deliberate and formal concession of legislative liberties was an act of the deepest interest. When Sandys, after a year's service, resigned his office as treasurer, a struggle ensued on the election of his successor. The meeting was numerously attended; and, as the courts of the company were now become the schools of debate, many of the distinguished leaders of parliament were present. King James attempted to decide the struggle; and a mes-

---

[1] Sir Edwin Sandys' Speech, reported in Stith, p. 166.
[2] Supplies for 1620, p. 11, annexed to State of Virginia, 1620.
[3] Stith, p. 196; State of Virginia, 1622, p. 6, &c.

sage was communicated from him, nominating four candidates, one of whom he desired should receive the appointment. The company resisted the royal interference as an infringement of their charter; and while James exposed himself to the disgrace of an unsuccessful attempt at usurpation, the choice of the meeting fell upon the earl of Southampton, the early friend of Shakspeare. Having thus vindicated their own rights, the company proceeded to redress former wrongs, and to provide colonial liberty with its written guarantees.[1]

In the case of the appeal to the London company from a sentence of death pronounced by Argall, the friends of that officer had assembled, with the earl of Warwick at their head, and had voted, that trial by martial law is the noblest kind of trial, because soldiers and men of the sword were the judges. This opinion was now reversed and the rights of the colonists to trial by jury amply sustained.[2] Nor was it long before the freedom of the northern fisheries was equally asserted; and the early history of New-England will explain with what success the monopoly of a rival corporation was opposed.[3]

The company had silently approved, yet never expressly sanctioned the colonial assembly which had been convened by Sir George Yeardley. It was in July, 1621, that a memorable ordinance[4] established for the colony a written constitution. The

---

[1] Stith, p. 176—181.
[2] Ibid, p. 181, 182.
[3] Ibid, p. 185; Gorges' Description, c. xvii.—xxii.
[4] Hening, v. i. p. 110, 111; Stith's Appendix, p. 32; Hazard, v. i. p. 131—133. Compare Chalmers, p. 54, 55; Story's Commentaries, v. i. p. 26.

form of government prescribed for Virginia was analogous to the English constitution, and was, with some modifications, the model of the systems, which were afterwards introduced into the various royal provinces. Its purpose was declared to be "the greatest comfort and benefit to the people, and the prevention of injustice, grievances and oppression." Its terms are few and simple; a governor, to be appointed by the company; a permanent council, likewise to be appointed by the company; a general assembly, to be convened yearly, and to consist of the members of the council, and of two burgesses to be chosen from each of the several plantations by their respective inhabitants. The assembly might exercise full legislative authority, a negative voice being reserved to the governor; but no law or ordinance would be valid, unless ratified by the company in England. With singular justice and a liberality without example, it was further ordained, that, after the government of the colony shall have once been framed, no orders of the court in London shall bind the colony, unless they be in like manner ratified by the general assembly. The courts of justice were required to conform to the laws and manner of trial, used in the realm of England.

Such was the constitution, which Sir Francis Wyatt, the successor of the mild but inefficient Yeardley, was commissioned to bear to the colony. The system of representative government and trial by jury, was thus established in the new hemisphere as an acknowledged right; the colonists, ceasing to

176   THE VIRGINIANS ACQUIRE CIVIL FREEDOM.

CHAP. IV.
1621.

depend as servants on a commercial company, now became freemen and citizens. The ordinance was the basis, on which Virginia erected the superstructure of its liberties. Its influences were wide and enduring, and can be traced through all following years of the history of the colony. It constituted the plantation, in its infancy, a nursery of freemen; and succeeding generations learned to cherish institutions, which were as old as the first period of the prosperity of their fathers. The privileges, which were now conceded, could never be wrested from the Virginians; and, as new colonies arose at the south, their proprietaries could hope to win emigrants only by bestowing franchises as large, as those enjoyed by their elder rival. The London company merits the fame of having acted as the successful friend of liberty in America. It may be doubted, whether any public act during the reign of King James was of more permanent or pervading influence; and it reflects glory on the earl of Southampton, Sir Edwin Sandys, and the patriot party of England, who, unable to establish guarantees of a liberal administration at home, were careful to connect popular freedom so intimately with the life, prosperity and state of society of Virginia, that they never could be separated.

[1] The oldest book, printed on Virginia, is in our Cambridge Library, though not mentioned in the catalogue. It is a thin quarto, in Black Letter, by John Smith, printed in 1608. "A True Relation of such occurrences and accidents of note, as hath hapned in Virginia since the first planting of that Collony, which is now resident in the South part thereof, till the last returne."

CHAPTER V.

SLAVERY. DISSOLUTION OF THE LONDON COMPANY.

WHILE Virginia, by the concession of a representative government, was constituted the asylum of liberty, by one of the strange contradictions in human affairs, it became the abode of hereditary bondsmen. The unjust, wasteful and unhappy system was fastened upon the rising institutions of America, not by the consent of the corporation, nor the desires of the emigrants; but, as it was introduced by the mercantile avarice of a foreign nation, so it was subsequently riveted by the policy of England, without regard to the interests or the wishes of the colony.

The traffic of Europeans in negro slaves was fully established before the colonization of the United States, and had existed a half century before the discovery of America. In the middle ages the Venetians,[1] in their commercial intercourse with the ports of unbelieving nations, purchased Christians and infidels in every market, where they were exposed; and sold them again to the Arabs in Sicily and Spain.

---

[1] Heeren on the Crusades, in Historische Werke, v. ii. p. 260. Heeren cites C. A. Marin, Storia civile e politica del commerzio de' Veneziani; Venezia, 1789, 8 vols.; v. i. p. 206, and v. ii. p. 55. I have never met with the work of Marin.

CHAP. V.

The commerce was denounced by the see of Rome;[1] but avarice triumphed, and the prohibition[2] became limited to the sale of Christians into bondage among the infidels. Christian avarice continued to supply the slave market of the Saracens. In England, the Anglo-Saxon nobility sold their servants as slaves to foreigners; and so tempting was the gain, that the terrors of religion were required to restrain the commerce.[3] Even after the conquest, slaves were exported from England to Ireland,[4] till the reign of Henry II., when the Irish, in a national synod, to remove a pretext for an invasion, decreed the emancipation of all English slaves within the island.[5]

1102.

1415. It was not long after the first conquests of the Portuguese in Barbary, that their maritime enterprize conducted their navy to the ports of Western
1441. Africa; and the first ships, which sailed so far south as Cape Blanco, returned, not with negroes, but with Moors. The subjects of this importation were treated, not as laborers, but rather as strangers, from whom information respecting their native country was to be derived; Antony Gonzalez, who had
1443. brought them to Portugal, was commanded to restore

---

[1] Heeren on the Crusades.
[2] Hallam, in Middle ages, c. ix. part i. near the end, cites a law of Carloman, ut mancipia Christiana paganis non vendantur.
[3] Concilium Londinense, extracted from William of Malmesbury and Eadmer, in Wilkins' Coucilia magnæ Britanniæ, &c. folio, v. i. p. 383. Ne quis illud nefarium negotium, quo hactenus homines in Anglia solebant velut bruta animalia venundari, deinceps ullatenus facere præsumat.
[4] Giraldus Cambrensis, in Wilkins, v. i. p. 471. Anglorum namque populus, adhuc integro eorum regno, communis gentis vitio, liberos suos venales exponere, et, priusquam inopiam ullam aut inediam sustinerent, filios proprios et cognatos in Hiberniam vendere consueverant. Decretum est igitur, ut Angli ubique per insulam, servitutis vinculo mancipati, in pristinam revocentur libertatem.
[5] Compare Lyttleton's History of the Life of Henry II., v. iii. p. 70.

ORIGIN OF NEGRO SLAVERY IN EUROPE.

them to their ancient homes. He did so, and the Moors gave him as their ransom, not gold only, but "black Moors" with curled hair. Thus negro slaves came into Europe; and mercantile cupidity immediately observed, that negroes might become an object of lucrative commerce. New ships were despatched without delay.[1] Spain also engaged in the traffic; the historian of her maritime discoveries even claims for her the unenviable distinction of having anticipated the Portuguese in introducing negroes into Europe.[2] The merchants of Seville imported gold dust and slaves from the western coast of Africa;[3] and negro slavery, though the severity of bondage was mitigated in its character by benevolent legislation,[4] was established in Andalusia, and "abounded in the city of Seville," before the enterprize of Columbus was conceived.[5]

The maritime adventurers of those days, joining the principles of pirates with the bold designs of heroism, esteemed the wealth of the countries which they might discover, as their rightful plunder; and the inhabitants, if civilized, as their subjects, if barbarous, as their slaves, by the laws of successful warfare. Even the Indians of Hispaniola were im-

---

[1] Galvano's Discoveries of the World, in Hakluyt, v. iv. p. 413.
[2] Navarette, Colleccion. Introduccion, s. xix.
[3] MS. History of the Reign of Ferdinand and Isabella, the Catholic, of Spain. See above, p. 7, note 1.
[4] Zuñiga, Annales de Sevilla, pp. 373, 374. The passage is a very remarkable one. "Avia años que desde los Puertos de Andaluzia se frequentava navegacion à los costas de Africa, y Guinea, de donde se traian esclavos, de que ya abundava esta ciudad, &c. &c. p. 373. Eran en Sevilla los negros tratados con gran benignidad, desde el tiempo de el Rey Don Henrique Tercero, &c. &c. p. 374. I owe the opportunity of consulting Zuñiga to W. H. Prescott, of Boston.
[5] Irving's Columbus, v. ii. p. 351, 352; Herrera, d. i. l. iv. c. xii.

ported into Spain. Cargoes of the natives of the north were early and repeatedly kidnapped. The coasts of America, like the coasts of Africa, were visited by ships in search of laborers; and there was hardly a convenient harbor on the whole Atlantic frontier of the United States, which was not entered by slavers.[1] The native Indians themselves were ever ready to resist the treacherous merchant; the freemen of the wilderness, unlike the Africans, among whom slavery had existed from immemorial times, would never abet the foreign merchant, or become his factors in the nefarious traffic. Fraud and force remained, therefore, the means by which, near Newfoundland or Florida, on the shores of the Atlantic or among the Indians of the Mississippi valley, Cortereal and Vazquez de Ayllon, Porcallo and Soto, with private adventurers whose names and whose crimes may be left unrecorded, transported the natives of North America into slavery in Europe and the Spanish West Indies. The glory of Columbus himself did not escape the stain; enslaving

1494. five hundred native Americans, he sent them to Spain, that they might be publicly sold at Seville.[2] The

---

[1] Compare Justin Martyr d'Anghiera, d. vii. c. i. and ii. in Hakluyt, v. v. p. 404, 405. 407. In citing, perhaps for the last time, the venerable historian of the Affairs of the Ocean, I have given him his whole name. He is called d'Anghiera, not because he was born there; for his native town was Arona, where he first saw the light in 1455; but because it was the name of his family, derived from the place of its origin. There is, then, a slight inaccuracy in a note of Irving, Life of Columbus, Appendix, No. 27, v. iii. p. 367, of first American edition. The error may be corrected from Tiraboschi, Storia della Letterat. Ital. t. vii. p. 1011, or Navarette, Introduccion, s. xlv., and the note of de la Roquette, in the French translation of Navarette, t. i. p. 161.

[2] Irving's Columbus, b. viii. c. v. v. ii. p. 84—86. First Am. edition.

generous Isabella commanded the liberation of the Indians held in bondage in her European possessions.[1] Yet her active benevolence extended neither to the Moors, whose valor had been punished by slavery, nor to the Africans; and even her compassion for the New World implied no hostility to the condition of servitude itself; it was rather the transient compassion, which relieves the miserable who are in sight; not the deliberate application of a just principle. For the commissions for making discoveries, issued a few days before and after her interference to rescue those whom Columbus had enslaved, reserved for herself and Ferdinand a fourth part[2] of the slaves, which the new kingdoms might contain. The slavery of Indians was recognized as lawful.[3]

The practice of selling the natives of North America into foreign bondage, continued for nearly two centuries; and even the sternest morality pronounced the sentence of slavery and exile on the captives, whom the field of battle had spared. The excellent Winthrop enumerates Indians among his bequests.[4] A scanty remnant of the Pequod tribe[5] in Connecticut, the captives treacherously made by Waldron in New-Hampshire,[6] the harmless fragments of the tribe of Annawon,[7] the orphan offspring of King Philip

---

[1] For the cédula, liberating the Indians, sold into bondage, por mandado de nuestro Almirante de las Indias, see Navarette, Coleccion, v. ii. p. 246, 247.

[2] Esclavos, é negros, é loros que en estos nuestros reinos sean habidos é reputados por esclavos, &c. Navarette, v. ii. p. 245, and again, v. ii. p. 249.

[3] See a cédula on a slave contract, in Navarette, v. iii. p. 514, 515, given June 20, 1501.

[4] Winthrop's N. England, Appendix, v. ii. p. 360.

[5] Ibid, v. i. p. 234.

[6] Belknap's Hist. of N. Hampshire, v. i. p. 75, Farmer's edition.

[7] Baylies' Memoir of Plymouth, part iii. p. 190.

himself,[1] were all doomed to the same hard destiny of perpetual bondage. The clans of Virginia[2] and Carolina, for more than a hundred years, were hardly safe against the kidnapper. The universal public mind was long and deeply vitiated.

It was not Las Casas, who first suggested the plan of transporting African slaves to Hispaniola; Spanish slaveholders, as they emigrated, were accompanied by their negroes. The emigration may at first have been contraband; but a royal edict soon permitted negro slaves, born in slavery among Christians, to be transported to Hispaniola.[3] Thus the royal ordinances of Spain authorized negro slavery in America. Within two years, there were such numbers of Africans in Hispaniola, that Ovando, the governor of the island, entreated that the importation might no longer be permitted.[4] The Spanish government attempted to disguise the crime by forbidding the introduction of negro slaves, who had been bred in Moorish families,[5] and allowing only those, who were said to have been instructed in the Christian faith, to be transported to the West Indies, under the plea, that they might assist in converting the infidel nations. But the idle pretence was soon abandoned; for should faith in Christianity be punished by perpetual bondage in the colonies? And would the purchaser be scrupulously inquisitive of

[1] Davis on Morton's Memorial, Appendix, p. 454, 455; Baylies' Memoir of Plymouth, part iii. p. 190, 191.
[2] Hening's Statutes at large, v. i. p. 481, 482. The act, forbidding the crime, proves, what is indeed undisputed, its previous existence. Lawson's Carolina.
[3] Herrera, d. i. l. iv. c. xii.
[4] Irving's Columbus, Appendix, No. 26, v. iii. p. 372, first American edition.
[5] Herrera, d. i. l. vi. c. xx.

NEGRO SLAVERY IN THE WEST INDIES.

the birth-place and instruction of his laborers? The system was already riveted and was not long restrained by the scruples of men in power. King Ferdinand himself sent from Seville fifty slaves[1] to labor in the mines; and, because it was said, that one negro could do the work of four Indians, the direct traffic in slaves between Guinea and Hispaniola was enjoined by a royal ordinance,[2] and deliberately sanctioned by repeated decrees.[3] Was it not natural that Charles V., a youthful monarch, surrounded by rapacious courtiers, should have readily granted licenses to the Flemings to transport negroes to the colonies? The benevolent Las Casas, who had seen the native inhabitants of the New World vanish away, like dew, before the cruelties of the Spaniards, who felt for the Indians all that an ardent charity and the purest missionary zeal could inspire, and who had seen the African thriving in robust[4] health under the sun of Hispaniola, returning from America to plead the cause of the feeble Indians, suggested the expedient,[5] that negroes might still further be employed to perform the severe toils, which they alone could endure. The avarice of the Flemish

CHAP. V.

1510.

1511.
1512-3

1516.

1517.

---

[1] Herrera, d. i. l. viii. c. ix.
[2] Ibid, d. i. l. ix. c. v. Herrera is explicit. The note of the French translator of Navarette, t. i. p. 203, 204, needs correction. A commerce in negroes, sanctioned by the crown, was surely not contraband.
[3] Irving's Columbus, v. iii. p. 372.
[4] Ibid, v. iii. p. 370, 371.
[5] The merits of Las Casas have been largely discussed. The controversy seems now concluded.

Irving's Columbus, v. iii. p. 367—378. Navarette, Introduccion, s. lviii. lix. The Memoir of Las Casas still exists in manuscript. Herrera, d. ii. l. ii. c. xx. Robertson's America, v. i. b. iii. It may yet gratify curiosity to compare Grégoire, Apologie de B. Las Casas, in Mem. de l' Inst. Nat. An. viii.; and the excellent discourse of Verplanck, in New-York Historical Collections, v. iii. p. 49—53, and p. 102—105.

CHAP. V.

1517.

greedily seized on the expedient; the board of trade at Seville was consulted, to learn how many slaves would be required. It had been proposed to allow four for each Spanish emigrant; deliberate calculation fixed the number, esteemed necessary, at four thousand. The monopoly[1] of annually importing that number of slaves into the West Indies was eagerly seized by La Bresa, a favorite of the Spanish monarch, and was sold to the Genoese, who purchased their cargoes of Portugal. We shall, at a later period, have occasion to observe a stipulation for this lucrative monopoly, forming an integral part in a treaty of peace, established by a European Congress; and shall witness the sovereign of the most free state in Europe stipulating for a fourth part of the profits of the abominable commerce.[2] Thus a hasty benevolence, too zealous to be just, attempted to save the natives of America by sanctioning an equal oppression of another race. But covetousness, and not a mistaken benevolence, established the slave trade; which existed and had nearly received its development, before the charity of Las Casas was heard in defence of the Indians. Reason,[3] policy,[4] and religion alike condemned the

---

[1] Herrera, d. ii. l. ii. c. xx.
[2] Southey's History of Brazil, v. iii. p. 136. Queen Anne reserved to herself one fourth part of the contract for slaves, and the king of Spain another fourth. The queen of England soon disposed of her share to the South Sea Company.
[3] Inter dominum et servum nulla amicitia est; etiam in pace belli tamen jura servantur. Quintus Curtius, l. vii. c. viii. John Locke, who yet seems to have sanctioned slavery in Carolina, gives a similar definition of it. "The perfect condition of slavery is the state of war continued between a lawful conqueror and a captive." Compare, also, Montesquieu de l' Esprit des Lois, l. xv. c. v., on negro slavery.
[4] See A.Q. Review, for Dec. 1832, for the effects of slavery in Virginia.

traffic. It was never sanctioned by the see of Rome. Pope Alexander III.,[1] in the very darkness of the middle ages, had written, that, "nature having made no slaves, all men have an equal right to liberty." Even Leo X., though his voluptuous life, making of his pontificate a continued carnival, might have deadened the sentiments of humanity and justice, declared,[2] that "not the Christian religion only, but nature herself cries out against the state of slavery." And Paul III., in two separate briefs,[3] imprecated a curse on the Europeans, who should enslave Indians, or any other class of men. It even became usual for Spanish vessels, when they sailed on a voyage of discovery, to be attended by a priest, whose benevolent duty it was, to prevent the kidnapping of the aborigines.[4] The legislation of independent America has been emphatic[5] in denouncing the hasty avarice, which entailed the anomaly of negro slavery in the midst of liberty. Ximenes, the gifted coadjutor of Ferdinand and Isabella, the stern grand inquisitor, the austere but ambitious Franciscan, saw in advance the danger, which it required centuries

---

[1] See his letter to Lupus, king of Valencia, in Historiæ Anglicanæ Scriptores, in folio; Londini, 1652; t. i. p. 580. Cum autem omnes liberos natura creasset, nullus conditione naturæ fuit subditus servituti.

[2] Grahame's United States, v. ii. p. 18; Clarkson's History of the Abolition of the Slave Trade, v. i. p. 35, American edition. Clarkson, v. i. p. 33, 34, says that Charles V. lived to repent his permission of slavery and to order emancipation. The first is probable; yet Herrera, d. ii. l. ii. c. xx., denounces not slavery, but the monopoly of the slave trade.

[3] See the Brief, in Remesal, Hist. de Chiappa, l. iii. c. xvi. and xvii.

[4] T. Southey's West Indies, v. i. p. 126.

[5] Walsh's Appeal, octavo, Philadelphia, 1819, p. 306—342; Belknap's letter to Tucker, i. Mass. Historical Collections, v. iv. p. 190—211.

186   HAWKINS THE FIRST ENGLISH SLAVE MERCHANT.

CHAP. V.

to reveal, and refused to sanction the introduction of negroes into Hispaniola; believing[1] that the favorable climate would increase their numbers, and infallibly lead them to a successful revolt. A severe retribution has clearly manifested his sagacity; Hayti, the first spot in America that received African slaves, was the first to set the example of African liberty.

1562. The odious distinction of having first interested England in the slave trade, belongs to Sir John Hawkins. He had fraudulently transported a large cargo of Africans to Hispaniola; the rich returns of sugar, ginger and pearls, attracted the notice of Queen
1567. Elizabeth; and when a new expedition was prepared, she was induced, not only to protect, but to share the traffic.[2] In the accounts, which Hawkins himself gives[3] of one of his expeditions, he relates, that he set fire to a city, of which the huts were covered with dry palm leaves, and, out of eight thousand inhabitants, succeeded in seizing two hundred and fifty. The deliberate and even self-approving frankness, with which this act of atrocity is related, and the lustre which the fame of Hawkins acquired, display in the strongest terms the depravity of public sentiment in the age of Elizabeth. The leader in these expeditions was not merely a man of courage; in all other emergencies he knew how to pity the unfortunate, even when they were not his countrymen, and

---

[1] Irving's Columbus, v. iii. p. 374, 375.
[2] Compare Hakluyt, v. ii. p. 351, 352, with v. iii. p. 594. Hewitt's Carolina, v. i. p. 20—26;
Keith's Virginia, p. 31; Anderson's History of Commerce.
[3] Hakluyt, v. iii. p. 618, 619. Compare Mackintosh's England, v. iii. p. 178, American edition.

to relieve their wants with cheerful liberality.¹ Yet the commerce, on the part of the English, in the Spanish ports, was by the laws of Spain illicit, as well as by the laws of morals detestable; and when the sovereign of England participated in its hazards, its profits and its crimes, she became at once a smuggler and a slave merchant.²

A ship of one Thomas Keyser and one James Smith, the latter a member of the church of Boston, first brought upon the colonies the guilt of participating in the traffic in African slaves. They sailed "for Guinea to trade for negroes;"³ but throughout Massachusetts the cry of justice was raised against them as malefactors and murderers; Richard Saltonstall, a worthy assistant, felt himself moved by his duty as a magistrate, to denounce the act of stealing negroes as "expressly contrary to the law of God and the law of the country;"⁴ the guilty men were committed for the offence;⁵ and, after advice with the elders, the representatives of the people, bearing "witness against the heinous crime of man stealing," ordered the negroes to be restored at the public charge "to their native country, with a letter expressing the indignation of the general court" at their wrongs.⁶

Conditional servitude, under indentures or covenants, had from the first existed in Virginia. The

[margin: CHAP. V. 1645. 1646.]

---

¹ Hakluyt, v. iii. p. 418, 419, and 612—614.
² Lingard's England, v. viii. p. 306, 307.
³ Winthrop's New-England, v. ii. p. 243, 244, 245.
⁴ Winthrop's New-England, v. ii. p. 379, 380.
⁵ Colony Records, v. iii. p. 45; Savage on Winthrop, v. ii. p 245.
⁶ Colony Laws, c. xii. p. 53

CHAP. V.

servant stood to his master in the relation of a debtor, bound to discharge the costs of emigration by the entire employment of his powers for the benefit of his creditor. Oppression early ensued; men who had been transported into Virginia at an expense of eight or ten pounds, were sometimes sold for forty, fifty, or even threescore pounds.[1] The supply of white servants became a regular business; and a class of men, nicknamed spirits, used to delude professed idlers into embarking for America, as to a land of spontaneous plenty.[2] White servants came to be in Barbadoes a usual article of traffic; like the negroes, they were to be purchased on shipboard, as men buy horses at a fair. In 1672, the price, where five years of service were due, was about ten pounds; while a negro was worth twenty or twenty-five pounds.[3] So usual was this manner of dealing in Englishmen, that not the Scots only, who were taken in the field of Dunbar, were sent into involuntary servitude in New-England,[4] but the royalist prisoners of the battle of Worcester,[5] and the leaders in the insurrection of Penruddoc,[6] were shipped to America. At the corresponding period in Ireland, the crowded exportation of Irish catholics was a frequent event, and was attended by cruel aggravations, hardly inferior to the usual atrocities of the

[1] Smith, v. i. p. 105.
[2] Bullock's Virginia, 1649, p. 14.
[3] Blome's Jamaica, 1672, p. 84 and p. 16.
[4] See the letters of Cromwell and Cotton, in Hutchinson's Collection, p. 233—235.
[5] Suffolk County Records, v. i. p. 5 and 6. The names of two hundred and seventy are recorded. The lading of the John and Sarah was "ironwork, household stuff, and other provisions for planters, and Scotch prisoners." Recorded May 14, 1652.
[6] Hume's England, c. lxi.

NEGRO SLAVERY IN VIRGINIA.

African slave trade.[1] In 1685, when nearly a thousand of the prisoners, condemned for participating in the insurrection of Monmouth, were sentenced to transportation, some gentlemen of influence at court, among others Sir Christopher Musgrave, begged of the monarch the convicted insurgents as a merchantable commodity, and satisfied their avarice by the sale of their countrymen into slavery.[2]

The condition of apprenticed servants in Virginia differed from that of slaves chiefly in the duration of their bondage; and the laws of the colony favored their early emancipation.[3] But this state of labor easily admitted the introduction of perpetual servitude. The commerce of Virginia had been at first monopolized by the company; but as its management for the benefit of the corporation led to frequent dissensions, it was in 1620 laid open to free competition.[4] In the month of August of that year, just fourteen months after the first representative assembly of Virginia, four months before the Plymouth colony landed in America, and less than a year before the concession of a written constitution, a Dutch man-of-war entered James River, and landed twenty negroes for sale.[5] This is, indeed, the sad epoch of the introduction of negro slavery within the English colonies; but the traffic would have been checked in its infancy, had its profits remained with the Dutch. Thirty years after this first importation of

---

[1] Lingard's England, v. xi. p. 131, 132.
[2] Hallam's England, v. iii. p. 92.
[3] Hening, v. i. p. 257.
[4] Stith, p. 171.
[5] Beverley's Virginia, p. 35. Stith, p. 182; Chalmers, p. 49; Burk, v. i. p. 211; and Hening, v. i. p. 146, all rely on Beverley.

CHAP. V.

Africans, the increase had been so inconsiderable, that to one black, Virginia contained fifty whites;[1] and, at a later period, after seventy years of its colonial existence, the number of its negro slaves was proportionably much less than in several of the free states at the time of the war of independence. It is the duty of faithful history, to trace events, not only to their causes, but to their authors; and we shall hereafter inquire, what influence was ultimately extended to counteract the voice of justice, the cry of humanity, and the remonstrances of colonial legislation. The negro race was from the first regarded with disgust, and its union with the whites was forbidden under ignominious penalties.[2] For many years, the Dutch were principally concerned in the slave trade in the market of Virginia; the immediate demand for laborers may, in part, have blinded the eyes of the planters to the ultimate evils of slavery;[3] though the laws of the colony, at a very early period, discouraged its increase by a special tax upon female slaves.[4]

1621. If Wyatt, on his arrival in Virginia, found the evil of negro slavery engrafted on the social system, he brought with him the memorable ordinance, on which the fabric of colonial liberty was to rest, and which was interpreted by his instructions[5] in a manner, the most favorable to the independent rights of the col-

[1] ii. Mass. Hist. Coll. v. ix. p. 105. A New Description of Virginia.
[2] Hening, v. i. p. 146.
[3] This may be inferred from a paper on Virginia, in Thurloe, v. v. p. 81, or Hazard, v. i. p. 601.
[4] Hening, v. ii. p. 84, Act liv. March, 1662. The statute implies, that the rule already existed.
[5] Ibid, v. i. p. 114—118. They are also in Stith, p. 194—196; and Burk, v. i. p. 224—227.

onists. Justice was established on the basis of the laws of England; and an amnesty of ancient feuds proclaimed. The order to search for minerals betrays the continuance of lingering hopes of finding gold; while the injunction to promote certain kinds of manufactures was ineffectual, because labor could otherwise be more profitably employed.

The business which occupied the first session under the written constitution, related chiefly to the encouragement of domestic industry; and the culture of silk particularly engaged the attention of the assembly.[1] But legislation, though it can favor industry, cannot create it. When soil, men and circumstances combine to render a manufacture desirable, legislation can protect the infancy of enterprize against the unequal competition with established skill. The culture of silk, long, earnestly and frequently recommended to the attention of Virginia,[2] is successfully pursued, only when a superfluity of labor exists in a redundant population. In America, the first wants of life left no labor without a demand; silkworms could not be cared for, where every comfort of household existence required to be created. Still less was the successful culture of the vine possible. The company had repeatedly sent vine-dressers, who had been set to work under the terrors of martial law; and whose efforts were continued after the establishment of regular government. But the toil was in vain. The extensive culture of the vine, unless singularly favored by climate, succeeds

[1] Hening, v. i. p. 119.   [2] Virgo Triumphans, p. 35.

CHAP. V.

only in a dense population; for a small vineyard requires the labor of many hands. It is a law of nature, that, in a new country under the temperate zone, corn and cattle will be raised, rather than silk or wine.

1621. The first culture of cotton in the United States deserves commemoration. This year the seeds were planted as an experiment; and their "plentiful coming up" was, at that early day, a subject of interest in America and England.[1]

Nor did the benevolence of the company neglect to establish places of education and provide for the support of religious worship. The bishop of London collected and paid a thousand pounds towards a university; which, like the several churches of the colony, was liberally endowed with domains.[2] Public and private charity were active;[3] but the lands were never occupied by productive laborers; and the system of obtaining a revenue through a permanent tenantry could meet with no success, for it was not in harmony with the condition of colonial society.

1622. Between the Indians and the English there had been quarrels, but no wars. From the first landing of colonists in Virginia, the power of the natives was despised; their strongest weapons were such arrows as they could shape without the use of iron, such hatchets as could be made from stone; and an English mastiff seemed to them a terrible adversary.[4]

---

[1] George Thorp's letter of May 17, 1621, in a marginal note in Purchas, v. iv. p. 1789.
[2] Stith, p. 162. 166. 172, 173.
[3] Memorial of Religious Charitie, in the State of Virginia, 1622, p. 51—54; Stith, p. 162.
[4] Smith, v. ii p. 68; Stith, p. 211.

NUMBER AND POWER OF THE ABORIGINES.

Nor were their numbers considerable. Within sixty miles of Jamestown, it is computed, there were no more than five thousand souls, or about fifteen hundred warriors. The whole territory of the clans, which listened to Powhatan as their leader or their conqueror, comprehended about eight thousand square miles, thirty tribes, and twenty-four hundred warriors; so that the Indian population amounted to about one inhabitant to a square mile.[1] The natives, naked and feeble compared with the Europeans, were no where concentrated in considerable villages; but dwelt dispersed in hamlets, with from forty to sixty in each company. Few places had more than two hundred; and many had less.[2] It was also unusual for any large portion of these tribes to be assembled together. An idle tale of an ambuscade of three or four thousand is perhaps an error for three or four hundred; otherwise it is an extravagant fiction, wholly unworthy of belief.[3] Smith once met a party, that seemed to amount to seven hundred; and, so complete was the superiority conferred by the use of fire-arms, that with fifteen men he was able to withstand them all.[4] The savages were therefore regarded with contempt or compassion.[5] No uniform care had been taken to conciliate

[1] Smith, v. i. p. 129. Compare Jefferson's Notes on Virginia; Quære, xi. p. 129; True Declaration of Virginia, p. 10. "The extent of a hundred miles was scarce peopled with two thousand inhabitants."
[2] Smith, v. ii. p. 66; Purchas, v. iv. p. 1790; State of Virginia in 1622, p. 19; Heylin's Cosmography, edition of 1677, b. iv. p. 96.
[3] Smith, v. i. p. 177, abundantly refuted by what "Smith writ with his own hand," v. i. p. 129. Burk, v. i. p. 311, 312, condemned too hastily.
[4] Smith's History of Virginia, v. i. p. 129.
[5] Bullock's Virginia Examined, p. 12.

their good will; although their condition had been improved by some of the arts of civilized life. The degree of their advancement may be judged by the intelligence of their chieftain. A house having been built for Opechancanough after the English fashion, he took such delight in the lock and key, that he would lock and unlock the door a hundred times a day, and thought the device incomparable.[1] When Wyatt arrived, the natives expressed a fear, lest his intentions should be hostile; he assured them of his wish to preserve inviolable peace; and the emigrants had no use for fire-arms except against a deer or a fowl. Confidence so far increased, that the old law, which made death the penalty for teaching the Indians to use a musket, was forgotten; and they were now employed as fowlers and huntsmen.[2] The plantations of the English were widely extended in unsuspecting confidence, along the James river and towards the Potomac, wherever rich grounds invited to the culture of tobacco;[3] nor were solitary places, remote from neighbors, avoided; since there would there be less competition for the ownership of the soil.

Powhatan, the father of Pocahontas, remained, after the marriage of his daughter, the firm friend of the English. He died in 1618; and his younger brother was now the heir to his influence. Should the native occupants of the soil consent to be driven from their ancient patrimony? Should their feebleness submit patiently to contempt, injury and the loss of their lands? The desire of self-preservation,

[1] Smith, v. ii. p. 68; Stith, p. 211. [3] Beverley, p. 38; Burk, v. i. p.
[2] Ib. v. ii. p. 103; Beverley, p. 38.   231, 232.

the necessity of self-defence, seemed to demand an active resistance; to preserve their dwelling-places, the English must be exterminated; in open battle the Indians would be powerless; conscious of their weakness, they could not hope to accomplish their end except by a preconcerted surprise. The crime was one of savage ferocity; but it was suggested by their situation. They were timorous and quick of apprehension, and consequently treacherous; for treachery and falsehood are the vices of cowardice. The attack was prepared with impenetrable secrecy. To the very last hour the Indians preserved the language of friendship; they borrowed the boats of the English to attend their own assemblies; on the very morning of the massacre, they were in the houses and at the tables of those, whose death they were plotting. At length, on the twenty-second of March, at mid-day, at one and the same instant of time, the Indians fell upon an unsuspecting population, which was scattered through distant villages, extending one hundred and forty miles, on both sides of the river.[1] The onset was so sudden, that the blow was not discerned till it fell. None were spared; children and women, as well as men, the missionary, who had cherished the natives with untiring gentleness, the liberal benefactors, from whom they had received daily benefits, all were murdered with indiscriminate barbarity and every aggravation of cruelty. The savages fell upon the dead bodies, as if it had been possible to commit on them a fresh murder.[2]

[1] State of Virginia, 1622, p. 19.   [2] Smith, v. ii. p. 67.

CHAP. V.
1622.

In one hour three hundred and forty-seven persons were cut off. Yet the carnage was not universal; and Virginia was saved from so disastrous a grave.[1] The night before the execution of the conspiracy, it was revealed by a converted Indian to an Englishman, whom he wished to rescue; Jamestown and the nearest settlements were well prepared against an attack; and the savages, as timid as they were ferocious, fled with precipitation from the appearance of wakeful resistance. In this manner, the most considerable part of the colony was saved.[2] A year after the massacre, there still remained two thousand five hundred men;[3] the total number of the emigrants had exceeded four thousand.[4] The immediate consequences of this massacre were disastrous. Public works were abandoned;[5] the culture of the fields was much restricted; the settlements were reduced from eighty plantations to less than eight.[6] Sickness prevailed among the dispirited colonists, who were now crowded into narrow quarters; some even returned to England. But plans of industry were eventually succeeded by schemes of revenge; and a war of extermination ensued. In England, the news, far from dispiriting the adventurers, awakened

[1] On the massacre; A Declaration of the State of Virginia, with a relation of the barbarous massacre, &c. &c. 1622. This is the groundwork of the narrative in Smith, v. ii. p. 65—76, and of Purchas, v. iv. p. 1788—1791. Compare Stith, p. 208—213; Burk, v. i. p. 232—244.
[2] State of Virginia, in 1622, p. 18. Purchas, v. iv. p. 1792, says one thousand eight hundred survived; probably inexact. Compare Holmes, v. i. p. 178, note.
[3] Stith's History of Virginia, p. 281.
[4] Ibid, p. 219.
[5] Ibid, p. 218.
[6] Purchas, v. iv. p. 1792; Virginia's Verger, in Purchas, v. iv. p. 1816; Stith, p. 235; Burk, v. i. p. 244.

them to strong feelings of compassionate interest; CHAP. the purchase of Virginia was endeared by the sacrifice of so much life; and the blood of the victims 1622. became the seed of the plantation.¹ New supplies and assistance were promptly despatched; even King James, for a moment, affected a sentiment of generosity, and, like the churl, gave from the tower of London presents of arms, which had been thrown by as good for nothing in Europe. They might be useful, thought the monarch, against the Indians! He also made good promises, which were never fulfilled.² The city of London contributed to repair the losses of the Virginians; and many private persons displayed an honorable liberality.³ Smith volunteered his services to protect the planters, overawe the savages, and make discoveries; the company had no funds, and his proposition was never made a matter of public discussion or record; but some of the members, with ludicrous cupidity, proposed, he should have leave to go at his own expense, if he would grant the corporation one half of the pillage.⁴ There were in the colony much loss and much sorrow; but never any serious apprehensions of discomfiture from the Indians. The midnight surprise, the ambuscade by day, might be feared; the Indians promptly fled on the least indications of watchfulness and resistance. There were not wanting men, who now advocated an entire subjection of those, whom leniency could not win; and the example of Spanish

[1] Stith, p. 233.
[2] Burk, v. i. p. 248, 249.
[3] Stith, 232, 233.
[4] Smith, v. ii. p. 79—81; Stith, p. 234; Burk, v. i. p. 249, 250; Belknap's Am. Biog. v. i. p. 314, 315.

CHAP. V.
1622.

cruelties was cited with applause.¹ Besides, a natural instinct had led the Indians to select for their villages the pleasantest places, along the purest streams, and near the soil that was most easily cultivated. Their rights of property were no longer much respected; their open fields and villages were now appropriated by the colonists, who could plead the laws of war in defence of their covetousness.² Treachery also was employed. The tangled woods, the fastnesses of nature, were the bulwarks to which the savages retreated. Pursuit would have been vain; they could not be destroyed except as they were lulled into security and induced to return to

1623. their old homes.³ In July of the following year, the inhabitants of the several settlements, in parties, under commissioned officers, fell upon the adjoining savages;⁴ and a law of the general assembly commanded, that in July of 1624, the attack should be

1630. repeated.⁵ Six years later, the colonial statute book proves that schemes of ruthless vengeance were still meditated; for it was sternly insisted, that no peace should be concluded with the Indians,⁶ a law, which remained in force till a treaty in the administration

1632. of Harvey.⁷

Meantime, a change was preparing in the relations of the colony with the parent state. A corporation, whether commercial or proprietary, is, perhaps, the worst of sovereigns. Gain is the object, which leads

¹ Stith, p. 233, is unjust upon Smith, v. ii. p. 71, 72.
² Smith, v. ii. p. 71, 72.
³ Stith, p. 303.
⁴ Burk, v. i. p. 275.
⁵ Hening, v. i. p. 123, Act, No. 32.
⁶ Ibid, v. i. p. 153.
⁷ Burk, v. ii. p. 37.

to the formation of those companies, and which constitutes the interest, most likely to be fostered. If such a company be wisely administered, its colonists are made subservient to commercial avarice. If, on the other hand, the interests of the company are sacrificed, the colonists, not less than the proprietors, are pillaged for the benefit of faithless agents. Where an individual is the sovereign, there is room for an appeal to magnanimity, to benevolence, to the love of glory; where the privilege of self-government is enjoyed, a permanent interest is sure to gain the ultimate ascendancy; but corporate ambition is deaf to mercy, and insensible to shame.

The Virginia colony had been unsuccessful. A permanent settlement had been made; but only after a vast expenditure of money, and a great sacrifice of human life. Angry factions distract unsuccessful institutions; and the London company was now rent by two parties, which were growing more and more embittered. As the shares in the unproductive stock were of little value, the contests were chiefly for power; and were not so much the wranglings of disappointed merchants, as the struggle of political parties. The meetings of the company, which now consisted of a thousand adventurers, of whom two hundred or more usually appeared at the quarter courts,[1] were the scenes for freedom of debate, where the party, which in parliament advocated the cause of liberty, triumphed in its opposition to the decrees of the privy council on subjects, connected with the

[1] Stith, p. 282—286.

CHAP. V.
1623.

rights of Virginia. The unsuccessful party in the company naturally found an ally in the king; it could hope for success only by establishing the supremacy of his prerogative; and the monarch, dissatisfied at having entrusted to others the control of the colony, now desired to recover the influence, of which he was deprived by a charter of his own concession. Besides, he disliked the freedom of debate. "The Virginia courts," said Gondemar, the Spanish envoy, to King James, "are but a seminary to a seditious parliament."[1] Yet the people of England, regarding only the failure of their extravagant hopes in the American plantations, took little interest in the progress of the controversy, which now grew up between the monarch and the corporation; and the inhabitants of the colony were still more indifferent spectators of the strife, which related, not to their liberties, but to their immediate sovereign.[2] Besides, there was something of retributive justice in the royal proceedings. The present proprietors enjoyed their privileges in consequence of a wrong done to the original patentees; and now suffered no greater injury, than had been before inflicted for their benefit.[3]

1622.

At the meeting for the choice of officers, in 1622, King James once more attempted to control the elections, by sending a message, nominating four candidates, out of whom they were to choose their treasurer. The advice of the king was disregarded,

[1] A New Description of Virginia, ii. Mass. Hist. Collections, v. ix. p. 113.
[2] Jefferson's Notes on Virginia, p. 152, 153.
[3] Smith, v. ii. p. 107.

and a great majority re-elected the earl of Southampton.[1] Unable to get the control of the company by overawing their assemblies, the monarch now resolved upon the sequestration of the patent; and raised no other question, than how the unjust design could most plausibly be accomplished, and the law of England be made the successful instrument of tyranny. The allegation of grievances, set forth by the court faction in a petition to the king, was fully refuted by the company, and the whole ground of discontent was answered by an explanatory declaration.[2] Yet commissioners were appointed to engage in a general investigation of the concerns of the corporation; the records were seized; the deputy-treasurer imprisoned; and private letters from Virginia intercepted for inspection.[3] Smith was particularly examined; his honest answers plainly exposed the defective arrangements of previous years, and favored the cancelling of the charter as an act of benevolence to the colony.[4]

The result surprised every one; the king, by an order in council, made known, that the disasters of Virginia were a consequence of the ill government of the company; that he had resolved, by a new charter, to reserve to himself the appointment of the officers in England; a negative on appointments in Virginia; and the supreme control of all colonial affairs. Private interests were to be sacredly pre-

---

[1] Burk, v. i. p. 257.
[2] The Declaration is in Burk, v. i. p. 316—330. See Stith, p. 276, 277, and p. 291—297.
[3] Stith, p. 298; Burk, v. i. p. 268; Smith, v. ii. p. 108; Rymer, v. xvii. p. 490—493.
[4] Smith, v. ii. p. 103—108.

served; and all grants of land to be renewed and confirmed. Should the company resist the change, its patent would be recalled.[1] This was in substance a proposition to revert to the charter originally granted.

It is difficult to obtain a limitation of authority from a corporate body; an aristocracy is, of all forms of government, the most tenacious of life, and the least flexible in its purposes. The company heard the order in council with amazement; it was read three several times, and after the reading, for a long while, no man spoke a word. Should they tamely surrender privileges, which were conceded according to the forms of law, had been possessed for many years, and had led them to expend large sums of money, that had as yet yielded no return? The corporation was inflexible, for it had no interest to yield. It desired only a month's delay, that all its members might take part in the final decision. The privy council peremptorily demanded a decisive answer within three days; and, at the expiration of that time, the surrender of the charter was strenuously refused.[2] The liberties of the company were a trust, which might be yielded to superior force, but could not be freely abandoned without dishonor.

But the decision of the king was already taken; and commissioners were appointed to proceed to Virginia, to examine into the state of the plantation, to ascertain what expectations might be conceived,

---

[1] Burk, v. i. p. 269; Stith, p. 303—304. [2] Stith, p. 294—296; Burk, v. i. p. 269—271.

and to discover the means, by which good hopes were to be realized.¹ John Harvey and Samuel Matthews, both distinguished in the annals of Virginia, were of the number of the committee.

It now only remained to issue a writ of quo warranto against the company. It was done; and, at the next quarter court, the adventurers, seven only opposing, confirmed the former refusal to surrender the charter, and made preparations for defence.² For that purpose their papers were for a season restored; while they were once more in the hands of the company, they were fortunately copied; and the copy, having been purchased by a Virginian, was consulted by Stith, and gave to his history the authority of an original record.³

While these things were transacting in England, the commissioners, early in the year, arrived in the colony. A meeting of the general assembly was immediately convened; and, as the company had refuted the allegations of King James, as opposed to their interests, so the colonists replied to them, as contrary to their honor and good name. The principal prayer was, that the governors might not have absolute power; and that the liberty of popular assemblies might be retained; "for," say they, "nothing can conduce more to the public satisfaction and the public utility."⁴ To urge this solicitation, an agent was appointed to repair to England. The manner in which the expenses of the mission

---

¹ Burk, v. i. p. 272, and note; Chalmers, p. 62 and p. 76.
² Stith, p. 298, 299.
³ Burk, v. i. p. 274, 275; Hening, v. i. p. 76.
⁴ Burk, v. i. p. 276, 277.

were borne, marks colonial times and manners, and the universality of the excitement. A tax of four pounds of the best tobacco was levied upon every male, who was above sixteen years and had been in the colony a twelvemonth.[1] The commissioner unfortunately died on his passage to Europe.[2]

The spirit of liberty had planted itself deeply among the Virginians. It had been easier to root out the staple produce of their plantations, than to wrest from them their established franchises. The movements of the colonial government display the spirit of the place and the aptitude of the English colonies for liberty. A faithless clerk, who had been suborned by one of the commissioners to betray the secret consultations of the Virginians, was promptly punished. In vain was it attempted, by means of intimidation and promises of royal favor, to obtain a petition for the revocation of the charter. It was under that charter, that the assembly was itself convened; and it prudently rejected a proposition, which might have endangered its own existence. The colonial assembly proceeded to memorable acts of legislation.[3]

The rights of property were strictly maintained against arbitrary taxation. "The governor shall not lay any taxes or ympositions upon the colony, their lands or commodities, other way than by the authority of the general assembly, to be levied and ymployed as the said assembly shall appoynt." Thus

---

[1] Hening's Statutes at Large, v. i. p. 128, Act 35.
[2] Burk, v. i. p. 277.
[3] Hening, v. i. p. 122—128; Burk, v. i. p. 278—286; Stith, p. 318—322.

Virginia, the oldest colony, was the first to set the example of a just and firm legislation on the management of the public money. We shall see other colonies imitate the example, which could not be excelled. The rights of personal liberty were likewise asserted, and the power of the governor circumscribed. The several governors had in vain attempted, by penal statutes, to promote the culture of corn; the true remedy was now discovered by the colonial legislature. "For the encouragement of men to plant store of corn, the price shall not be stinted, but it shall be free for every man to sell it as deare as he can." The reports of controversies in England, rendered it necessary to provide for the public tranquillity by an express enactment, "that no person within the colony, upon the rumor of supposed change and alteration, presume to be disobedient to the present government." The law was dictated by the emergency of the times; and during the struggle in London, the administration of Virginia was based upon a popular decree. These laws, so judiciously framed, show how readily, with the aid of free discussion, men become good legislators on their own concerns; for wise legislation is the enacting of proper laws at proper times; and no criterion is so nearly infallible as the fair representation of the interests to be affected.

While the commissioners were urging the colonists to renounce their right to the privileges, which they exercised so well, the English parliament assembled; and a gleam of hope revived in the company, as it forwarded an elaborate petition[1] to the grand inquest of the kingdom. It is a sure proof of the unpopularity of the corporation, that it met with no support from the commons;[2] but Sir Edwin Sandys, more intent on the welfare of Virginia, than the existence of the company, was able to secure for the colonial staple complete protection against foreign tobacco, by a petition of grace,[3] which was followed by a royal proclamation.[4] The people of England could not have given a more earnest proof of their disposition to foster the plantations in America, than by restraining all competition in their own market for the benefit of the American planter.

Meantime, the commissioners arrived from the colony, and made their report to the king.[5] They enumerated the disasters, which had befallen the infant settlement; they eulogized the fertility of the soil and the salubrity of the climate; they aggravated the neglect of the company in regard to the encouragement of staple commodities; they declared the plantations to be of great importance to the nation, and a monument of the reign of King James; they expressed a preference for the original constitution of 1606; they declared, that the alteration of the charter to so popular a course and so many hands, referring, not to the colonial franchises, but, to the democratic form of the London company,

[1] Stith, p. 324—328.
[2] Chalmers, p. 65, 66; Burk, v. i. p. 291.
[3] Stith, p. 398, refers to the nine grievances; erroneously. See Cobbett's Parl. Hist. v. i. p. 1489—1497. The commons acted by petition. Hazard, v. i. p. 193.
[4] Hazard, v. i. p. 193—196.
[5] Ibid, v. i. p. 190, 191; Burk's History of Virginia, v. i. p. 291, 292.

could lead only to confusion and contention; and they promised prosperity only by a recurrence to the original instructions of the monarch.

Now, therefore, nothing but the judicial decision remained. The decree, which was to be pronounced by judges, who held their office by the tenure of the royal pleasure,[1] could not long remain doubtful; and at the trinity term of the ensuing year, judgment was given against the treasurer and company,[2] and the patents were cancelled.

Thus the company was dissolved. It had fulfilled its high destinies; it had confirmed the colonization of Virginia, and had conceded a liberal form of government to Englishmen in America. It could accomplish no more. The members were probably willing to escape from a concern, which promised no emolument and threatened an unprofitable strife; the public acquiesced in the fall of a corporation, which had of late maintained but a sickly and hopeless existence; and the friends of the colony well knew, that a body, rent by internal factions and opposed by the whole force of the English government, could never succeed in fostering Virginia. The fate of the London company found little sympathy; in the domestic government of the colony, it produced no change whatever. So far as the business of the

---

[1] Story's Com. v. i. p. 27.
[2] Stith, p. 329, 330, doubts if judgment were passed. The doubt may be removed. "Before the end of the same term, a judgment was declared by the Lord Chief Justice Ley against the company and their charter, only upon a failer, or mistake in pleading." See a Short Collection of the most Remarkable Passages from the originall to the Dissolution of the Virginia Company. London, 1651, p. 15. See, also, Hazard, v. i. p. 191; Chalmers, p. 62; Proud's Pennsylvania, v. i. p. 107.

colony was to be transacted in England, it was entrusted to a large committee, composed, in part, of members of the privy council, and clothed with very extensive powers. To this committee the charter and all other papers of the company were ordered to be delivered;[1] and it was invested with the powers, which had before rested with the corporation. To the liberties of Virginia, the abolition of the charter brought no immediate diminution; Sir Francis Wyatt, though he had been an ardent friend of the London company, was confirmed in the government of the province; and he and his council, far from being rendered absolute, were only empowered to govern "as fully and amplye as any governor and council resident there, at any time within the space of five years now last past."[2] This term of five years was precisely the period of representative government; and the limitation could not but be interpreted as sanctioning the continuance of popular assemblies. The king, in appointing the council in Virginia, refused to nominate the embittered partisans of the court faction; but formed the administration on the principles of accommodation.[3] These moderate measures appear, it is true, to have been designed as temporary. The vanity of the monarch claimed the opportunity of establishing for the colony a code of fundamental laws; but death prevented the royal legislator from attempting the task, which would have furnished his self-complacency so grateful an occupation.

[1] Hazard, v. i. p. 186. 188.
[2] Ibid, v. i. p. 192.
[3] Ibid, v. i. p. 189. 192; Burk, v. ii. p. 11, from ancient records.

CHAPTER VI.

RESTRICTIONS ON COLONIAL COMMERCE.

ASCENDING the throne in his twenty-fifth year, Charles I. inherited the principles and was governed by the favorite of his father. The rejoicings in consequence of his recent nuptials, the reception of his bride, and preparations for a parliament, left him little leisure for American affairs. Virginia was esteemed by the monarch as the country, producing tobacco; its inhabitants were valued at court as planters; and prized according to the revenue derived from the staple of their industry. The plantation, no longer governed by a chartered company, was become a royal province and an object of favor; and, as it enforced conformity to the church of England, it could not be an object of suspicion to the clergy or the court. The king felt an earnest desire to heal old grievances, to secure the personal rights and property of the colonists, and to promote their prosperity.[1] Franchises were neither conceded nor restricted; for it did not occur to his pride, that, at that time, there could be in an American province anything like established privileges or vigorous politi-

[1] Hazard, v. i. p. 204.

cal life; nor was he aware that the seeds of liberty were already germinating on the borders of the Chesapeake. His first Virginian measure was a proclamation[1] on tobacco; confirming to Virginia and the Somer isles the exclusive supply of the British market; under penalty of the censure of the star-chamber for disobedience. In a few days a new proclamation[2] appeared; in which it was his evident design to secure the profits, that might before have been engrossed by the corporation. After a careful declaration of the forfeiture of the charters, and consequently of the immediate dependence of Virginia upon himself, a declaration, aimed against the claims of the London company and not against the franchises of the colonists, the monarch proceeded to announce his fixed resolution of becoming, through his agents, the sole factor of the planters. Indifferent to their constitution, it was his principal aim to monopolize the profits of their industry; and the politieal rights of Virginia were established as usages by his salutary neglect.[3]

There is no room to suppose, that Charles nourished the design of suppressing the colonial assemblies. For some months, the organization of the government was not changed; and when Wyatt, on the death of his father, obtained leave to return to Scotland, Sir George Yeardley was appointed his successor. This appointment was in itself a guarantee, that, as "the former interests of Virginia were to be

[1] Hazard, v. i. p. 202, 203.
[2] Ibid, v. i. p. 203—205.
[3] Burk's History of Virginia, v. ii. p. 14, 15.

VIRGINIA RETAINS ITS FRANCHISES.

kept inviolate,"[1] so the representative government, the chief political interest, would be maintained; for it was Yeardley, who had had the glory of introducing the system. In the commission now issued,[2] the monarch expressed his desire to benefit, encourage and perfect the plantation; "the same means, that were formerly thought fit for the maintenance of the colony," were continued; and the power of the governor and council was limited, as it had before been done in the commission of Wyatt, by a reference to the usages of the last five years. In that period representative liberty had become the custom of Virginia. The words were interpreted as favoring the wishes of the colonists; and King Charles, intent only on increasing his revenue, confirmed, perhaps unconsciously, the existence of a popular assembly. The colony prospered; Virginia rose rapidly in public estimation; in one year, a thousand emigrants arrived; and there was an increasing demand for all the products of the soil.[3]

The career of Yeardley was now closed by death. Posterity will ever retain a grateful recollection of the man, who first convened a representative assembly in the western hemisphere; the colonists, announcing his decease in a letter to the privy council, gave at the same time a eulogy on his virtues; the surest evidence of his fidelity to their interests.[4] The day after his burial, Francis West was elected his successor;[5] for the council was authorized to elect

[1] Letter of the privy council, in Burk, v. ii. p. 18.
[2] Hazard, v. i. p. 230—234.
[3] Burk, v. ii. p. 23.
[4] Burk, v. ii. p. 22, 23.
[5] Hening, v. i. p. 4.

the governor "from time to time, as often as the case shall require."¹

1628. But if any doubts existed of the royal assent to the continuance of colonial assemblies, they were soon removed by a letter of instructions, which the king addressed to the governor and council. After much cavilling in the style of a purchaser, who undervalues the wares which he wishes to buy, the monarch arrives at his main purpose, and offers to contract for the whole crop of tobacco; desiring, at the same time, that an assembly might be convened to consider his proposal.² This is the first recognition, on the part of a Stuart, of a representative assembly in America. Hitherto, the king had, fortunately for the colony, found no time to take order for its government. His zeal for an exclusive contract led him to observe and to sanction the existence of an elective legislature. The assembly, in its answer, firmly protested against the monopoly; and rejected the conditions, which they had been summoned to approve.³ The independent reply of the assembly was signed by the governor, by five members of the council, and by thirty-one burgesses. The Virginians, happier than the people of England, enjoyed a faithful representative government, and, through the resident planters who composed the council, they repeatedly elected their own governor. When West designed to embark for Europe, his place was supplied by election.⁴

June 16.

1629. Mar. 26.

[1] Hazard, v. i. p. 233.
[2] Burk, v. ii. p. 19, 20; Hening, v. i. p. 129.
[3] Hening, v. i. p. 134—136; Burk, v. ii. p. 24.
[4] Hening, v. i. p. 4. 137.

SIR JOHN HARVEY'S ADMINISTRATION.

No sooner had the news of the death of Yeardley reached England, than the king proceeded to issue a commission[1] to John Harvey. The tenor of the instrument offered no invasions of colonial freedom; but, while it renewed the limitations which had previously been set to the executive authority, it permitted the council in Virginia, which had common interests with the people, to supply all vacancies, occurring in their body. In this way direct oppression was rendered impossible.

CHAP. VI.
1628.

It was during the period, which elapsed between the appointment of Harvey and his appearance in America, that Lord Baltimore visited Virginia. The zeal of religious bigotry pursued him as a Romanist;[2] and the intolerance of the colony led to memorable results. Nor should we, in this connexion, forget the hospitable plans of the southern planters; the people of New-Plymouth were invited to abandon the cold and sterile clime of New-England, and plant themselves in the milder regions on the Delaware Bay.[3]

1628, to 1629.

It was probably in the autumn of 1629 that Harvey arrived in Virginia.[4] Till October, the name of Pott appears as governor;[5] Harvey met his first assembly of burgesses in the following March.[6] He had for several years been a member of the council; and, as at an earlier day he had been a willing instrument in the hands of the faction, to which Virginia ascribed its earliest griefs and continued to bear

1630.
Mar. 24.

---

[1] Hazard, v. i. p. 234—239.
[2] Records, in Burk, v. ii. p. 24, 25.
[3] Ibid, v. ii. p. 32.
[4] Chalmers, p. 118.
[5] Hening, v. i. p. 4.
[6] Ibid, v. i. p. 147.

a deep-rooted hostility, his appointment could not but be unpopular. The colony had esteemed it a special favor from King James, that, upon the substitution of the royal authority for the corporate supremacy, the government had been entrusted to impartial agents; and, after the death of Yeardley, two successive chief magistrates had been elected in Virginia. The appointment of Harvey implied a change of power among political parties; it gave authority to a man, whose connections in England were precisely those, which the colony regarded with the utmost aversion. As his first appearance in the colony, in 1623, had been with no friendly designs, so now he was the support of those, who desired large grants of land and unreasonable concessions of separate jurisdictions; and he preferred the interests of himself, his partisans and patrons to the welfare and quiet of the colony. The extravagant language, which exhibited him as a tyrant, without specifying his crimes, was the natural hyperbole of political excitement; and when historians, receiving the account and interpreting tyranny to mean arbitrary taxation, drew the inference, that he convened no assemblies, trifled with the rights of property, and levied taxes according to his caprice, they were betrayed into extravagant errors. Such a procedure would have been impossible. He had no soldiers at his command; no obsequious officers to enforce his will; and the Virginians would never have made themselves the instruments of their own oppression. The party, opposed to Harvey, was

SIR JOHN HARVEY'S ADMINISTRATION. 215

deficient neither in capacity, nor in colonial influence; and while arbitrary power was rapidly advancing to triumph in England, the Virginians, during the whole period, enjoyed the benefit of independent colonial legislation;[1] through the agency of their representatives, they levied and appropriated all taxes,[2] secured the free industry of their citizens,[3] guarded the forts with their own soldiers at their own charge,[4] and gave to their statutes the greatest possible publicity.[5] When the defects and inconveniences of infant legislation were remedied by a revised code, which was published with the approbation of the governor and council,[6] all the privileges which the assembly had ever claimed, were carefully confirmed.[7] Indeed, they seem never to have been questioned.

CHAP. VI.

1630, to 1635.

---

[1] As an opposite statement has received the sanction, not of Oldmixon, Chalmers and Robertson only, but of Marshall and of Story, (see Story's Commentaries, v. i. p. 28, "without the slightest effort to convene a colonial assembly,") I deem it necessary to state, that many of the statutes of Virginia under Harvey still exist, and that, though many others are lost, the first volume of Hening's Statutes at Large proves, beyond a question, that assemblies were convened, at least, as often as follows:—

1630, March, H. v. i. p. 147—153.
1630, April, ibid, 257.
1632, February, ibid, 153—177.
1632, September, ibid, 178—202.
1633, February, ibid, 202—209.
1633, August, ibid, 209—222.
1634, ibid, 223.
1635, ibid, 223.
1636, ibid, 229.
1637, ibid, 227.
1639, ibid, 229—230.
1640, ibid, 268.
1641, June, H. v. i. p. 259—262.
1642, January, ibid, 267.
1642, April, ibid, 230.
1642, June, ibid, 269.

Considering how imperfect are the early records, it is surprising that so considerable a list can be established. The instructions to Sir William Berkeley do not first order assemblies; but speak of them as of a thing established. At an adjourned session of Berkeley's first legislature, the assembly declares "its meeting exceeding *customary* limits, in this place used." Hening, v. i. p. 236. This is a plain declaration, that assemblies were the custom and use of Virginia at the time of Berkeley's arrival. If any doubts remain, it would be easy to multiply arguments and references.

[2] Hening, v. i. p. 171, Act 38.
[3] Ibid, p. 172, Act 40.
[4] Ibid, p. 175, Acts 57 and 58.
[5] Ibid, p. 177, Act 68.
[6] Ibid, p. 179.
[7] Ibid, p. 180—202. See par-

CHAP. VI.
1635.

Yet the administration of Harvey was disturbed by divisions, which grew out of other causes than infringements of the constitution. The community would hardly have been much disturbed, because fines were exacted with too relentless rigor;[1] but the whole colony of Virginia was in a state of excitement and alarm in consequence of the dismemberment of its territory by the cession to Lord Baltimore. As in many of the earlier settlements, questions about land-titles were agitated with passion; and there was reason to apprehend the increase of extravagant grants, that would again include the soil, on which settlements had already been made without the acquisition of an indisputable legal claim. In Maryland, the early settlers had refused to submit, and a skirmish had ensued, in which the blood of Europeans was shed for the first time on the waters of the Chesapeake; and Clayborne, defeated and banished from Maryland as a murderer and an outlaw, sheltered himself in Virginia, where he had long been a member of the council. There the contest was renewed; and Harvey, far from attempting to enforce the claims of Virginia against the royal grant, sent Clayborne to England to answer for the crimes with which he was charged. The colonists were indignant, that their governor should thus, as it seemed to them, betray their interests; and as the majority of the council favored their wishes, " Sir John Harvey was thrust out of his government; and

ticularly Acts 34, 35, 36. 39. 46. 57, 58. 61.
[1] Beverley, p. 48; Bullock, p. 10.

SIR JOHN HARVEY'S ADMINISTRATION.

Captain John West appointed to the office, till the king's pleasure be known." An assembly was summoned in May, to receive complaints against Harvey; but he had in the mean time consented to go to England, and there meet his accusers.[1]

CHAP. VI.

The commissioners appointed by the council to manage the impeachment of Harvey, met with no favor in England, and were not even admitted to a hearing.[2] Harvey immediately re-appeared to occupy his former station; and was followed by a new commission, by which his powers were still limited to such as had been exercised during the period of legislative freedom. General assemblies continued to be held; but the vacancies in the council, which had been filled in Virginia, were henceforward to be supplied by appointment in England.[3] Harvey remained in office till 1639.[4] The complaints, which have been brought against him, will be regarded with some degree of distrust, when it is considered, that the public mind of the colony, during his administration, was controlled by a party, which pursued him with implacable hostility. In April, 1642, two months only after the accession of Berkeley, a public document declares the comparative happiness of

1636.

Jan. 3.

---

[1] Hening's Statutes, v. i. p. 223, and p. 4; Bullock's Virginia, in Oldmixon, v. i. p. 240. Oldmixon himself is wholly unworthy of trust. Beverley, p. 48, is not accurate. Campbell's Virginia, p. 60. A modest and valuable little book.—Chalmers, p. 118, 119, is betrayed into error by following Oldmixon. Burk, v. ii. p. 41, 42. Compare Bullock's Virginia examined, p. 10. Robertson, in his History of Virginia, after the dissolution of the company, furnishes a tissue of inventions. Keith, p. 143, 144, places in 1639 the occurrences of 1635. His book is superficial.
[2] Burk, v. ii. p. 45. Yet Burk corrected but one half of the errors of his predecessors.
[3] Hazard, v. i. p. 400—403.
[4] Campbell's Virginia, p. 61; Hening's Statutes, v. i. p. 4.

218   SIR FRANCIS WYATT'S ADMINISTRATION.

CHAP. VI. the colony under the royal government; a declaration, which would hardly have been made, if Virginia had so recently and so long been smarting under intolerable oppression.[1]

1639. Nov.
1640. Jan.
At length he was superseded; and Sir Francis Wyatt[2] appointed in his stead. Early in the next year, he convened a general assembly. History has recorded many instances, where a legislature has altered the scale of debts; in modern times, it has frequently been done by debasing the coin, or by introducing paper money. In Virginia, debts had been contracted to be paid in tobacco; and when the article rose in value, in consequence of laws, restricting its culture, the legislature of Virginia did not scruple to provide a remedy, by enacting that "no man need pay more than two thirds of his debt during the stint;"[3] and that all creditors should take "forty pounds for a hundred."[4] Probably the members of the legislature and the council were themselves much in debt.[5]

1641. Aug. 9.
After two years, a commission[6] was issued to Sir William Berkeley. Historians, reasoning from the revolutions, which took place in England, that there had been corresponding attempts at oppression and corresponding resistance in Virginia, have delighted

---

[1] Hening's Statutes at Large, v. i. p. 231.
[2] Rymer's Foedera, v. xx. p. 484; Hazard, v. i. p. 477; Savage on Winthrop, v. ii. p. 160, 161. A note by Savage settles a question. Hening, v. i. p. 224, and p. 4; Campbell's Virginia, p. 61. But Keith, and Beverley, and Chalmers, and even Burk and Marshall, were ignorant of such a governor as Wyatt, in 1639; and represent Berkeley as the immediate successor of Harvey.
[3] Hening, v. i. p. 226, Act 8.
[4] Ibid, p. 225, Act 1.
[5] Bullock's Virginia Examined, p. 10, 11.
[6] Hazard, v. i. p. 477—480; Rymer, v. xx. p. 484—486.

to draw a contrast, not only between Harvey and the new governor, but between the institutions of Virginia under their respective governments; and Berkeley is said to have "restored the system of freedom," and to have "effected an essential revolution."[1] I cannot find that his appointment was marked by the slightest concession of new political privileges; except that the council recovered the right of supplying its own vacancies; and the historians, who make an opposite statement, are wholly ignorant of the intermediate administration of Wyatt; a government, so suited to the tastes and habits of the planters, that it passed silently away, leaving almost no impression on Virginia history, except in the archives of its statutes. The commission of Berkeley was exactly analogous to those of his predecessors.

The instructions[2] given him, far from granting franchises to the Virginians, imposed new, severe and unwarrantable restrictions on the liberty of trade; and, for the first time, England claimed that monopoly of colonial commerce,[3] which was ultimately enforced by the navigation act, and which never ceased to be a subject of dispute till the war of independence. The nature of those instructions will presently be explained.

It was in February, 1642, that Sir William Berkeley, arriving in the colony, assumed the government. His arrival must have been nearly simultaneous with the adjournment of the general assembly, which

[1] Chalmers, p. 120, 121.
[2] Ibid, p. 131—133.
[3] See Instructions, in Chalmers, Nos. 14 and 15.

was held in the preceding January.¹ He found the American planters in possession of a large share of the legislative authority, and he confirmed them in the enjoyment of franchises, which a long and uninterrupted succession had rendered familiar. Immediately after his arrival, he convened the colonial legislature. The utmost harmony prevailed; the memory of factions was lost in a general amnesty of ancient griefs. The lapse of years had so far effaced the divisions, which grew out of the dissolution of the company, that when George Sandys, an agent of the colony and an opponent of the royal party in England, presented a petition to the commons, praying for the restoration of the ancient patents,² the assembly promptly disavowed the design; and, after a full debate, opposed it by a solemn protest.³ The whole document breathes the tone of a body, accustomed to public discussion and the independent exercise of legislative power. They assert the necessity of the freedom of trade, "for freedom of trade," say they, "is the blood and life of a commonwealth." And they defended their preference of self-government through a colonial legislature, by a conclusive argument. "There is more likelyhood, that such as are acquainted with the clime and its accidents may upon better grounds prescribe our advantages, than such as shall sit at the helm in

---

¹ The acts of that session are lost; but are referred to in Hening, v. i. p. 267—269, in the acts 49, 50, 51, 52. The statutes, of course, call the year 1641; as the year then began in March.

² Chalmers, p. 121; Hening's Statutes at Large, v. i. p. 230.

³ Hening's Statutes at Large, v. i. p. 230—236; Burk's Virginia, v. ii. p. 68—74.

England."[1] In reply to their urgent petition, the king immediately declared his purpose not to change a form of government, in which they "received so much content and satisfaction."[2]

The Virginians could now deliberately perfect their civil condition. Condemnations to service had been a usual punishment; these were abolished. In the courts of justice, a near approach was made to the laws and customs of England. Religion was provided for; the law about land-titles adjusted;[3] an amicable treaty with Maryland successfully matured; and peace with the Indians confirmed. Taxes were assessed, not in proportion to numbers, but to men's abilities and estates. The spirit of liberty, displayed in the English parliament, was transmitted to America; and the rights of property, the freedom of industry, the solemn exercise of civil franchises, seemed to be secured to themselves and their posterity. "A future immunity from taxes and impositions," except such as should be freely voted for their own wants, "was expected as the fruits of the endeavors of their legislature."[4] As the restraints, with which colonial navigation was threatened, were not enforced,[5] they attracted no attention; and Virginia enjoyed nearly all the liberties, which a monarch could concede, and retain his supremacy.

Believing themselves secure of all their privileges, the triumph of the popular party in England, did not

---

[1] Hening's Statutes at Large, v. i. p. 233.
[2] Chalmers, p. 133, 134; Burk, v. ii. p. 74.
[3] Keith's Virginia, p. 145; Hening, v. i. p. 237, 238.
[4] Hening, v. i. p. 237, 238.
[5] Chalmers, p. 124.

alter the condition, or the affections of the Virginians. The commissioners appointed by parliament, with unlimited authority over the plantations,[1] found no favor in Virginia. They promised, indeed, freedom from English taxation; but this immunity was already enjoyed. They gave the colony liberty to choose its own governor; but it had no dislike to Berkeley; and though there was a party for the parliament, yet the king's authority was maintained.[2] The sovereignty of Charles had ever been mildly exercised.

The greatest invasion of private rights was committed by the Virginians themselves; it was by their own act, that religious liberty was restrained. If the king had issued orders, that the oaths of allegiance and supremacy should be administered, the general assembly had ever, of its own accord, been zealous to preserve the unity of doctrine and worship after the forms of the English church.[3] It was now specially ordered, that no minister should preach or teach, publicly or privately, except in conformity to the constitutions of the church of England,[4] and non-conformists were banished from the colony. Strange intolerance, which attempted to shut the wildernesses of Virginia against dissenters, and could not suffer the untamed soil to be rendered arable by the discipline of puritan culture! The unsocial spirit of mutual intolerance prevented a frequent intercourse between Virginia and New-England. It was

---

[1] Hazard, v. i. p. 533—535. [3] Hening's Statutes at Large, v.
[2] Winthrop's Journal, v. ii. p. i. p. 268.
159, 160, and the note of Savage. [4] Act 64, Hening, v. i. p. 277.

in vain, that the faithful ministers, who had been invited from Boston by the puritan settlements in Virginia, carried letters from Winthrop, written to Berkeley and his council by order of the general court of Massachusetts. "The hearts of the people were much inflamed with desire after the ordinances;" but the missionaries were silenced by the state and ordered to leave the country.[1] Sir William Berkeley was "a courtier and very malignant towards the way of the churches" in New-England.

While Virginia thus displayed, though with comparatively little bitterness, the intolerance, which for centuries had almost universally prevailed throughout the Christian world, a scene of distress was prepared by the vindictive ferocity of the natives, with whom a state of hostility had been of long continuance. In 1643, it was enacted by the assembly, that no terms of peace should be entertained with the Indians; whom it was usual to distress by sudden marches against their settlements. But the Indians had now heard of the dissensions in England, and taking counsel of their passions, rather than of their prudence, they resolved on one more attempt at a general massacre; believing that, by midnight incursions, the destruction of the cattle and the fields of corn, they might succeed in famishing the remnant of the colonists, whom they should not be able to murder by surprise. On the eighteenth

---

[1] Winthrop's Journal, v. ii. p. 77, 78. 95, 96, and 164, 165; Hubbard's New-England, p. 410, 411; Wonder-working Providence, b. iii. c. xi. in ii. Mass. Hist. Coll. v. viii. p. 29; Hening, v. i. p. 275.

day of April,[1] the time appointed for the carnage, the unexpected onset was begun upon the frontier settlements. But hardly had the Indians steeped their hands in blood, before they were dismayed by the recollection of their own comparative weakness; and trembling for the consequences of their treachery, they feared to continue their design, and fled to a distance from the colony. The number of victims had been three hundred. Measures were promptly taken by the English for protection and defence; and a war was vigorously conducted. The aged Opechancanough was easily made prisoner; and the venerated monarch of the sons of the forest, so long the undisputed lord of almost boundless hunting grounds, died in miserable captivity of wounds, inflicted by a brutal soldier. In his last moments, he chiefly regretted his exposure to the contemptuous gaze of his enemies.[2]

So little was apprehended, when the English were once on their guard, that, two months after the massacre, Berkeley embarked for England, leaving Richard Kemp as his successor.[3] A border warfare continued; marches up and down the Indian country were ordered; yet so weak were the natives, that though the careless traveller and the straggling

---

[1] The reader is cautioned against the inaccuracies of Beverley, Oldmixon, and, on this subject, of Burk. See Winthrop's Journal, v. ii. p. 165. Compare the note of Savage; whose sagacious conjecture is confirmed in Hening, v. i. p. 290, Act 4, session of February, 1645.

[2] On the massacre, there are three contemporary guides: The statutes of the time, in Hening, v. i.; The Perfect Description of Virginia, in ii. Mass. Hist. Coll. v. ix. p. 115—117, and the Reports of the exiled Puritans, in Winthrop, v. ii. p. 165.

[3] Hening, v. i. p. 4. 282, and 286.

huntsman were long in danger of being intercepted,[1] yet ten men were considered a sufficient force to protect a place of danger.[2]

About fifteen months after Berkeley's return from England, articles of peace were established between the inhabitants of Virginia and Necotowance, the successor of Opechancanough.[3] Submission and a cession of lands were the terms, on which the treaty was purchased by the original possessors of the soil; who now began to vanish away from the immediate vicinity of the settlements of their too formidable invaders. It is one of the surprising results of moral power, that language, composed of fleeting sounds, retains and transmits the remembrance of past occurrences long after every other monument has passed away. Of the labors of the Indians on the soil of Virginia, there remains nothing so respectable as would be a common ditch for the draining of lands;[4] the memorials of their former existence are found only in the names of the rivers and the mountains. Unchanging nature retains the appellations, which were given by those, whose villages have disappeared, and whose tribes have become extinct.

Thus the colony of Virginia acquired the management of all its concerns; war was levied, and peace concluded, and territory acquired, in conformity to the acts of the representatives of the people. Possessed of security and quiet, abundance of land, a

---

[1] Hening, v. i. p. 300, 301, Act 3.
[2] Ibid, p. 285, 286, Act 5.
[3] Ibid, p. 323—326. Compare Drake's Indian Biography, b. iv. p. 22—24; Johnson's Wonder-working Providence, b. iii. c. xi. in ii. Mass. Hist. Coll. v. viii. p. 30.
[4] Jefferson's Notes, p. 132.

CHAP. VI.
1646.

free market for their staple, and, practically, all the rights of an independent state, having England for its guardian against foreign oppression, rather than its ruler, the colonists enjoyed all the prosperity, which a virgin soil, equal laws, and general uniformity of condition and industry, could bestow. Their numbers increased; the cottages were filled with children, as the ports were with ships and emigrants. At Christmas, 1648, there were trading in Virginia, ten ships from London, two from Bristol, twelve Hollanders, and seven from New-England.[1] The number of the colonists was already twenty thousand; and they, who had sustained no griefs, were not tempted to engage in the feuds, by which the mother country was divided. They were attached to the cause of Charles, not because they loved monarchy, but because they cherished the liberties, of which he had left them in the undisturbed possession; and,

1649. after his execution, though there were not wanting some who favored republicanism, the government recognized his son[2] without dispute. The loyalty of the Virginians did not escape the attention of the royal exile; from his retreat in Breda he transmitted

1650. June. to Berkeley a new commission,[3] and Charles the Second, a fugitive from England, was still the sovereign of Virginia.

Oct. 3.

But the parliament did not long permit its authority to be denied. Having, by the vigorous energy and fearless enthusiasm of republicanism, triumphed

---

[1] New Description of Virginia, p. 15, in ii. Mass. Hist. Coll. v. ix. p. 118.
[2] Hening's Statutes at Large, v. i. p. 359, 360, Act 1.
[3] Chalmers, p. 122.

over all its enemies in Europe, it turned its attention to the colonies; and a memorable ordinance[1] at once empowered the council of state to reduce the rebellious colonies to obedience, and, at the same time, established it as a law, that foreign ships should not trade at any of the ports "in Barbadoes, Antigua, Bermudas and Virginia." Maryland which was not expressly included in the ordinance, had taken care to acknowledge the new order of things;[2] and Massachusetts, alike unwilling to encounter the hostility of parliament, and jealous of the rights of independent legislation, by its own enactment, prohibited all intercourse with Virginia, till the supremacy of the commonwealth should be established; although the order, when it was found to be injurious to commerce, was promptly repealed, even whilst royalty still triumphed at Jamestown.[3] But would Virginia resist the fleet of the republic? Were its royalist principles so firm, that they would animate the colony to a desperate war with England? The lovers of monarchy indulged the hope, that the victories of their friends in the Chesapeake would redeem the disgrace, that had elsewhere fallen on the royal arms; many partisans of Charles had come over as to a place of safety; and the honest governor Berkeley, than whom "no man meant better," was so confirmed in his confidence, that he wrote to the king, almost inviting him to America.[4] The ap-

CHAP. VI.

1650. Oct. 3.

1651. May 7.

Oct. 14.

[1] Hazard, v. i. p. 637, 638; Parliamentary History, v. iii. p. 1357. The commentary of Chalmers, p. 123, is that of a partisan lawyer.
[2] Langford's Refutation, p. 6, 7.
[3] Hazard, v. i. p. 553 and 558.
[4] Clarendon, b. xiii. v. iii, p. 466.

proach of the day of trial was watched with the deepest interest.

1651. But while the preparations were yet making for the reduction of the colonies, which still preserved an appearance of loyalty, the commercial policy of England underwent an important revision, and the new system, as it was based upon the permanent interests of English merchants and ship-builders, obtained a consistency and durability, which could never have been gained by the feeble selfishness of the Stuarts.

It is the ancient fate of colonies to be planted by the daring of the poor and the hardy; to struggle into being through the severest trials; to be neglected by the parent country during the season of poverty and weakness; to thrive by the unrestricted application of their powers and enterprize; and then by their prosperity to tempt oppression. The Greek colonies early attained opulence and strength, because they were always free; the new people at its birth was independent and remained so; the emigrants were dismissed, not as servants, but as equals.[1] They were the natural, not the necessary, allies of the mother country. They spoke the same dialect, revered the same Gods, cherished the same customs and laws; but they were politically independent.[2] Freedom, stimulating exertion, invited them to stretch their settlements from the shores of the Euxine to the Western Mediterranean; and urged

---

[1] Thucydides, b. i. c. xxxiv. οὐ γὰρ ἐπὶ τῷ δοῦλοι, ἀλλ' ἐπὶ τῷ ὅμοιοι εἶναι ἐκπέμπονται.

[2] Grotius, De Jure Belli et Pacis, l. ii. c. x.

them forward to wealth and prosperity, commensurate with their boldness and the vast extent of the domains which they occupied. The colonies of Carthage, on the contrary, were subjected to a different system. When they had attained sufficient consideration to merit attention, the mother state insisted upon a monopoly of their commerce. The colonial system is as old as colonies and the spirit of commercial gain and political oppression.[1]

No sooner had Spain and Portugal entered on maritime discovery, and found their way round the cape of Good Hope and to America, than a monopoly of the traffic of the world was desired. Greedily covetous of the whole, they could with difficulty agree upon a division, not of a conquered province, the banks of a river, a neighboring territory, but of the oceans, and the commerce of every people and empire along the wide margin of their waters. They claimed, that on the larger seas the winds should blow only to fill their sails; that the islands and continents of Asia, of Africa, and the New World, should be fertile only to freight the ships of their merchants; and, having denounced the severest penalties against any, who should infringe the rights which they claimed, they obtained the sanction of religion to adjust their differences, and to bar the ocean against the intrusion of competitors.[2]

---

[1] Brougham's Colonial Policy, v. i. p. 21—23; Dionysius Halicarnassus, l. iii. But of all on the subject, Heeren's Ideen, fourth edition, part ii. p. 91—108, particularly p. 96—98.

[2] Bull of Alexander VI., May 4, 1493, in Navarette, v. ii. p. 32 and 34. "Sub excommunicationis latæ sententiæ pœna," &c. &c.

CHAP. VI.

The effects of this severity are pregnant with instruction. Direct commerce with the Spanish settlements was punished by the Spaniards with confiscation and the threat of eternal wo. The moral sense of mariners revolted at the extravagance; since forfeiture, imprisonment and excommunication were to follow the attempt at the fair exchanges of trade, since the freebooter and the pirate could not suffer more, than was menaced against the merchant who should disregard the maritime monopoly, the seas became infested by reckless buccaniers, the natural offspring of colonial restrictions. Rich Spanish settlements in America were pillaged; fleets attacked and captured; predatory invasions were even made on land to intercept the loads of gold, as they came from the mines; and men, who might have acquired honor and wealth in commerce, if commerce had been permitted, now displayed a sagacity of contrivance, coolness of execution, and capacity for enduring hardships, which won them the admiration of their contemporaries, and, in a better cause, would have won them the perpetual praises of the world.

1607. In Europe, the freedom of the sea was vindicated against the claims of Spain and Portugal by a nation, hardly yet recognized as an independent state, occupying a soil, of which much had been redeemed by industry, and driven by the stern necessity of a dense population to seek for resources upon the sea.

1612. The most gifted of her sons defended the liberty of commerce; and appealed to the judgment of all free governments and nations against the maritime restrictions, which humanity denounced as contrary to the principles of social intercourse; which justice derided as infringing the clearest natural rights; which enterprize rejected as a monstrous usurpation of the ocean and the winds. The relinquishment of navigation in the East Indies was required as the price at which her independence should be acknowledged, and she preferred to defend her separate existence by her arms, rather than purchase security by circumscribing the courses of her ships. The nation, which by its position was compelled to acquire skill in commerce, and, in its resistance to monopoly, was forced by competition to obtain an advantage, succeeded in gaining the maritime ascendency. While the inglorious James of England, immersed in vanity and pedantry, was negotiating about points of theology, while the more unhappy Charles was wasting his strength in vain struggles against the liberties of his subjects, the Dutch, a little nation, which had been struck from the side of the vast empire of Spain, a new people, scarcely known as possessed of nationality, had, by their superior skill, begun to engross the carrying trade of the world. Their ships were soon to be found in the harbors of Virginia; in the West Indian archipelago; in the south of Africa, among the tropical islands of the Indian Ocean, and even in the remote harbors of China and Japan. Already their trading houses were planted on the Hudson and the coast of Guinea, in Java and Brazil. One or two rocky islets in the West Indies, in part neglected by the Spaniards as unworthy of culture, were occupied by these daring merchants; and furnished a convenient shelter for a large contraband traffic with the terra firma. So great was the naval success of Holland, that it engrossed the commerce of the European nations themselves; English mariners sought employment in Dutch vessels, with which the ports of England were filled; English ships lay rotting at the wharves; English ship-building was an unprofitable vocation. The freedom and the enterprize of Holland had acquired maritime power and skill and wealth, such as the vast monopoly of Spain had never been able to command.[1]

The causes of the commercial greatness of Holland were forgotten in envy at her success. She ceased to appear as the antagonist of Spain, and the gallant champion of the freedom of the seas; she was now envied as the successful rival. The eloquence of Grotius was neglected; as well as the pretensions of Spain disregarded;[2] and the English government resolved to protect the English merchant.[3] Cromwell desired to confirm the maritime power of his country; and St. John, a puritan and a republican, proposed in parliament the act of navigation,[4] rightly entitled, "Goods from foreign parts, by whom to be imported." Henceforward, the

---

[1] Holland possessed Goree on the coast of Guinea in 1617, built Batavia in 1621, gained all the spice islands soon after 1623, occupied Curaçoa in 1634, Brazil, 1636, Malacca, 1641, Ceylon, 1644.

[2] J. Q. Adams' Review.

[3] Heeren on the British continental interest. Works, v. i. p. 156.

[4] Parl. History, v. iii. p. 1374, 1375; Clarendon, l. xiii.

commerce between England and her colonies, as well as between England and the rest of the world, was to be conducted in ships, solely owned and principally manned by Englishmen. Foreigners might bring to England nothing but the products of their own respective countries, or those, of which their countries were the established staples. In vain did the Dutch expostulate against the act as a breach of commercial amity; the parliament replied, that it knew the interests of England, and could not repeal laws to please a neighbor.[1]

A naval war soon followed, which Cromwell eagerly desired, and Holland as earnestly endeavored to avoid. The spirit of each people was kindled with the highest national enthusiasm; the commerce of the world was the prize contended for; the ocean was the scene of the conflict; and the annals of recorded time had never known so many great naval actions in such quick succession. This was the war in which Blake and Ayscue and De Ruyter gained their glory; in which Tromp fixed a broom to his mast in bravado, as if he would sweep the English flag from the seas.[2]

Cromwell was not disposed to trammel the industry of Virginia, and Maryland, and New-England. His ambition aspired to make England the commercial emporium of the world. His plans extended to the possession of the harbors in the Spanish Netherlands; France was obliged to pledge her aid to con-

---
[1] Clarendon, b. xiii. v. iii. p. 458; Parl. History, v. iii. p. 1378. [2] Hume's History of England, c. lx.

quer, and her consent to yield Dunkirk, Mardyke and Gravelines; and Dunkirk, in the summer of 1658, was given up to his ambassador by the French king in person. Nor was this all; he desired the chief harbors in the North Sea, and the Baltic; and an alliance with Sweden, made not simply from a zeal for protestantism, was to secure him Bremen, and Helsingör, and Dantzig, as his reward.[1] In the West Indies, his genius had planned the capture of Jamaica, which succeeded; and the attempt at the reduction of Hispaniola, then the chief possession of Spain among the islands, failed only through the incompetency or want of concert of his agents.

It is as the rival of Holland, the successful antagonist of Spain, the protector of English shipping, that Cromwell has claims to glory. The crown passed from the brow of his sons; his wide plans for the possession of commercial places on the continent, were defeated; Dunkirk was restored; the monarchy, which he subverted, was re-established; the nobility, which he humbled, recovered its pride; Jamaica and the Act of Navigation are the permanent monuments of Cromwell.

The protection of English shipping, thus permanently established as a part of the British commercial policy, was the successful execution of a scheme, which many centuries before had been prematurely attempted. A new and a far less justifiable encouragement was soon demanded, and English merchants began to insist upon the en-

[1] Heeren's Works, v. i. p. 158.

tire monopoly of the commerce of the colonies. This question had but recently been agitated in parliament. It was within the few last years, that England had acquired colonies; and as, at first, they were thought to depend upon the royal prerogative, the public policy with respect to them can be found only in the proclamations, charters and instructions, which emanated from the monarch.

CHAP. VI.

1655.

The prudent forecast of Henry VII. had considered the advantages, which might be derived from a colonial monopoly; and while ample privileges were bestowed on the adventurers, who sailed for the New World, he stipulated, that the exclusive staple of its commerce should be made in England.[1] A century of ill success had checked the extravagance of hope; and as the charters of Gilbert and of Raleigh had contained little but concessions, suited to invite those eminent men to engage with earnestness in the career of western discoveries, so the first charter for Virginia expressly admitted strangers to trade with the colony on payment of a small discriminating duty.[2] On the enlargement of the company, the intercourse with foreigners was still permitted; nor were any limits assigned to the commerce in which they might engage.[3] The last charter was equally free from unreasonable restrictions on trade; and, by a confirmation of all former privileges, it permitted to foreign nations the traffic, which it did not expressly sanction.[4]

1606.

1609.

1612.

[1] Hazard, v. i. p. 10 and 13, 14; Biddle's Cabot, p. 309.
[2] Charter, s. 13, in Hen. v. i. p. 63.
[3] Second Charter, s. 21, in Hening, v. i. p. 94, 95.
[4] Third Charter, s. 21, ib. p. 109.

At an early period of his reign, before Virginia had been planted, King James found in his hostility to the use of tobacco a convenient argument for the excessive tax, which a royal ordinance imposed on its consumption.[1] When the weed had evidently become the staple of Virginia, the Stuarts cared for nothing in the colony so much as for a revenue to be derived from an impost on its produce. Whatever false display of zeal might be made for religion, the conversion of the heathen, the organization of the government, and the establishment of justice, the subject of tobacco was never forgotten. The sale of it in England was strictly prohibited, unless the heavy impost had been paid;[2] a proclamation enforced the royal decree;[3] and, that the tax might be gathered on the entire consumption, by a new proclamation,[4] the culture of tobacco was forbidden in England and Wales, and the plants, already growing, were ordered to be uprooted. Nor was it long before the importation and sale of tobacco required a special license from the king.[5] In this manner, a compromise was effected between the interests of the colonial planters and the monarch; the former obtained the exclusive supply of the English market, and the latter succeeded in imposing an exorbitant duty.[6] In the ensuing parliament, Lord Coke did not fail to remind the commons of the usurpations of authority on the part of the monarch, who had

---

[1] Hazard, v. i. p. 49, 50.
[2] May 25. Hazard, v. i. p. 89.
[3] Nov. 10. Ibid, p. 90.
[4] Hazard, v. i. 93.
[5] April 7. Hazard, v. i. p. 89—91. June 29. Ibid, p. 93—96.
[6] Stith, p. 168—170; Chalmers, p. 50. 52. 57.

COMMERCIAL POLICY OF THE STUARTS.

taxed the produce of the colonies, without the consent of the people and without an act of the national legislature;[1] and Sandys, and Diggs, and Farrar, the friends of Virginia,. procured the substitution of an act for the arbitrary ordinance.[2] In consequence of the dissensions of the times, the bill, which had passed the house, was left among the unfinished business of the session; nor was the affair adjusted, till, as we have already seen, the commons, in 1624, again expressed their regard for Virginia by a petition, to which the monarch readily attempted to give effect.[3]

The first colonial measure[4] of King Charles related to tobacco; and the second proclamation,[5] though its object purported to be the settling of the plantation of Virginia, partook largely of the same character. In a series of public acts, King Charles attempted during his reign to procure a revenue from this source. The authority of the star-chamber was invoked to assist in filling his exchequer by new and onerous duties on tobacco;[6] his commissioners were ordered to contract for all the product of the colonies;[7] though the Spanish tobacco was not steadily excluded.[8] All colonial tobacco was soon ordered to be sealed;[9] nor was its importation permitted except with special license;[10] and we have

CHAP. VI.

1621. April 18.

1624.

1625.

1626.

1627.

---

[1] Debates of the Commons in 1620 and 1621, v. i. p. 169. This minute work was sent me by I. P. Davis, of Boston.
[2] Ibid, p. 269—271, and 296; Chalmers, p. 51. 70—74.
[3] Hazard, v. i. p. 193—198 and 198—202.
[4] Ibid, p. 202, 203.
[5] Ibid, p. 203—205.
[6] March 2, 1626. Ibid, p. 224—230.
[7] Jan. 1627. Rymer, v. xviii. p. 831.
[8] Feb. 1627. Ibid, p. 848.
[9] March, 1627. Ibid, p. 886.
[10] August, 1627. Rymer, v. xviii. p. 920.

238   COMMERCIAL POLICY OF THE STUARTS.

CHAP. VI.

1628.

1631.

1633.

1634.

1639.

seen, that an attempt was made, by a direct negotiation with the Virginians, to constitute the king the sole factor of their staple.[1] The measure was defeated by the firmness of the colonists; and the monarch was left to issue a new series of proclamations, constituting London the sole mart of colonial tobacco;[2] till, vainly attempting to regulate the trade,[3] he declared "his will and pleasure to have the sole pre-emption of all the tobacco" of the English plantations.[4] He long adhered to his system with resolute pertinacity.[5]

The measures of the Stuarts were ever unsuccessful; because they were directed against the welfare of the colonists, and were not sustained by popular interests in England. After the long continued efforts, which the enterprize of English merchants and the independent spirit of English planters had perseveringly defied, King Charles, on the appointment of Sir William Berkeley, devised the expedient, which was destined to become so celebrated. No vessel, laden with colonial commodities, might sail from the harbors of Virginia for any ports but those of England, that the staple of those commodities might be made in the mother country; and all trade with foreign vessels, except in case of necessity, was forbidden.[6] This system, which the instructions of Berkeley commanded him to introduce, was ultimately successful; for it sacrificed no rights

[1] Hening, v. i. p. 129 and 134.
[2] Jan. 1631. Rymer, v. xix. p. 235.
[3] Ibid, p. 474 and 522.
[4] June 19. Hazard, v. i. p. 375.
[5] August, 1639. Rymer, v. xx. p. 348.
[6] Chalmers, p. 132, 133.

but those of the colonists, while it identified the interests of the English merchant and the English government, and leagued them together for the oppression of those, who, for more than a century, were too feeble to offer effectual resistance.

The Long Parliament was more just; it attempted to secure to English shipping the whole carrying trade of the colonies, but with the free consent of the colonies themselves; offering an equivalent, which the legislatures in America were at liberty to reject.[1]

1646.
Jan. 23.

The memorable ordinance of 1650 was a war measure, and extended only to the colonies, which had adhered to the Stuarts. All intercourse with them was forbidden, except to those, who had a license from parliament or the council of state. Foreigners were rigorously excluded;[2] and this prohibition was designed to continue in force even after the suppression of all resistance. While, therefore, the navigation act secured to English ships the entire carrying trade with England, in connexion with the ordinance of the preceding year, it conferred a monopoly of colonial commerce.

1650.

1651.

But this state of commercial law was essentially modified by the manner, in which the authority of the English commonwealth was established in the Chesapeake. The republican leaders of Great Britain, conducting with true magnanimity, suffered the fever of party to subside, before decisive measures were adopted; and then two of the three commission-

[1] Hazard, v. i. p. 634, 635.   [2] Ibid, p. 636—638.

240   VIRGINIA CAPITULATES TO THE COMMONWEALTH.

CHAP. VI.
1651.
Sept. 26.

ers, whom they appointed, were taken from among the planters themselves. The instructions given them, were such as Virginians might carry into effect; for they constituted them the pacificators and benefactors of their country. In case of resistance, the cruelties of war were threatened.[1] If Virginia would but adhere to the commonwealth, she might be the mistress of her own destiny.

1652. Mar.

What opposition could be made to the parliament, which, in the moment of its power, voluntarily proposed a virtual independence? No sooner had the Guinea frigate anchored in the waters of the Chesapeake, than "all thoughts of resistance were laid aside,"[2] and the colonists, having no motive to contend for a monarch, whose fortunes seemed irretrievable, were earnest only to assert the freedom of their own institutions. It marks the character of the Virginians, that they refused to surrender to force; but yielded by a voluntary deed and a mutual compact. It was agreed upon the surrender, that the "PEOPLE OF VIRGINIA" should have all the liberties of the freeborn people of England; should entrust their business as formerly to their own grand assembly; should remain unquestioned for their past loyalty; and should have "as free trade as the people of England." No taxes, no customs, might be levied, except by their

---

[1] Let the reader consult the instructions themselves, in Thurloe, v. i. p. 197, 198, or in Hazard, v. i. p. 556—558, rather than the commentary of Chalmers or Grahame.

[2] Clarendon, b. xiii. p. 466, 467. It is strange how much error has been introduced into Virginia history, and continued, even when means of correcting it were abundant and easy of access. Clarendon relates the matter rightly. See also Strong's Babylon's Fall, p. 2, 3, and Langford's Refutation, p. 6, 7.

own burgesses; no forts erected, no garrisons maintained, but by their own consent.[1] In the settlement of the government, the utmost harmony prevailed between the burgesses and the commissioners; it was the governor and council only, who had any apprehensions for their safety, and who scrupulously provided a guarantee for the security of their persons and property, which there evidently had existed no design to injure.[2]

These terms, so favorable to liberty and almost conceding independence, were faithfully observed till the restoration. Historians[2] have, indeed, drawn gloomy pictures of the discontent, which pervaded a colony, that remained loyal to the last, and have represented that discontent as heightened by commercial oppression. The statement is a pure fiction. The colony of Virginia enjoyed liberties as large as the favored New-England; and displayed an equal degree of fondness for popular sovereignty and political independence. The executive officers became elective; and so evident were the designs of all parties to promote an amicable settlement of the government, that Richard Bennett, himself a commissioner of the parliament, was unanimously elected governor.[3] Under the administration of Berkeley, he had been com-

---

[1] Hening, v. i. p. 363—365, and 367, 368; Jefferson's Notes on Virginia; Hazard, v. i. p. 560—564; Burk, v. ii. p. 85—91.

[2] Beverley, Chalmers, Robertson, Marshall. Even the accurate and learned Holmes has transmitted the error. Compare Jared Sparks, in North American Review, v. xx. new series, p. 433—436.

[3] Hening, v. i. p. 371. See Stith, p. 199, who tells the story rightly. Strange that historians would not take a hint from the accurate Stith.

CHAP. VI.

1652. April.

May 5.

May 6.

1655. Mar. 31.

pelled to quit Virginia; and now not the slightest effort at revenge was attempted.[1] The act which constituted the government, claimed for the assembly the privilege of defining the powers which were to belong to the governor and council; and the public good was declared to require, "that the right of electing all officers of this colony should appertain to the burgesses," as to "the representatives of the people."[2] It had been usual for the governor and council to sit in the assembly; the expediency of the measure was questioned, and a temporary compromise ensued; they retained their former right, but were required to take the oath, which was administered to the burgesses.[3] Thus the house of burgesses acted as a convention of the people; exercising supreme authority, and distributing power as the public welfare required.[4]

Nor was this an accidental and transient arrangement. Cromwell never made any appointments for Virginia; not one governor acted under his commission.[5] When Bennett retired from office, the assembly itself elected his successor; and Edward Diggs, who had before been chosen of the council,[6] received the suffrages.[7] The commissioners in the colony[8] were rather engaged in settling the affairs and adjusting the boundaries of Maryland, than in controlling the destinies of Virginia.

---

[1] Langford's Refutation, p. 3. On Bennett, compare ii. Mass. Hist. Coll. v. ix. p. 118. He was of the council in 1646. Hening, v. i. p. 322.
[2] Hening, v. i. p. 372.
[3] Ibid, p. 373.
[4] Hening's Note, v. i. p. 369.
[5] Hening, v. i. Preface, p. 13.
[6] Ibid, p. 388. November, 1654.
[7] Ibid, p. 408. Compare, also, Hening, v. i. p. 5, and also p. 426.
[8] Ibid, p. 428 and 432; Hazard, v. i. p. 594.

The right of electing the governor continued to be claimed by the representatives of the people,[1] and "worthy Samuel Matthews, an old planter, of nearly forty years' standing," who had been "a most deserving commonwealth's man, kept a good house, lived bravely and was a true lover of Virginia,"[2] was next honored with the office. But the worthy old gentleman had too exalted ideas of his station; and, in conjunction with the council, became involved in an unequal contest with the very assembly, by which he had been elected. The burgesses had enlarged their power by excluding the governor and council from their sessions, and, having thus reserved to themselves the first free discussion of every law, had voted an adjournment till November. The governor and council, by message, declared the dissolution of the assembly. The legality of the dissolution was denied;[3] and, after an oath of secrecy, every burgess was enjoined not to betray his trust by submission. Matthews yielded, reserving a right of appeal to the protector.[4] When the house unanimously voted the governor's answer unsatisfactory,[5] he expressly revoked the order of dissolution; but still referred the decision of the dispute to Cromwell. The members of the assembly, apprehensive of a limitation of colonial liberty by the reference of a political question to England, determined on a solemn assertion of their independent powers. A committee was appointed, of which John Carter, of Lancaster, was the chief;

CHAP. VI.

1658.

April 1.

[1] Hening, v. i. p. 431.
[2] ii. M. Hist. Coll. v. ix. p. 119.
[3] Hening's Note, v. i. p. 430.
[4] Hening, v. i. p. 496, 497, and 500, 501.
[5] Ibid, p. 501.

CHAP. VI.
1658.

and a complete declaration of popular sovereignty was solemnly made. This was followed by an unusual exercise of power. The governor and council had ordered the dissolution of the assembly; the burgesses now decreed the former election of governor and council to be void. Having thus exercised, not merely the right of election, but the more extraordinary right of removal, they re-elected Matthews, "who by us," they add, "shall be invested with all the just rights and privileges belonging to the governor and captain-general of Virginia." The governor submitted, and acknowledged the validity of his ejection by taking the new oath, which had just been prescribed. The council was organized anew; and the spirit of popular liberty established all its claims.[1]

1658.
1659. Mar.

The death of Cromwell made no change in the constitution of the colony. The message of the governor duly announced the event to the legislature.[2] It has pleased some English historians to ascribe to Virginia a precipitate attachment to Charles II. On the present occasion, the burgesses deliberated in private, and unanimously resolved, that Richard Cromwell should be acknowledged.[3] But it was a more interesting question, whether the change of protector in England would endanger liberty in Virginia. The letter from the council had left the government to be administered according to former usage. The assembly declared itself satisfied with

[1] Hening, v. i. p. 504, 505.
[2] See the names of the members, in Hening, v. i. p. 506, 507.
[3] Hening, v. i. p. 511. Mar. 1659.

the language.¹ But that there might be no reason to question the existing usage, the governor was summoned to come to the house; where he appeared in person, deliberately acknowledged the supreme power of electing officers to be, by the present laws, resident in the assembly, and pledged himself to join in addressing the new protector for special confirmation of all existing privileges. The reason for this extraordinary proceeding is assigned; "that what was their privilege now, might be the privilege of their posterity."² The frame of the Virginia government was deemed worthy of being transmitted to remote generations.

On the death of Matthews, the Virginians were without a chief magistrate, just at the time when the resignation of Richard had left England without a government. The burgesses, who were immediately convened, resolving to become the arbiters of the fate of the colony, enacted, "that the supreme power of the government of this country shall be resident in the assembly; and all writs shall issue in its name, until there shall arrive from England a commission, which the assembly itself shall adjudge to be lawful."³ This being done, Sir William Berkeley was elected governor;⁴ and, acknowledging the validity of the acts of the burgesses, whom, it was expressly agreed, he could in no event dissolve, he accepted the office to which he had been chosen, and recognized, without a scruple, the authority to which he owed his elevation. "I am," said he, "but a

---

[1] Hening, v. i. p. 511.
[2] Ibid, p. 511, 512.
[3] Ibid, p. 530, Act 1. Mar. 1660.
[4] Ibid, p. 530, 531, and 5.

servant of the assembly."[1] Virginia did not lay claim to absolute independence; but anxiously awaited the settlement of affairs in England.[2]

The legislation of the colony had taken its character from the condition of the people, who were essentially agricultural in their pursuits; and it is the interest of society in that state to discountenance contracting debts. Severe laws for the benefit of the creditor are the fruits of commercial society; Virginia possessed not one considerable town, and her statutes favored the independence of the planter, rather than the security of trade. The representatives of colonial landholders voted "the total ejection of mercenary attornies."[3] By a special act, emigrants were safe against suits, designed to enforce engagements that had been made in Europe;[4] and colonial obligations might be easily satisfied by a surrender of property.[5] Already large landed proprietors were frequent; and plantations of two thousand acres were not unknown.[6]

During the suspension of the royal government in England, Virginia attained unlimited liberty of commerce, which she regulated by independent laws. The ordinance of 1650 was rendered void by the act of capitulation; the navigation act of Cromwell was not designed for her oppression, and was not enforced within her borders. If an occasional confiscation took place, it was done by the authority of

[1] Smith's History of New-York, p. 27.
[2] See the note of Hening, in v. i. p. 526—529.
[3] Hening, v. i. p. 275. 302. 313.
[4] Ibid, p. 256, 257.
[5] Ibid, p. 294.
[6] Virginia's Cure, p. 2 and 8.

349. 419. 482. 495, and preface, p. 18.

VIRGINIA AND ITS INHABITANTS. 247

the colonial assembly.¹ The war between England and Holland necessarily interrupted the intercourse of the Dutch with the English colonies; but if, after the treaty of peace, the trade was considered contraband, the English restrictions were entirely disregarded.² A remonstrance, addressed to Cromwell, demanded an unlimited liberty; and we may suppose, that it was not refused, for, some months before Cromwell's death, the Virginians "invited the Dutch and all foreigners" to trade with them, on payment of no higher duty, than that which was levied on such English vessels, as were bound for a foreign port.³ Proposals of peace and commerce between New-Netherlands and Virginia were discussed without scruple by the respective colonial governments; and at last a special statute of Virginia extended to every Christian nation, in amity with England, a promise of liberty to trade and equal justice.⁴ At the restoration, Virginia enjoyed freedom of commerce with the whole world.

Religious liberty advanced under the influence of independent domestic legislation. Conformity to the church of England had, in the reign of Charles, been enforced by measures of disfranchisement and exile.⁵ Under the commonwealth, all things respecting parishes and parishioners were referred to their own ordering.⁶ Unhappily, the extravagance of a few wild fanatics, who, under the name of qua-

CHAP. VI.

1656.

1658. Mar.

1660.

1658. Mar. 1.

---

¹ Hening, v. i. p. 382, 383.
² Thurloe, v. v. p. 80; Hazard, v. i. p. 599—602.
³ Hening, v. i. p. 469.
⁴ Smith, p. 27; Hen. v. i. p. 450.
⁵ Hening, v. i. p. 123. 144. 149. 155. 180. 240. 268, 269. 277.
⁶ Ibid, p. 433, Act 1. 1658.

CHAP. VI.
kers, were charged with avowing doctrines, than which none are more offensive to the society of Friends, gave such umbrage, that Virginia was still excited to an act of intolerance. All quakers were banished; and they, who should obstinately persist in returning, were ordered to be prosecuted as felons.[1]

Virginia was the first state in the world, composed of separate townships, diffused over an extensive surface, where the government was organized on the principle of universal suffrage. All freemen without exception were entitled to vote. An attempt was once made to limit the right to house-keepers;[2] but the public voice reproved the restriction; the very next year, it was decided to be "hard and unagreeable to reason, that any person shall pay equal taxes and yet have no votes in elections;" and the electoral franchise was restored to all freemen.[3] Servants, when the time of their bondage was completed, at once became electors; and might be chosen burgesses.[4]

1655.

1656.

Thus Virginia established upon her soil the supremacy of the popular branch, the freedom of trade, the independence of religious societies, the security from foreign taxation, and the universal elective franchise. If, in following years, she departed from either of these principles, and yielded a reluctant consent to change, it was from the influence of foreign authority. Virginia had herself

[1] Hening, v. i. p. 532, 533, Act 6. 1660.
[2] Ibid, preface, p. 19, 20 and p. 412, Act 7. March, 1655.
[3] Hening, v. i. p. 403, Act 16. March, 1656.
[4] Virginia's Cure, printed in 1662, p. 18.

VIRGINIA AND ITS INHABITANTS.

established a nearly independent democracy. Prosperity advanced with freedom; dreams of new staples and infinite wealth were indulged;[1] while the population of Virginia at the epoch of the restoration, may have been about thirty thousand. Many of the recent emigrants had been royalists in England, good officers in the war, men of education, of property, and of condition. But the waters of the Atlantic divided them from the political strifes of Europe; their industry was employed in making the best advantage of their plantations; the interests and liberties of Virginia, the land, which they adopted as their country, were dearer to them than the monarchical principles, which they had espoused in England;[2] and therefore no bitterness could exist between the partisans of the Stuarts and the friends of republican liberty. Virginia had long been the home of its inhabitants. "Among many other blessings," said their statute book,[3] "God Almighty hath vouchsafed increase of children to this colony; who are now multiplied to a considerable number;" and the huts in the wilderness were as full as the birds-nests of the woods.

The genial climate and transparent atmosphere delighted those, who had come from the denser air of England. Every object in nature was new and wonderful. The loud and frequent thunder-storms

[1] E. Williams' Virginia, and Virginia's Discovery of Silkworms, 1650, quarto.
[2] Clarendon, b. xiii. v. iii. p. 466. 467; Walsh's Appeal, p. 31.
[3] Hening, v. i. 336. "A very numerous generation of Christian children born in Virginia, who naturally are of beautiful and comely persons, and generally of more ingenious spirits than those of England." Virginia's Cure, p. 5.

were phenomena, that had been rarely witnessed in the colder summers of the north; the forests, majestic in their growth and free from underwood, deserved admiration for their unrivalled magnificence; the purling streams and the frequent rivers, flowing between alluvial banks, quickened the ever pregnant soil into an unwearied fertility; the strangest and the most delicate flowers grew familiarly in the fields; the woods were replenished with sweet barks and odors; the gardens matured the fruits of Europe, of which the growth was invigorated and the flavor improved by the activity of the virgin mould. Especially the birds with their gay plumage and varied melodies inspired delight; every traveller expressed his pleasure in listening to the mocking-bird, which carolled a thousand several tunes, imitating and excelling the notes of all its rivals. The humming-bird, so brilliant in its plumage and so delicate in its form, quick in motion yet not fearing the presence of man, haunting about the flowers like the bee gathering honey, rebounding from the blossoms out of which it sips the dew, and as soon returning "to renew its many addresses to its delightful objects," was ever admired as the smallest and the most beautiful of the feathered race. The rattle-snake, with the terrors of its alarms and the power of its venom; the opossum, soon to become as celebrated for the care of its offspring as the fabled pelican; the noisy frog, booming from the shallows like the English bittern; the flying squirrel; the myriads of pigeons, darkening the air with the immensity of their flocks, and, as men believed, breaking with their weight the boughs of trees on which they alighted, were all honored with frequent commemoration and became the subjects of the strangest tales. The concurrent relation of all the Indians justified the belief, that, within ten days' journey towards the setting of the sun, there was a country, where gold might be washed from the sand; and where the natives themselves had learned the use of the crucible;[1] but definite and accurate as were the accounts, inquiry was always baffled; and the regions of gold remained for two centuries an undiscovered land.

Various were the employments by which the calmness of life was relieved. One idle man, who had been a great traveller, and who did not remain in America, beguiled the ennui of his seclusion by translating the whole of Ovid's Metamorphoses.[2] To the man of leisure, the chase furnished a perpetual resource. It was not long before the horse was multiplied in Virginia; and to improve that noble animal was early an object of pride, soon to be favored by legislation. Speed was especially valued; and the planter's pace became a proverb.

Equally proverbial was the hospitality of the Virginians. Labor was valuable; land was cheap; competence promptly followed industry. There was no need of a scramble; abundance gushed from the earth for all. The morasses were alive with water-

---

[1] E. Williams, Virginia, &c. p. 17. Comp. Silliman's Journal, on the mines of N. C. v. xxiii. p. 8, 9. [2] Rymer, v. xviii. p. 676, 677.

CHAP. fowl; the forests were nimble with game; the woods
VI. rustled with covies of quails and wild turkies, while
they rung with the merry notes of the singing-birds;
and hogs, swarming like vermin, ran at large in
troops. It was "the best poor man's country in the
world." "If a happy peace be settled in poor
England," it had been said, "then they in Virginia
shall be as happy a people as any under heaven."[1]
But plenty encouraged indolence. No domestic
manufactures were established; every thing was
imported from England. The chief branch of industry, for the purpose of exchanges, was tobacco
planting; and the spirit of invention was enfeebled
by the uniformity of pursuit.

[1] ii. M. Hist. Coll. v. ix. p. 116.

CHAPTER VII.

COLONIZATION OF MARYLAND.

The limits of Virginia, by its second charter, extended two hundred miles north of Old Point Comfort; and therefore included all the soil, which subsequently formed the state of Maryland. It was long before the country towards the head of the Chesapeake was explored; settlements in Accomack were extended; and commerce was begun with the tribes which Smith had been the first to visit. Porey, the secretary of the colony, "made a discovery into the great bay," as far as the river Patuxent, which he ascended; but his voyage probably extended no further to the north. The English settlement of a hundred men, which he is represented to have found already established,[1] was rather a consequence of his voyage; and seems to have been on the eastern shore, perhaps within the limits of Virginia.[2] The hope "of a very good trade of furs," animated the adventurers; and if the plantations advanced but slowly, there is yet evidence, that commerce with the Indians was earnestly pursued under the sanction of the colonial government.[3]

---

[1] Chalmers, p. 206.
[2] Purchas, v. iv. p. 1784; Smith, v. ii. p. 61—64.
[3] Relation of Maryland, p. 4; Smith's History of Virginia, v. ii. p. 63 and 95.

EARLIEST SETTLEMENTS IN MARYLAND.

CHAP. VII.

An attempt was made to obtain a monopoly of this commerce[1] by William Clayborne, whose resolute and enterprizing spirit was destined to exert a powerful and long continued influence. His first appearance in America was as a surveyor,[2] sent by the London company to make a map of the country. At the fall of the corporation, he had been appointed by King James a member of the council;[3] and, on the accession of Charles, was continued in office, and, in repeated commissions, was nominated secretary of state.[4] At the same time, he received authority from the governors of Virginia to discover the source of the bay of the Chesapeake, and, indeed, any part of that province, from the thirty-fourth to the forty-first degree of latitude.[5] It was, therefore, natural, that he should become familiar with the opportunities for traffic, which the country afforded; and the jurisdiction and the settlement of Virginia seemed about to extend to the forty-first parallel of latitude, which was then the boundary of New-England. Upon his favorable representation, a company was formed in England for trading with the natives; and, through the agency of Sir William Alexander, the Scottish proprietary of Nova Scotia, a royal license was issued, sanctioning the commerce, and conferring on Clayborne powers of government over those, who should make themselves the companions of his voyages.[6] Harvey enforced the commands of his sovereign, and confirmed the license

1621.
1624.
1625.
1627, to 1629.
1631. May 16.
1632. Mar. 8.

---

[1] Rel. of Maryland, 1635, p. 10.
[2] Hening, v. i. p. 116.
[3] Hazard, v. i. p. 189.
[4] Ibid, p. 234 and 239.
[5] Papers in Chalmers, p. 227.
[6] Chalmers, p. 227, 228.

by a colonial commission.[1] The Dutch plantations were esteemed to border upon Virginia. After long experience as a surveyor, and after years employed in discoveries, Clayborne, now acting under the royal license, formed establishments, not only on Kent Island, in the heart of Maryland, but also near the mouth of the Susquehannah.[2] Thus the colony of Virginia anticipated the extension of its commerce and its limits; and, as mistress of all the vast and commodious waters of the Chesapeake, and of the soil on both sides of the Potomac, indulged the hope of obtaining the most brilliant commercial success, and rising into powerful opulence, without the competition of a rival.

It was the peculiar fortune of the United States, that they were severally colonized by men, in origin, religious faith and purposes, as various, as the climes which are included within their limits. Before Virginia could complete its settlements and confirm its claims to jurisdiction over the country north of the Potomac, a new government was erected, on a foundation as extraordinary, as its results were benevolent. Sir George Calvert had early become interested in colonial establishments in America. A native of Yorkshire,[3] educated at Oxford,[4] with a mind enlarged by extensive travel, on his entrance into life befriended by Sir Robert Cecil, advanced to the honors of knighthood, and at length employed as one

1580.

---

[1] Chalmers, p. 228, 229.
[2] Hazard, v. i. p. 430; Relation of Maryland, p. 34; Thurloe, v. v. p. 486; Hazard, v. i. p. 630; Maryland Papers, in Chalmers, p. 233.
[3] Fuller's Worthies, p. 201.
[4] Wood's Athenæ Oxonienses, p. 522, 523.

CHAP. VII.

1619.
1621.

1624.

of the two secretaries of state,[1] he not only secured the consideration of his patron and his sovereign,[2] but the good opinion of the world. He was chosen by an immense majority to represent in parliament his native county of Yorkshire.[3] His knowledge of business, his industry, and his fidelity are acknowledged by all historians. He lived in an age, when religious controversy still continued to be active, and when the increasing divisions among protestants were spreading a general alarm. His mind sought relief from controversy in the bosom of the Roman Catholic church; and preferring the avowal of his opinions to the emoluments of office, he resigned his place and made an open profession of his conversion. King James was never bitter against the catholics, who respected his pretensions as a monarch; Calvert retained his place in the privy council, and was advanced to the dignity of an Irish peerage. He had, from early life, shared in the general enthusiasm of England in favor of American plantations; he had been a member of the great company for Virginia; and, while he was secretary of state, he had obtained a special patent for the southern promontory of Newfoundland. How zealous he was in selecting suitable emigrants, how earnest to promote habits of domestic order and economical industry, how lavishly he expended his estate in advancing the interests of his settlement on the rugged shores of Avalon,[4] is related by those who have written of

[1] Stow, edition of 1631, p. 1031.
[2] Winwood, v. ii. p. 58, and v. iii. p. 318 and 337.
[3] Debates of 1620 and 1621, v. i. p. 175.
[4] Whitbourne's Newfoundland,

LIFE AND CHARACTER OF SIR GEORGE CALVERT.

his life. He desired, as a founder of a colony, not present profit, but a reasonable expectation; and, perceiving the evils of a common stock, he cherished enterprize by leaving each one to enjoy the results of his own industry. But numerous difficulties prevented success in Newfoundland; parliament had ever asserted the freedom of the fisheries,[1] which his grants tended to impair; the soil and the climate proved less favorable, than had been described in the glowing and deceptive pictures of his early agents; and the incessant danger of attacks from the French, who were possessed of the circumjacent continent, spread a gloom over the future. Twice, it is said, did Lord Baltimore, in person, visit his settlement; with ships, manned at his own charge, he repelled the French, who were hovering round the coast with the design of annoying the English fishermen; and, having taken sixty of them prisoners, he secured a temporary tranquillity to his countrymen and his colonists. But, notwithstanding this success, he found all hopes of a thriving plantation in Avalon to be vain. Why should the English emigrate to a rugged and inhospitable island, surrounded by a hostile power, when the hardships of colonizing the milder regions of Virginia had already been encountered; and a peaceful home might now be obtained without peril?

in the Cambridge Library. Also Purchas, v. iv. p. 1882—1891; Collier on Calvert; Fuller's Worthies of Yorkshire, p. 201, 202; Wood's Athenæ Oxonienses, v. ii. p. 522, 523; Lloyd's State Worthies, in Biog. Brit. article Calvert; Chalmers, p. 201.
[1] Chalmers, p. 84. 100. 114, 115, 116. 130.

CHAP. VII.

Lord Baltimore looked to Virginia, of which the climate, the fertility, and the advantages were so much extolled. Yet, as a papist, he could hardly expect a hospitable welcome in a colony, from which the careful exclusion[1] of Roman Catholics had been originally avowed as a special object, and where the statutes of the provincial legislature, as well as the commands of the sovereign, aimed at a perpetual religious uniformity. When Lord Baltimore visited Virginia in person, the zeal of the assembly immediately ordered the oaths of allegiance and supremacy to be tendered him. It was in vain that he proposed a form, which he was willing to subscribe; the government firmly insisted upon that which had been chosen by the English statutes, and which was purposely framed in such language as no catholic could adopt. A letter was transmitted from the assembly to the privy council, explanatory of the dispute, which had grown out of the intolerance of European legislation.[2] It was evident, that Lord Baltimore could never hope for quiet in any attempt at establishing a colony within the jurisdiction of Virginia.

1628, and 1629.

1629. Oct.

But the country beyond the Potomac seemed to be as yet untenanted by any but the scattered hordes of the native tribes. The cancelling of the Virginia patents had restored to the monarch the ample authority of his prerogative over the soil; he might now sever a province from the colony, to which he had at first assigned a territory so vast; and it was not diffi-

[1] Hazard, v. i. p. 72. History of Virginia, v. ii. p. 94
[2] Ancient Records, in Burk's —27.

cult for Calvert, a man of such moderation, that all parties were taken with him,[1] sincere in his character, disengaged from all interests, and a favorite with the royal family, to obtain a charter for domains in that happy clime. The nature of the document itself and concurrent opinion, leave no room to doubt, that it was penned by the first Lord Baltimore himself; although it was finally issued for the benefit of his son.

The fundamental charter[2] of the colony of Maryland, however it may have neglected to provide for the power of the king, was the sufficient frankpledge of the liberties of the colonist, not less than of the rights and interests of the proprietary. The ocean, the fortieth parallel of latitude, the meridian of the western fountain of the Potomac, the river itself from its source to its mouth, and a line drawn due east from Watkin's Point to the Atlantic, these were the limits of the territory, which was now erected into a province, and from Henrietta Maria, the daughter of Henry IV. and wife of Charles I., received the name of Maryland. The country, thus described, was given to Lord Baltimore, his heirs and assigns, as to its absolute lord and proprietary; to be holden by the tenure of fealty only, paying a yearly rent of two Indian arrows, and a fifth of all gold and silver ore, which might be found. Yet the absolute authority was conceded rather with

---

[1] Collier on Calvert.
[2] The charter may be found in Hazard, v. i. p. 327—337, in Bacon's Laws of Maryland at Large. It is appended in English to the Relation of Maryland, 1635. It has been commented upon by Chalmers, p. 202—205; very diffusely by McMahon, p. 133—183; by Story, v. i. p. 92—94, and many others.

reference to the crown, than the colonists; for the charter, unlike any patent which had hitherto passed the great seal of England, secured to the emigrants themselves an independent share in the legislation of the province, of which the statutes were to be established with the advice and approbation of the majority of the freemen or their deputies. Representative government was indissolubly connected with the fundamental charter; and it was especially provided, that the authority of the absolute proprietary should not extend to the life, freehold, or estate of any emigrant. These were the features, which endeared the proprietary government to the people of Maryland; and, but for these, the patent would have been as worthless as those of the London company; of Warwick, of Gorges, or of Mason. It is a singular fact, that the only proprietary charters, productive of considerable emolument to their owners, were those, which conceded popular liberty. Sir George Calvert was a Roman Catholic; yet, far from guarding his territory against any but those of his persuasion, as he had taken from himself and his successors all arbitrary power, by establishing the legislative franchises of the people, so he took from them the means of being intolerant in religion, by securing to all present and future liege people of the English king, without distinction of sect or party, free leave to transport themselves and their families to Maryland. Christianity was by the charter made the law of the land, but no preference was given to any sect; and equality in religious rights, not less than in civil freedom, was assured. A monopoly of the fisheries had formerly been earnestly resisted by the commons of England; to avoid all dispute on this point, Calvert, in his charter, expressly renounced any similar claim. As a catholic, he needed to be free from the jurisdiction of his neighbor; Maryland was carefully separated from Virginia, nor was he obliged to obtain the royal assent to the appointments or the legislation of his province, nor even to make a communication of the results. So far was the English monarch from reserving any right of superintendence in the colony, he left himself without the power to take cognizance of what transpired; and, by an express stipulation, covenanted, that neither he, nor his heirs, nor his successors, should ever, at any time thereafter, set any imposition, custom, or tax whatsoever upon the inhabitants of the province. Thus was conferred on Maryland an exemption from English taxation forever. Sir George Calvert was a man of sagacity, and an observing statesman. He had beheld the arbitrary administration of the colonies; and, against any danger of future oppression, he provided the strongest defence, which the promise of a monarch could afford. Some other rights were conferred on the proprietary, the advowson of churches; the power of creating manors and courts baron, and of establishing a colonial aristocracy on the system of sub-infeudation. But these things were practically of little moment. Even in Europe, feudal institutions appeared like the decrepitude of age amidst the vigor and enterprize of a new and more peaceful civilization; they could not be perpetuated in the lands of their origin; far less could they renew their youth in America. Sooner might the oldest oaks in Windsor forest be transplanted across the Atlantic, than the social forms, which Europe itself was beginning to reject as antiquated and rotten. But the seeds of popular liberty, contained in the charter, would find, in the New World, the very soil, best suited to quicken them into life and fruitfulness.

Calvert deserves to be ranked among the most wise and benevolent law-givers of all ages. He was the first in the history of the Christian world to seek for religious security and peace by the practice of justice, and not by the exercise of power; to plan the establishment of popular institutions with the enjoyment of liberty of conscience; to advance the career of civilization by recognizing the rightful equality of all Christian sects. The asylum of papists was the spot, where, in a remote corner of the world, on the banks of rivers, which, as yet, had hardly been explored, the mild forbearance of a proprietary adopted religious freedom as the basis of the state.

Before the patent could be finally adjusted and pass the great seal, Sir George Calvert died;[1] leaving a name, against which the breath of calumny has hardly whispered a reproach. The petulance of his adversaries could only taunt him with being "an Hispaniolized papist."[2] His son, Cecil Calvert, succeeded to his honors and fortunes. For him, the

---

[1] Chalmers, p. 201.   [2] Wilson, in Kennett, v. iii. p. 705.

heir of his father's intentions,¹ not less than of his father's fortunes, the charter of Maryland was published and confirmed; and he obtained the high distinction of successfully performing, what the colonial companies had hardly been able to achieve. At a vast expense, he planted a colony, which for several generations descended as a patrimony to his heirs.

Virginia regarded the severing of her territory with apprehension, and before any colonists had embarked under the charter of Baltimore, her commissioners had in England remonstrated against the grant as an invasion of her commercial rights, an infringement on her domains, and a discouragement to her planters. In Strafford, Lord Baltimore found a friend; for Strafford had been the friend of the father,² and the remonstrance was in vain; the privy council sustained the proprietary charter, and, advising the parties to an amicable adjustment of all disputes, commanded a free commerce and a good correspondence between the respective colonies.³

Nor was it long before gentlemen of birth and quality resolved to adventure their lives and a good part of their fortunes in the enterprize of planting a colony under so favorable a charter. Lord Baltimore, who, for some unknown reason, abandoned his purpose of conducting the emigrants in person, appointed his brother to act as his lieutenant; and, on Friday, the twenty-second of November, with a small but favoring gale, Leonard Calvert and

---

[1] The charter asserts it.
[2] Chalmers, p. 209.
[3] Hazard, v. i. p. 337; Bozman, p. 381 and 265; Chalmers, p. 231.

about two hundred people, most of them Roman Catholic gentlemen and their servants, in the Ark and the Dove, a ship of large burden, and a pinnace, set sail for the northern bank of the Potomac. Having staid by the way in Barbadoes and St. Christopher, it was not till February of the following year, that they arrived at Point Comfort, in Virginia; where, in obedience to the express letters of King Charles, they were welcomed by Harvey with courtesy and humanity. Clayborne also appeared, but it was as a prophet of ill omen, to attempt to terrify the company by sounding an alarm of the fixed hostility of the natives.

Leaving Point Comfort, Calvert sailed into the Potomac; and with the pinnace ascended the stream. A cross was planted on an island, and the country claimed for Christ and for England. At about forty-seven leagues above the mouth of the river, he found the village of Piscataqua; an Indian settlement nearly opposite Mount Vernon. The chieftain of the tribe would neither bid him go nor stay; "he might use his own discretion." It did not seem safe for the English to plant the first settlement so high up the river; Calvert descended the stream, examining, in his barge, the creeks and estuaries nearer the Chesapeake; he entered the river, which is now called St. Mary's, and which he named St. George's; and, about four leagues from its junction with the Potomac, he anchored at the Indian town of Yoacomoco. The native inhabitants, having already suffered from the superior power of the Susquehannahs, who occupied the district between the bays, had already resolved to remove into places of more security in the interior; and many of them had begun to migrate before the English arrived. To Calvert, the spot seemed convenient for a plantation; it was easy, by presents of cloth and axes, of hoes and knives, to gain the good will of the natives, and to purchase their rights to the soil, which they were preparing to abandon. They readily gave consent, that the English should immediately occupy one half of their town, and, after the harvest, should become the exclusive tenants of the whole. Mutual promises of friendship and peace were made; so that, upon the twenty-seventh day of March, the catholics took quiet possession of the little place; and religious liberty obtained a home, its only home in the wide world, at the humble village, which bore the name of St. Mary's.

Three days after the landing of Calvert, the Ark and the Dove anchored in the harbor. Sir John Harvey soon arrived on a visit; the native chiefs, also, came to welcome or to watch the emigrants; and were so well received, that they resolved to give perpetuity to their league of amity with the English. The Indian women taught the wives of the new comers to make bread of maize; the warriors of the tribe instructed the huntsmen how rich were the forests of America in game, and joined them in the chase. And, as the season of the year invited to the pursuits of agriculture, and the English had come into possession of ground already subdued, they were able, at once, to possess cornfields and gardens, and prepare the wealth of successful husbandry. Virginia, from its surplus produce, could furnish a temporary supply of food; and all kinds of domestic cattle. No sufferings were endured; no fears of want were excited; the foundation of the colony of Maryland was peacefully and happily laid. Within six months, it had advanced more than Virginia had done in as many years. The proprietary continued with great liberality to provide every thing, that was necessary for the comfort and protection of the colony, and spared no costs to promote its interests. In the two first years, he expended upwards of forty thousand pounds sterling.[1] But far more memorable was the character of the Maryland institutions. Every other country in the world had persecuting laws; "I will not," such was the oath for the governor of Maryland, "I will not by myself or any other, directly or indirectly, trouble, molest, or discountenance, any person professing to believe in Jesus Christ, for or in respect of religion."[2] Under the mild institutions and munificence of Baltimore, the dreary wilderness soon bloomed with the swarming life and activity of prosperous settlements; the Roman Catholics, who were oppressed by the laws of England, were sure to find a peaceful asylum in the quiet harbors of the Chesapeake; and there too protestants were sheltered against protestant intolerance.

Such were the beautiful auspices under which the

[1] Chalmers, p. 205—208; McMahon, p. 196—198.
[2] Chalmers' Political Annals, p. 235.

province of Maryland started into being; its prosperity and its peace seemed assured; the interests of its people and its proprietary were united; and, for some years, its internal peace and harmony were undisturbed. Its history is the history of benevolence, gratitude and toleration. No domestic factions disturbed its harmony. Every thing breathed peace but Clayborne. Dangers could only grow out of external causes, and were eventually the sad consequences of the revolution in England.

Twelve months had not elapsed before the colony of Maryland was convened for legislation. Probably all the freemen of the province were present in a strictly popular assembly. The laws of the session are no longer extant; but we know, that the necessity of vindicating the jurisdiction of the province against the claims of Clayborne was deemed a subject, worthy of the general deliberation and of a decisive act.[1] For he had been roused, by confidence in his power, to resolve on maintaining his possessions by force of arms. The earliest annals of Maryland are defaced by the accounts of a bloody skirmish on one of the rivers near the isle of Kent. Several lives were lost in the affray; but Clayborne's men were defeated and taken prisoners. Clayborne himself had fled to Virginia; and when he was reclaimed by the government of Maryland, Harvey, though he seems himself to have favored Baltimore, sent the fugitive with the witnesses to England.[2]

---

[1] Chalmers, p. 210 and 232. Bacon, in his Laws at Large, makes no mention of this assembly.

[2] Bozman, p. 260—262; Burk, v. ii. p. 40, 41; Chalmers, p. 209, 210. 232; McMahon, p. 12.

268   ESTABLISHMENT OF LEGISLATIVE LIBERTY.

CHAP. VII.

1638. Jan.

When a colonial assembly was next convened, it passed an act of attainder against Clayborne; for he had not only derided the powers of the proprietary, but had scattered jealousies among the Indians, and infused a spirit of disobedience into the inhabitants of Kent island. Now that he had fled, his estates were seized, and were declared forfeited to the laws, which he had contemned as invalid.[1] In England, Clayborne attempted to gain a hearing for his wrongs; and, partly by false representations, still more by the influence of Sir William Alexander, succeeded, for a season, in procuring the favorable disposition of Charles. But when the whole affair came to be referred to the commissioners for the plantations, it

1639. April.

was found, that, on received principles, the right of the king to confer the soil and the jurisdiction of Maryland could not be controverted; that the earlier license to traffic did not vest in Clayborne any rights, which were valid against the charter; and therefore that the isle of Kent belonged absolutely to Lord Baltimore, who alone could permit plantations to be established, or commerce with the Indians to be conducted, within the limits of his territory.[2]

Yet the people of Maryland were not content with vindicating the limits of their province; they were jealous of their liberties. The charter had secured to them the right of advising and approving in legislation. Did Lord Baltimore alone possess the right of originating laws? The people of Maryland re-

[1] Chalmers' Political Annals, p. 210.   [2] Bozman, p. 330—344; Chalmers, p. 212. 232—235.

jected the code, which the proprietary, as if holding the exclusive privilege of proposing statutes, had prepared for their government; and, asserting their equal rights of legislation, they, in their turn, enacted a body of laws, which they proposed for the assent of the proprietary: — so uniformly active in America was the spirit of popular liberty. How discreetly it was exercised, cannot now be known; for the laws, which were then enacted, were never ratified, and are therefore not to be found in the provincial records.[1]

In the early history of the United States, nothing is more remarkable, than the uniform attachment of each colony to its franchises; and popular assemblies burst every where into life with a consciousness of their importance, and an immediate capacity for efficient legislation. The first assembly of Maryland had vindicated the jurisdiction of the colony; the second had asserted its claims to original legislation; the third, which was now convened, examined its obligations, and, though not all its acts were carried through the forms essential to their validity, it yet displayed the spirit of the people and the times by framing a declaration of rights. Acknowledging the duty of allegiance to the English monarch, and securing to Lord Baltimore his prerogatives, it likewise confirmed to the inhabitants of Maryland all the liberties, which an Englishman can enjoy at home; established a system of representative gov-

---

[1] Bacon, 1637; Chalmers' Political Annals, p. 211; Bozman, p. 299—318, and 394—399; McMahon, p. 145.

ernment; and asserted for the general assemblies in the province all such powers, as may be exercised by the commons of England.[1] Indeed, throughout the whole colonial legislation of Maryland, the body representing the people, in its support of the interests and civil liberties of the province, was never guilty of timidity or treachery.[2] It is strange, that religious bigotry could ever stain the statute-book of a colony, founded on the basis of the freedom of conscience. An apprehension of some remote danger of persecution seems even then to have hovered over the minds of the Roman Catholics; and, at this session, they secured to their church its rights and liberties. Those rights and those liberties, it is plain from the charter, could be no more than the tranquil exercise of the Romish worship. The constitution had not yet attained a fixed form; thus far it had been a species of democracy under a hereditary patriarch. The act,[3] constituting the assembly, marks the transition from a democracy to a representative government. At this session, any freeman, who had taken no part in the election, might attend in person; henceforward, the governor might summon his friends by special writ; while the people were to choose as many delegates as "the freemen should think good." As yet there was no jealousy of power, no strife for place. While these laws prepared a frame of government for future generations, we are reminded of the feebleness and

[1] Bacon, 1638-9, c. i. ii.
[2] McMahon, p. 149.
[3] Bacon, 1638-9, c. i.; Griffith's Maryland, p. 7.

poverty of the state, where the whole people were obliged to contribute to "the setting up of a water-mill."¹

The restoration of the charter of the London company would have endangered the separate existence of Maryland; yet we have seen Virginia, which had ever been jealous of the division of its territory, defeat the attempt to revive the corporation. Meantime, the legislative assembly of Maryland, in the grateful enjoyment of happiness, seasonably guarded the tranquillity of the province against the perplexities of an "interim," by providing for the security of the government in case of the death of the proprietary. Commerce also was fostered; and tobacco, the staple of the colony, subjected to inspection.

Nor was it long before the inhabitants recognized Lord Baltimore's "great charge and solicitude in maintaining the government and protecting them in their persons, rights and liberties;" and therefore, "out of desire to return some testimony of gratitude," they freely granted "such a subsidy, as the young and poor estate of the colony could bear."² Maryland, at that day, was unsurpassed for happiness and liberty. Conscience was without restraint; a mild and liberal proprietary conceded every measure which the welfare of the colony required; domestic union, a happy concert between all the branches of government, an increasing emigration, a productive

---

[1] Bacon, 1638-9; Chalmers, p. 213, 214; Griffith's Sketches of the Early History of Maryland, p. 8. [2] Bacon, 1641-2, c. v.

commerce, a fertile soil, which Heaven had richly favored with rivers and deep bays, united to perfect the scene of colonial felicity and contentment. Ever intent on advancing the interests of his colony, Lord Baltimore invited the puritans of Massachusetts to emigrate to Maryland, offering them lands and privileges, and "free liberty of religion;" but Gibbons, to whom he had forwarded a commission, was "so wholly tutored in the New-England discipline," that he would not advance the wishes of the Irish peer; and the people, who subsequently refused Jamaica and Ireland, were not now tempted to desert the bay of Massachusetts for the Chesapeake.[1]

But secret dangers existed. The aborigines, alarmed at the rapid increase of the Europeans, vexed at being frequently over-reached by the cupidity of traders, not yet entirely recovered from the jealousies, which the malignant Clayborne had infused, commenced hostilities; for the Indians, ignorant of the remedy of redress, always plan retaliation. After a war of frontier aggressions, marked by no decisive events, peace was re-established on the usual terms of submission and promises of friendship, and rendered durable by the prudent legislation of the assembly and the firm humanity of the government. The pre-emption of the soil was reserved to Lord Baltimore;[2] kidnapping an Indian made a capital offence; and the sale of arms prohibited as a felony.[3] A regulation of intercourse with the natives

[1] Winthrop's New-England, v. ii. p. 148, 149.
[2] Bacon, 1649, c. iii.
[3] Ibid, c. vi.

was the surest preventive of war; the wrongs of an individual were ascribed to the nation; the injured savage, ignorant of peaceful justice, panted only for revenge; and thus the obscure villainy of some humble ruffian, whom the government would willingly punish for his outrages, might involve the colony in the horrors of savage warfare.

But the restless Clayborne, urged, perhaps, by the conviction of having been wronged, and still more by the hope of revenge, proved a far more dangerous enemy. Now that the civil war in England left nothing to be hoped from royal patronage, he declared for the popular party, and, with the assistance of one Ingle, who obtained sufficient notoriety to be proclaimed a traitor to the king,[1] he was able to promote a rebellion. By the very nature of the proprietary frame of government, the lord paramount could derive physical strength and resources only from his own private fortunes, or from the willing attachment of his lieges. His power depended on a union with his people. In times of peace, this condition was eminently favorable to the progress of liberty; the royal governors were often able, were still more often disposed, to use oppressive and exacting measures; the deputies of the proprietaries were always compelled to struggle for the assertion of the interests of their employer; they could never become successful aggressors on the liberties of the people. Besides, the crown, always jealous of the immense powers which had been carelessly lavished on the

---

[1] Bacon's Preface; Chalmers, p. 217.

CHAP. VII.
1643.

proprietary, was usually willing to favor the people in every reasonable effort to improve their condition, or limit the authority of the intermediate sovereign. At present, when the commotions in England left every colony in America almost unheeded, and Virginia and New-England were pursuing a course of nearly independent legislation, the power of the proprietary was almost as feeble as that of the king. The other colonies took advantage of the period to secure and advance their liberties; in Maryland, the effect was rather to encourage the insubordination of the restless; and Clayborne was able to excite an insurrection. Early in 1645, the rebels were triumphant; unprepared for an attack, the governor was compelled to fly, and more than a year elapsed, before the assistance of the well-disposed could enable him to resume his power and restore tranquillity. The insurgents distinguished the period of their dominion by disorder and misrule, and most of the records were then lost or embezzled.[1] Peace was confirmed by the wise clemency of the government; the offences of the rebellion were concealed by a general amnesty;[2] and the province was rescued, though not without expense,[3] from the distresses and confusion, which had followed a short but vindictive and successful insurrection.

1644.
1645.
1646. Aug.

1647, to 1649.

1649. April.

The controversy between the king and the parliament advanced; the overthrow of the monarchy seemed about to confer unlimited power in England

---

[1] Bacon's Preface; Chalmers, p. 217, 218; Burk, v. ii. p. 112; McMahon, p. 202.
[2] Bacon's Laws at Large, 1650, c. xxiv.
[3] Ibid, 1649, c. ix.

upon the embittered enemies of the Romish church; and, as if with a foresight of impending danger, and an earnest desire to stay its approach, the Roman Catholics of Maryland, with the earnest concurrence of their governor and of the proprietary, determined to place upon their statute-book an act for the religious freedom, which had ever been sacred on their soil. "And whereas the enforcing of the conscience in matters of religion," such was the sublime tenor of a part of the statute, "hath frequently fallen out to be of dangerous consequence in those commonwealths where it has been practised, and for the more quiet and peaceable government of this province, and the better to preserve mutual love and amity among the inhabitants, no person within this province, professing to believe in Jesus Christ, shall be any ways troubled, molested, or discountenanced, for his or her religion, or in the free exercise thereof." Thus did the early star of religious freedom appear as the harbinger of day; though, as it first gleamed above the horizon, its light was still colored and obscured by the mists and exhalations of morning. The greatest of English poets, when he represents the ground teeming with living things at the word of the Creator, paints the moment, when the forms, so soon to be instinct with perfect life and beauty, are yet emerging from the inanimate earth, and when but

> half appeared
> The tawny lion pawing to get free;
> ———— then springs as broke from bonds,
> And rampant shakes his brinded mane.

So it was with the freedom of religion in the United

States. The clause for liberty in Maryland extended only to Christians; and was introduced by the proviso, "except as in this present act is before declared and set forth."[1] And it had already been declared, that "whatsoever person shall blaspheme God, that is, curse him, or shall deny our Savior Jesus Christ to be the Son of God, or shall deny the Holy Trinity, the Father, Son, and Holy Ghost, or the Godhead of any of the sayd three persons of the Trinity, or the Unity of the Godhead, or shall use and utter any reproachful speeches, words, or language, concerning the Holy Trinity, or any of the sayd three persons thereof, shall be punished with death." Nowhere in the United States is religious opinion now deemed a proper subject for penal enactments. The only fit punishment for error is refutation. God needs no avenger in man. The foolhardy levity of shallow infidelity proceeds from a morbid passion for notoriety, or the miserable malice that finds pleasure in giving annoyance. The laws of society should do no more than reprove the breach of its decorum. Blasphemy is the crime of despair. One hopeless sufferer commits suicide; another curses Divine Providence for the evil which is in the world, and of which he cannot solve the mystery. The best medicine for intemperate grief is compassion; the keenest rebuke for ribaldry, contempt.

But the design of the law of Maryland was undoubtedly to favor freedom of conscience; and some

---

[1] N. B. These words are omitted in Bacon's abstract of the law. See Bacon, 1649, c. i. "A true copy" of the law is printed by Langford, p. 27—32, and I follow the authentic document.

years after it had been confirmed, the apologist of Lord Baltimore could assert, that his government, in conformity with his strict and repeated injunctions, had never given disturbance to any person in Maryland for matter of religion;[1] that the colonists enjoyed freedom of conscience, not less than freedom of person and estate, as amply as ever any people did in any place of the world.[2] The disfranchised friends of prelacy from Massachusetts and the puritans from Virginia, were welcomed to an equality of political rights in the Roman Catholic province of Maryland.[3]

An equal union prevailed between all branches of the government in explaining and confirming the civil liberties of the colony. In 1642, Robert Vaughan, in the name of the rest of the burgesses, had desired, that the house might be separated, and thus a negative secured to the representatives of the people. Before 1649, this change had taken place; and it was confirmed by a statute.[4] The dangerous prerogative of declaring martial law was also limited to the precincts of the camp and the garrison;[5] and a perpetual act declared, that no tax should be levied upon the freemen of the province, except by the vote of their deputies in a general assembly. "The strength of the proprietary" was confidently reposed "in the affections of his people."[6] Well might the freemen of Maryland place upon their records a

---

[1] Langford, p. 11.
[2] Ibid, p. 5.
[3] Chalmers' Political Annals, p. 219.
[4] Bacon, 1649, c. xii. and note, 1650, c. i.
[5] Bacon, 1650, c. xxvi.
[6] Ibid, 1650, c. xxv.

declaration of their gratitude "as a memorial to all posterities," and a pledge that succeeding generations would faithfully "remember" the care and industry of Lord Baltimore in advancing "the peace and happiness of the colony."[1]

But the revolutions in England could not but affect the destinies of the colonies; and while New-England and Virginia vigorously advanced their liberties under the salutary neglect, Maryland was involved in the miseries of a disputed government. The people were ready to display every virtue of good citizens; but doubts were raised as to the authority to which obedience was due; and the government, which had been a government of benevolence, good order and toleration, was, by the force of circumstances, soon abandoned to the misrule of bigotry and the anarchy of a disputed sovereignty. When the throne and the peerage had been subverted in England, it might be questioned, whether the mimic monarchy of Lord Baltimore should be permitted to continue? When hereditary power had ceased in the mother country, might it properly exist in the colony? It seemed uncertain, if the proprietary could maintain his position; and the scrupulous puritans hesitated to take an unqualified oath of fealty, with which they might be unable to comply.[2] Englishmen were no longer lieges of a sovereign, but members of a commonwealth; and, but for the claims of Baltimore, Maryland would equally enjoy the benefits of republican liberty. Great as was the

[1] Bacon, 1650, c. xxiii.   [2] Strong's Babylon's Fall, p. 1, 2.

MARYLAND IN THE TIMES OF THE COMMONWEALTH. 279

temptation to assert independence, it would not have prevailed, could the peace of the province have been maintained. But who, it might well be asked, was the sovereign of Maryland? The distinction was claimed by four separate aspirants. Virginia[1] was ever ready to revive its rights to jurisdiction beyond the Potomac, and Clayborne had already excited attention by his persevering opposition;[2] Charles II., incensed against Lord Baltimore for his adhesion to the rebels and his toleration of schismatics, had issued a commission to Sir William Davenant;[3] Stone was the active deputy of Lord Baltimore; and parliament had already appointed its commissioners.

In the ordinance[4] for the reduction of the rebellious colonies, Maryland had not been included; if Charles II. had been inconsiderately proclaimed by a temporary officer, the offence had been expiated;[5] and, as assurances had been given of the fidelity of Stone to the commonwealth, no measures against his authority were designed.[6] Yet the commissioners were instructed to reduce "all the plantations within the bay of the Chesapeake;"[7] and it must be allowed, that Clayborne might find in the ambiguous phrase, intended, perhaps, to include only the settlements of Virginia, a sufficient warrant to stretch his authority to Maryland. The commissioners accordingly entered the province; and, after much altercation with

1650.

1651.
Sept.

1652.

---

[1] Hazard, v. i. p. 620—630; McMahon, p. 207, 208.
[2] Bacon, 1650, c. xvii.
[3] Langford's Refutation, p. 3, 4; Grahame's U. S. v. i. p. 117, 118.
[4] Hazard, v. i. p. 636.
[5] McMahon, p. 203.
[6] Langford, p. 6 and 7.
[7] Thurloe, v. i. p. 198; Hazard, v. i. p. 557.

CHAP. VII.

1652.
June.

1653.
April.

1654.

July.

Stone, depriving him of his commission from Lord Baltimore, and changing the officers of the province, they at last established a compromise. Stone, with three of his council, was permitted to retain the executive power till further instructions should arrive from England.[1]

The dissolution of the Long Parliament threatened a change in the political condition of Maryland; for, it was argued, the only authority, under which Bennett and Clayborne had acted, had expired with the body, from which it was derived.[2] In consequence, Stone, Hatton and his friends, re-instated the rights of Lord Baltimore in their integrity; displacing all officers of the contrary party, they introduced the old council, and declared the condition of the colony, as settled by Bennett and Clayborne, to have been a state of rebellion.[3] A railing proclamation to that effect was published to the puritans in their church meeting.

The measures were rash and ill-advised. No sooner did Clayborne and his colleague learn the new revolution, than they hastened to Maryland; where it was immediately obvious, that they could be met by no effectual resistance. Unable to persuade Stone, "in a peaceable and loving way," to abandon the claims of Lord Baltimore, they yet compelled him to surrender his commission and the government into their hands. This being done,

---

[1] Strong's Babylon's Fall, p. 2 and 3; Langford's Reply, p. 7 and 8; Bacon's Preface; McMahon, p. 204, 205; Chalmers, p. 122.

[2] Langford, p. 10; Strong, p. 3.

[3] Strong, p. 3; Hazard, v. i. p. 626. The date is there 1653. It was in 1654, as Strong asserts. McMahon, p. 206, cites Hazard doubtingly. Bacon, 1654, c. xlv.

MARYLAND DURING THE PROTECTORATE.

Clayborne and Bennett appointed a board of ten commissioners, to whom the administration of Maryland was entrusted.[1]

Intolerance followed upon this arrangement; for parties in Maryland had necessarily become identified with religious sects. The puritans, ever the friends of popular liberty, hostile to monarchy, and equally so to a hereditary proprietary, contended earnestly for every civil liberty; but had neither the gratitude to respect the rights of the government, by which they had been received and fostered, nor magnanimity to continue the toleration, to which alone they were indebted for their residence in the colony. A new assembly, convened at Patuxent, acknowledged the authority of Cromwell, but it also exasperated the whole Romish party by their wanton disfranchisement. An act concerning religion, confirmed the freedom of conscience, provided the liberty were not extended to "popery, prelacy,[2] or licentiousness" of opinion. Yet Cromwell, remote from the scene of strife, was not betrayed by his religious prejudices into an approbation of the ungrateful decree. He commanded the commissioners "not to busy themselves about religion, but to settle the civil government."[3]

When the proprietary heard of these proceedings, he felt indignant at the want of firmness, which his lieutenant had displayed.[4] The pretended assembly was esteemed "illegal, mutinous and usurped;" and

---

[1] Strong, p. 3, 4, 5; Langford, p. 11, 12; McMahon, p. 206; Chalmers, p. 223.
[2] Bacon, 1654, c. iv.
[3] Chalmers, p. 236.
[4] Hazard, v. i. p. 629; Strong.

Lord Baltimore and his officers determined, under the powers, which the charter conferred, to vindicate his supremacy.[1] In the latter end of January, on the arrival of a friendly ship, it was immediately noised abroad, that his patent had been confirmed by the protector; and orders began again to be issued for the entire restoration of his authority. Papists and others[2] were commissioned by Stone to raise men in arms; and the leaders of this new revolution were able to surprise and get possession of the provincial records. They marched, also, from Patuxent towards Anne Arundel, the chief seat of the republicans, who insisted on naming it Providence. The inhabitants of Providence and their partisans gathered together with the zeal that belongs to the popular party, and with the courage in which puritans were never deficient. Vain were proclamations, promises and threats. The party of Stone was attacked and utterly discomfited; he himself was taken prisoner; and would have been put to death but for the respect and affection borne him by the soldiers, on whom his execution was enjoined. He was kept a prisoner during most of the administration of Cromwell.[3]

A friend to Lord Baltimore, then in the province, begged of the protector no other boon, than that he would " condescend to settle the country by declaring

[1] Langford, p. 9, 10.
[2] Strong, p. 5.
[3] On this occasion, were published, Strong's Babylon's Fall in Maryland, and Langford's Just and Clear Refutation of a scandalous pamphlet, entitled, Babylon's Fall in Maryland, 1655. Both are minute, and, in the main, agree. Compare Chalmers; McMahon, p. 207; Hazard, v. i. p. 621 —628, and 629, 630; Bacon's Pref.

MARYLAND DURING THE PROTECTORATE.

his determinate will."[1] And yet the same causes, which led Cromwell to neglect the internal concerns of Virginia, compelled him to pay but little attention to the disturbances in Maryland. On the one hand, no steps were taken to invalidate the patent, in right of which the proprietary might exercise the government; on the other hand, Cromwell corresponded with his commissioners, and expressed no displeasure at their exercise of power.[2] The right to the jurisdiction of Maryland remained, therefore, a disputed question. Fuller, Preston and the others, appointed by Clayborne, actually possessed authority; while Lord Baltimore commissioned[3] Josias Fendall to appear as his lieutenant. Fendall had, the preceding year, been engaged in exciting an insurrection, under pretence of instructions from Stone; he now appeared as an open insurgent. But he was unsuccessful; and little is known of his "disturbance," except that it occasioned a heavy public expenditure.[4]

Yet the confidence of Lord Baltimore was continued to Fendall, who received anew an appointment to the government of the province. For a season, there was a divided rule; Fendall was acknowledged by the catholic party in the city of St. Mary's; and the commissioners were sustained by the puritans of St. Leonard's. At length, the conditions of a compromise were settled; and the government of the whole province was surrendered to the agent of the proprietary. Permission to retain arms; an indem-

CHAP. VII.
1655.
1656. July 10.
1657. Sept.
Nov. 18.
1658.
Mar. 24.

[1] Barber, in Langford, p. 15.
[2] Thurloe, v. i. p. 724, and v. iv. p. 55. Hazard, v. i. p. 594, quotes but one of the rescripts.
[3] McMahon, p. 211.
[4] Bacon, 1657, c. viii.

nity for arrears; relief from the oath of fealty; and a confirmation of the acts and orders of the recent puritan assemblies; these were the terms of the surrender, and prove the influence of the puritans.[1]

Fendall was a weak and impetuous man, but I cannot find any evidence, that his administration was stained by injustice. Most of the statutes enacted during his government, were thought worthy of being perpetuated. The death of Cromwell left the condition of England uncertain, and might well diffuse a gloom through the counties of Maryland. For ten years the unhappy province had been distracted by dissensions, of which the root had consisted in the claims, that Baltimore had always asserted, and had never been able to establish. What should now be done? England was in a less settled condition than ever. Would the son of Cromwell permanently hold the place of his father? Would Charles II. be restored? Did new revolutions await the colony? new strifes with Virginia, the protector, the proprietary, the king? Wearied with long convulsions, a general assembly saw no security but in asserting the power of the people, and constituting the government on the expression of their will. Accordingly, just one day before that memorable session of Virginia, when the people of the ancient dominion adopted a similar system of independent legislation, the representatives of Maryland, convened in the house of Robert Slye, voted themselves

---

[1] Bacon's Preface, and 1658, c. Proceedings, in McMahon, note i.; McMahon, p. 211, and Council to p. 14.

a lawful assembly, without dependence on any other power in the province. The burgesses of Virginia had assumed to themselves the election of the council; the burgesses of Maryland refused to acknowledge the rights of the body claiming to be an upper house. In Virginia, Berkeley yielded to the public will; in Maryland, Fendall permitted the power of the people to be proclaimed. The representatives of Maryland, having thus successfully settled the government, and hoping for tranquillity after years of storms, passed an act, making it felony to disturb the order which they had established. No authority would henceforward be recognized, except the assembly, and the king of England.[1] The light of peace promised to dawn upon the province.

Thus was Maryland, like Virginia, at the epoch of the restoration, in full possession of liberty, based upon the practical assertion of the sovereignty of the people. Like Virginia, it had so nearly completed its institutions, that, till the epoch of its final separation from England, it hardly made any further advances towards freedom and independence.

Men love liberty, even if it be turbulent; and the colony had increased, and flourished, and grown rich, in spite of domestic dissensions. Its population, in 1660, is variously estimated at eight thousand,[2] and at twelve thousand.[3]

---

[1] Bacon, 1659-60; McMahon, p. 212; Chalmers, p. 224, 225; Griffith, p. 18; Ebeling, v. v. p. 709. The German historian is remarkably temperate. All the others have been unjust to the legislature of Maryland.

[2] Fuller's Worthies, printed in 1662.

[3] Chalmers, p. 226.

CHAPTER VIII.

THE PILGRIMS.

THE settlement of New-England was a result of the Reformation;[1] not of the contest between the new opinions and the authority of Rome, but of implacable differences between protestant dissenters and the established Anglican church.

Who will venture to measure the consequences of actions by the humility or the remoteness of their origin? The mysterious influence of that power, which enchains the destinies of states, overruling the decisions of sovereigns and the forethought of statesmen, often deduces the greatest events from the least commanding causes. A Genoese adventurer, discovering America, changed the commerce of the world; an obscure German, inventing the printing-press, rendered possible the universal diffusion of increased intelligence; an Augustin monk, denouncing indulgences, introduced a schism in religion and changed the foundations of European politics; a young French refugee, skilled alike in theology and civil law, in the duties of magistrates and the dialectics of religious controversy, entering the republic of Geneva, and

---

[1] Heeren on the Reformation, Historische Werke, v. i. p. 102, 103.

conforming its ecclesiastical discipline to the principles of republican simplicity, established a party, of which Englishmen became members, and New-England the asylum. The enfranchisement of the mind from religious despotism led directly to inquiries into the nature of civil government; and the doctrines of popular liberty, which sheltered their infancy in the wildernesses of the newly discovered continent, within the short space of two centuries have infused themselves into the life-blood of every rising state from Labrador to Chili, established outposts at the mouth of the Oregon and in Liberia, and, making a proselyte of enlightened France, have disturbed all the ancient governments of Europe, and awakened the public mind to resistless action from the shores of Portugal to the palaces of the Czars.

The trading company of the west of England, incorporated in the same patent[1] with Virginia, possessed too narrow resources or too little enterprize for success in establishing colonies. The Spaniards, affecting an exclusive right of navigation in the seas of the new hemisphere, captured and confiscated a vessel,[2] which Popham, the chief justice of England, and Gorges, the governor of Plymouth, had, with some others, equipped for discovery. But a second and almost simultaneous expedition from Bristol encountered no disasters; and the voyagers, on their return, increased public confidence, by re-

---

[1] See above, p. 137; Chalmers, p. 79.
[2] Purchas, v. iv. p. 1827 and 1832, and ff.; Gorges' Briefe Naration, c. iv. p. 4—6; Prince's N. E. Chronology, p. 113, 114; ii. Mass. Historical Collections, v. ix. p. 3, 4.

CHAP. VIII.

newing the favorable reports of the country, which they had visited.[1] The spirit of adventure was not suffered to slumber; the lord chief justice displayed persevering vigor; for his honor was interested in the success of the company, which his influence had contributed to establish; Gorges,[2] the companion and friend of Raleigh, was still reluctant to surrender his sanguine hopes of fortune and domains in America;

1607. and, in the next year, two ships were despatched to Northern Virginia, commanded by Raleigh Gilbert, and bearing emigrants for a plantation under the presidency of George Popham.[3] After a tedious

Aug. 8.
voyage, the adventurers reached the coast of America near the mouth of the Kennebec; and, offering public thanks to God for their safety, began their settlement under the auspices of religion, with a government, framed, as if for a permanent colony. Rude cabins, a storehouse, and some slight fortifica-

Dec. 5.
tions were rapidly prepared, and the ships sailed for England, leaving forty-five emigrants in the plantation, which was named St. George. But the winter was intensely cold; the natives, at first friendly, became restless; the storehouse caught fire and part of the provisions was consumed; the emigrants grew weary of their solitude; they lost Popham, their president, "the only one[4] of the company that died

---

[1] Gorges, c. v. p. 6.
[2] The name of Gorges occurs in Hume, c. xliv.; Lingard, v. viii. p. 449. Compare Belknap's Biography, v. i. p. 347—354. Gorges was ever a sincere royalist.
[3] Gorges, c. vii. viii. ix. p. 8—11; Purchas, v. iv. p. 1828; Smith, v. ii. p. 173—175; Belknap's Biog. v. i. p. 350—354; i. Mass. Hist. Coll. v. i. p. 251, 252; Williamson's History of Maine, v. i. p. 197 —203; Prince, p. 116, 117, 118, 119; Hubbard's N. E. p. 36, 37.
[4] Chalmers, p. 79, writes: "*they looked at the numerous graves of*

COLONY AT SAGADAHOC.

there;" the ships, which revisited the settlement with supplies, brought news of the death of the chief justice, the most vigorous friend of the settlement in England; and Gilbert, the sole in command at St. George, had, by the decease of his brother, become heir to an estate, which invited his presence. So the plantation was abandoned; and the colonists, returning to England, "did coyne many excuses," and sought to conceal their own deficiency of spirit by spreading exaggerated accounts of the rugged poverty of the soil, and the inhospitable severity of the climate.[1] But the Plymouth company was dissatisfied with their pusillanimity; Gorges esteemed it a weakness to be frightened at a blast. The idea of a settlement in these northern latitudes was no longer terriffic. The American fisheries also constituted a prosperous and well established business. Three years had elapsed, since the French had been settled in their huts at Port Royal; and the ships, which carried the English from the Kennebec, were on the ocean at the same time with the little squadron of the French, who succeeded in building Quebec, the very summer in which Maine was deserted. Indeed, but a few seasons passed away, before the crew of a British vessel had the hardihood to defy an American winter at Port Nelson, in Hudson's Bay.

CHAP. VIII.

1608.

1612.

The fisheries and the fur-trade were not relinquished; vessels were annually employed in traffic

---

the dead;" drawing on his imagination for embellishments. Compare ii. Mass. Hist. Coll. v. ix. p. 4. Chalmers, p. 79, names among those who died, "Gilbert, their chief." An error.

[1] Sir W. Alexander's Map of New-England, p. 30.

290   JOHN SMITH IN NEW-ENGLAND.

CHAP. VIII.

1614. April

with the Indians; and once,[1] at least, perhaps oftener, a part of a ship's company remained during a winter on the American coast. But new hopes were awakened, when Smith, who had already obtained distinction in Virginia, and who had, with rare sagacity, discovered, and, with unceasing firmness, asserted, that colonization was the true policy of England, with two ships, set sail for the coast, north of the lands granted by the Virginia patent. The expedition was a private[2] adventure of "four merchants of London and himself;" and was very successful. The freights were profitable; the health of the mariners did not suffer; and the whole voyage was accomplished in less than seven months. While the sailors were busy with their hooks and lines, Smith examined the shores from the Penobscot to Cape Cod, prepared a map of the coast,[3] and named the country New-England, a title which Prince Charles confirmed. The French could boast with truth, that New-France had been colonized, before New-England obtained a name; Port Royal was older than Plymouth, Quebec than Boston. Yet the voyage was not free from crime. After Smith had departed for England, Thomas Hunt, the master of the second ship, kidnapped a large party of Indians, and, sailing for Spain, sold "the poor innocents" into slavery. It is singular, how good is educed from evil; one of the number, escaping from captivity,

[1] Gorges, c. x. p. 12; Prince, p. 119.
[2] Chalmers, p. 80, erroneously attributes the expedition to the Plymouth company. See Smith, in iii. Mass. Hist. Coll. v. iii. p. 19; and in his Historie, v. ii. p. 175, 176; Purchas, v. iv. 1828.
[3] Map, in iii. Mass. Historical Collections, v. iii.

made his way to London, and, in 1619, was restored to his own country, where he subsequently became an interpreter for English emigrants.[1]

Encouraged by commercial success, Smith next endeavored, in the employment of Sir Ferdinando Gorges, and of friends in London, members of the Plymouth company, to establish a colony. Sixteen men[2] were all, whom the adventurers destined for the occupation of New-England. The attempt was unsuccessful. Smith was forced by extreme tempests to return. Again renewing his enterprize, he suffered from the treachery of his companions, and was, at last, intercepted by French pirates. His ship was taken away; he himself escaped alone, in an open boat, from the harbor of Rochelle.[3] The severest privations in a new settlement would have been less wearisome, than the labors, which his enthusiasm now prompted him to undertake. Having published a map and a description of New-England, he spent many months[4] in visiting the merchants and gentry of the west of England to excite their zeal for enterpize in America; he proposed to the cities, mercantile profits, to be realized in short and safe voyages; to the noblemen, vast dominions; from men of small means, his earnestness concealed the hard-

CHAP. VIII.

1615.

1617.

---

[1] Smith's Description of New-England, p. 47; Smith's Generall Historie, v. ii. p. 176; Morton's Memorial, p. 55, and Davis on Morton; Prince, p. 132; Mourt's Relation, in i. M. H. Coll. v. viii. p. 238; Plantation of N. England, in ii. Mass. Historical Collections, v. ix. p. 6 and 7.

[2] Williamson's Maine, v. i. p. 212. The learned and very valuable historian of Maine confounds this design of Smith to found a colony with his previous voyage for trade and discovery.

[3] Smith, v. ii. p. 205—215; and in iii. M. Hist. Coll. v. iii. p. 20, 21.

[4] Smith, v. ii. p. 218.

ships of emigrants, and, upon the dark ground, drew a lively picture of the rapid advancement of fortune by colonial industry, of the abundance of game, the delights of unrestrained liberty; the pleasures to be derived from "angling and crossing the sweet air from isle to isle, over the silent streams of a calm sea."[1] The attention of the western company was excited; they began to form vast plans of colonization; Smith was appointed admiral of the country for life; and a renewal of the letters patent, with powers analogous to those possessed by the southern company, became an object of eager solicitation.

1618. But a new charter was not obtained without vigorous opposition. "Much difference there was betwixt the Londoners and the Westerlings,"[2] since each was striving to engross all the profits to be derived from America; while the interests of the nation were boldly sustained by others, who were desirous, that no monopoly should be conceded to either company. The remonstrances of the Virginia corporation[3] and a transient regard for the rights of the country, could delay, but not defeat a measure, that was sustained by the personal favorites of the monarch.

1620. Nov. 3. After two years' entreaty, the ambitious adventurers gained every thing which they had solicited; and King James issued to forty of his subjects, some of them members of his household and his government, the most wealthy and powerful of

[1] Smith's Generall Historie, v. ii. p. 201. 84, 85; Gorges; Purchas, v. iv. p. 1830, 1831.
[2] Smith, in iii. Mass. Hist. Collections, v. iii. p. 21; Hubbard, p. [3] Stith's Virginia, p. 185; Hazard, v. i. p. 390.

the English nobility, a patent,[1] which, in American annals, and, even in the history of the world, has but one parallel. The adventurers and their successors were incorporated as "The Council established at Plymouth, in the county of Devon, for the planting, ruling, ordering and governing New-England, in America." The territory, conferred on the patentees in absolute property, with unlimited jurisdiction, the sole powers of legislation, the appointment of all officers and all forms of government, extended, in breadth, from the fortieth to the forty-eighth degree of north latitude, and, in length, from the Atlantic to the Pacific; that is to say, nearly all the inhabited British possessions to the north of the United States, all New-England, New-York, half of New-Jersey, very nearly all Pennsylvania, and the whole of the country to the west of these states, comprising, and, at the time, believed to comprise,[2] much more than a million of square miles, and capable of sustaining far more than two hundred millions of inhabitants, were, by a single signature of King James, given away to a corporation within the realm, composed of but forty individuals. The grant was absolute and exclusive; it conceded the land and islands; the rivers and the harbors; the mines and the fisheries. Without the leave of the council of Plymouth, not a ship might sail into a harbor from Newfoundland to the latitude of Philadelphia; not a

CHAP. VIII.
1620.

---

[1] Trumbull's Connecticut, v. i. p. 546—567; Hazard, v. i. p. 103—118; Baylies, v. i. p. 160—185. Compare Hubbard, c. xxx.; Chalmers, p. 81—85.

[2] Smith, in iii. Mass. Hist. Coll. v. iii. p. 31, estimates the land at one million one hundred and twenty thousand square miles; a computation far below the truth.

skin might be purchased in the interior; not a fish might be caught on the coast; not an emigrant might tread the soil. No regard was shown for the liberties of those, who might become inhabitants of the colony; they were to be ruled, without their own consent, by the corporation in England. The patent favored only the cupidity of the proprietors; and possessed all the worst features of a commercial monopoly. A royal proclamation was soon issued, enforcing its provisions; and a revenue was already considered certain from an onerous duty on all tunnage, employed in the American fisheries.[1] The results, which grew out of the concession of this charter, form a new proof, if any were wanting, of that mysterious connexion of events, by which Providence leads to ends, that human councils had not conceived. The patent left the emigrants at the mercy of the unrestrained power of the corporation; and it was under concessions from that plenary power, confirmed, indeed, by the English monarch, that institutions, the most favorable to colonial liberty, were established. The patent yielded every thing to the avarice of the corporation; the very extent of the grant rendered it of little value. The jealousy of the English nation, incensed at the concession of vast monopolies by the exercise of the royal prerogative, immediately prompted the house of commons to question the validity of the grant;[2] and the French nation, whose traders had been annually sending

[1] Smith, in iii. Mass. Hist. Coll. v. iii. p. 32; Smith's Generall Historie, v. ii. p. 263.

[2] Chalmers, p. 100—102; Parliamentary Debates, 1620-1, v. i. p. 260. 318, 319.

home rich freights of furs, while the English were disputing about charters and commissions, derided the tardy action of the British monarch in bestowing lands and privileges, which their own sovereign, seventeen years before, had appropriated.[1] The patent was designed to hasten plantations, in the belief that men would eagerly throng to the coast and put themselves under the protection of the council; and, in fact, adventurers were delayed through fear of infringing the rights of a powerful company.[2] While the English monopolists were wrangling about their exclusive privileges, the first permanent colony on the soil of New-England was established without the knowledge of the corporation, and without the aid of King James.

The Reformation in England, an event which had been long and gradually prepared among the people by the opinions and followers of Wickliffe, and in the government by increasing and successful resistance to the usurpations of ecclesiastical jurisdiction, was at length abruptly established during the reign and in conformity with the passions of a despotic monarch. The acknowledgement of the right of private judgment,[3] far from being the cause of the separation from Rome was one of its latest fruits. Luther was more dogmatical than his opponents; though the deep philosophy, with which his mind

---

[1] Smith, in iii. Mass. Historical Collections, v. iii. p. 20.
[2] Ibid, p. 32; Smith's Generall Historie, v. ii. p. 263.
[3] Under Edward VI. intolerance sanctioned by law. See Rymer, v. xv. p. 182. 250, under Elizabeth. Rymer, v. xv. p. 740 and 741. Compare Lingard, v. vii. p. 286, 287; Hallam's Constitutional History of England, v. i. p. 130, 131, 132, 133.

296   THE REFORMATION IN ENGLAND.

CHAP. VIII.
1522.

was imbued, repelled the use of violence to effect conversion in religion. He was wont to protest against propagating reform by persecution and massacres; and, with wise moderation, an admirable knowledge of human nature, a familiar and almost ludicrous quaintness of expression, he would deduce from his great principle of justification by faith alone the sublime doctrine of the freedom of conscience.[1]

1553. Yet Calvin, many years after, anxiously engaged in dispelling ancient superstitions, was still fearful of the results of sceptical reform, and, in his opinions on heresy and its punishment, shared the unhappy error of his time.[2]

In England, so far was the freedom of private inquiry from being recognized as a right, the means
1534. of forming a judgment on religious subjects was denied. A law[3] which prohibited the sale of bound books imported from the continent, excluded the writings of the reformers, and insulated England from the defenders of the protestant cause. The
Nov. 4. act of supremacy,[4] which effectually severed the

---

[1] Nollem vi et cæde pro evangelio certari. Compare the passages from Luther's Seven Sermons, delivered in March, 1522, at Wittenberg, quoted in Planck's Geschichte des Protestantischen Lehrbegriffs, b. ii. p. 68—72. Summa summarum! Predigen will ichs, sagen will ichs, schreiben will ichs, aber zwingen, dringen mit Gewalt will ich niemand; denn der Glaube will willig, ungenöthigt und ohne Zwang angenommen werden. I have quoted these words, which are in harmony with Luther's doctrines and his works, as a reply to those,

who, like Turner, in his History, v. iii. p. 135, erroneously charge the great German reformer with favoring persecution.

[2] Servetus was burned, October 27, 1553.

[3] 25. Henry VIII. c. xv.; Statutes of the Realm, folio, 1817, v. iii. p. 456. It purports to be a tariff law, made to protect "the expert in the craft of printing and binding" against foreign competition.

[4] 25. Henry VIII. c. xix. xx. xxi. Statutes v. iii. p. 460—471.; 26. Henry VIII. c. i. iii. xiii. Statutes, v. iii. p. 492, 493—499. 508, 509.

English nation from the Roman see, contained no clause, favorable to religious liberty. The king of England was now the pope in his own dominions; and heresy was still accounted the greatest of all crimes.[1] The right of correcting errors of religious faith became, by the suffrage of parliament, a branch of the royal prerogative; and, as the active minds of the people were continually proposing new schemes of doctrine, a law, alike arrogant in its pretensions and vindictive in its menaces, was, after great opposition in parliament,[2] enacted "for abolishing diversity of opinions."[3] All the Roman Catholic doctrines were asserted except the supremacy of Rome. The pope could praise Henry VIII. for his orthodoxy, while he excommunicated him for his disobedience. He commended to the wavering emperor the English sovereign as a model for the soundness of his belief, and anathematized him only for his contumacy.[4] It was Henry's pride, to defy the authority of the Roman bishop, and yet to enforce the doctrines of the Roman church. He was as tenacious of his reputation for catholic orthodoxy, as of his claim to spiritual dominion. He disdained submission, and detested heresy.

Nor was Henry VIII. slow to sustain his new prerogatives. He rejected the advice of the commons,

---

Lingard, v. iv. p. 266—270, and v. vi. p. 281—283.
[1] Henry's Great Britain, v. xii. p. 53; Turner's England, v. ii. p. 349—353; Mackintosh's England, v. ii. p. 147—150.
[2] Strype's Memorials, v. i. p. 352.
[3] 31. Henry VIII., c. xiv. Statutes, v. iii. p. 739—743; Lingard, v. vi. p. 380—386, Bossuet, Hist. des Variations, l. vii. c. xxiv.—xl.; Henry's Great Britain, v. xii. p. 84.
[4] Fra Paolo, l. i. v. i. p. 82.

CHAP. VIII. as of "brutes and inexpert folks," of men, as unfit to advise him, as "blind men are to judge of colors.'" According to ancient usage, no sentence of death, awarded by the ecclesiastical courts, could be carried into effect, until a writ had been obtained from the king. The regulation had been adopted in a spirit of mercy, securing to the temporal authorities the power of restraining persecution.[2] The heretic might appeal from the atrocity of the priest to the mercy of the sovereign. But now what hope could remain, when the two authorities were united; and the law, which had been enacted as a protection of the subject, was become the powerful instrument of tyranny! The establishment of the English church under the king, was sustained by inexorable persecutions. No virtue, no eminence, conferred security. Not the forms of worship merely, but the minds of men were declared subordinate to the government; faith, not less than ceremony, was to vary with the acts of parliament. Death was denounced against the catholic, who denied the king's supremacy, and the Lutheran, who doubted his creed. Had Luther been an Englishman, he himself would probably have perished by fire.[3] Henry always adhered to his old religion;[4] he believed its most extravagant doctrines to the last, and died in the Roman, rather than in the protestant faith.[5] But the awakening intelligence of a great nation could not be terrified into a passive lethargy.

[1] Lord Herbert's Henry VIII. p. 418, 419.
[2] Neal's Puritans, v. i. p. 55.
[3] Turner's England, v. iii. p. 140.
[4] Turner's England, v. ii. p. 352.
[5] Bossuet, Hist. des Variations, l. viii. c. iii. iv. and xxiv.—xl; Henry's Gt. Britain, v. xii. p. 107.

The environs of the court displayed no resistance to the capricious monarch; a subservient parliament yielded him absolute authority in religion;[1] but the public mind was roused to independence.

The accession of Edward VI. led the way to the establishment of protestantism in England, and, at the same time, gave life to the germs of the difference, which was eventually to divide the English. A change in the reformation had already been effected among the Swiss, and especially at Geneva. Luther had based his reform upon the sublime but simple truth, which lies at the basis of morals; the paramount value of character and purity of conscience; the superiority of right dispositions over ceremonial exactness; or, as he expressed it, justification by faith alone. But he hesitated to deny the real presence, and was indifferent to the observance of external ceremonies. Calvin, with sterner dialectics, sanctioned by the influence of the purest life, and by his power as the ablest writer of his age, attacked the Roman doctrines respecting the communion, and esteemed as a commemoration the rite, which the catholics reverenced as a sacrifice. Luther acknowledged princes as his protectors, and, in the ceremonies of worship, favored magnificence as an aid to devotion; Calvin was the guide of Swiss republics, and avoided, in their churches, all appeals to the senses as a crime against religion. Luther resisted the Roman church for its immorality; Calvin for its idolatry. Luther exposed the folly of

[1] 37. Henry VIII. c. xvii. Statutes, v. iii. p. 1009.

superstition; Calvin shrunk from its criminality with impatient horror. Luther permitted the cross and the taper, pictures and images, as things of indifference; Calvin demanded a spiritual worship in its utmost purity.

The reign of Edward, giving safety to protestants, soon brought to light, that both sects of the reformed church existed in England. The one party, sustained by Cranmer, desired moderate reforms; the other, countenanced by the protector, were the implacable adversaries of the ceremonies of the Roman church. It was still attempted to enforce[1] uniformity by menaces of persecution; but the most offensive of the Roman doctrines were expunged from the liturgy. The tendency of the public mind favored a greater simplicity in the forms of devotion; the spirit of inquiry was active; not a rite of established worship, not a point in church government, escaped unexamined; not a vestment nor a ceremony remained, of which the propriety had not been denied. A more complete reform was demanded; and the friends of the established liturgy expressed in the prayer-book itself a wish for its furtherance.[2] The party, strongest in numbers, pleaded expediency for retaining much that had been sanctioned by ancient usage; while abhorrence of superstition excited the other party to demand the boldest innovations. The austere principle was now announced, that not even a

---

[1] Lingard, v. vii. p. 286, 287; 2 and 3 Edward VI. c. i. Statutes, v. iv. 36—39; Rymer, v. xv. 181—183, and 250—252.

[2] Neal's Puritans, v. i. p. 121; Neal's History of New-England, v. i. p. 51.

ceremony should be tolerated, unless it was enjoined by the word of God.¹ And this was puritanism. The church of England, at least, in its ceremonial part, was established by an act of parliament, or a royal ordinance; puritanism, zealous for independence, admitted no voucher but the bible; a fixed rule, which they would allow neither parliament, nor hierarchy, nor king to interpret. The puritans adhered to the established church as far as their interpretations of the bible seemed to warrant; but no farther, not even in things of indifference. They would yield nothing in religion to the temporal sovereign; they would retain nothing, that seemed a relic of the religion, which they had renounced. In these views they were sustained by the reformers of the continent. Bucer and Peter Martyr² both complained of the backwardness of the reformation in England; Calvin wrote in the same strain.³ When Hooper, who had gone into exile in the latter years of Henry VIII., was appointed bishop of Gloucester, he, for a time, refused⁴ to be consecrated in the vestments, which the law required; and his refusal marks the era, when the puritans first existed as a separate party. They demanded a thorough reform; the established church desired to check the propensity to

1550.
July.

---

¹ So Cartwright, a few years later, in his Reply to Whitgift, p. 27: "In matters of the church, there may be nothing done but by the word of God."

In his Sec. Reply, 1675, p. 81: "It is not enough, that the Scripture speaketh not against them, unless it speak for them."

² Strype's Memo. v. ii. c. xxviii.
³ Hallam's England, v. i. p. 140.
⁴ Strype's Memorials, v. ii. p. 226, and Repository, v. ii. p. 118—132; Hallam's England, v. i. p. 141; Neal's Puritans, v. i. p. 108—113; Prince, p. 282—307. Prince has written with great diligence and distinctness.

change. The strict party repelled all union with the catholics; the politic party aimed at conciliating their compliance. The churchmen, with, perhaps, a wise moderation, differed from the ancient forms as little as possible, and readily adopted the use of things indifferent; the puritans could not sever themselves too widely from the Roman usages, and sought glaring occasions to display their antipathy. The surplice and the square cap, for several generations, remained things of importance; for they became the badges of a party. They were rejected as the livery of superstition. The unwilling use of them was evidence of religious servitude.

The reign of Mary involved both parties in danger; but they, whose principles wholly refused communion with Rome, were placed in the greatest peril. Rogers and Hooper, the first martyrs of protestant England, were puritans; and it may be remarked, that, while Cranmer, the head and founder of the English church, desired, almost to the last, by delays, recantations and entreaties, to save himself from the horrid death to which he was doomed, the puritan martyrs never sought, by concessions, to escape the flames. For them, compromise was itself apostacy. The offer of pardon could not induce Hooper to waver; nor the pains of a lingering death impair his fortitude. He suffered by a very slow fire; at length, says the faithful narrator, he died as quietly as a child in his bed.

A large part of the English clergy returned to their submission to the see of Rome; others firmly adhered to the reformation, which they had adopted from conviction; and very many, who had taken advantage of the laws[1] of Edward, sanctioning the marriage of the clergy, had, in their wives and children, given hostages for their fidelity to the protestant cause. Multitudes, therefore, hurried into exile to escape the grasp of vindictive bigotry; but even in foreign lands, two parties among the emigrants were visible; and the sympathies of a common exile could not immediately eradicate the rancor of religious divisions. The one party[2] aimed at renewing abroad the forms of discipline, which had been sanctioned by the English parliaments in the reign of Edward; the puritans, on the contrary, endeavored to sweeten exile by a complete emancipation from the ceremonies, which they had reluctantly observed. The sojourning in Frankfort was embittered by the anger of consequent divisions; but Time, the great calmer of the human passions, softened the asperities of controversy; and a reconciliation of the two parties was prepared by concessions[3] to the puritans. For the circumstances of their abode on the continent were well adapted to strengthen the influence of the stricter sect. While the companions of their exile had, with the most bitter intolerance, been rejected by Denmark and Northern Germany,[4] the English emi-

[1] 2 and 3 Edward VI. c. xxi., 5 and 6 Edward VI. c. xii. in Statutes, v. iv. p. 67, and 146, 147; Strype's Memorials, v. iii. p. 108.
[2] Discourse of the Troubles in Frankfort.
[3] Ibid, edition of 1642, p. 160, 161, 162, 163. "We will joyne with you to be suitors for the reformation and abolishing of all offensive ceremonies." Prince, p. 287, 288. The documents refute the contrary opinion expressed by Hallam, Const. Hist. v. i. p. 233.
[4] Planck's Geschichte des Pro-

CHAP. VIII.

grants received in Switzerland the kindest welcome; their love for the rigorous austerity of a spiritual worship was confirmed by the stern simplicity of the republic; and some of them had enjoyed in Geneva the instructions and the friendship of Calvin.

1558.

On the death of Mary, the puritans returned to England, with still stronger antipathies to the forms of worship and the vestures, which they now repelled as associated with the cruelties of Roman intolerance at home, and which they had seen so successfully rejected by the churches of Switzerland. The pledges, which had been given at Frankfort and Geneva, to promote further reforms, were redeemed.[1] But the controversy did not remain a dispute about ceremonies; it was modified by the personal character of the English sovereign, and became identified with the political parties in the state. The first act of parliament in the reign of Elizabeth declared the supremacy[2] of the crown in the state ecclesiastical; and the uniformity of common prayer was soon established under the severest penalties.[3] In these enactments, the common zeal to assert the protestant ascendency, left out of sight the scruples of the puritans.

The early associations of the younger daughter of Henry VIII. led her to respect the faith of the catholics, and to love the magnificence of their worship. She publicly thanked one of her chaplains,

testantischen Lehrbegriffs, b. v. t. ii. p. 35—45, and 69.
[1] Prince, p. 288.
[2] 1 Elizabeth, c. i. Statutes, v. iv. p. 350—355; Hallam's England, v. i. p. 152; Mackintosh, v. iii. p. 45, 46.
[3] 1 Elizabeth, c. ii.; Hallam's England, v. i. p. 153; Mackintosh's England, v. iii. p. 46, 47.

who had asserted the real presence; and, on a revision of the creed of the English church, the tenet of transubstantiation was no longer expressly rejected. To calm the fury of religious intolerance, let it be forever remembered, that the doctrine of the real presence, which, by the statutes of the realm in the reign of Edward VI., Englishmen were punished for believing, and in that of Henry VIII. were burned at the stake for denying, was in the reign of Elizabeth left undecided, as a question of national indifference. She long struggled to retain images, the crucifix, and tapers in her private chapel; she was inclined to offer prayers to the Virgin; she favored the invocation of saints.[1] She insisted upon the continuance of the celibacy of the clergy, and, during her reign, their marriages took place only by connivance.[2] For several years, she desired and was able to conciliate the catholics into a partial conformity.[3] The puritans denounced concession to the papists, even in things indifferent; but during the reign of her sister, Elizabeth had conformed in all things, and she still retained an attachment for many tenets, that were deemed the most objectionable. Could she, then, favor the party of rigid reform?

Besides the influence of early education, the love of authority would not permit Elizabeth to cherish the new sect among protestants; a sect which had

---

[1] Burnett, part ii. b. iii. No. 6; Heylin, p. 124; Neal's Puritans, v. i. p. 191, 192; Mackintosh, v. iii. p. 161; Hume, c. xlv.; Hallam, v. i. p. 124.
[2] Neal's Puritans, v. i. p. 205, 206; Strype's Parker, p. 107.
[3] Southey's Book of the Church, v. i. p. 257, 258.

risen in defiance of all ordinary powers of the world, and which could justify its existence only on a strong claim to natural liberty.[1] The catholics were friends to monarchy, if not to the monarch; they upheld the forms of regal government, if they were not friends to the person of the queen. But the puritans were the harbingers of a revolution; the hierarchy charged them with seeking a popular state; and Elizabeth openly declared, that they were more perilous than the Romanists.[2] At a time when the readiest mode of reaching the minds of the common people was through the pulpit, and when the preachers would often speak with plainness and homely energy on all the events of the day, their claim to "the liberty of prophesying" was similar to the modern desire for the liberty of the press; and the free exercise of private judgment threatened, not only to disturb the uniformity of the national worship, but to impair the royal authority and erect the dictates of conscience into a tribunal, before which sovereigns might be arraigned.[3] The queen long desired to establish the national religion mid-way between sectarian licentiousness and Roman supremacy; and when her policy in religion was once established, the pride of authority would brook no opposition. By degrees she occupied politically the position of the head of protestantism; catholic sovereigns conspired against her kingdom; the convocation of cardinals proposed measures for her de-

[1] Burke on Taxation.
[2] Southey's Book of the Church, v. ii. p. 294, 295.
[3] Cartwright's Second Reply, p. 158—170.

position; the pope, in his excommunications, urged her subjects to rebellions. Then it was, that, as the Roman Catholics were no longer treated with forbearance, so the queen, struggling, from regard to her safety, to preserve unity among her friends, became inveterately hostile to the puritans, as to mutineers in the camp.

The popular voice was not favorable to a rigorous enforcement of the ceremonies. In the first protestant convocation of the clergy under Elizabeth, though the square cap and the surplice found in the queen a resolute friend, and though there were in the assembly many, who, at heart, preferred the old religion, the proposition to abolish a part of the ceremonies was lost in the lower house by the majority of a single vote.[1] Nearly nine years passed away, before the thirty-nine articles, which were then adopted, were confirmed by parliament; and the act, by which they were finally established, required assent to those articles only, which concern the confession of faith and the doctrine of the sacraments;[2] a limitation, which the puritans interpreted in their favor. The house of commons often displayed an earnest zeal for a further reformation;[3] and its active interference was prevented only by the authority of the queen.

When rigorous orders for enforcing conformity were first issued,[4] the puritans were rather excited

---

[1] Strype's Annals, v. i. p. 338, 339; Hallam's England, v. i. p. 238; Prince, p. 289—293.
[2] Strype's Annals, v. ii. p. 71.
[3] Prince, p. 300.
[4] Strype's Annals, v. i. p. 460, 461; Appendix to Strype's Parker, b. ii. Do. 24.

CHAP. VIII.

1567. June.

1574. June 26.

1575. Feb. 15.

1583.

to defiance than intimidated. Of the London ministers, about thirty refused subscription,[1] and men began to speak openly of a secession from the church.[2] At length, a separate congregation was formed; immediately the government was alarmed; and the leading men and several women were sent to Bridewell for a year.[3] In vain did some of the best English statesmen of the day favor moderation. Grindall had so sincere a reluctance to persecute, that he was himself charged with secretly favoring puritanism. The temper of the times is marked by his reply. He denied the charge, not as a falsehood only, but as a calumny, declaring, that "some incarnate, never-sleeping devil had wrought him this wrong." The charge of leniency he repelled as a slander on his office; and claimed sincerity in persecution as essential to his good name.[4] He succeeded in becoming arch-bishop. Yet Grindall was by nature averse to violence, and when placed at the head of the English clergy, continued till his death to merit the censure of moderation.

---

[1] Strype's Annals, v. i. p. 462.

[2] Grindall, in Prince; Cartwright's Second Reply, p. 38. "Not for hatred to the estates of the church of England, but for love to a better."

How little the early puritans knew of the true results of their doctrines of independence of the state in religious matters, is evident from such passages as these from Cartwright's Second Reply. "𝕳𝖊𝖗𝖊𝖙𝖎𝖐𝖊𝖘 𝖔𝖚𝖌𝖍𝖙𝖊 𝖙𝖔 𝖇𝖊 𝖕𝖚𝖙 𝖙𝖔 𝖉𝖊𝖆𝖙𝖍𝖊 𝖓𝖔𝖜𝖊. 𝕴𝖋 𝖙𝖍𝖎𝖘 𝖇𝖊 𝖉𝖔𝖚𝖇𝖙𝖋𝖊, 𝖆𝖓𝖉 𝖊𝖝𝖙𝖗𝖊𝖒𝖊, 𝕴 𝖆𝖒 𝖈𝖔𝖓𝖙𝖊𝖓𝖙𝖊 𝖙𝖔 𝖇𝖊 𝖘𝖔 𝖈𝖔𝖚𝖓𝖙𝖊𝖉 𝖜𝖎𝖙𝖍𝖊 𝖙𝖍𝖊 𝖍𝖔𝖑𝖞𝖊 𝕲𝖔𝖘𝖙𝖊." p. 115. "𝕴 𝖉𝖊𝖓𝖎𝖊 𝖙𝖍𝖆𝖙 𝖚𝖕𝖕𝖔𝖓 𝖗𝖊- pentance ther oughte to follow any pardon of deathe." p. 116. "𝕿𝖍𝖊 magistrates which punish murther and are loss in punishing the breaches of the first table, begynne at the wronge end." p. 117. The writer continues, displaying the most intense and most consistent bigotry.

[3] Strype's Life of Parker, p. 242; Strype's Grindall, p. 114, 115.

[4] Murdin's State Papers, p. 275, in Mackintosh's Continuator, v. iii. p. 261. Had Prince seen this letter, he would hardly have called Grindall a puritan. See Prince, p. 298.

The puritans, as a body, had avoided a separation from the church. They had desired a reform, and not a schism. When, by espousing a party, a man puts a halter round his neck, and is thrust out from the career of public honor, it is the rash, and the least cautious, and, therefore, the least persevering, who will be the first to display their opinions. So it was in the party of the puritans. There began to grow up among them a class of men, who carried opposition to the church of England to the farthest extreme, and refused to hold communion with a church, of which they condemned the ceremonies and the government. The most noisy advocate of these opinions was Brown, a man of rashness, possessing neither true courage nor constancy; zealous, but fickle; dogmatical, but not profound. He has acquired historical notoriety, because his hot-headed indiscretion urged him to undertake the defence of separation. He suffered much oppression; he was often imprisoned; he was finally compelled to go into exile. The congregation, which he had gathered, and which banished itself with him, was composed of persons hasty and unstable like himself; it was soon dispersed by its own dissensions. Brown eventually purchased a living in the English church by conformity.[1] He could sacrifice his own reputation; "he forsook the Lord, so the Lord forsook him."[2] The principles, of which the intrepid assertion had alone given him distinction, lay deeply

---

[1] Fuller's Church History, b. ix. p. 167, 168 and 169; Neal's Puritans, v. i. p. 376—378.

[2] John Robinson's Justification of Separation, p. 54. A tract of great merit, containing doctrines,

CHAP. VIII.

rooted in the public mind; and, as they had not derived life from his support, they did not suffer from his apostacy.

1582. From this time there was a division among the opponents of the church of England. The puritans acknowledged its merits, but desired its reform; the separatists denounced it as an idolatrous institution, false to Christianity and to truth; the puritans considered it as the temple of God, in which they were to worship, though its altars might need purification; the separatists regarded the truths, which it might profess, as holy things in the custody of the profane, the Ark of the Lord in the hands of Philistines. The enmity between the divisions of the party eventually became bitter. The puritans reproached the Brownists for their ill-advised precipitancy, and were in their turn censured for paltering cowardice. The one party abhorred the ceremonies, which were the bequests of popery; the other party reprobated the establishment itself. The puritans desired to amend; the Brownists, to destroy. The feud became bitter in England, and eventually led to great political results; but the controversy could not be continued beyond the Atlantic, for it required to be nourished by the presence of the hierarchy.

1583. Sept. 23.

The accession of Whitgift marks the epoch of extreme and consistent rigor in the public councils; for the new arch-bishop was sincerely attached to the English church; and, from a regard to religion,

which necessarily led to the assertion of the freedom of conscience. I use the copy, which once belonged to William Bradford, and which is now in the library of Robinson's church.

enforced the conformity, which the queen desired as the best support of her power. He was a strict disciplinarian; and wished to govern the clergy of the realm, as he would rule the members of a college. Subscriptions were now required to points, which before had been eluded;[1] the kingdom rung with the complaints for deprivation; the most learned and diligent of the ministry[2] were driven from their places; and those, who were introduced to read the liturgy, were so ignorant, that few of them could preach. Did men listen to their deprived pastors in the recesses of the forests, the offence, if discovered, was visited by fines and imprisonment. A court of high commission was established for the detection and punishment of non-conformity, and was invested with powers as arbitrary as those of the Spanish inquisitors.[3] Men were obliged to answer, on oath, every question proposed, either against others or against themselves. In vain did the sufferers murmur; in vain did parliament disapprove the commission, which was alike illegal and arbitrary; in vain did Burleigh remonstrate against a system so intolerant, that "the inquisitors of Spain used not so many questions to trap their preys."[4] The archbishop would have deemed forbearance a weakness; and the queen was ready to interpret any freedom in religion as a treasonable denial of her supremacy. Two men were hanged for so trivial an offence as

CHAP. VIII.

1583.

1584. July 1.

1583.

---

[1] Neal's Puritans, v. i. p. 396.
[2] Hallam's England, v. i. p. 270.
[3] Strype's Annals, v. iii. p. 180; Hallam's England, v. i. p. 271—273; Rymer, v. xvi. p. 291—297, June 15, 1596, and 546—551, August 26, 1603; Mackintosh, v. iii. p. 261, 262; Lingard, v. vii. p. 266.
[4] Burleigh to Whitgift. Strype's Whitgift, p. 157.

the distribution of Brown's tract on the liberty of prophesying.[1]

The party thus persecuted were the most efficient opponents of popery. "The puritans," said Burleigh, "are over squeamish and nice, yet their careful catechising and diligent preaching, lessen and diminish the papistical numbers."[2] But for the puritans, the old religion would have retained the affections of the multitude. If Elizabeth reformed the court, the ministers, whom she persecuted, reformed the commons. That the English people became protestant is due to the puritans. How, then, could the party be subdued? The spirit of brave and conscientious men can not be broken. No part is left but to tolerate or destroy. Extermination could alone produce conformity. In a few years, it was said in parliament, that there were in England twenty thousand of those, who frequented conventicles.[3] It was proposed to banish them, as the Moors had been banished from Spain; and as the Huguenots were afterwards driven from France. This measure was not adopted; but a law of savage ferocity, ordering those, who, for a month, should be absent from the English service, to be interrogated as to their belief, menaced the obstinate non-conformists with exile or with death.[4]

Holland offered an asylum against the bitter se-

---

[1] Strype's Annals, v. iii. p. 186; Fuller's Church History of Britain, b. ix. p. 169.
[2] Somer's Tracts, fourth collection, v. i. p. 103.
[3] D'Ewes' Jour. p. 517; Strype's Whitgift, p. 417; Neal's Puritans, v. i. p. 516.
[4] 35 Eliz. c. i. Stat. v. iv. p. 841—843; Parl. Hist. p. 863; Neal's Puritans, v. i. p. 513—515; Neal's New-England, v. i. p. 60.

verity of this statute. A religious society, founded by the independents at Amsterdam, continued to exist for a century, and served as a point of hope for the exiles. But, through the influence of Whitgift, Henry Barrow, a gentleman, and John Greenwood, a minister, though true hearted and loyal, as well as pious, were selected as examples, and hanged at Tyburn.[1]

1593
April 6.

The queen repented that she had sanctioned the execution. Her age and the prospect of favor to puritanism from her successor, conspired to check the spirit of persecution. The leaders of the church became more prudent; and by degrees bitterness subsided. The independents had, it is true, been nearly exterminated; but the number of the non-conforming clergy, after forty years of molestation, had increased; their popularity was more deeply rooted, and their enmity to the established order was irreconcileable. They now began to constitute a powerful political party; they inquired into the nature of government; in parliament they opposed monopolies, limited the royal prerogatives, and demanded a reform of ecclesiastical abuses. "The precious spark of liberty," says an historian who was never accused of favoring the puritans, "had been kindled and was preserved by the puritans alone." Victorious over her foreign enemies, Elizabeth never could crush the religious sect, of which the increase seemed dangerous to the state. Her

[1] Strype's Whitgift, p. 414, &c.; Roger Williams' Truth and Peace, Neal's Puritans, v. i. p. 526, 527; p. 237.

career was full of glory abroad; it was unsuccessful against the progress of opinion at home. In the latter years of her reign, her popularity declined; and her death was the occasion of little regret. "In four days," says an early historian, "she was forgotten."[1] The multitude, fond of change, welcomed her successor with shouts; but when the character of that successor was better known, they persuaded themselves, that they had revered Elizabeth to the last, and that her death had been honored by inconsolable grief.

The accession of King James would, it was believed, introduce a milder system; and the puritans might hope even for favor. But the personal character of the new monarch could not inspire confidence.

The pupil of Buchanan was not destitute of learning nor unskilled in rhetoric. Protected from profligate debauchery by the austerity of public morals in Scotland, and incapable of acting the part of a statesman, he had aimed at the reputation of a "most learned clerk;" and had been so successful, that Bacon,[2] with equivocal flattery, pronounced him incomparable for learning among kings, and Sully, who knew him well, esteemed him the wisest fool in Europe.—The man of letters, who possesses wealth without the capacity for active virtue, often learns to indulge in the vacancy of contemplative enjoyments, and, slumbering on his post, abandons himself to pleasant dreams. This is the euthanasia of his honor. The reputation of King James was lost

---

[1] Carte's England, v. iii. p. 707. [2] Bacon's Works, v. iv. p. 436.

more ignobly. At the mature age of thirty-six he ascended the throne of England, and, for the first time acquiring the opportunity of displaying the worthlessness of his character, he exulted in the freedom of self-indulgence; in idleness and gluttony. The French ambassador despised him for his frivolous amusements;[1] gross licentiousness in his vicinity was unreproved; and the manners of the palace were so coarsely profligate, that even the women of his court appeared in his presence in a state of disgusting inebriety.[2]

The life of James, as a monarch, was full of meannesses. Personal beauty became the qualification of a minister of state. The interests of England were sacrificed, that his son might marry the daughter of a powerful king. His passions were as feeble as his will. His egregious vanity desired perpetual flattery; and no hyperboles excited his distrust. He boasted, that England, even in the days of Elizabeth, had been governed by his influence; by proclamation, he forbad the people to talk of state affairs,[3] and in reply to the complaints of his commons, he declared, that he was and would be the father of their country.[4]

Dissimulation is the vice of those, who have neither true judgment nor courage. King James, from his imbecility, was false; and sometimes vindicated his falsehood, as though deception and cunning had been worthy of a king. But he was an awkward

---

[1] Lingard's Eng. v. ix. p. 107.
[2] Harrington's Nugæ Antiquæ, v. i. p. 348—350.
[3] Rapin's England, v. ii. p. 202; Sully's Memoirs, l. xv.
[4] Cobbett's Parl. Hist. v. i. p. 1504.

liar, rather than a crafty dissembler.[1] He could, before parliament, call God to witness his sincerity, when he was already resolved on being insincere. His cowardice was such, that he feigned a fondness for Carr, whose arrest for murder he had secretly ordered. He was afraid of his wife; could be governed by being overawed; and was easily intimidated by the vulgar insolence of Buckingham.[2] In Scotland, he solemnly declared his attachment[3] to the puritan discipline and doctrines; but it was from his fear of open resistance. The pusillanimous man assents from cowardice, and recovers boldness with the assurance of impunity.

Demonology was a favorite topic with King James. He demonstrated with erudition the reality of witchcraft; through his solicitation it was made, by statute, a capital offence; he could tell "why the devil doth work more with auncient women than with others;" and hardly a year of his reign went by, but some helpless crone perished on the gallows, to satisfy the vanity and confirm the dialectics of the royal author.

There was no room to doubt the sincere attachment of King James to protestantism.[4] His mind had been early and deeply imbued with the doctrines of Calvin. He prided himself on his skill in theological learning, and challenged the praise of Europe as a subtle controversialist. With the whole force of English diplomacy, he suggested the propriety of

---

[1] Hallam's History of England, v. i. p. 404.
[2] Clarendon's Rebellion, v. i. p. 16; Hume's History of England, c. xlix.
[3] Calderwood's Church of Scotland, p. 286.
[4] Bentivoglio, Relazione di Fiandra, parte ii. c. iii. Op. Storiche, v. i. p. 206, 207.

burning an Arminian professor of Holland;[1] while he, at the same time, refuted the errors of the heretic in a harmless tract. Arians were, by his order, burned at the stake; he disputed with a wretched man, whom, after the discussion, he consigned to the flames.[2] He long favored Calvinism, but he loved arbitrary power better than the tenets of Knox, and, when the Arminians in England favored royalty, King James became an Arminian. He steadily adhered to his love of flattery and his love of ease; but he had no fixed principles of conduct or belief.

Such was the character of the king of England at a period, when the limits of royal authority were not as yet clearly defined. Such was the man, to whose decision the puritans must refer the consideration of their claims. Would he be faithful to the principles, in which he had been educated? He had called the church of Scotland "the sincerest kirk of the world;" he had censured the service of England as "an evil said mass."[3] Would he retain for puritans the favor, which he had promised?

There were not wanting statesmen, whose more profound philosophy favored a liberal toleration. Lord Bacon, in whose vigorous mind the truths of political wisdom had been sown by Burleigh in deep furrows, cherished the established worship, and yet advised concessions,[4] regarding the church as the eye

---

[1] Winwood's Memorials, v. iii. p. 290. 293. 295. 298. 316. 339. 357, and other places; Rapin's England, v. ii. p. 179, 180.
[2] Lingard's England, v. ix. p. 217, 218; Prince, p. 127.
[3] Calderwood, p. 286, year, 1590.
[4] Bacon's Works, v. ii. p. 541. Hume, in Appendix to James I., and Grahame, v. i. p. 253, charge Bacon with intolerance; as I think, most unjustly.

of England, in which there might yet be a blemish. The divisions in religion seemed to him a less evil than the violent measures of prevention. The wound, said he, is not dangerous, unless we poison it with our remedies.—The wrongs of the puritans may hardly be dissembled or excused.—The silencing of ministers for the sake of enforcing the ceremonies, is, in this scarcity of good preachers, a punishment that lighteth upon the people.—The bishops should keep one eye open to look upon the good, that those men do.—On subjects of religion, he says of himself, he was always for moderate counsels.[1] Nor did he fear inquiry; for he esteemed controversy "the wind, by which truth is winnowed."

But what relation could subsist between such philosophy, and the selfish arrogance of King James? The tolerant views of Bacon were disregarded in his own time; like L'Hopital and Grotius, he scattered the seeds of truth, which were not to ripen till a late generation. The English hierarchy had feared, in the new monarch, the approach of a "Scottish mist;" but apprehension was soon dispelled.[2] The borders of Scotland were hardly passed, before James began to identify the interests of the English church with those of his prerogative. No bishop, no king, was a maxim often in his mouth. Whitgift was aware, that the puritans were too numerous to be borne down; "I have not been greatly quiet in mind," said the disappointed arch-bishop, "the

[1] Bacon, Of Church Controversies. Of the Pacification of the Church, first published in 1604. Apothegms. Works, v. ii. p. 516. 541. 517. 462.
[2] Neal's Puritans, v. ii. p. 30.

vipers are so many." But James was not as yet fully conscious of their strength. While he was in his progress to London, more than seven hundred of them presented the "millenary petition" for a redress of ecclesiastical grievances.[1] He was never disposed to favor the puritans, but a decent respect for the party to which he had belonged, joined to a desire of displaying his talents for theological debate, induced him to appoint a conference at Hampton Court.

The conference was distinguished on the part of the king by a strenuous vindication of the church of England. Refusing to discuss the question of the power of the church in things indifferent, he substituted authority for argument, and where he could not produce conviction, demanded obedience. "I will have none of that liberty as to ceremonies; I will have one doctrine, one discipline, one religion in substance and in ceremony. Never speak more to that point, how far you are bound to obey."[2]

The puritans desired permission occasionally to assemble, and at their meetings to have the liberty of free discussions; but the king, prompt to discover, that concessions in religion would be followed by greater political liberty, interrupted the petition:—"You are aiming at a Scot's presbytery, which agrees with monarchy as well as God and the devil; then

---

[1] Hume's England, c. xlv; Neal's Puritans, v. ii. p. 31, 32.
[2] Barlow's Sum and Substance of the Conf. at Hampton Court, p. 71. I chiefly follow this account, which I find in the New-England Library of Prince, though more favorable to the king and bishops than they deserved. Hallam, v. i. p. 404. See Nugæ Antiquæ, v. i. p. 180, 181, 182, for an account more disgraceful to James. Yet Harrington was a friend to the church.

CHAP. VIII.
1604.

Jack and Tom and Will and Dick shall meet and at their pleasures censure me and my council and all our proceedings. Then Will shall stand up and say, it must be thus; then Dick shall reply and say, nay, marry, but we will have it thus; and therefore, here I must once more reiterate my former speech, and say, le roi s' avisera; the king alone shall decide."[1] Turning to the bishops, he avowed his belief, that the hierarchy was the firmest support of the throne. Of the puritans he added; "I will make them conform, or I will harry them out of the land, or else worse,"[2] "only hang them; that's all." This closed the day's debate.

Jan. 18.

On the last day of the conference the king defended the necessity of subscription, concluding, that "if any would not be quiet and show their obedience, they were worthy to be hanged." The high commission and the use of inquisitorial oaths equally found in him an advocate. He argued for despotic authority and its instruments.[3] A few alterations in the book of common prayer were the only reforms, which the conference effected. It was agreed, that a time should be set, within which all should conform; if any refused to yield before the time expired, they were to be removed.[4] The king had insulted the puritans with vulgar rudeness and indecorous jests;[5] but his self-complacency was satisfied. He had talked much Latin;[6] he had spoken a part of the

[1] Barlow, p. 79; Neal's Puritans, v. ii. p. 43, 44; Lingard, v. ix. p. 30; Hume, c. xlv.
[2] Barlow, p. 83.
[3] Ibid, p. 90—92.
[4] Barlow, p. 101.
[5] Neal's Puritans, v. ii. p. 45.
[6] Nugæ Antiquæ, v. i. p. 181; Montague, in Winwood's Memorials, v. iii. p. 13—16.

time in the presence of the nobility of Scotland and England, willing admirers of his skill in debate and of his marvellous learning; and he was elated by the eulogies of the churchmen, who paid full tribute to the vanity of their royal champion. "Your majesty speaks by the special assistance of God's spirit," said the aged Whitgift. Bishop Bancroft, on his knees, exclaimed, that his heart melted for joy, "because God had given England such a king, as, since Christ's time, has not been;"[1] and, in a foolish letter, James boasted that "he had soundly peppered off the puritans."[2]

Whitgift, the arch-bishop, a man of great consistency of character, estimable for his learning, respected and beloved by his party, did not long survive the conference. He earnestly desired not to live till the next parliament should assemble, for the puritans would have the majority; and grief,[3] it is thought, hastened his death, six weeks after the close of the conference, and only eleven months after the death of Elizabeth.

1604.
Feb. 29.

In the parliament, which soon assembled, the party opposed to the church asserted their liberties with such tenacity and vigor, that King James began to hate them as embittering royalty itself. "I had rather live like a hermit in the forest," he writes, "than be a king over such a people as the pack of puritans are, that over-rules the lower house."[4] At the opening of the session, he had in vain pursued the policy

---

[1] Barlow, p. 93, 94; Lingard, v. ix. p. 32; Neal's Purit. v. ii. p. 45.
[2] Strype's Whitgift, App. p. 239.
[3] Fuller's Chh. Hist. b. x. p. 25.
[4] Hallam, v. i. p. 408—420, especially the letter at p. 419. Note.

of attempting a union between the old religion and the English church, and had offered "to meet the catholics in the mid-way," while he had added, that "the sect of puritans is insufferable in any well-governed commonwealth."[1] It was equally in vain, that, at the next session of parliament, he expressed himself with more vindictive decision; declaring the Roman Catholics to be faithful subjects, but expressing detestation of the puritans, as worthy of fire for their opinions.[2] The commons of England resolutely favored the sect, which was their natural ally in the struggle against despotism.

Far different was the spirit which actuated the convocation of the clergy. They were very ready to decree against obstinate puritans excommunication and all its consequences.[3] Bancroft, the successor of Whitgift, required[4] conformity with unrelenting rigor; King James issued a proclamation[5] of equal severity; and it is asserted,[6] perhaps with considerable exaggeration, yet by those, who had opportunities of judging rightly, that, in the year 1604 alone, three hundred puritan ministers were silenced, imprisoned, or exiled. But the oppressed party was neither intimidated nor weakened; the moderate men, who assented to external ceremonies as to things indifferent, were unwilling to enforce them by relentless severity; and they resisted not the square

---

[1] Neal's Puritans, v. ii. p. 51, 52; Rapin's England, v. ii. p. 165, 166.
[2] Prince, p. 111; Neal, v. ii. p. 52.
[3] Constitution and Canons Ecclesiastical; Neal's Puritans, v. ii. p. 57—60; Prince, p. 107, 108.
[4] Bancroft's Letter, in Neal, v. ii. p. 67.
[5] Prince, p. 109. See the Canons.
[6] Calderwood, in Neal's N. England, v. i. p. 73. Compare a note in Neal's Puritans, v. ii. p. 64.

cap and the surplice, but the compulsory imposition of them. Yet the clergy proceeded with a consistent disregard of the national liberties. The importation of foreign books was impeded; and a severe censorship of the press was exercised by the bishops. Frivolous acts were denounced as ecclesiastical offences. At a later convocation, they proceeded to draw up a series of canons,[1] denying every doctrine of popular rights, asserting the superiority of the king to the parliament and the laws, and admitting, in their zeal for absolute monarchy, no exception to the duty of passive obedience. Thus the opponents of the church became the sole guardians of popular liberty; the lines of the contending parties were distinctly drawn; the established church and the monarch, on the one side, were arrayed against the puritan clergy and the people. A war of opinion began; immediate success was obtained by the established authority; but the contest would be transmitted to the next generation. Would victory ultimately belong to the churchmen or to the puritans? To the monarch or the people? The interests of European liberty were at issue on the contest.

CHAP. VIII.

1606.

Towards the close of the reign of Elizabeth, there had existed in the North of England a congregation of Separatists, men, who despaired of effecting in the church of England the changes, which their consciences demanded, and who preferred, "whatever it might cost them, as the Lord's free people, to join themselves, by covenant, into a church state."

1622.

[1] Bishop Overall's Convocation Book, (not printed till 1690.)

CHAP. Though Calvinists in their faith, according to the
VIII.
straitest system, they renounced all attachment to
human authority, and reserved an entire and perpetual liberty of forming their principles and practice from the light, that inquiry might shed upon their minds. The history of their wrongs, their pilgrimages, and their success, written by William Bradford, who shared their fortunes and became their leader, has unfortunately perished; but copious extracts from the work have been preserved by the careful Thomas Prince, who merits the gratitude of the inquirer, not less for his judgment and research as an annalist, than for his pious care in collecting and preserving the memorials of the fathers of New-England.[1]

1606. The reformed church, under Robinson, could not hope to escape persecution; and its members were harassed by imprisonments, search-warrants, trivial prosecutions, and the various malice of intolerance.

1607. It is the very nature of the bigotry, which insists

---

[1] I follow in my narration, exclusively, the contemporary authors; Robinson's Apology; Gov. Bradford, in Prince, and the few extracts in Hutchinson, v. ii. Appendix, No. 1; Mourt's Relation; Winslow's Good Newes; Fragments of Bradford's Letter Book; John Smith's Histories and Tracts; the few documents in Hazard, v. i. I have compared the views of the earlier writers, Hubbard and C. Mather. The English authors, Ogilby, Oldmixon, Neal, Burk, Chalmers, furnish nothing of additional value, and most of them are not trustworthy. De Laet is too concise. Of late American writers, I have examined Hutchinson in his Appendix, Belknap's excellent Biographies, Baylies' Memoirs, Thacher's Plymouth, and the very valuable commentary of Davis on Morton. I have consulted the Church Records under the roof of the present pastor of Robinson's church. The Old Colony Records are in good order. The worthy Rossiter Cotton, as register of deeds, has them in his office. May the station, which has been in his family more than one hundred and twenty years, remain to his son and grandson. Hardly a dynasty in Europe has enjoyed so safe a succession.

upon conformity, that the execution of its will is attended with atrocities, which were never designed to be sanctioned; for the enforcement of persecuting laws devolves upon the fanatic or the savage. Men of humane feelings shun the service, which is coveted either by the reckless agents of arbitrary power, or by the envenomed adversaries of the suffering sect. Hence the severity of religious persecution usually surpasses the intention of its authors; and the peaceful members of the church of John Robinson, despairing of finding rest in England, resolved to seek safety in exile.

But whither should they go? Holland, in its controversy with Spain, had displayed republican virtues, and, in the reformation of its churches, had chiefly inclined to the discipline of Calvin. England had been its ally in its greatest dangers; the states, at one time, had almost become a part of the English dominions; the "cautionary" towns were still garrisoned by English regiments, some of which were friendly to the separatists; and William Brewster, the ruling elder of the church, had himself served as a diplomatist in the Low Countries. Common sympathies, therefore, attracted the emigrants to Holland.

The departure from England was effected with much suffering and hazard. The first attempt was prevented; but the magistrates checked the ferocity of the subordinate officers; and, after a month's arrest of the whole company, seven only of the principal men were detained in prison.

CHAP. VIII.

1608.

The next spring, the design was renewed. An unfrequented heath, in Lincolnshire, was the place of secret meeting. As if it had been a crime to escape from persecution, the embarkation was to be made under the shelter of darkness. After having encountered a night storm, just as a boat was bearing a part of the emigrants to their ship, a company of horsemen appeared in pursuit, and seized on the helpless women and children, who had not yet adventured on the surf. "Pitiful it was to see the heavy case of these poor women in distress; what weeping and crying on every side." But when they were apprehended, it seemed impossible to punish and imprison wives and children for no other crime, than that they would go with their husbands and fathers. They could not be sent home, for "they had no homes to go to;" so that, at last, the magistrates were "glad to be rid of them on any terms," "though, in the mean time, they, poor souls, endured misery enough." Such was the flight of Robinson and Brewster, and their followers, from the land of their fathers.

1608.
1609.

Their arrival in Amsterdam was but the beginning of the eventful wanderings of the PILGRIMS. They soon removed to Leyden, where, for eleven years, they continued to live in great harmony. A clear and well written apology of their church was published by Robinson; his fame attracted new members from England; his congregation inspired the nuncio of Rome with respect;[1] and, but for fear of

---

[1] Bentivoglio, Relazione di Fiandra, parte ii. c. xi.

offending King James, they would have met with public favor from the Dutch. In the disputes against Arminianism, Robinson was selected as the champion of orthodoxy, and disputed with a skill, which his friends, at least, considered triumphant.

CHAP. VIII.
1617.

But, notwithstanding the distinction, which was thus acquired, the desires of the company were unsatisfied. They were restless from the consciousness of ability to act a more important part on the theatre of the world. The career of maritime discovery had, meantime, been pursued with daring intrepidity and rewarded with brilliant success. The voyages of Gosnold and Smith and Hudson, the enterprize of Raleigh and Delaware and Gorges, the compilations of Eden and Willes and Hakluyt, had filled the commercial world with wonder; while weighty reasons, often and seriously discussed, inclined the Pilgrims to change their abode. They had been bred to the pursuits of husbandry, and in Holland they were compelled to learn mechanical trades; Brewster became a printer; Bradford, who had been educated as a farmer, learned the art of dying silk. The language of the Dutch never became pleasantly familiar; and their manners still less so. The climate was not grateful to the aged; and the close occupation in mechanical trades was detrimental to the young. The dissoluteness of the disbanded soldiers and mariners, who had grown licentious in the recent wars, filled the English with anxiety, lest their children should become contaminated; and they were moved by an enlightened desire of improving their condition, and the honorable ambition of becoming the founders of a state.

1617. "Upon their talk of removing, sundry of the Dutch would have them go under them, and made them large offers;" but the Pilgrims were attached to their nationality as Englishmen, and to the language of their line. A secret, but deeply seated love of their country led them to the generous purpose of recovering the protection of England by enlarging her dominions. They were "restless" with the desire to live once more under the government of their native land.

Whither should they go to acquire a province for King James? The beautiful fertility and immeasurable wealth of Guiana had been exhibited in dazzling colors by the brilliant eloquence of Raleigh. But the terrors of the tropical climate, the wavering pretensions of England to the soil, and the proximity of bigotted catholics, led them rather to look towards Virginia; and Robert Cushman and John Carver repaired to England to obtain consent of the London company to their emigration. The envoys were favorably received; and a patent and ample liberties were cheerfully promised. Assured of the special approbation of Sir Edwin Sandys, they declined completing their negotiation, till they could consult the multitude, with whose interests they were entrusted. The Pilgrims, following the principles of democratic liberty, transmitted to the company their request, signed by the hands of the greatest part of the congregation. "We are well weaned," added

Robinson and Brewster, "from the delicate milk of our mother country, and inured to the difficulties of a strange land; the people are industrious and frugal. We are knit together as a body in a most sacred covenant of the Lord, of the violation whereof we make great conscience, and by virtue whereof we hold ourselves straitly tied to all care of each other's good, and of the whole. It is not with us as with men, whom small things can discourage."

The messengers of the Pilgrims continued to be received with great kindness by the Virginia company; they also sought for the favor of the king. But in vain did they transmit an account of their principles; in vain was high influence at court exerted in their behalf. Even while the negotiations were pending, a royal declaration constrained the puritans of Lancashire to conform or leave the kingdom; and nothing more could be obtained for the wilds of America, than an informal promise of neglect. No public act of toleration could be wrung from the English monarch.

The bigotry of the English hierarchy was a great discouragement to the church at Leyden. The dissensions in the Virginia corporation occasioned further delay; but, as the influence of Sir Edwin Sandys, the friend of the puritans, prevailed, a patent was at length granted to the Pilgrims under the company's seal. It was taken in the name of one, who failed to accompany the expedition; and was never of the least service to those, who had obtained it with much toil and cost.

CHAP. VIII.
1619.

One more negotiation remained to be completed. The Pilgrims were not possessed of sufficient capital for the execution of their schemes. The reports of Smith, the efforts of Gorges, the confidence in wealth to be derived from fisheries, had made American expeditions a subject of consideration with English merchants; and the agents from Leyden were able to form a partnership between their employers and men of business in London. The terms of the contract were deemed exceedingly severe. The whole company constituted a numerous partnership; the services of each emigrant were rated as a capital of ten pounds, and belonged to the company; all profits were to be reserved, till the end of seven years, when the whole amount, and all houses and lands, gardens and fields, were to be divided among the shareholders according to their respective interests. The London merchant, who risked one hundred pounds, would receive for his money ten-fold more than the pennyless emigrant for his entire services. This arrangement threatened a seven years' check to the pecuniary prosperity of the community; yet, as it did not interfere with civil rights, or religion, it did not intimidate the Pilgrims.[1]

1620.

And now the English at Leyden, trusting in God and in themselves, made ready for their departure.

[1] "Under the influence of this wild notion, the colonists of New-Plymouth, in imitation of the primitive Christians, threw all their property into a common stock." Robertson's America, b. x. One of the many errors, with which the volume of Robertson teems. There was no attempt at imitating the primitive Christians; the partnership was a consequence of negotiations with British merchants; the colonists preferred the system of private property, and acted upon it, as far and as soon as was possible.

The Speedwell, a ship of sixty tuns, was purchased in London; the Mayflower, a vessel of one hundred and eighty tuns, was hired in England. These could hold but a minority of the congregation; and Robinson was therefore detained at Leyden, while Brewster, the teaching elder, conducted the emigrants. Every enterprize of the Pilgrims began from God. A solemn fast was held. "Let us seek of God," said they, "a right way for us, and for our little ones, and for all our substance." Anticipating their high destiny and the sublime doctrines of liberty, that would grow out of the principles, on which their religious tenets were established, Robinson gave them a farewell, breathing a noble spirit of Christian liberty, such as was hardly then known in the world.

CHAP. VIII.

1620. July.

"I charge you before God and his blessed angels, that you follow me no farther, than you have seen me follow the Lord Jesus Christ. The Lord has more truth yet to break forth out of his holy word. I cannot sufficiently bewail the condition of the reformed churches, who are come to a period in religion, and will go at present no further than the instruments of their reformation.—Luther and Calvin were great and shining lights in their times, yet they penetrated not into the whole counsel of God. —I beseech you, remember it, 'tis an article of your church covenant, that you be ready to receive whatever truth shall be made known to you from the written word of God."

The Pilgrims were accompanied by most of the

brethren from Leyden to Delft-Haven; where the night was passed "in friendly and Christian converse." As the morning dawned, Robinson, kneeling in prayer by the sea-side, gave to their embarkation the sanctity of a religious rite. A prosperous wind soon wafts the vessel to Southampton, and, in a fortnight, the Mayflower and the Speedwell, freighted with the first colony for New-England, leave Southampton for America. But they had not gone far upon the Atlantic, before the smaller vessel was found to need repairs; and they enter the port of Dartmouth. After the lapse of eight precious days, they again weigh anchor; the coast of England recedes; already they are unfurling their sails on the broad ocean, when the captain of the Speedwell, with his company, dismayed at the dangers of the enterprize, once more pretends, that his ship is too weak for the service. They put back to Plymouth, to dismiss their treacherous companions, though the loss of the vessel was "very grievous and discouraging." The timid and the hesitating were all freely allowed to abandon the expedition. Having thus winnowed their numbers of the cowardly and the disaffected, the little band of resolute men, some with their wives and children, in all, but one hundred and two souls, went on board the single ship, which was hired only to convey them across the Atlantic; and, on the sixth day of September, 1620, thirteen years after the first colonization of Virginia, two months before the concession of the grand charter of Plymouth, without any warrant from the sovereign of England, without any useful charter from a corporate body, the passengers in the Mayflower, under the guidance of a faithless captain, who had received a bribe to thwart their purposes, set sail for a new world, where the past could offer no favorable auguries.

Had New-England been colonized immediately on the discovery of the American continent, the old English institutions would have been planted under the powerful influence of the Roman Catholic religion; had the settlement been made under Elizabeth, it would have been before activity of mind in religion had conducted to a corresponding activity of mind in politics. The Pilgrims were Englishmen, protestants, exiles for religion; men disciplined by misfortune, cultivated by opportunities of extensive observation, equal in rank as in rights, and bound by no code, but that which was imposed by religion, or might be created by the public will.

The eastern coast of the United States abounds in beautiful and convenient harbors, in majestic bays and rivers; the first Virginia colony, sailing along the shores of North-Carolina, was, by a favoring storm, driven into the magnificent bay of the Chesapeake; the Pilgrims, having selected as the place for their settlement the mouth of the Hudson, the best position on the whole coast, were, by the treachery of their captain, conducted to the most barren and inhospitable part of Massachusetts. After a long and boisterous voyage of sixty-three days, during which one person had died, they espied land, and in two days more, were safely moored in the harbor of Cape Cod. Dutch cupidity and English intolerance combined to effect the first settlement of New-England.

Yet, before they landed, the manner in which their government should be constituted, was considered; and, as some were observed "not well affected to unity and concord," they formed themselves into a body politic by a solemn voluntary compact.

Nov. 11.
"In the name of God, amen; we, whose names are underwritten, the loyal subjects of our dread sovereign King James, having undertaken for the glory of God, and advancement of the Christian faith, and honor of our king and country, a voyage to plant the first colony in the northern parts of Virginia, do by these presents, solemnly and mutually, in the presence of God, and one of another, covenant and combine ourselves together, into a civil body politic, for our better ordering and preservation, and furtherance of the ends aforesaid; and by virtue hereof, to enact, constitute, and frame such just and equal laws, ordinances, acts, constitutions, and offices, from time to time, as shall be thought most convenient for the general good of the colony. Unto which we promise all due submission and obedience."

This instrument was signed by the whole body of men, forty-one in number, who, with their families, constituted the one hundred and one, the whole colony, "the proper democracy," that arrived in New-England. John Carver was immediately and unanimously chosen governor for the year.

Men, who emigrate, even in well-inhabited districts, pray that their journey may not be in winter. Wasted by the rough and wearisome voyage, ill-supplied with provisions, the English fugitives found themselves, at the opening of winter, on a barren and bleak coast, in a severe climate, with the ocean on one side and the wilderness on the other. There were none to show them kindness or bid them welcome. The nearest French settlement was at Port Royal; it was five hundred miles to the English plantation at Virginia. As they attempted to disembark, the water was found so shallow, that they were forced to wade; and, in the freezing weather, the very act of getting on land sowed the seeds of consumption and inflammatory colds. The bitterness of mortal disease was their welcome to the inhospitable shore.

The season was already fast bringing winter, and the spot for the settlement remained to be chosen. The shallop was unshipped, and it was a real disaster to find, that it needed repairs. The carpenter made slow work, so that sixteen or seventeen weary days elapsed, before it was ready for service. But Standish and Bradford, and others, impatient of the delay, determined to explore the country by land. "In regard to the danger," the expedition "was rather permitted than approved." Much hardship was endured; but what discoveries could be made in Truro and near the banks of Paomet creek? The first expedition in the shallop was likewise unsuccessful; "some of the people, that died that

CHAP. VIII.
1620.

winter, took the original of their death" in the enterprize; "for it snowed and did blow all the day and night, and froze withal." The men, who were set on shore, "were tired with marching up and down the steep hills and deep vallies, which lay half a foot thick with snow." A heap of maize was discovered; and further search led to a burial-place of the Indians; but they found "no more corn, nor any thing else but graves."

Dec. 6.

At length, the shallop was again sent out, with Carver, Bradford, Winslow, Standish, and others, with eight or ten seamen. The cold was severe; the spray of the sea froze as it fell on them, and made their clothes like coats of iron. That day they reached Billingsgate Point at the bottom of the bay of Cape Cod, on the western shore of Wellfleet harbor. The next morning the company divided; those on shore find a burial-place, graves, and four or five deserted wigwams; but neither people, nor any place, inviting a settlement. Before night, the whole party met by the sea-side, and encamped on land together near Namskeket, or Great Meadow Creek.

Dec. 7.

Dec. 8.

The next day they rose at five; their morning prayers were finished; when, as the day dawned, a war-whoop and a flight of arrows announced an attack from Indians. They were of the tribe of the Nausites, who knew the English as kidnappers; but the encounter was without further result. Again the boat's crew give thanks to God, and steer their bark along the coast for the distance of fifteen leagues.

But no convenient harbor is discovered. The pilot of the boat, who had been in these regions before, gives assurance of a good one, which might be reached before night; and they follow his guidance. After some hours' sailing, a storm of snow and rain begins; the sea swells; the rudder breaks; the boat must now be steered with oars; the storm increases; night is at hand; to reach the harbor before dark, as much sail as possible is borne; the mast breaks into three pieces; the sail falls overboard; but the tide is favorable. The pilot, in dismay, would have run the boat on shore in a cove full of breakers; "about with her," exclaimed a sailor, "or we are cast away." They get her about immediately, and passing over the surf, they enter a fair sound; and get under the lee of a small rise of land. It is dark and the rain beats furiously; yet the men are so wet and cold and weak, they slight the danger to be apprehended from the savages, and, after great difficulty, kindle a fire on shore.

Morning, as it dawned, showed the place to be a small island within the entrance of a harbor. The day was required for rest and preparations. Time was precious; the season advancing; their companions were left in suspense. The next day was the "Christian Sabbath." Nothing marks the character of the Pilgrims more fully, than that they kept it sacredly, though every consideration demanded haste.

On Monday, the eleventh day of December, Old Style, the exploring party of the forefathers land at Plymouth. A grateful posterity has marked the rock, which first received their footsteps. The consequences of that day are constantly unfolding themselves, as time advances. It was the origin of New-England; it was the planting of the New-England institutions. Inquisitive historians[1] have loved to mark every vestige of the Pilgrims; poets[2] of the purest minds have commemorated their virtues; the noblest genius has been called into exercise to display their merits worthily, and to trace the consequences of their daring enterprize.

The spot, when examined, seemed to invite a settlement, and, in a few days, the Mayflower was safely moored in its harbor. In memory of the hospitalities, which the company had received at the last English port, from which they had sailed, this oldest New-England colony obtained the name of Plymouth. The system of civil government had been established by common agreement; the character of the church had for many years been fixed by a sacred covenant. As the Pilgrims landed, their institutions were already perfected. Democratic liberty and independent Christian worship at once existed in America.

---

[1] Hubbard, Prince, Hutchinson, Belknap, Freeman, Davis, Baylies, Thacher.

[2] Should this volume meet the eye of Mrs. Hemans, I hope she will not disregard a sincere expression of respect from one, who admires alike her rare abilities, and the noble use, to which they are applied. The popular poet, who adds the charm of beautiful language to the sentiment of morality and truth, enjoys an influence, of which the remote extent may hardly be known to its author. I have heard the hymns of Heber sung by drovers on Lake Erie, and seen the favorite poems of Mrs. Hemans in the village newspapers of the remote interior. Happy the nation, of which the writers are filled with elevated thought and tastes! Happy the people, which expresses its faith in immortality in the chorus of its every day songs!

After some days, they began to build; a difficult task for men, of whom one half were wasting away with consumptions and lung-fevers. For the sake of haste, it was agreed, that every man should build his own house; but frost and foul weather were great hindrances; they could seldom work half of the week; and tenements were erected as they could be, in the short intervals of sunshine between showers of sleet and snow-storms.

On the third of March, a south wind brought warm and fair weather. "The birds sang in the woods most pleasantly." But it was not till spring had far advanced, that the mortality began to cease. It was afterwards remarked, with modest gratitude, that of the survivors, very many lived to an extreme old age. A shelter, not less than comfort, had been wanting; the living had been scarce able to bury the dead; the well not sufficient to take care of the sick. At the season of greatest distress, there were but seven able to render assistance. The benevolent Carver had been appointed governor; at his first landing, he had lost a son; soon after the departure of the Mayflower for England, his health sunk under a sudden attack; and his wife, broken-hearted, followed him in death. William Bradford, the historian of the colony, was soon chosen his successor. The record of misery was kept by the graves of the governor and half the company.

But if sickness ceased to prevail, the hardships of privation and want remained to be encountered. In the autumn, an arrival of new emigrants, who came

CHAP. VIII. unprovided with food, compelled the whole colony, for six months in succession, to subsist on half allowance only. "I have seen men," says Winslow, "stagger by reason of faintness for want of food." They were once saved from famishing by the benevolence of fishermen off the coast. Sometimes they

1622. suffered from oppressive exactions on the part of ships, that sold them provisions at the most exorbitant prices. Nor did their miseries soon terminate.

1623. Even in the third year of the settlement, their victuals were so entirely spent, that "they knew not at night where to have a bit in the morning." Tradition declares, that, at one time, the colonists were reduced to a pint of corn, which, being parched and distributed, gave to each individual only five kernels; but

July. rumor falls short of reality; for three or four months together, they had no corn whatever. When a few of their old friends arrived to join them, a lobster, or a piece of fish, without bread or any thing else but a cup of fair spring water, was the best dish, which the hospitality of the whole colony could offer.

1624. Neat cattle were not introduced till a later day.
Mar. Yet during all this season of self-denial and suffering, the cheerful confidence of the Pilgrims in the mercies of Providence remained unshaken.

The system of common property had occasioned grievous discontents; the influence of law could not compel regular labor like the uniform impulse of personal interest; and even the threat of "keeping back their bread" could not change the character of the idle. After the harvest of 1623, there was no general want of food; in the spring of that year, it had been agreed, that each family should plant for itself; and parcels of land, in proportion to the respective numbers, were assigned for culture, though not for inheritance. This arrangement produced contented labor and universal industry; "even women and children now went into the field to work." The next spring, every person obtained a little land in perpetual fee. The necessity of the case, and the common interest, demanded a slight departure from the severe agreement with the English merchants. Before many harvests, so much corn was raised, that it began to form a profitable article of commerce, and the Indians, preferring the chase to tillage, abandoned culture, and looked to the colonists for their supply. The intercourse between the Plymouth colony and the Indians soon assumed the character of commercial familiarity. The exchange of European manufactures for beaver and other skins, was almost the only pursuit, which promised to be lucrative.

The spot, to which Providence had directed the planters, had, a few years before, been rendered entirely a desert by a pestilence, which had likewise swept over the neighboring tribes, and desolated almost the whole sea-board of New-England. Where the Pilgrims landed, there were the traces of a previous population, but not one living inhabitant. Smokes from fires in the remote distance alone indicated the vicinity of natives. Miles Standish, "the best linguist" among the Pilgrims, as well as the best soldier, with an exploring party, was able to discover wigwams, but no tenants. Yet a body of Indians from abroad was soon discovered, hovering near the settlement; though disappearing, when pursued. The colony, therefore, assumed a military organization; and Standish, a man of the greatest courage, the devoted friend of the church, which he never joined, was appointed to the chief command. But dangers were not at hand.

One day, Samoset, an Indian, who had learned a little English of the fishermen at Penobscot, boldly entered the town, and, passing to the rendezvous, exclaimed in English, "Welcome Englishmen." He belonged to the Wampanoags, a tribe which was destined to become memorable in the history of New-England. In the name of his nation, he bade the strangers possess the soil, which there was no one of the original occupants alive to claim. After some little negotiation, in which an Indian, who had been carried away by Hunt, had learned English in England, and had, in an earlier expedition, returned to his native land, acted as an interpreter, Massassoit himself, the sachem of the tribe, possessing the country north of Narragansett Bay, and between the rivers of Providence and Taunton, came to visit the Pilgrims, who, with their wives and children, now amounted to no more than fifty. The chieftain of a race, as yet so new to the Pilgrims, was received with all the ceremonies, which the condition of the colony permitted. A treaty of friendship was soon completed in few and unequivocal terms. The parties promised to abstain from mutual injuries, and to deliver up offenders; the colonists were to receive assistance, if attacked; to render it, if Massassoit should be attacked unjustly. The treaty included the confederates of the sachem; it is the oldest act of diplomacy recorded in New-England; it was concluded in a day, and, being founded on reciprocal interests, was sacredly kept for more than half a century. Massassoit desired the alliance, for the powerful Narragansetts were his enemies; his tribe, moreover, having become habituated to some English luxuries, were willing to establish a traffic; while the emigrants obtained peace, security, and the opportunity of a lucrative commerce.

CHAP. VIII.

1621.

An embassy from the little colony to their new ally, performed, not with the pomp of modern missions, but through the forests and on foot, and received, not to the luxuries of courts, but to a share in the abstinence of savage life, confirmed the treaty of amity, and prepared the way for a trade in furs. The marks of devastation from a former plague were visible, wherever the envoys went, and they witnessed the extreme poverty and feebleness of the natives.

July.

The influence of the English over the aborigines was rapidly extended. A sachem, who menaced their safety, was himself compelled to sue for mercy; and nine chieftains subscribed an instrument of submission to King James. The bay of Massachusetts and harbor of Boston were fearlessly explored. Canonicus, the wavering sachem of the Narragansetts,

Aug.

Sept. 13.

whose territory had escaped the ravages of the pestilence, had at first desired to treat of peace. A bundle of arrows, wrapped in the skin of a rattlesnake, was now the token of his hostility. But when Bradford stuffed the skin with powder and shot and returned it, his courage quailed, and he desired to be in amity with a race of men, whose weapons of war were so terrible. The hostile expedition, which caused the first Indian blood to be shed, grew out of a quarrel, in which the inhabitants of Plymouth were involved by another colony.

For who will define the limits to the graspings of avarice? The opportunity of gain by the fur-trade had been envied the planters of New-Plymouth; and Weston, who had been active among the London adventurers in establishing the Plymouth colony, now desired to engross the profits, which he already deemed secure. A patent for land near Weymouth, the first plantation in Boston Harbor, was easily obtained; and a company of sixty men were sent over. Helpless at their arrival, they intruded themselves, for most of the summer, upon the unrequited hospitality of the people of Plymouth. In their plantation, they were soon reduced to necessity by their want of thrift; their injustice towards the Indians provoked hostility; and a plot was formed for the entire destruction of the English. But the grateful Massassoit revealed the design to his allies; and the planters at Weymouth were saved by the wisdom of the older colony and the intrepid gallantry of Standish. It was "his capital exploit." Some of the rescued men went to Plymouth; some sailed for England. One short year saw the beginning and end of the Weymouth plantation. "Certainly the best works and of greatest merit for the public," observes Lord Bacon, "have proceeded from the unmarried or childless men." The great English philosopher was himself a childless man; and all-powerful self-love confirmed his remark. Weston's men, after having boasted of their strength, as far superior to Plymouth, which was weakened, they said, by the presence of children and women, owed their deliverance to the colony, which had many women, children, and weak ones with them.

The danger from Indian hostilities was early removed; the partnership with English merchants occasioned greater inconvenience. Robinson and the rest of his church, at Leyden, were suffering from deferred hopes, and were longing to rejoin their brethren in America. The adventurers in England refused to provide them a passage, and attempted, with but short success, to force upon the colonists a clergyman, more friendly to the established church; thus outraging at once the affections and the religious scruples of those, whom they had pledged themselves to cherish. Divisions ensued; and the partners in England, offended by opposition, and discouraged at the small returns from their investments, deserted the interests of their associates in America. A ship was even despatched to rival them in their business; goods, which were sent for their supply, were sold to them at an advance of seventy per cent. The curse of usury, which always falls so heavily upon new settlements, did not spare them; for, being left without help from the partners, they were obliged to borrow money at fifty per cent., and at thirty per cent. interest. At last, the emigrants themselves succeeded in purchasing the entire rights of the English adventurers; the common property was equitably divided; and agriculture established immediately and completely on the basis of private possessions. For a six years' monopoly of the trade, eight of the most enterprizing men assumed all the engagements of the colony; so that the cultivators of the soil became really freeholders; neither debts nor rent-day troubled them.

The colonists of Plymouth had exercised self-government, without the sanction of a royal patent. Yet their claim to their lands was valid, according to the principles of English law, as well as natural justice. They had received a welcome from the aborigines; and the council of Plymouth, through the mediation of Sir Ferdinand Gorges,[1] immediately issued a patent to John Pierce for their benefit. But the trustee, growing desirous of becoming lord proprietary and holding them as tenants, obtained a new charter, which would have caused much difficulty, had not his misfortunes compelled him to transfer his rights to the company. When commerce extended to the Kennebec, a patent for the adjacent territory was easily procured. The same year, Allerton was again sent to London to negotiate an

---

[1] Gorges' Description, p. 24; Briefe Narration, c. xxii.

enlargement of both the grants; and he obtained from the council of Plymouth concessions equal to all his desires. But it was ever impossible to obtain a charter from the king; so that, according to the principles adopted in England, the planters, with an unquestionable property in the soil, had no right to assume a separate jurisdiction. It was therefore in the virtues of the colonists themselves, that their institutions found a guarantee for stability. They never doubted their authority to punish for small offences; it was only after some scruples, that they inflicted capital punishment. Their doubts being once removed, they exercised the same authority as the charter governments. Death was, by subsequent laws, made the penalty for several crimes; but was never inflicted except for murder. House-breaking and highway robbery were offences unknown in their courts, and too little apprehended to make them subjects of severe legislation.

The progress of population was very slow. The lands in the vicinity were not fertile; and at the end of ten years the colony contained no more than three hundred souls. Few as were their numbers, they had struck deep root, and would have out-lived every storm, even if they had been followed by no other colonies in New-England. Hardly were they planted in America, when their enterprize began to take a wide range; before Massachusetts was settled, they had acquired rights at Cape Ann, as well as an extensive domain on the Kennebec; and they were the first to possess an English settlement on the banks of the Connecticut. The excellent Robinson died at Leyden, before the faction in England would permit his removal to Plymouth; his heart was in America, where his memory will never die. The remainder of his people, and with them his wife and children, emigrated, so soon as means could be provided to defray the costs. "To enjoy religious liberty was the known end of the first comers' great adventure into this remote wilderness;" and they desired no increase, but from the friends of their communion. Yet their residence in Holland had made them acquainted with various forms of Christianity; a wide experience had emancipated them from bigotry; and they were never betrayed into the excesses of religious persecution, though they sometimes permitted a disproportion between punishment and crime.

The frame of civil government in the Old Colony was of the utmost simplicity. A governor was chosen by general suffrage; whose power, always subordinate to the general will, was, at the desire of Bradford, specially restricted by a council of five, and afterwards of seven, assistants. In the council, the governor had but a double vote. For more than eighteen years, "the whole body of the male inhabitants" constituted the legislature; the state was governed, like our towns, as a strict democracy; and the people were frequently convened, to decide on executive, not less than on judicial questions. At length, the increase of population, and its diffusion over a wider territory, led to the introduction of the representative system, and each town sent its committee to the general court. We shall subsequently find the colony a distinct member of the earliest American Confederacy; but it is chiefly as guides and pioneers, that the fathers of the Old Colony merit gratitude.

Through scenes of gloom and misery, the Pilgrims showed the way to an asylum for those, who would go to the wilderness for the purity of religion or the liberty of conscience. They set the example of colonizing New-England, and formed the mould for the civil and religious character of its institutions. Enduring every hardship themselves, they were the servants of posterity, the benefactors of succeeding generations. In the history of the world, many pages are devoted to commemorate the heroes, who have besieged cities, subdued provinces, or overthrown empires. In the eye of reason and of truth, a colony is a better offering than a victory; the citizens of the United States should rather cherish the memory of those, who founded a state on the basis of democratic liberty; the fathers of the country; the men, who, as they first trod the soil of the New World, scattered the seminal principles of republican freedom and national independence. They enjoyed, in anticipation, the thought of their extending influence, and the fame, which their grateful successors would award to their virtues. "Out of small beginnings," said Bradford, "great things have been produced; and as one small candle may light a thousand, so the light here kindled hath shone to many, yea in some sort to our whole nation." — "Let it not be grievous to you," such was the consolation offered from England to the Pilgrims in the season of their greatest sufferings, "let it not be grievous to you, that you have been instruments to break the ice for others. The honor shall be yours to the world's end."

CHAPTER IX.

THE EXTENDED COLONIZATION OF NEW-ENGLAND.

THE council of Plymouth for New-England, having obtained of King James the boundless territory and the immense monopoly which they had desired, had no further obstacles to encounter but the laws of nature and the remonstrances of parliament. No tributaries tenanted their countless millions of uncultivated acres; and exactions upon the vessels of English fishermen were the only means of acquiring an immediate revenue from America. But the spirit of the commons indignantly opposed the extravagant pretensions of the favored company; and demanded for every subject of the English king the free liberty of engaging in a pursuit, which was the chief source of wealth to the merchants of the west. "Shall the English," said Sir Edwin Sandys, the statesman, so well entitled to the enduring gratitude of Virginia, "be debarred from the freedom of the fisheries, a privilege, which the French and Dutch enjoy? It costs the kingdom nothing but labor; employs shipping; and furnishes the means of a lucrative commerce with Spain."—"The fishermen hinder the plantations," replied Calvert; "they choke the harbors with their ballast, and waste the forests by improvident use. America is not annexed to the realm, nor within the jurisdiction of parliament; you have therefore no right to interfere." — "We may make laws for Virginia," rejoined another member, intent on opposing the flagrant benevolence of the king, and wholly unconscious of asserting, in the earliest debate on American affairs, the claim of parliament to that absolute sovereignty, which the colonies never acknowledged, and which led to the war of the revolution; "a bill, passed by the commons and the lords, if it receive the king's assent, will control the patent." The charter, argued Sir Edward Coke, with ample reference to early statutes, was granted without regard to previously existing rights; and is therefore void by the established laws of England. So the friends of the liberty of fishing in the commons triumphed over the advocates of the royal prerogative, though the parliament was dissolved, before a bill could be carried through all the forms of legislation.

Yet enough had been done to infuse vigor into mercantile enterprize; in the second year after the settlement of Plymouth, five and thirty sail of vessels went to fish on the coasts of New-England, and made good voyages. The monopolists appealed to King James; and the monarch, preferring to assert his own extended prerogative, rather than to regard the spirit of the house of commons, issued a proclamation, which forbad any to approach the northern coast of America, except with the special leave of the company of Plymouth, or of the privy council. It was monstrous thus to attempt to seal up a large portion of an immense continent; it was impossible to carry the ordinance into effect; and here, as so often, despotism caused its own fall. By desiring strictly to enforce its will, it provoked a conflict in which it was sure of being defeated.

But the monopolists endeavored to establish their claims. One Francis West was despatched with a commission as admiral of New-England, for the purpose of excluding from the American seas such fishermen as came without a license. But his feeble authority was derided; the ocean was a wide place over which to keep sentry. The mariners refused to pay the tax, which he imposed; and his ineffectual authority was soon resigned. In England, the attempt occasioned the severest remonstrances, which did not fail to make an impression on the ensuing parliament.

The patentees, alike prodigal of charters and tenacious of their monopoly, having given to Robert Gorges, the son of Sir Ferdinand, a patent for a tract, extending ten miles on Massachusetts Bay, and thirty miles into the interior, now appointed him lieutenant-general of New-England, with power " to restrain interlopers," not less than to regulate the affairs of the corporation. His patent was never permanently used; though the colony at Weymouth was renewed, to meet once more with ill fortune. He was attended by Morrell, an episcopal clergyman, who was provided with a commission for the superintendence of ecclesiastical affairs. Instead of establishing a hierarchy, Morrell, remaining in New-England about a year, wrote a description of the country in verse; while the civil dignity of Robert Gorges ended in a short-lived dispute with Weston. They came to plant a hierarchy and a general government, and they produced only a fruitless quarrel and a dull poem.

1624.

But when parliament was again convened, the controversy against the charter was once more renewed; and the rights of liberty found an inflexible champion in the aged Sir Edward Coke, who now expiated the sins of his early ambition by devotion to the interests of the people. It was in vain that the patentees relinquished a part of their pretensions; the commons resolved, that English fishermen shall have fishing with all its incidents. "Your patent," thus Gorges was addressed by Coke from the speaker's chair, "contains many particulars contrary to the laws and privileges of the subject; it is a monopoly, and the ends of private gain are concealed under color of planting a colony." "Shall none," observed the veteran lawyer in debate, "shall none visit the sea-coast for fishing? This is to make a monopoly upon the seas, which wont to be free. If you alone are to pack and dry fish, you attempt a monopoly of the wind and the sun." It was in vain for Sir George Calvert to resist. The bill passed without amendment; though it never received the royal assent.[1]

Mar. 17.

---

[1] The original authorities, Debates of the Commons, 1620-1, v. i. p. 258. 260, 261. 318, 319; Journal of Commons, in Chalmers, p. 100—102, and 103, 104; Sir F. Gorges' Narration; Morrell, in i.

The determined opposition of the house, though CHAP. it could not move the king to overthrow the corpora- IX. tion, paralyzed its enterprize; many of the patentees 1624. abandoned their interest; so that the Plymouth company now did little except issue grants of domains; and the cottages, which, within a few years, were sprinkled along the coast from Cape Cod to the bay of Fundy, were the consequence of private adventure.

The territory between the river of Salem and the Kennebec became, in a great measure, the property of two enterprizing individuals. We have seen, that Martin Pring was the discoverer of New-Hampshire; 1603. and that Smith had examined and extolled the deep 1614. waters of the Piscataqua. Sir Ferdinand Gorges, the 1620. most energetic member of the council of Plymouth, always ready to encounter risks in the cause of colonizing America, had not allowed repeated ill success to chill his confidence and decision; and now he found in John Mason, "who had been governor of a plantation in Newfoundland, a man of action," like himself. It was not difficult for Mason, who had 1621. been elected an associate and secretary of the Mar. 9. council, to obtain a grant of the lands between Salem river and the farthest head of the Merrimac; but he did no more with his vast estate, than give it a name. The passion for land increased; and Gor- 1622. ges and Mason next took a patent for Laconia, the Aug. 10. whole country between the sea, the St. Lawrence, the Merrimac, and the Kennebec; a company of

Mass. Hist. Coll. v. i. p. 125—139; 151—155. I have also compared Smith, in iii. Mass. Hist. Collec- Prince, Morton, Hutchinson, Bel-tions, v. iii. p. 25; Hazard, v. i. p. knap, and Chalmers.

356 COLONIZATION OF NEW-HAMPSHIRE.

CHAP. IX.

1623.

English merchants was formed; and under its auspices permanent plantations were established on the banks of the Piscataqua.[1] Portsmouth and Dover are among the oldest towns in New-England. Splendid as were the anticipations of the proprietaries, and lavish as was their enthusiasm in liberal expenditures, the immediate progress of the plantations was inconsiderable, and, even as fishing stations, they do not seem to have prospered.

1628.

When the country on Massachusetts Bay was granted to a company, of which the zeal and success were soon to overshadow all the efforts of proprieta-

1629. Nov. 7.

ries and merchants, it became expedient for Mason to procure a new patent; and he now received a fresh title[2] to the territory between the Merrimac and Piscataqua in terms, which, in some degree, interfered with the pretensions of his neighbors on the south. This was the patent for New-Hampshire; and was pregnant with nothing so signally as suits at law. The country had been devastated by the mutual wars of the tribes, and the same wasting pestilence which left New-Plymouth a desert; no notice seems to have been taken of the rights of the natives; nor did they now issue any deed of their

1630. lands;[3] but the soil in the immediate vicinity of Do-
1631. ver, and afterwards of Portsmouth, was conveyed to the planters themselves, or to those, at whose expense

---

[1] Gorges' Narrative, c. xxiv.; Hubbard, p. 614—616; Prince, p. 215; Adams' Annals of Portsmouth, p. 9, 10; Williamson's Maine, v. i. p. 222, and ff.; Belknap's New-Hampshire, c. i. A truly valuable work, highly creditable to American literature.
[2] Hazard, v. i. p. 290—293.
[3] Savage on Winthrop, v. i. p. 405, and ff.

COLONIZATION OF NEW-HAMPSHIRE.

the settlement had been made.¹ A favorable impulse was thus given to the little colonies; and houses now began to be built on the "Strawberry Bank" of the Piscataqua. But the progress of the town was slow; Josselyn² described the whole coast as a mere wilderness, with here and there a few huts scattered by the sea-side; and thirty years after its settlement, Portsmouth made only the moderate boast of containing "between fifty and sixty families."³

When the grand charter, which had established the council of Plymouth, was about to be revoked, Mason extended his pretensions to the Salem river, the southern boundary of his first territory; and obtained of the expiring corporation a corresponding patent. There is room to believe, that the king would, without scruple, have confirmed the grant,⁴ and conferred upon him the powers of government, as absolute lord and proprietary; but the death of Mason cut off all the hopes, which his family might have cherished of territorial aggrandizement and feudal supremacy. His widow in vain attempted to manage the colonial domains; the costs exceeded the revenue; the servants were ordered to provide for their own welfare; the property of the great landed proprietor was divided among them for the payment of arrears; and Mason's American estate was completely ruined.⁵ Neither king nor proprietary troubled the few inhabitants of New-Hampshire;

---

¹ Adams' Annals of Portsmouth, p. 17—19.
² Josselyn's Voyages, p. 20.
³ Farmer's Belknap, p. 434.
⁴ Ibid, p. 431.
⁵ Belknap, c. ii.

they were left to take care of themselves; the best dependence for states, as well as for individuals.

The enterprize of Sir Ferdinand Gorges, though sustained by stronger expressions of royal favor, and continued with indefatigable perseverance, was not followed by much greater success. We have seen a colony established, though but for a single winter, on the shores which Pring had discovered, and Weymouth had been the first to explore. After the bays of New-England had been more carefully examined by the same daring adventurer, who sketched the first map of the Chesapeake, the coast was regularly visited by fishermen and traders. A special account of the country was one of the fruits of Hakluyt's inquiries, and was published in the collections of Purchas. At Winter Harbor, near the mouth of Saco river, Englishmen, under Richard Vines, again encountered the severities of the inclement season; and not long afterwards, the mutineers of the crew of Rocraft lived from autumn till spring on Monhegan island. The earliest navigators, intent only on their immediate objects, neither desired nor merited glory, and have left few memorials of their presence in Maine; it is not, perhaps, possible to ascertain the precise time, when the rude shelters of the fishermen on the sea-coast began to be tenanted by permanent inmates, and the fishing stages of a summer to be transformed into the regular establishments of trade.[1]

[1] For the early history of Maine, the original authorities are in Purchas, v. iv.; the Relation of the President and Council for New-England; Josselyn's Voyages; and the Narration, which Gorges himself composed in his old age. Materials may be found also in Sullivan's History; and far better in the elaborate and most minute work

COLLISION WITH FRANCE ON THE EASTERN FRONTIER.

The first observers could not but admire the noble rivers and secure bays, which invited commerce, and gave the promise of future opulence; but if hamlets were soon planted near the mouths of the streams; if forts were erected to protect the merchant and the mariner, agriculture received no encouragement; and so many causes combined to check the growth of the country, that, notwithstanding its natural advantages, nearly two centuries glided away, before the scattered settlements along the sea-side rose into a succession of busy marts, sustained and enriched by the thriving villages of a fertile interior.

The settlement at Piscataqua could not quiet the ambition of Gorges. As a protestant and an Englishman, he was almost a bigot, both in patriotism and in religion. Unwilling to behold the Roman Catholic church and the French monarch obtain possession of the eastern coast of North America, his first act with reference to the territory of the present state of Maine was, to invite the Scottish nation to become the guardians of its frontier. Sir William Alexander, a man of influence with King James, and already filled with the desire of engaging in colonial adventure, seconded a design, which promised to establish his personal dignity and interest; and he obtained, without difficulty, a patent for all the territory east of the river St. Croix, and south of the St. Lawrence.[1] The whole region, which constituted

of Williamson. I have also derived advantage from Geo. Folsom's Saco and Biddeford, and W. Willis's Portland. Williamson, v. i. p. 227, describes Saco as a permanent settlement in 1623; I incline rather to the opinion of Willis and Folsom.

[1] The patent is in Hazard v. i. p. 134—145, in Purchas, v. iv. p.

360 COLLISION WITH FRANCE ON THE EASTERN FRONTIER.

CHAP. IX.

but a fragment of what the French had already called Acadia, was designated in English geography by the name of Nova Scotia. Thus were the seeds of future wars scattered broadcast by the unreasonable pretensions of England; for James now gave

1603. away lands, which, already and with a better title on the ground of discovery, had been granted by Henry IV. of France, and which had been immediately occupied by his subjects; nor could it be supposed, that the reigning French monarch would esteem his rights to his rising colonies invalidated by a parchment under the Scottish seal, or prove himself so forgetful of honor, as to discontinue the protection of the emigrants, who had planted themselves in America on the faith of the crown.[1]

Yet immediate attempts were made to effect a

1622. Scottish settlement. One ship, despatched for the purpose, did but come in sight of land, and then declining the perilous glory of colonization, returned to the permanent fishing station on Newfoundland.

1623. The next spring, a second ship arrived; but the two vessels in company, hardly possessed courage to sail to and fro along the coast, and make a partial survey of the harbors and the adjacent lands. The formation of a colony was postponed; and a brilliant eulogy of the soil, climate and productions of Nova Scotia, was the only compensation for the delay.[2]

1625. May.

The marriage of Charles I. with Henrietta Maria, promised between the rival claimants of the wilds of

---

1871. See, also, Sir Ferdinand Gorges' Narration, c. xxiv.
[1] Chalmers, p. 92.
[2] Purchas' Pilgrims, v. iv. p. 1872; Charlevoix, v. i. p. 274; De Laet, p. 62.

Acadia such friendly relations, as would lead to a peaceful adjustment of jarring pretensions. Yet even at that period the claims of France were not recognized by England; and a new patent confirmed to Sir William Alexander all the prerogatives, with which he had been lavishly invested.[1]

The citizens of a republic are so accustomed to see the legislation and the destinies of their country controlled only by public opinion, as formed and expressed in masses, that they can hardly believe the extent, in which the fortunes of European nations have been moulded by the caprices of individuals; how often the wounded vanity of a courtier, or an unsuccessful passion of a powerful minister, has changed the foreign relations of a kingdom. The feeble monarch of England, having twice abruptly dissolved parliament, and having vainly resorted to illegal modes of taxation, had forfeited the confidence of his people, and while engaged in a war with Spain, was destitute of money and of credit. It was at such a moment, that the precipitate gallantry of the favorite Buckingham, eager to thwart the jealous Richelieu, to whom he was as far inferior in the qualities of a statesman, as he was superior in youth, manners, and personal beauty, hurried England into an unnecessary and disastrous conflict with France. The siege of Rochelle invited the presence of an English fleet; but the expedition was fatal to the honor and the objects of Buckingham.

Hostilities were no where successfully attempted,

---

[1] Hazard, v. i. p. 206 and ff.

CHAP. IX.
1628.

except in America. Port Royal fell easily into the hands of the English; the conquest was no more than the acquisition of a small trading station. It was a bolder design to attempt the reduction of Canada. Sir David Kirk and his two brothers, Louis and Thomas, were commissioned to ascend the St. Lawrence, and Quebec received a summons to surrender. The garrison, destitute alike of provisions and of military stores, had no hope but in the character of Champlain, its commander; his answer of proud defiance concealed his weakness; and the intimidated

1629. assailants withdrew. But Richelieu sent no seasonable supplies; the garrison was reduced to extreme suffering and the verge of famine; and when the squadron of Kirk re-appeared before the town, the English were welcomed as deliverers. Favorable terms were demanded and promised; and Quebec capitulated. Thus did England, one hundred and thirty years before the enterprize of Wolf, make the conquest of the capital of New-France; that is to say, she gained possession of a barren rock and a few wretched hovels, tenanted by a hundred miserable men, who were now but beggars for bread of their vanquishers. Yet the event might fairly be deemed of importance, as pregnant with consequences; and the English admiral could not but admire the position of the fortress. Not a port in North America remained to the French; from Long Island to the Pole, England was without a rival.[1]

[1] Mémoires, in Hazard, v. i. p. 285—287; Charlevoix, v. i. p. 259 and ff. Compare, also, Haliburton's N. Scotia, v. i. p. 43. 46, &c.

But before the conquest of Canada was achieved, CHAP. IX. peace had been proclaimed between the contending states; and an article in the treaty promised the restitution of all acquisitions, made subsequent to April 14, 1629.[1] The possession of New-France would have been too dearly purchased by the dishonor of falsehood; and it was readily agreed to restore Quebec.[2] Perhaps an indifference to the issue prevailed in France; but the pride of honor and of religion seconded the claims to territory; and the genius of Richelieu succeeded in obtaining the restitution, not of Canada only, but of Cape Breton and the undefined Acadia.[3] The event has been frequently deplored; but misery ensued, because neither the boundaries of the rival nations were distinctly marked, nor the spirit of the compact honestly respected.

1629. May.

1632. Mar. 29.

While the eastern provinces of America were thus recovered by the firmness and ability of the French minister, very different causes delayed the colonization of Maine. Hardly had the little settlement, which claimed the distinction of being the oldest plantation on that coast, gained a permanent existence, before a succession of patents distributed the whole territory from the Piscataqua to the Penobscot among various proprietors. The grants were couched in vague language, and were made in hasty succession, without deliberation on the part of the

1628.

1629 to 1631.

[1] Rushworth, v. ii. p. 24.
[2] Hazard, v. i. p. 314, 315.
[3] Charlevoix, v. i. p. 273; Winthrop, v. i. p. 13; Hazard, v. i. p. 319, 320; Williamson, v. i. p. 246,
247; Dummer's Memorial, in iii. M. H. Coll. v. i. p. 232, is an *ex parte* statement, unworthy to be cited as an authority.

council of Plymouth, and without any firm purpose of establishing colonies on the part of those, for whose benefit they were issued. The consequences were obvious. As the neighborhood of the indefinite possessions of France foreboded the border feuds of a controverted jurisdiction, so the domestic disputes about land-titles and boundaries threatened perpetual lawsuits. At the same time enterprize was wasted by its diffusion over too wide a surface. Every harbor along the sea was accessible; the groups of cabins were scattered at wide intervals without any common point of attraction; and the agents of such proprietaries as aimed at securing a revenue from colonial rents, were often, perhaps, faithless, were always unsuccessful. How feeble were the attempts at planting towns, is evident from the nature of the tenure, by which the lands near the Saco were held; the condition of the grant was the introduction of fifty settlers within seven years! Agriculture was hardly attempted. A district of forty miles square, named Lygonia, and stretching from Harpswell to the Kennebunk, was set apart for the first colony of farmers; but when a vessel of sixty tuns brought over the emigrants, who were to introduce the plough into the regions on Casco Bay, the earlier resident adventurers treated their scheme with derision. The musket and the hook and line were more productive than the implements of husbandry; the few members of the unsuccessful company remained but a single year in a neighborhood, where the culture of the soil was so little esteemed;

and, embarking once more, sought a home among the rising settlements of Massachusetts. Except for the wealth to be derived from the forest and the sea, the coast of Maine would not at that time have been tenanted by Englishmen; and this again was fatal to the expectations of the proprietaries; since furs might be gathered and fish taken without the payment of quit-rents or the purchase of lands.[1]

Yet a pride of character sustained in Gorges an unbending hope; and he clung to the project of territorial aggrandizement. When Mason limited himself to the country west of the Piscataqua, and while Sir William Alexander obtained of the Plymouth company a patent for the eastern extremity of the United States, Gorges, alike undismayed by previous losses and by the encroaching claims of the French, who had already advanced their actual boundary to the Penobscot, succeeded in soliciting the whole district, that lies between the Kennebec and the boundary of New-Hampshire. The earnestness of his designs is apparent from his appointment as governor-general of New-England. If an unforeseen accident prevented his embarkation for America, and relieved Massachusetts of its apprehensions, he at least sent his nephew, William Gorges, to govern his territory. That officer repaired to the province without delay. Saco may have contained one hundred and fifty inhabitants, when the first court ever duly organized on the soil of Maine,

1635.
Feb. 3.

1636.

[1] Hubbard's Narrative, p. 204; 318, &c.; Williamson, v. i. p. 237 Willis, p. 13. 17, &c.; Folsom, p. and ff.; Gorges, p. 48, 49.

was held within its limits.[1] Before that time, there may have been some voluntary combinations among the settlers themselves; but there had existed on the Kennebec no jurisdiction of sufficient power to prevent or to punish bloodshed among the traders.[2] William Gorges remained in the country less than two years; the six puritans of Massachusetts and Connecticut, who received a commission to act as his successors, declined the trust,[3] and the infant settlements, again abandoned to the anarchy in which they had been planted, resolved to entreat Massachusetts to extend over them its protecting jurisdiction.[4]

1637.

1638.

1639.
April 3.

But such an event was to be longer delayed; for a royal charter now constituted Gorges, in his old age, the lord proprietary of the country; and his ambition immediately soared to the honor of establishing boroughs, framing schemes of colonial government, and enacting a code of laws. The veteran royalist, clearly convinced of the necessity of a vigorous executive, had but dim conceptions of popular liberty and rights; and he busied himself in making such arrangements as might have been expected from an old soldier, who was never remarkable for sagacity, had never seen America, and who, now in his dotage, began to act as a law-giver for a rising state in another hemisphere.[5]

Such was the condition of the settlements at the North at a time when the region, which lies but a

---

[1] Documents in Folsom, p. 49—52; Josselyn, p. 200.
[2] Hubbard, p. 167, 168; Winthrop.
[3] Winthrop; Hubbard, p. 261, 262; Williamson, v. i. p. 268.
[4] Williamson, v. i. p. 271.
[5] Gorges, p. 50 and ff.; Williamson, v. i. c. vi.

little nearer the sun, was already converted by the CHAP. energy of religious zeal into a busy, well organized, and even opulent state. The early history of Massachusetts is the history of a class of men, as remarkable for their qualities and their influence on public happiness, as any by which the human race has ever been diversified.

The settlement near Weymouth was revived; a 1624. new plantation was begun near Mount Wollaston, 1625. within the present limits of Quincy; and the merchants of the West continued their voyages to the islands of New-England. But these things were of feeble influence compared with the consequences of 1624. the attempt at a permanent establishment near Cape Ann; for White, a minister of Dorchester, a Puritan but not a Separatist, breathed into the enterprize a higher principle than that of the desire of gain. Roger Conant, having already left New Plymouth for Nantasket, through a brother in England, who was a friend of White, obtained the agency of the 1625. adventure. A year's experience proved to the company, that their speculation must change its form, or it would produce no results; the merchants, therefore, paid with honest liberality all the persons, whom they had employed, and abandoned the unprofitable scheme. But Conant, a man of extraordinary vigor, "inspired as it were by some superior instinct," and confiding in the active friendship of 1626. White, succeeded in breathing a portion of his sublime courage into his three companions; and making choice of Salem, as opening a convenient place of

CHAP. IX.

refuge for the exiles for religion, they resolved to remain as the sentinels of puritanism on the bay of Massachusetts.[1]

The design of a plantation was now ripening in the mind of White and his associates in the southwest of England. About the same time some friends in Lincolnshire fell into discourse about New-England; imagination swelled with the thought of planting the pure gospel among the quiet shades of America; it seemed better to depend on the benevolence of uncultivated nature and the care of Providence, than to endure the constraints of the English laws and the severities of the English hierarchy; and who could doubt, that at the voice of undefiled religion, the wilderness would change to a Paradise for a people, who lived under a bond with the Omnipresent God? After some deliberation, persons in London and the West Country were made acquainted with the design.[2]

1627.

1628.
Mar.
19.

The council for New England, itself incapable of the generous purpose of planting colonies, was ever ready to make sale of patents, which had now become their only source of revenue. Little concerned even at making grants of territory, which had already been purchased,[3] they sold to Sir Henry Roswell, Sir John Young, Thomas Southcoat, John

---

[1] Hubbard, p. 102. 106—108. Prince, p. 224. 229. 231. 235, 236. Cotton Mather, b. i. c. iv. 8. 3.

[2] Dudley to the Countess of Lincoln in i. Mass. Hist. Coll. v. viii. p. 37. The Countess of Lincoln to whom Dudley wrote, was "the approved lady Briget," the sister-in-law, and *not the mother* of the Lady Arbella. Savage on Winthrop, v. i. p. 2. Walpole's Royal and Noble Authors, v. ii. p. 272—275. The mother of Arbella was an authoress.

[3] Chalmers, p. 135.

COLONIZATION OF MASSACHUSETTS.

Humphrey, John Endicot, and Simon Whetcomb, gentlemen of Dorchester,[1] a belt of land, stretching from the Atlantic to the Pacific, extending three miles south of the River Charles and the Massachusetts bay, and three miles north of every part of the river Merrimac.[2] The zeal of White sought and soon found other and powerful associates in and about London,[3] kindred spirits, men of religious fervor, uniting the emotions of enthusiasm with unbending perseverance in action, Winthrop, Dudley, Johnson, Pynchon, Eaton, Saltonstall, Bellingham, so famous in colonial annals, besides many others, men of fortune, and friends to colonial enterprise, who desired to establish a plantation of "the best" of their countrymen on the shores of New England, in a safe seclusion, which the corruptions of human superstition might never invade. Three of the original purchasers parted with all their rights; Humphrey, Endicot and Whetcomb, retained an equal interest with the new partners.[4]

The company, already possessing the firmness of religious zeal and the resources of mercantile opulence, and having now acquired a title to an extensive territory, immediately prepared for the emigration of a colony; and Endicot, a man of dauntless courage and that cheerfulness which accompanies courage, benevolent though austere, firm though choleric, of a rugged nature, which the sternest form

---

[1] Hubbard, p. 108.
[2] Prince, p. 247. The charter repeats the boundaries.
[3] Hubbard, p. 109. Mather, b. i. c. iv. S. 3.
[4] Prince, p. 247. Col. Records.

of puritanism had not served to mellow, was selected as "a fit instrument to begin this wilderness work."¹ His wife and family were the companions of his voyage, the hostages of his fixed attachment to the New World. His immediate attendants, and those whom the company sent over the same year, in all, not far from one hundred in number,² were welcomed by Conant and his faithful associates to gloomy forests and unsubdued fields. Yet even then the spirit of enterprize predominated over the melancholy, which is impressed upon nature in its savage state; and seven or more threaded a path through the woods to the neck of land which is now Charlestown. English courage had preceded them; they found there one English hovel already tenanted.³

When the news reached London of the safe arrival of the emigrants, the number of the adventurers had already been much enlarged. The "Boston men" next lent their strength to the company;⁴ and the puritans throughout England began to take an interest in the efforts which invited the imagination to indulge in delightful visions. Interest was also made to obtain a royal charter, with the aid of Bellingham and of White, an eminent lawyer, who advocated the design. The Earl of Warwick had always been the friend of the company; Gorges had seemed to favor its advancement;⁵ and Lord Dorchester, then

---

¹ Johnson, b. i. c. ix. Hutchinson's Coll. p. 51, 52. p. 250, in Edward Everett's Address, p. 18, 19.
² Hubbard, p. 110. Higginson's N. E. Plantation, in i. Mass. Hist. Coll. v. i. p. 123. Dudley's Letter.
⁴ Colony Records.
⁵ Prince, p. 254. Gorges' Description, p. 25. Gorges' Narrative, c. xxvi. p. 40, 41.
³ Charlestown Records in Prince,

CHARTER FOR THE MASSACHUSETTS COLONY.

one of the secretaries of state, is said[1] to have exerted a powerful influence in its behalf. At last, after much labor and large expenditures,[2] the patent[3] for the Company of the Massachusetts Bay passed the seals.

The charter, which bears the signature of Charles I., and which was cherished for more than half a century as the most precious boon, established a corporation, like other corporations within the realm. The associates were constituted a body politic by the name of the Governor and Company of the Massachusetts Bay in New England. The administration of its affairs was entrusted to a Governor, Deputy, and eighteen assistants, who were to be annually elected by the stockholders, or members of the corporation. Four times a year, or oftener if desired, a general assembly of the freemen was to be held; and to these assemblies, which were invested with the necessary powers of legislation, inquest, and superintendence, the most important affairs were referred. No provision required the assent of the king to render the acts of the body valid; in his eye it was but a trading corporation, not a civil government; its doings were esteemed as indifferent as those of any guild or company in England; and if powers of jurisdiction in America were conceded, it was only from the nature of the business, in which the stockholders were to engage.

---

[1] Chalmers alone asserts it.
[2] Letter in Hazard, v. i. p. 237.
[3] The patent is at the State House in Boston, and is printed in Colony Laws, in Hutchinson's Coll. and in Hazard.

CHAP. IX.

For the charter designedly granted great facilities for colonization. It allowed the company to transport to its American territory any persons, whether English or foreigners, who would go willingly, would become lieges of the English king, and were not restrained " by especial name." It empowered, but it did not require,[1] the governor to administer the oaths of supremacy and allegiance; yet it was far from conceding to the patentees the privilege of freedom of worship. Not a single line alludes to such a purpose; nor can it be implied by a reasonable construction from any clause in the charter. The omission of an express guarantee left religious liberty unprovided for and unprotected. The instrument confers on the colonists the rights of English subjects; it does not confer on them new and greater rights. On the contrary, they are strictly forbidden to make laws or ordinances, repugnant to the laws and statutes of the realm of England. The express concession of power to administer the oath of supremacy, demonstrates that universal religious toleration was not designed; and the freemen of the corporation, it should be remembered, were not at that time Separatists. Even Higginson, and Hooker, and Cotton were still min-

[1] Grahame, v. i. p. 244, 245, is right as to that fact and no further. On the contested question he follows Neal, while Chalmers and Robertson have sustained an opposite view. I have written with confidence, because I have been favored with an ample, and to my mind, a conclusive opinion on the subject from the author of the Commentaries on the Constitution of the U. S.; whose opinions derive their weight less from his eminent station than from his profound learning and genius. The European who would understand our form of government, must study the Commentaries of Story.

isters of the church of England; nor could the patentees foresee, nor the English government anticipate, how wide a departure from English usages, would grow out of the emigration of puritans to America.[1]

The political condition of the colonists was not deemed by king Charles a subject worthy of his consideration. Full legislative and executive authority was conferred not on the emigrants but on the company, of which the emigrants could not be active members, so long as the charter of the corporation remained in England. The associates in London were to establish ordinances, to settle forms of government, to name all necessary officers, to prescribe their duties, and to establish a criminal code. Massachusetts was not erected into a province, to be governed by laws of its own enactment; it was reserved for the corporation to decide, what degree of civil rights its colonists should enjoy. The charter on which the freemen of Massachusetts succeeded in erecting a system of independent representative liberty, did not secure to them a single privilege of self-government; but left them, as the Virginians had been left, without one valuable franchise, at the mercy of a corporation within the realm. This was so evident, that some of those, who had already emigrated, clamored that they were become slaves.[2]

---

[1] The editor of Winthrop did me the kindness to read to me unpublished letters, which are in his possession, and which prove that the Puritans in England were amazed as well as alarmed at the boldness of their brethren in Massachusetts.

[2] Hazard, v. i. p. 257.

CHAP. IX.
1629.

It was equally the right of the corporation, to establish the terms on which new members should be admitted to its freedom. Its numbers could be enlarged or changed only by its own consent.

It was perhaps implied, though it was not expressly required, that the affairs of the company should be administered in England; yet the place for holding the courts was not specially appointed. What if the corporation should vote the emigrants to be freemen, and call a meeting beyond the Atlantic? What if the governor, deputy, assistants, and freemen should themselves emigrate, and thus break down the distinction between the colony and the corporation? The history of Massachusetts is the counterpart to that of Virginia; the latter obtained its greatest liberty by the abrogation of the charter of its company; the former by a transfer of its charter and a daring construction of its powers by the successors of the original patentees.

The charter had been granted in March; in April preparations were hastening for the embarkation of new emigrants. The government which was now established for Massachusetts, merits commemoration, though it was never duly organized. It was to consist of a governor and counsellors; of whom eight out of the thirteen were appointed by the corporation in England; three were to be named by these eight; and, as it was said, to remove all grounds of discontent, the choice of the remaining two counsellors was granted to the colonists as a liberal boon. The board, when thus constituted, was invested with all the powers of legislation, justice, and administration. Such was the inauspicious dawn of civil and religious liberty on the Bay of Massachusetts.[1]

Benevolent instructions to Endicot were at the same time issued. "If any of the salvages," such were the orders long and uniformly followed in all changes of government, and placed on record more than half a century before William Penn proclaimed the principles of peace on the borders of the Delaware, " pretend right of inheritance to all or any part of the lands granted in our patent, we pray you endeavor to purchase their tytle, that we may avoid the least scruple of intrusion." " Particularly publish, that no wrong or injury be offered to the natives."[2]

The departure of the fleet for America was now anxiously desired. The colonists were to be cheered by the presence of religious teachers; and the excellent and truly catholic John Higginson, an eminent non-conforming minister, receiving an invitation to conduct the emigrants, esteemed it as a call from heaven.[3] The propagation of the gospel among the heathen was earnestly desired; in pious sincerity they resolved if possible to redeem these wrecks of human nature; the colony seal was an Indian, erect, with an arrow in his right hand, and the motto, "Come over and help us;"[4]—a device of

---

[1] Col. Records. Hazard, v. i. p. 256—268, and 268—271. Bentley in i. Mass. Hist. Coll. v. vi. 235, 236.
[2] Hazard, v. i. p. 263. 277.
[3] Hutchinson's Coll. p. 24, 25. Hubbard, p. 112.
[4] Douglass, v. i. p. 409. Douglass is almost as rash as Oldmixon.

CHAP. IX.
1629.

which the appropriateness has been lost by the modern substitution of the favorite line of Algernon Sidney;—and three additional ministers attended the expedition. The company of emigrants was winnowed before sailing; and servants of ill life were discharged. "No idle drone may live amongst us;"[1] was the spirit as well as the law of the dauntless community, which was to turn the sterility of New-England into a cluster of wealthy states.

May.

As the ships were bearing Higginson and his followers out of sight of their native land, they remembered it, not as the scene of their sufferings from intolerance, but as the home of their fathers and the dwelling place of their friends. They did not say "Farewell Babylon! farewell Rome! but, FAREWELL DEAR ENGLAND."[2]

It was in the last days of June, that the little band of two hundred arrived at Salem; where the "corruptions of the English church" were never to be planted, and where a new "reformation" was to be reduced to practice. They found neither church nor town; eight or ten pitiful hovels, one more stately tenement for the Governor, and a few cornfields were the only proofs, that they had been preceded by their countrymen. The whole body of old and new planters now amounted to three hundred; of whom one third joined the infant settlement at Charlestown.[3]

[1] Hazard, v. i. p. 283, 284. 256.
[2] Mather, b. iii. c. i. S. 12.
[3] Higginson's whole account is, of course, the highest authority.
See Hutchinson's Collection, p. 32—50, and i. Mass. Hist. Coll. v. i. p. 117—124. Charlestown Records in Prince, p. 261.

ESTABLISHMENT OF RELIGIOUS INDEPENDENCE.

To the great European world the few tenants of the mud-hovels and log-cabins at Salem might appear too insignificant to merit notice; to themselves they were as the chosen emissaries of God; outcasts from England yet favorites with heaven; destitute of security, of convenient food and shelter, and yet blessed beyond all mankind, for they were the depositories of the purest truth, and the selected instruments to kindle in the wilderness the beacon of pure religion, of which the undying light should not only penetrate the wigwams of the heathen, but spread its benignant beams across the darkness of the whole civilized world. The emigrants were not so much a body politic, as a church in the wilderness; with no benefactor around them but nature, no present sovereign but God. An entire separation was made between state and church; religious worship was established on the basis of the independence of each separate religious community; all officers of the church were elected by its members; and these rigid Calvinists, of whose rude intolerance the world has been filled with malignant calumnies, established a covenant, cherishing, it is true, the severest virtues, but without one tinge of fanaticism. It was an act of piety not of study; it favored virtue not superstition; inquiry and not submission. The people were enthusiasts but not bigots.[1] The church was self-constituted.[2] It did not ask the assent of the king; or recognize him as its head; its officers were set apart

CHAP. IX.

1629.

July 20.

Aug. 6.

[1] See the covenant in Neal's N. E. v. i. 141—143, and in Bentley's Salem, App. No. iv.
[2] Hubbard, p. 116—120. Prince, p. 263, 264. Neal's N. England, v. i. p. 144.

and ordained among themselves ;[1] it used no liturgy; it rejected unnecessary ceremonies; and reduced the simplicity of Calvin to a still plainer standard. The motives, which controlled their decisions, were so deeply seated in the very character of their party, that the doctrine and discipline, then established at Salem, remained the rule of puritans in New England.

There existed even in this little company a few individuals, to whom the new system was unexpected; and in John and Samuel Browne, they found able leaders. Both were members of the colonial council, they had been favorites of the corporation in England; and one of them an experienced and meritorious lawyer, had been a member of the board of Assistants in London.[2] They declared their dissent from the church of Higginson; and at every risk of union and tranquillity, they insisted upon the use of the English liturgy. But should the emigrants give up the very purpose for which they had crossed the Atlantic? Should not even the forests of Massachusetts be safe against the intrusion of the hierarchy, before which they had fled? They were, in one sense, a garrison, set for the defence of the territory against insincere friends not less than open foes. They deemed the coëxistence of their liberty and of prelacy impossible; anticipating invasions of their rights, they feared to find in the adherents of the establishment, persons, who would act as spies in the

[1] Felt's Annals of Salem, p. 573. An accurate and useful work, the fruit of much original research.
[2] Hazard, v. i. p. 267. 269.

camp and betray them to their persecuting adversaries; the form of religion, from which they had suffered, was therefore attacked, not as a sect but as a tyranny.[1] The charter had conferred on the company the right of expelling from its colonial domains every person, whose presence seemed a detriment to its welfare;[2] and the instructions from the company required the enforcement of the provision.[3] Finding it to be a vain attempt to persuade the Brownes to relinquish their resolute opposition, and believing that their speeches tended to produce disorder and dangerous feuds, Endicot sent them to England in the returning ships; and faction, deprived of its leaders, died away.[4]

Winter brought disease and the sufferings incident to early settlements. Above eighty, almost half of the emigrants, died before spring;[5] lamenting only, that they were removed from the world before beholding the perfect establishment of their religion. Higginson himself fell a victim to a hectic fever; the future prosperity of New England, and the glories of the many churches, which were to adorn and gladden the wilderness, were the cheering visions, that in the hour of death floated before his eyes.[6]

The Brownes returned to England, breathing in-

---

[1] Montesquieu, L. xxv. c. ix. Hutchinson, quoting the remark, omits the best part of it.
[2] Colony Laws, p. 15, 16.
[3] "If any prove incorrigible, ship such persons home by the Lyon's Whelp." Hazard, v. i. p. 263.
[4] Prince, p. 264. Bentley, p. 241, 242. Mather, b. i. c. 4. S. 3. Eliot, in i. Mass. Hist. Coll. v. ix. p. 3—6. Chalmers, 144—146. Neal's N. E. v. i. p. 144, 145. The liberal Ebeling, v. i. p. 869, defends the measure.
[5] Dudley, p. 38. Prince, p. 271.
[6] Mather, b. iii. c. i. S. 14

effectual menaces.[1] The ships also carried with them a description of New England by Higginson; a tract, of which three editions were published within a few months, so intense an interest in the new colony had been diffused throughout the realm.

For the concession of the Massachusetts Charter seemed to the puritans like a summons from Heaven, inviting them to America. There the gospel might be taught in its purity; and the works of nature would alone be the safe witnesses of their devotions. England by her persecutions proved herself weary of her inhabitants, who were now esteemed more vile, than the earth on which they trod. Habits of expense degraded men of moderate fortune; and even the schools, which should be the fountains of living waters, had become corrupt. The new world shared in the Providence of God; it had claims, therefore, to the benevolence and exertions of man. What nobler work, than to abandon the comforts of England, and plant the church in the remote citadel, which the advocates of a false religion should never scale?

But was it right, a scrupulous conscience demanded, to fly from persecutions? Yes, they answered, for persecutions might lead their posterity to abjure the truth. The certain misery of their wives and children was the most gloomy of their forebodings; and it must have been a stern sensé of duty, which could command the powerful emotions of nature to be silent, and set aside all considerations of physical

[1] Hazard, v. i. p. 287. 289.

evils as the fears of too carnal minds. The rights of the natives offered an impediment more easily removed; much land had been desolated by the plague; and the good leave of the Indians might be purchased. The ill success of other plantations could not chill the rising enthusiasm; former enterprize had aimed at profit; the present object was purity of religion; the earlier settlements had been filled with a lawless multitude; it was now proposed to form " a peculiar government," and to colonize " the best." Such were the " Conclusions"[1] which were privately circulated among the puritans of England.

On the suggestion of the generous Matthew Cradock, the governor of the company,[2] it was proposed that the charter should be transferred to those of the freemen, who should themselves inhabit the colony; and the question immediately became the most important, that could be debated. An agreement was at once formed at Cambridge in England between men of fortune and education, that they would themselves embark for America, if, before the last of September, the whole government should be legally transferred to them and the other freemen of the company, who should inhabit the plantation.[3] The plan was sufficient to excite in the family of John Winthrop and in many of the purest men in England, the desire to emigrate. "I shall call that my

1629.
July 28.

Aug. 24.

---

[1] Hutchinson's Coll. p. 27—31. Mather, b. i. c. iv. S. 5.
[2] Prince, p. 262. Savage on Winthrop, v. i. p. 2. I have carefully consulted the Colony Records, which are in general in a good state of preservation, and which are diffuse on the subject of the transfer of the charter.
[3] Hutchinson's Coll. p. 25, 26.

country," said the younger Winthrop to his father, "where I may most glorify God, and enjoy the presence of my dearest friends. Therefore herein I submit myself to God's will and yours, and dedicate myself to God and the company, with the whole endeavors, both of body and mind. The Conclusions, which you sent down, are unanswerable; and it cannot but be a prosperous action, which is so well allowed by the judgments of God's prophets, undertaken by so religious and wise worthies in Israel, and indented to God's glory in so special a service."[1] Two days after the contract had been executed, the subject was again brought before the court. A serious debate ensued, and continued the next day, when it was fully and with general consent declared, that the government and the patent should be transferred beyond the Atlantic and settled in New England.[2]

This vote was simply a decision of the question, where the future meetings of the company should be held; and yet it effectually changed a commercial corporation into an independent provincial government. The measure was believed to be consistent with the principles of the charter. The corporation did not sell itself; the corporation emigrated. They could not assign the patent; but they could call a legal meeting at London or on board ship in

---

[1] Winthrop, v. i. p. 359, 360. The publicity of the admirable letter is due to Savage.

[2] Records, v. i. p. 31.; "soe far as it may be done legally." Yet Sept. 29, 1629, a committee was raised "to take advice of Learned Counsell, whether the same may be legally done or no." Records, v. i. p. 33.

an English harbor; and why not in the port of Salem as well as at the Isle of Wight? In a cabin or under a tree at Charlestown, as well as at the house of Goffe in London? The propriety of the measure in a juridical point of view, cannot be sustained;[1] but whatever may be thought of the legality of the decision, it certainly conferred no new franchises or power on the emigrants, unless they were already members of the company; it admitted no new freemen; it gave to Massachusetts a present government; but the corporation, though it was to meet in New England, retained in its full integrity the right conferred by the charter, of admitting freemen according to its pleasure. The manner in which that power was to be exercised, would control the early political character of Massachusetts.

At the court, convened for the purpose of appointing officers who would emigrate, John Winthrop, a man approved for piety, liberality and wisdom, was chosen governor, and the whole board of assistants selected for America. Yet as the hour of departure drew near, the consciousness of danger spread such terrors, that even the hearts of the strong began to fail. One and another of the magistrates declined. It became necessary to hold a court at Southampton for the election of three substitutes among the assistants; and of these three one never went. Even after they had embarked, a court was held on board the Arbella, and Thomas Dudley was chosen Deputy Governor in the place of Humphrey, who staid be-

[1] Story's MS. opinion.

hind.[1] Dudley emigrated, and had hardly reached America, before he repented that he had come; the country had been described in too favorable colors.[2] It was principally the calm decision of Winthrop which sustained the courage of his companions.[3]

The whole number of ships employed during the season was seventeen; and they carried over not far from fifteen hundred souls. About eight hundred, all of them puritans, inclined to the party of the independents, many of them men of high endowments, large fortune, and the best education, scholars, well versed in all the learning of the times, clergymen, who ranked among the most eloquent and pious in the realm, embarked with Winthrop for their asylum, bearing with them the charter, which was to be the basis of their liberties.[4] Religion did not expel the feelings of nature; before leaving Yarmouth they pub-

---

[1] Records, v. i. p. 54. Prince, p. 264. 266, 267. 270. 272. 274, 275. Hutchinson, v. i. p. 23, 24.
[2] Dudley's Letter as before.
[3] Ibid. i. Mass. H. Coll. v. viii. 38.
[4] For the history of Massachusetts in the remainder of this chapter, the Records of the Colony were a principle source. The History of Winthrop in the incomparably accurate edition and with the Commentary of Savage is of still greater historical value and of equal authenticity. Hubbard, Mather, Prince, Neal, Oldmixon, and Chalmers, are of little service in comparison. The Mass. Hist. Coll. are rich in authentic materials, none of which I have neglected. The excellent Letter of Dudley, Winthrop's Correspondence, Johnson's Wonderworking Providence, have been carefully consulted, and shorter tracts and letters almost without number. Hutchinson's Collection is full of important documents for the history of N. E. His history is an excellent guide; but I have followed the contemporaries of the events which I describe. Snow, Felt, and Francis, have treated their respective subjects with ability and research. Besides the recent edition of the Colony Laws, I have before me the folio of 1660. Many documents are in Hazard. Many more are on file in the State House; and I have examined hundreds of them; gleaning but little new information, where men like Prince and Savage had been gathering before me. The original materials for the early history of New England are exceedingly copious; the circumstances, attending every considerable event may be traced with minuteness.

lished to the world the grounds of their removal, and bade an affectionate farewell to the church of England and to the land of their nativity. "Our hearts," say they, "shall be fountains of tears for your everlasting welfare, when we shall be in our poor cottages in the wilderness."

The emigrants were a body of sincere believers, desiring purity of religion, and not a colony of philosophers, bent upon universal toleration; reverence for the peculiarities of their faith led them to a land, which was either sterile or overgrown with an unprofitable vegetation. They emigrated to a new hemisphere, where distance might protect them from inquisition; to a soil of which they had purchased the exclusive possession, with a charter of which they had acquired the entire control, for the sake of reducing to practice the doctrines of religion and the forms of civil liberty, which they cherished more than life itself. They constituted a corporation to which they themselves might establish at their pleasure the terms of admission. They held in their own hands the key to their asylum, and maintained their right of closing its doors against the enemies of its harmony and its safety.

In June and July the ships which bore Winthrop and his immediate companions, arrived to a scene of gloom; such of the earlier emigrants as had survived the previous winter, were poor and weak from sickness; their corn and bread were hardly enough for a fortnight's supply. Instead of offering a welcome, they thronged to the new comers to be fed. Nearly

CHAP. IX.
1630.

two hundred servants, who had been sent over at a great expense, received their liberty, free from all engagements; their labor, such was the excessive scarcity, was worth less than the cost of their maintenance.

The selection of places for the new plantations became the immediate care. The bay and the adjoining rivers were examined; if Charlestown was the place of the first sojourning, it was not long before the fires of civilization, never more to be quenched, were kindled in Boston and the adjacent villages. The dispersion of the company was esteemed a grievance; but no time was left for long deliberation; and those who had health began to build. Yet sickness delayed the progress of the work; and death often withdrew the laborer from the fruit of his exertions. Every hardship was encountered. The emigrants lodged at best in tents of cloth and in miserable hovels; they beheld their friends "weekly, yea almost daily, drop away before their eyes;" in a country abounding in secret fountains, they perished for the want of good water. Many of them had been accustomed to plenty and ease, the refinements of cultivated life and the conveniences of luxury. Woman was there to struggle against unforeseen hardships, unwonted sorrows; the men who defied trials for themselves, were miserable at beholding those whom they cherished, dismayed by the horrors which

Aug. encompassed them. The virtues of Arbella Johnson, a daughter of the house of Lincoln, could not break through the gloomy shadows that surrounded her;

and as she had been ill before her arrival, grief soon hurried her to the grave. Her husband, one of the first men in the colony, zealous for pure religion, in life "the greatest furtherer of the plantation," and by his bequests a benefactor of the infant state, was subdued by the force of disease and afflictions; but "he died willingly and in sweet peace," making a "most godly end." Winthrop lost a son, though not by disease. A hundred or more, some of them of the board of assistants, men who had enjoyed high consideration, and had been revered with confidence as the inseparable companions of the common misery or the common success, disheartened by the scenes of woe, and dreading famine and death, deserted Massachusetts and sailed for England. Before December two hundred at the least had died. Yet as the brightest lightnings are kindled in the darkest clouds, the general distress did but augment the piety and confirm the fortitude of the colonists. Their enthusiasm was softened by the mildest sympathy with suffering humanity; while a sincere religious faith kept guard against despondency and weakness. Not a hurried line, not a trace of repining, appears in their records; the congregations always assembled at the stated times, whether in the open fields or under the shade of an ancient tree; in the midst of want they abounded in hope; in the solitudes of the wilderness, they believed themselves in company with the Greatest, the most Benevolent of Beings. Honor is due not less to those who perished than to those who survived; to the martyrs the hour of death was an hour of triumph; such as is never witnessed in more tranquil seasons; just as there can be no gorgeous sunset, but when the vapors of evening gather in heavy masses round the west, to reflect the glories of declining day. For that placid resignation, which diffuses grace round the bed of sickness, and makes death too serene for sorrow and too beautiful for fear, no one was more remarkable than the daughter of Thomas Sharp, whose youth and sex, and as it seemed unequalled virtues, won the warmest eulogies of the austere Dudley. Even children caught the spirit of the place; and in their last hours awoke to the awful mystery of the impending change, awaited its approach in the tranquil confidence of faith, and went to the grave full of immortality. The survivors bore all things meekly, "remembering the end of their coming hither." "We here enjoy God and Jesus Christ," wrote Winthrop to his wife, whom pregnancy had detained in England, "and is not this enough? I thank God I like so well to be here, as I do not repent my coming. I would not have altered my course, though I had foreseen all these afflictions. I never had more content of mind."

Such were the scenes in the infant settlements of Massachusetts. In the two following years the colony had not even the comfort of receiving large accessions. In 1631 ninety only came over; a smaller number than had returned the preceding year. In 1632 no more than two hundred and fifty arrived. Men dreaded the hazards of the voyage and the wil-

ORGANIZATION OF THE GOVERNMENT.

derness; and waited to learn the success of the first CHAP. IX.
adventurers. Those who had deserted, excused
their cowardice by defaming the country. Dudley 1630.
wrote plainly of the hardships to be encountered;
and, moreover, the apprehension was soon raised and
never quieted, that the liberties of the colonists would
be subverted by the government in England.

Purity of religion and civil liberty were the objects
nearest the wishes of the emigrants. The first court Aug. 23.
of assistants took measures for the support of the
ministers. As others followed, the form of the administration was considered; that the liberties of the
people might be secured against the encroachments of
the rulers; "for," say they, "the waves of the sea
do not more certainly waste the shore, than the
minds of ambitious men are led to invade the liberties
of their brethren." By the charter, fundamental
laws were to be enacted in the assembly of all the
freemen of the colony; and a general court was ac- Oct. 19.
cordingly convened at Boston to settle the government. More than one hundred persons, many of
them old planters and members of no church, were
admitted to the franchises of the corporation; the
inconvenience of gathering the whole body for purposes of legislation became but the greater and the
more apparent; and the people did but reserve to
themselves the right of filling such vacancies as
might occur in the board of assistants. Thus the
government became for a season an elective aristocracy; the magistrates holding their offices for no
limited period, were to choose the governor and dep-

uty from among themselves; and were entrusted with every branch of political power.

1631. May 18. This arrangement was temporary. At the next general court the freemen began to revoke a part of the authority, of which they had been too lavish. The former ordinance was now modified by a declaratory act, which did not, it is true, limit the duration of office to a year, but reserved to the commons a right of annually making in the board such changes as a majority should desire. If the right thus asserted should not be exercised, the former magistrates remained in power without the formality of a new election. And a law of still greater moment, pregnant with evil and with good, was at the same time established. "To the end the body of the commons may be preserved of honest and good men, it was ordered and agreed, that for the time to come, no man shall be admitted to the freedom of this body politic but such as are members of some of the churches within the limits of the same." The principle of universal suffrage was the usage of Virginia; Massachusetts, resting for its defence on its unity and its enthusiasm, gave all power to the select band of religious votaries, into which the avenues could be opened only by the elders. The elective franchise was thus confined to a small proportion of the whole population, and the government rested on an essentially aristocratic foundation. But it was not an aristocracy of wealth; the polity was a sort of theocracy; the servant or the bondman, if he were a member of a church, might be a freeman of the company. Other states have limited the possession of political rights to the opulent; to free-holders; to the first-born; the colonists of Massachusetts had emigrated for the enjoyment of purity of religion; and, while they scrupulously refused to the clergy even the least shadow of political power, they deliberately entrusted the whole government to those of the laity, over whose minds the ministers would probably exercise an unvarying influence. It was the reign of the church; it was a commonwealth of the chosen people in covenant with God.

The motive of this limitation of the elective franchise lay in the dangers, which were apprehended from England; and which seemed to require a devoted union, confirmed by the strongest ties and consecrated by the holiest rites of religion. The public mind of the colony was in other respects ripening for the practice of democratic liberty. It could not rest satisfied with leaving the assistants in possession of all authority and of an almost independent existence; and the magistrates, with the exception of the passionate Ludlow, were willing to yield. It was, therefore, agreed, at the next general court, that the governor and assistants should be annually chosen. The people, satisfied with the recognition of their right, re-elected their former magistrates, and carried themselves with silence and modesty. The germ of a representative government was already visible; each town was ordered to choose two men, to appear at the next court of assistants, and concert a plan for the establishment of a public treasury.

The measure had become necessary; for the levy, made by the assistants alone, had already awakened alarm and opposition.

A transition to a more perfect form of government soon ensued. Two years had not elapsed, before the people had become yet more jealous of their liberties, and previous to the general court the freemen in each town, of themselves, as it were by a general impulse, chose deputies to consider in advance, what subjects should be brought before the general court. The charter also was carefully examined; the opinion of the governor was required in explanation of its provisions and the best mode of carrying them into effect. It was plain, that the legislative authority was reserved to the whole body of freemen; " the patent," thought Winthrop, " allows no deputies at all, but only by inference ;" yet the welfare of the colony would not permit the assembling of the whole people. The governor, therefore, proposed a select committee to be chosen by the respective towns, with power to amend the legislation of the assistants, to sanction assessments, and to dispose of lands. The advice was discreet; the conduct of the people was still better.

The day for the assembling of the general court arrived. The magistrates and the clergy were aware of the democratic tendencies of the freemen; and John Cotton, who had newly joined the colony, attempting by the exercise of professional influence to raise a barrier against the swelling tide, preached an election sermon against rotation in office. To eject an honest magistrate from his post was compared to the injustice of turning a private man out of his freehold. The question, having thus been decided in the pulpit, remained to be settled by the electors at the polls; and they reversed the opinion by choosing a new governor and deputy. The mode of taking the votes was at the same time reformed; and instead of the erection of hands, the ballot-box was now introduced. Thus "the people established a reformation of such things as they judged to be amiss in the government."

It was then decreed, that the whole body of the freemen should be convened only for the election of the magistrates; to whom in conjunction with the deputies to be chosen by the several towns, the powers of legislation and appointment were henceforward entrusted. Thus did the epidemic of America break out in Massachusetts just fifteen years after its first appearance in Virginia. The trading corporation had become a representative democracy.

The pride of newly acquired power proceeded to investigate the conduct of the first administration; and to censure the usurpations of authority by the assistants. But the laws which were dictated by a spirit of jealous liberty, are of far deeper interest. The people of Virginia in March, 1624, and perhaps at an earlier session, had asserted for its popular branch the exclusive right of laying taxes. It was now made the rule in Massachusetts, that the immediate representatives of the freemen alone might raise money or dispose of lands. Arbitrary taxation was strangled in the American colonies in their infancy. Thus early did they establish the principles, which at a greater hazard and for a greater object, were again and triumphantly declared after the lapse of nearly a century and a half. Thus early did the freemen of Massachusetts unconsciously echo back the voice of the people of Virginia; like the solitary mountain, replying to the thunder, or like deep, calling unto deep. The state was filled with the hum of village politicians; "the freemen of every town in the Bay were busy in inquiring into their liberties and privileges." With the exception of the principle of universal suffrage, now so happily established, the annual representative democracy was as perfect two centuries ago as it is to-day. The dangers which the enemies of popular liberty now feign to apprehend, were then considered imminent. "Elections cannot be safe there long," said the lawyer Lechford. The same prediction has been made these two hundred years; and all the while the civil government has remained secure. The public mind has been in perpetual agitation; like the vast rocking-stone, it is still easily shaken, even by slight and transient impulses; but after all its vibrations it follows the laws of the moral world and safely and steadily recovers its balance, as surely as that the power of gravity continues unchanged.

The people, full of excitement but not of faction, were earnest to obtain fixed guarantees of their rights, and desired to limit the discretion of the executive. They therefore demanded a written constitution; and a commission was accordingly appointed "to frame a body of grounds of laws in resemblance to a magna charta," to serve as a bill of rights. It marks the manners of the times, that the approbation of the ministers, as well as of the general court, was desired, before they should be received as valid.

The relative powers of the assistants and the deputies remained for nearly ten years the object of discussion and contest. Both parties received office at the hands of the people; but the former were elected by the freemen of the colony, the latter by the respective towns. The two bodies used to meet in convention; but the assistants claimed and exercised the right of a separate negative vote on all joint proceedings. Discontent ensued and increased in vehemence; the authority of the patricians was successfully maintained, sometimes by wise delays, sometimes by "a judicious sermon;" at last public excitement required a definite adjustment of the grievance; and an easy remedy was found by dividing the court in their consultations; the magistrates and the deputies, each constituting a separate branch, and each possessing a negative on the proceedings of the other.

The settlement of the controversy had required the interference of the clergy; the elders were summoned to attend the general court, and the question referred to their arbitrament. For the basis of the state was religion; the people had emigrated for the sake of enjoying it in its unadulterated forms; and the puritan church was the rock, on which the foundations of political independence rested. On what else could it have been built? What but the motive for the plantation could have been made the principle of its institutions?

The infirm man who is just recovering from disease, shrinks from the light which is grateful to the eye of health, and is chilled by the very air that gives new vigor to the strong. The same is true of men in masses. An unnatural irritability follows a train of sufferings; the men who have just escaped from persecutions for opinion's sake, shrink from contradiction as from the approach of peril; and are quick to discern the seeds of danger and the causes of alarm, where a healthier public feeling would have observed the progress of discussion with patience, or welcomed a discovery of truth with approbation. There was perpetual reason to dread an attack from the hierarchy of England; and the bulwark of religious enthusiasm was made the defence of the colony. It proved a sufficient defence; its energy in a community, where it ruled without opposition, could never be shaken by threats, nor cajoled by caresses, nor intimidated by the awards of dependant tribunals.

To the colonists the maintenance of their religious unity seemed essential to their cordial resistance to English attempts at oppression. And why, said they, should we not insist upon this union? We have come to the outside of the world for the privilege of living by ourselves; why should we open our asylum to those, in whom we can repose no confidence?

The world cannot call this persecution. We have been banished to the wilderness; is it an injustice to exclude our oppressors and those whom we dread as their allies, from the place which is to shelter us from their intolerance? Is it a great cruelty to expel from our abode the enemies of our peace or even the doubtful friend? Will any man complain at being driven from among banished men, with whom he has no fellowship, of being refused admittance to a gloomy place of exile?—The whole continent of America invited colonization; they claimed their own narrow domains for "the brethren." Their religion was their life; they welcomed none but its adherents; they could not tolerate the scoffer, the infidel, or the dissenter; and the presence of the whole people was required in their congregations. Such was the system inflexibly established and regarded as the only adequate guarantee of the rising liberties of Massachusetts.

While the state was thus connecting by the closest bonds the energy of its faith with its form of government, there appeared in its midst one of those clear minds, which sometimes bless the world by their power of receiving moral truth in its purest light, and of reducing the just conclusions of their principles to a happy and consistent practice. In February of the first year of the colony, but a few months after the arrival of Winthrop, and before either Cotton or Hooker had embarked for New-England, there arrived at Nantasket, after a stormy passage of sixty-six days, "a young minister, godly and zealous, having precious" gifts. It was Roger Williams. He was then but a little more than thirty years of age; but his mind had already matured a doctrine, which secures him an immortality of fame, as its application has given religious peace to the American world. He was a puritan, and a fugitive from English persecution; but his wrongs had not clouded his accurate understanding; in the capacious recesses of his mind he had revolved the nature of intolerance, and he, and he alone, had arrived at the great principle which is its sole effectual remedy. He announced his discovery under the simple proposition of the sanctity of conscience. The civil magistrate should restrain crime, but never control opinion; should punish guilt, but never violate the freedom of the soul. The doctrine contained within itself an entire reformation of theological jurisprudence; it would blot from the statute-book the crime of non-conformity; would quench the fires that persecution had so long kept burning; would repeal every law compelling attendance on public worship; would abolish tithes and all forced contributions to the maintenance of religion; would give an equal protection to every form of religious faith; and never suffer the authority of the civil government to be enlisted against the mosque of the mussulman or the altar of the fire-worshipper, against the Jewish synagogue or the Roman cathedral. It is wonderful with what distinctness Roger Williams deduced these inferences from his great principle, the consistency with which, like

Pascal and Edwards, those bold and profound reasoners on other subjects, he accepted every fair inference from his doctrines, and the circumspection with which he repelled every unjust imputation. In the unwavering assertion of his views he never changed his position; the sanctity of conscience was the great tenet, which, with all its consequences, he defended, as he first trod the shores of New-England; and in his extreme old age it was the last pulsation of his heart. But it placed the young emigrant in direct opposition to the whole system, on which Massachusetts was founded; and gentle and forgiving as was his temper, prompt as he was to concede every thing which honesty permitted, he always asserted his belief with temperate firmness and unbending benevolence.

So soon, therefore, as Williams arrived in Boston, he found himself among the New-England churches, but not of them. They had not yet renounced the use of force in religion; and he could not with his entire mind adhere to churches, which retained the offensive features of English legislation. What then was the commotion in the colony, when it was found that the people of Salem desired to receive him as their teacher? The court of Boston "marvelled" at the precipitate decision, and the people of Salem were required to forbear. Williams withdrew to the settlement of Plymouth, and remained there about two years. But his virtues had won the affections of the church of Salem; and the apostle of 1633. intellectual liberty was once more welcomed to their

400 INTELLECTUAL LIBERTY FINDS AN ADVOCATE.

CHAP. IX.

confidence. He remained the object of public jealousy. How mild was his conduct is evident from an example. He had written an essay on the nature of the tenure, by which the colonists held their lands in America; and he had argued, that an English patent could not invalidate the rights of the native inhabitants. The opinion sounded, at first, like treason against the cherished charter of the colony;

1634. Jan. 24.

Williams desired only that the offensive manuscript might be burned; and so effectually explained its purport, that the court applauded his temper, and declared " that the matters were not so evil, as at first they seemed."[1]

But the principles of Roger Williams led him into perpetual collision with the clergy and the government of Massachusetts. It had ever been their custom to respect the church of England, and in the mother country they frequented its service without scruple; yet its principles and its administration were still harshly exclusive. Williams would hold no communion with intolerance; for, said he, " the doctrine of persecution for cause of conscience is most evidently and lamentably contrary to the doctrine of Christ Jesus."

The magistrates insisted on the presence of every man at public worship; Williams reprobated the law;

---

[1] I derive the account of Roger Williams, in Massachusetts, exclusively from the Colony Records, Winthrop, John Cotton's diffuse quarto, and the letters and writings of Roger Williams himself. Yet I have carefully compared all that has been published about him by Hubbard, C. Mather, Prince, Callender, Hopkins, Backus, Bentley, Eliot, Dwight, Allen, Davis on Morton, Savage on Winthrop, Eddy, Felt, Upham, Knowles, and Christian Examiner for March, 1834.

the worst statute[1] in the English code was that which did but enforce attendance upon the parish church. To compel men to unite with those of a different creed he regarded as an open violation of their natural rights; to drag to public worship the irreligious and the unwilling, seemed only like requiring hypocrisy. "An unbelieving soul is dead in sin," such was his argument; and to force the indifferent from one worship to another, "was like shifting a dead man into several changes of apparell." "No one, should be bound to worship or," he added, "to maintain a worship against his own consent." "What," exclaimed his antagonists, amazed at his tenets; "is not the laborer worthy of his hire?" "Yes," replied he, "from them that hire him."

The magistrates were selected exclusively from the members of the church; with equal propriety, reasoned Williams, might "a doctor of physick or a pilot" be selected according to his skill in theology and his standing in the church.

It was objected to him, that his principles subverted all good government. The commander of the vessel of state, replied Williams, may maintain order on board the ship, and see that it pursues its course steadily, even though the dissenters of the crew are not compelled to attend the public prayers of their companions.

But the controversy finally turned on the question of the rights and duty of magistrates to guard the minds of the people against corruption, and to punish

---
[1] 35 Elizabeth, c. i. Statutes, v. iv. p. 841.

what would seem to them error and heresy. Magistrates, Williams asserted, are but the agents of the people, or its trustees, on whom no spiritual power in matters of worship can ever be conferred; since conscience belongs to the individual and is not the property of the body politic; and with admirable dialectics, clothing the great truth in its boldest form, he asserted that "the civil magistrate may not intermeddle even to stop a church from apostacy and heresy," that equal protection should be extended to every sect and every form of worship. With corresponding distinctness he foresaw the influence of his principles on society. "The removal of the yoke of soul-oppression," to use the words in which, at a later day, he confirmed his early view, "as it will prove an act of mercy and righteousness to the enslaved nations, so it is of binding force to engage the whole and every interest and conscience to preserve the common liberty and peace."[1]

1634. Nov. 27. The same magistrates, who punished Eliot, the apostle of the Indian race, for his freedom in censuring their measures, could not brook the independence of Williams; and the circumstances of the times seemed to them to justify their apprehensions. An intense jealousy was excited in England against

1634. Dec. Massachusetts; "members of the Generall Court received intelligence of some episcopal and malignant practises against the country;" and the magistrates on the one hand were scrupulously careful to avoid all unnecessary offense to the English govern-

---

[1] Hireling Ministry, p. 29.

ment, on the other were sternly consolidating their own institutions and even preparing for resistance. It was in this view that the Freeman's Oath was appointed; by which every freeman was obliged to pledge his allegiance not to King Charles but to Massachusetts. There was room for scruples on the subject; and an English lawyer would have questioned the legality of the measure. The liberty of conscience for which Williams contended, denied the right of a compulsory imposition of an oath;[1] when he was summoned before the court, he could not renounce his belief; and his influence was such "that the government was forced to desist from that proceeding." To the magistrates he seemed the ally of a civil faction; to himself he appeared only to make a frank avowal of the truth. In all his intercourse with the tribunals he spoke with the distinctness of settled convictions. He was fond of discussion; but he was never betrayed into angry remonstrance. If he was charged with pride, it was only for the novelty of his opinions.

The scholar who is accustomed to the pursuits of abstract philosophy, lives in a world of thought, far different from that by which he is surrounded. The range of his understanding is remote from the paths of common minds, and he is often the victim of the contrast. It is not unusual for the world to reject the voice of truth, because its tones are strange; to declare doctrines unsound, only because they are

---

[1] See his opinions, fully reduced to the form of a law, at Providence, in 1647, in ii. Mass. Hist. Coll. v. vii. p. 96.

new; and even to charge obliquity or derangement on the man, who brings forward principles which the many repudiate. Such has ever been the way of the world; and Socrates, and St. Paul, and Luther, and others of the most acute dialecticians, have been ridiculed as drivellers and madmen. The extraordinary developement of one faculty may sometimes injure the balance of the mind; just as the constant exercise of one member of the body injures the beauty of its proportions; or as the exclusive devotedness to one pursuit, politics for instance, or money, brushes away from conduct and character the agreeable varieties of light and shade. It is a very ancient remark, that folly has its corner in the brain of every wise man; and certain it is, that not the poets only like Tasso, but the clearest minds, Sir Isaac Newton, Pascal, Spinoza, have been deeply tinged with insanity. Perhaps Williams pursued his sublime principles with too scrupulous minuteness; it was at least natural for Bradford and his contemporaries, while they acknowledged his power as a preacher, to esteem him "unsettled in judgment."

The court at Boston remained as yet undecided; when the church of Salem, those who were best acquainted with Williams, taking no notice of the recent investigations, elected him to the office of their teacher. Immediately the evils inseparable on a religious establishment began to be displayed. The ministers got together and declared any one worthy of banishment, who should obstinately assert, that "the civil magistrate might not intermeddle even to stop a church from apostacy and heresy;" the magistrates delayed action, only that a committee of divines might have time to repair to Salem and deal with him and with the church in a church way. Meantime, the people of Salem were blamed for their choice of a religious guide: and a tract of land to which they had a claim, was withheld from them as a punishment.

The breach was therefore widened. To the ministers Williams frankly but temperately explained his doctrines; and he was armed at all points for their defence. As his townsmen had lost their lands in consequence of their attachment to him, it would have been cowardice on his part to have abandoned them; and the instinct of liberty led him again to the suggestion of a proper remedy. In conjunction with the church he wrote "letters of admonition unto all the churches whereof any of the magistrates were members, that they might admonish the magistrates of their injustice." The church members alone were freemen; Williams, in modern language, appealed to the people, and invited them to instruct their representatives to do justice to the citizens of Salem.

This last act seemed flagrant treason;[1] and at the next general court, Salem was disfranchised till an ample apology for the letter should be made. The town acquiesced in its wrongs and submitted; not an individual remained willing to justify the letter of remonstrance; the church of Williams would not

[1] Cotton calls it crimen majestatis laesae.

avow his great principle of the sanctity of conscience; even his wife, under a delusive idea of duty, was for a season influenced to disturb the tranquillity of his home by her reproaches.[1] Williams was left alone, absolutely alone. Anticipating the censures of the colonial churches, he declared himself no longer subjected to their spiritual jurisdiction. "My own voluntary withdrawing from all these churches, resolved to continue in persecuting the witnesses of the Lord, presenting light unto them, I confess it was mine own voluntary act; yea, I hope the act of the Lord Jesus," proclaiming truth as with the voice of a trumpet. When summoned to appear before the general court, he avowed his convictions in the presence of the representatives of the state, "maintained the rocky strength of his grounds," and declared himself "ready to be bound and banished and even to die in New England" rather than renounce the opinions which had dawned upon his mind in the clearness of light. At a time when Germany was the battle field for all Europe in the implacable wars of religion, when even Holland was bleeding with the anger of vengeful factions, when France was still to go through the fearful struggle with bigotry, when England was gasping under the despotism of intolerance, more than forty years before William Penn became an American proprietary, Roger Williams asserted the great doctrine of intellectual liberty. It became his glory to found a state upon that principle, and to stamp himself upon its

[1] Master John Cotton's Reply, p. 9.

rising institutions, in characters so deep that the CHAP. IX.
impress has remained to the present day, and, like
the image of Phidias on the shield of Minerva, can
never be erased without the total destruction of the
work. The principles which he first sustained
amidst the bickerings of a colonial parish, next asserted in the general court of Massachusetts, and
then introduced into the wilds on Narragansett Bay,
he soon found occasion to publish to the world, and 1644.
to defend as the basis of the religious freedom of
mankind; as the lark, that pleasant bird of the peaceful summer, "affecting to soar aloft, springs upward
from the ground, takes his rise from pale to tree,"
and at last surmounting the highest hills, utters his
clear carols through the skies of morning.[1] He was
the first person in modern Christendom to assert in
its plenitude the doctrine of the liberty of conscience,
the equality of opinions before the law; and in its
defense he was the harbinger of Milton, the precursor and the superior of Jeremy Taylor. For Taylor
limited his toleration to a few Christian sects;
the philanthropy of Williams compassed the earth;
Taylor favored partial reform, commended lenity,
argued for forbearance, and entered a special plea in
behalf of each tolerable sect; Williams would permit persecution of no opinion, of no religion, leaving
heresy unharmed by law, and orthodoxy unprotected
by the terrors of penal statutes. Taylor still clung
to the necessity of positive regulations enforcing re-

[1] The rhetoric is chiefly John Cotton's, who says jeeringly, what I repeat reverently. Reply, p. 2.

ligion and eradicating error; he resembled the poets who in their folly first declare their hero to be invulnerable and then clothe him in earthly armor; Williams was willing to leave Truth alone, in her own panoply of light,[1] believing that if in the ancient feud between Truth and Error, the employment of force could be entirely abrogated, Truth would have much the best of the bargain. It is the custom of mankind to award high honors to the successful inquirer into the laws of nature, to those who advance the bounds of human knowledge. We praise the man who first analyzed the air, or resolved water into its elements, or drew the lightning from the clouds; though the condition of physical investigations may have ripened the public mind at the time for the advancement in science. A moral principle has a much wider and nearer influence on human happiness; nor can any discovery of truth be of more direct benefit to society, than that which establishes a perpetual religious peace and spreads tranquillity through every community and every bosom. If Copernicus is held in perpetual reverence, because on his death bed he published to the world that the sun is the centre of our system, if the name of Kepler is preserved in the annals of human excellence for his sagacity in detecting the laws of the planetary motion, if the genius of Newton has been almost adored for dissecting a ray of light and weighing heavenly bodies, as in a balance, let there be for the name of Roger Williams at least some humble place among

---

[1] The expression is partly from Gibbon and Sir Henry Vane.

those who have advanced moral science and made themselves the benefactors of mankind.

But if the opinion of posterity is no longer divided, the members of the general court of that day pronounced against him the sentence of exile;[1] yet not by a very numerous majority. Some gentlemen who consented to his banishment, would never have yielded but for the persuasions of Cotton; and the judgment was vindicated not as a punishment for opinion, or as a restraint on freedom of conscience, but because the application of the new doctrine to the construction of the patent, to the discipline of the churches, and to the "oaths for making tryall of the fidelity of the people," seemed about "to subvert the fundamental state and government of the country."

Winter was at hand; Williams succeeded in obtaining permission to remain till spring; intending then to begin a plantation in Narragansett Bay. But the affections of the people of Salem revived and could not be restrained; they thronged to his house to hear him whom they were so soon to loose for ever; it began to be rumored, that he could not safely be allowed to found a new state in the vicinity; the people were "many of them much taken with the apprehension of his godliness;" there was evident danger that his opinions were contagious; that the infection would spread very widely. It was therefore resolved to remove him to England in a

[1] Winthrop, v. i. p. 170, 171. Cotton's Reply, p. 27. 29. Roger Colony Records, v. i. p. 163. John Williams' Account, ibid. p. 24. & ff.

ship that was just ready to set sail. A warrant was accordingly sent to him to come to Boston and embark. For the first time he declined the summons of the court. A pinnace was sent for him; the officers repaired to his house; he was no longer there. Three days before, he had left Salem, in winter snow and inclement weather, of which he remembered the severity even in his late old age. "For fourteen weeks he was sorely tost in a bitter season, not knowing what bread or bed did mean."[1] Often in the stormy night he had neither fire, nor food, nor company; often he wandered without a guide, and had no house but a hollow tree.[2] But he was not without friends. The same scrupulous respect for the rights of others, which had led him to defend the freedom of conscience, had made him also the champion of the Indians. He had already been zealous to acquire their language; and knew it so well that he could debate with them in their own dialect. During his residence at Plymouth he had often been the guest of the neighboring sachems; and now when he came in winter to the cabin of the chief of Pokanoket, he was welcomed by Massasoit, and "the barbarous heart of Canonicus, the chief of the Narragansetts, loved him as his son to the last gasp." "The ravens," he relates with gratitude, "fed me in the wilderness." And in requital for their hospitality, he was ever through his long life their friend and benefactor; the apostle of Christianity to them

[1] Roger Williams to Mason, in i. Mass. Hist. Coll. v. i. p. 276.
[2] Roger Williams' Key. Reprinted in R. I. Hist. Coll. v. i.

without hire, without weariness, and without impatience at their idolatry; the guardian of their rights; the pacificator, when their rude passions were inflamed; and their unflinching advocate and protector, whenever Europeans attempted an invasion of their rights.

He first pitched and began to build and plant at Seekonk. But Seekonk was found to be within the patent of Plymouth; on the other side of the water, the country opened in its unappropriated beauty; and there he might hope to establish a community as free as the other colonies.

It was in June that the lawgiver of Rhode-Island with five companions embarked on the stream; a frail Indian canoe contained the founder of an independent state and its earliest citizens. Tradition has marked the spring, near which they landed; it is the parent spot, the first inhabited nook of Rhode-Island. To express his unbroken confidence in the mercies of God, Williams called the place PROVIDENCE. "I desired," said he, "it might be for a shelter for persons distressed for conscience."[1]

In his new abode Williams could have less leisure for contemplation and study. "My time," he observes of himself, and it is a sufficient apology for the roughness of his style, as a writer on morals, "was not spent altogether in spiritual labors; but day and night, at home and abroad, on the land and

[1] Backus, v. i. p. 94. There is in Backus much evidence of diligent research and critical respect for documentary testimony. He deserves more reputation than he has had.

water, at the hoe, at the oar, for bread."[1] In the course of two years he was joined by others, who fled to his asylum. The land which was now occupied by Williams, was within the territory of the Narragansett Indians; it was not long before an Indian deed from Canonicus and Miantonomoh[2] made him the undisputed possessor of an extensive domain. Nothing displays more clearly the character of Roger Williams than the use which he made of his acquisition of territory. The soil he could claim as his "own, as truly as any man's coat upon his back;"[3] and he "reserved to himself not one foot of land, not one tittle of political power, more than he granted to servants and strangers." "He gave away his lands and other estate to them, that he thought were most in want, until he gave away all."[4] He chose to found a commonwealth in the unmixed forms of a pure democracy; where the will of the majority should govern the state. Yet "only in civil things;" God alone was respected as the ruler of conscience. To their more aristocratic neighbors, it seemed as if these fugitives "would have no magistrates;"[5] for every thing was as yet decided in convention of the people. This first system has had its influence on the whole political history of Rhode-Island; in no state in the world, not even in the agricultural state of Vermont, has the magistracy so little power or the representatives of the people so

---

[1] Bloody Tenent yet more Bloody, p. 38, in Knowles.
[2] Backus, vol. i. page 89, 90. Knowles, p. 106, 107.
[3] Backus, v. i. p. 290. Knowles, c. viii.
[4] Letter of Daniel Williams.
[5] Winthrop, v. i. p. 293. Hubbard, p. 338.

much. The annals of Rhode-Island, if written in the spirit of philosophy, would exhibit the forms of society under a peculiar aspect; had the territory of the state corresponded to the importance and singularity of the principles of its early existence, the world would have been filled with wonder at the phenomena of its history.

The most touching trait in the founder of Rhode-Island was his conduct towards his persecutors. Though keenly sensitive to the hardships which he had endured, he was far from harboring feelings of revenge towards those who banished him, and only regretted their delusion. "I did ever, from my soul, honor and love them, even when their judgment led them to afflict me."[1] In all his writings on the subject, he attacked the spirit of intolerance, the doctrine of persecution; and never his persecutors or the colony of Massachusetts. Indeed we shall presently behold him requite their severity by exposing his life at their request and for their benefit. It is not strange, then, if "many hearts were touched with relentings. That great and pious soul, Mr. Winslow, melted, and kindly visited me," says the exile, "and put a piece of gold into the hands of my wife, for our supply;"[2] the founder, the legislator, the proprietor of Rhode-Island, owed a shelter to the hospitality of an Indian chief; and his wife the means of sustenance to the charity of a stranger. The half-wise Cotton Mather concedes, that many judicious persons confessed him to have had the root of

[1] Winthrop and Savage, v. 1. p. 65. [2] Williams to Mason.

the matter in him; and his nearer friends, the immediate witnesses of his actions, declared him from "the whole course and tenor of his life and conduct to have been one of the most disinterested men that ever lived, a most pious and heavenly minded soul."[1]

Thus was Rhode-Island the offspring of Massachusetts; but her political connections were long influenced by the circumstance of her origin. The loss of the few emigrants who resorted to the new state, was not sensibly felt in the parent colony; for the bay of Massachusetts was already thronged with squadrons. The emigrants had from the first been watched in the mother country with intense interest; a letter from New-England was venerated "as a sacred script, or as the writing of some holy prophets; and was carried many miles, where divers came to hear it."[2] When the first difficulties had been surmounted, the stream of emigration flowed with a full current; "Godly people in England began to apprehend a special hand of providence in raising this plantation, and their hearts were generally stirred to come over."

1634.

The fame of its liberties extended widely; the Earl of Warwick offered his congratulations on its prosperity; and in a single year three thousand new settlers were added to the puritan colony. Among these was the fiery Hugh Peter, who had been pastor of a church of English exiles in Rotterdam; a republican of an enlarged spirit, great energy, and popular eloquence, tempering a spirit of active enterprize with solidity of judgment. At the same

1635.

[1] Callender, p. 17.   [2] ii. Mass. H. Coll. v. ii. p. xxix.

time came Henry Vane, the younger, a man of the purest mind; a statesman of spotless integrity; whose name the progress of intelligence and liberty will erase from the rubric of fanatics and traitors and insert high among the aspirants after truth and the martyrs for liberty. He had valued the "obedience of the gospel," more than the successful career of English diplomacy, and cheerfully "forsook the preferments of the court of Charles for the ordinances of religion in their purity in New-England." He was happy in the possession of an admirable genius, though naturally more inclined to contemplative excellence than to action; he was happy in the eulogist of his virtues, for Milton, ever so parsimonious of praise, reserving the majesty of his verse to celebrate the glories and vindicate the providence of God, was lavish of his encomiums on the youthful friend of religious liberty. But Vane was still more happy in attaining early in life a firmly settled theory of morals, and in possessing an energetic will, which made all his conduct to the very last conform to the doctrines he had espoused, turning his dying hour into a seal of the witness, which his life had ever borne with noble consistency to the freedom of conscience and the people. "If he were not superior to Hamden," says Clarendon, "he was inferior to no other man;" "his whole life made good the imagination, that there was in him something extraordinary,"[1]

The freemen of Massachusetts, pleased that a

---

[1] Clarendon, b. vii. and b. iii. v. ii. p. 379, and v. i. p. 186, 187, 188.

young man of such elevated rank and distinguished ability, should have adopted their creed and joined them in their exile, elected him their governor. The choice was unwise; for neither the age nor the experience of Vane entitled him to the distinction. He came but as a sojourner and not as a permanent resident; neither was he imbued with the colonial prejudices, the genius of the place; and his clear mind, unbiassed by previous discussions and fresh from the public business of England, saw distinctly what the colonists did not wish to see, the really wide difference between their practice under their charter and the meaning of that instrument on the principles of English jurisprudence.[1]

These latent causes of discontent could not but be eventually displayed; at first the arrival of Vane was considered an auspicious pledge for the emigration of men of the highest rank in England. Several of the English peers, especially Lord Say and Seal, and Lord Brooke, had begun to inquire into the character of the rising institutions, and to negotiate for such changes as would offer them inducements for removing to America. They demanded a division of the general court into two branches, that of assistants and of representatives, a change which was acceptable to the people, and which, from domestic reasons, was ultimately adopted; but they further required an acknowledgement of their own hereditary right to a seat in the upper house. The fathers of Massachusetts were disposed to conciliate

---

[1] I find proofs of this in Hutchinson's Coll. p. 72, 73. 76 and 83.

AN ORDER OF NOBILITY PROPOSED AND REJECTED. 417

these powerful friends; they promised them the honors of magistracy, would have readily conferred it on some of them for life, and actually began to make appointments on that tenure; but as for the establishment of hereditary dignity they answered by the hand of Cotton, "Where God blesseth any branch of any noble or generous family with a spirit and gifts fit for government, it would be a taking of God's name in vain to put such a talent under a bushel; and a sin against the honor of magistracy to neglect such in our public elections. But if God should not delight to furnish some of their posterity with gifts fit for magistracy, we should expose them rather to reproach and prejudice, and the commonwealth with them, than exalt them to honor, if we should call them forth, when God doth not, to public authority."[1] And thus the proposition for establishing hereditary nobility was defeated. The people, moreover, soon became uneasy at the concession of office during lifetime; the measure was dreaded as dangerous to public liberty; nor would they be quieted, till it was made a law, that those who were appointed magistrates for life, should yet not be magistrates except in those years, in which they might be regularly chosen at the annual election.[2]

The institutions of Massachusetts, which were thus endangered by the influence of men of rank in England, were likewise in jeopardy from the effects

[1] Hutchinson, v. i. p. 44, and 433—436. Hazard, v. i. p. 379.
[2] Winthrop, v. i. p. 184. 302. Hubbard, p. 244.

of religious divisions. The minds of the colonists were excited to intense activity on questions, which the nicest subtlety only could have devised, and which none but those experienced in the shades of theological opinions could long comprehend. For it goes with these opinions as with colors; of which the artist who works in mosaic, easily and regularly discriminates many thousand varieties, where the common eye can discern a difference only on the closest comparison. Boston and its environs were now employed in theological controversy; and the transports of enthusiasm sustained the toil of abstruse speculations. The most profound questions, which can relate to the mysteries of human existence and the laws of the moral world, questions, which the mind in the serenity of unclouded reflection may hardly aspire to solve, were discussed with passionate zeal; eternity was summoned to reveal its secrets; human tribunals pretended to establish for the Infinite Mind the laws, on which the destinies of the soul are to depend; the Holy Spirit was claimed by the most infatuated as the personal companion of man; and there were not wanting those who had become so assured of their acceptance with God, that, as they thought, no outward actions could obliterate the consciousness of the divine approbation. Cases also of insanity occurred. Strange inconsistency in human nature! The timid totter towards the precipice which they dread. I knew an aged man, who, urged by an excessive apprehension of the punishments of the unseen world, attempted suicide from despair; and two hundred years ago an unhappy mother, whose wits were turned from anxiety about her soul, threw her child into the water, that she might at least escape the agony of doubt, and feel sure of her damnation as an infanticide. Religious metaphysics occupied the thoughts of the whole colony; Christianity was at once become an exceedingly "subtle thing." Many persons fearlessly adopted the conclusions to which passion hurried them, and were in perpetual danger of making shipwreck of all religious faith in their headlong confidence; while a few restrained themselves within the limits of more rigid dialectics, and occasionally sounded their way, as they proceeded through the "dim and perilous" paths of speculative science.

Amidst the arrogance of spiritual pride, the vagaries of undisciplined imaginations, and the extravagances to which the intellectual power may be led in its pursuit of ultimate principles, the formation of two distinct parties may be perceived. The first consisted of the original settlers, the framers of the civil government and their adherents; they who were intent on a great practical purpose, the foundation and preservation of a commonwealth, who were satisfied with the established order of society, and were not disposed to retard the great objects of their emigration for the gratification of theorists and the nice disquisitions of acute theological learning. They had founded their government on the basis of the church, and church membership could be obtained only by an exemplary life. Professing the strictest doctrine of Calvinism, they yet conformed their judgments not to their theory, but to their actual condition. "The cracks and flaws in the new building of the reformation, thought they, portend a fall;"[1] they desired patriotism, union, and a common heart; they were earnest to confirm and build up the state, the child of their cares and their sorrows. They were reproached with being practical men; "under a covenant of works."

The leaders of the other party, Wheelwright and Anne Hutchinson, were individuals who had arrived after the civil government and religious discipline of the colony had been established; and on their main principles they claimed Vane, and Cotton, in whose house Vane was an inmate,[2] as their adherents. They came fresh from the study of the tenets of Geneva; and their pride consisted in following them with logical precision to all their consequences. Their eyes were not primarily directed to the institutions of Massachusetts, but to the doctrines of their religious system; their thoughts were not for the safety and the favorable exposition of the charter, but for the developement of Calvinism with accurate boldness. They asserted the certain salvation of every true Christian, a certainty consequent on predestination, not on faith, and still less on good actions. The divine choice was an absolute exercise of free grace, as little to be questioned as the decree, by which one particle of earth contributes to

---

[1] Shepherd's Lamentation, p. 2.   [2] Suffolk Probate Records, v. i. p. 72.

the production of a hateful weed, and another enters the composition of the fragrant rose; or, according to the eastern apologue, one drop of the descending rain joins the waters of the ocean, and the next is caught by a shell-fish and transformed to a pearl. Acceptance was the result of the unchanging will, the eternal counsels of God; an unqualified election, which not even the commission of the foulest sins could defeat,[1] and of which the chosen favorites of heaven receive evidence by an approving conscience, the direct revelation of God to the mind. A person of this sort might have asserted as a part of his religious creed his assurance of his own salvation.[2] For him penitence was become a foible, and despondency a crime. It was evident that these doctrines, which, when interpreted in one way, lead to internal excellence as the living and perpetual fountain of goodness, might, under another exposition, substitute the oracles of a fanatical or an unenlightened conscience for the rules of morality. Thus the same principles which were designed to promote the highest moral purity of contemplative existence, might be perverted to favor the grossest licentiousness; a perversion, which would have been reproved more sternly by none than by the proud but ascetic Calvin. There was, therefore, ample opportunity for the intolerance of captious logic; for misapprehensions and constructive charges of error. Men proved to their own satisfaction, that the doctrine of election was a de-

---

[1] Shepherd, p. 4, 5. Surely Shepherd would not misrepresent.
[2] Let the curious compare Bossuet, Hist. des Var. L. ix. c. i.—iv.

nial of the immortality of the soul; and, by the refinements of controversy, every harmless proposition became prolific of a brood of monstrous corollaries. What controversies between the parties ensued! What mutual criminations; what private discussions and public debates; what elaborate essays and replies, each duly fortified with apt citations of Scripture; how was the history of the Jews ransacked for parallels; how were errors and "unsavory speeches" exposed and confuted! Crowded conferences of women became the weekly fashion; and in these assemblies, the eloquent Anne Hutchinson, the paragon of religious "gossips," would amuse the ennui of colonial life by dogmatical disquisitions, well suited to excite her infatuated admirers. The tongues of fifty females were at once busy in discussing the doctrines and balancing the merits of the ministers; and the sessions of the general court were still worse employed; for it wasted its time in collecting the idle speeches of giddy devotees, and extracting sedition from the reproofs of a fast-day's sermon. He that should have listened with credulity to the parties, must have believed one of them, destitute of religious knowledge, and the other, bankrupt in morals.

Unfortunately the subject became of political importance; and Wheelwright, who strenuously maintained the truth of his opinions[1] and had never been confuted,[2] was, in spite of the remonstrance of Vane,

[1] Winthrop and Savage, v. i. p. 215. [2] Hutchinson's Collection, page 82.

censured by the general court for sedition; and at the ensuing choice of magistrates the religious divisions controlled the elections. Could it be doubted who would obtain the confidence of the people? In the midst of such high excitement, that even the pious Wilson climbed into a tree to harangue the people on election day, Winthrop and his friends, the fathers and founders of the colony, recovered the entire management of the government.[1] But the dispute infused its spirit into every thing; it interfered with the levy of troops for the Pequod war;[2] it influenced the respect shown to the magistrates; the distribution of town-lots; the assessment of rates; and at last the continued existence of the two opposing parties was considered inconsistent with the public peace. To prevent the increase of a faction, esteemed to be so dangerous, a law, somewhat analogous to the alien law in England, and to the European policy of passports, was enacted by the party in power; none should be received within the jurisdiction, but such as should be allowed by some of the magistrates. The dangers, which were simultaneously menaced from the episcopal party in the mother country, gave to the measure an air of magnanimous defiance; it was almost a proclamation of independence. As an act of intolerance it found in Vane an inflexible opponent, and, using the language of the times, he left a memorial of his dissent. "Scribes and pharisees, and such as are confirmed in any way

---

[1] Winthrop, v. i. p. 219, 220. Col. Records. Hutchinson's Coll. p. 63 and ff.

[2] Welde, p. 27. Mather, b. vii. c. iii. S. 5. Hutchinson's Coll. p. 80

of error," these are the remarkable words of the man, who soon embarked for England, where he afterwards pleaded in Parliament for the liberties of Catholics and Dissenters, "all such are not to be denyed cohabitation, but are to be pitied and reformed. Ishmael shall dwell in the presence of his brethren."

The friends of Wheelwright could not brook the censure of their leader; but they justified their indignant remonstrances by the language of fanaticism. "A new rule of practice by immediate revelations,"[1] was now to be the guide of their conduct; in other words, they slighted the decrees of the court, and avowed their determination to follow the impulses of conscience. But individual conscience is often the dupe of interest, and often but a more honorable name for self-will. The government feared, or pretended to fear, a disturbance of the public peace, a wild insurrection of lawless fanatics. A synod of the ministers of New-England was therefore assembled, to accomplish the difficult task of settling the true faith. Numerous opinions were harmoniously condemned; and the vagueness of language, so often the parent of furious controversy, now performed the office of a peace-maker. At last it was hardly possible to find any grounds of difference between the flexible Cotton and his equally orthodox opponents. The general peace of the colony being thus assured, the civil magistrates proceeded to pass sentence on the more resolute offenders. Wheelwright, Anne Hutchinson and Aspinwall were exiled from the territory

[1] Welde, p. 45, ed. 1692, or p. 42, ed. 1644.

EMIGRATION TO NEW-HAMPSHIRE AND RHODE-ISLAND.

of Massachusetts; and their adherents, who, it was CHAP. IX. feared " might upon some revelation, make a sudden insurrection," were, like. the tories during the war for independence, required to deliver up their arms.

So ended the Antinomian strife in New-England.[1] Many of the party emigrated to the neighboring colonies. Of these a considerable number, led by John Clarke and William Coddington, proceeded to the south; designing to make a plantation on Long Island, or near Delaware Bay. But Roger Williams welcomed them to his vicinity; and his own influence and the powerful name of Henry Vane prevailed with Miantonomoh, the chief of the Narragansetts, to obtain for them a gift of the beautiful island of Rhode-Island. The spirit of the institutions, established by this band of voluntary exiles on the soil, which they owed to the benevolence of the natives, was derived from natural justice; a social compact, signed after the manner of the precedent at New-Plymouth, so often imitated in America, founded the government upon the basis of the universal consent of every inhabitant; the forms of the administration were borrowed from the examples of the Jews;[2] and judges were chosen to rule the new Israel.

1638.
Mar.
24.

Mar.
7.

Wheelwright and his immediate friends removed to the banks of the Piscataqua; and, at the head of

---

[1] On this strife I have read the Col. Records; the decisions of the synod; the copious Winthrop; the Documents in Hutchinson's Coll.; Welde's Rise, Reign and Ruin; T. Shepherd's Lamentation; a fragment of Wheelwright's Sermon; and the statement of John Cotton himself, in his reply to Williams; also, Hubbard, C. Mather, Neal, Hutchinson, Callender, Backus, Savage and Knowles.
[2] Mass. Hist. Coll. v. i. p. 166 and ff. Callender, p. 29 and ff. Backus, v. i. p. 91. 96 and ff. Knowles, c. xi.

CHAP. IX.

1639.
Oct.
4.

tide waters on that stream, they founded the town of Exeter; one more little republic in the wilderness, organized on the principles of natural justice by the voluntary combination of the inhabitants.[1]

Such were the peaceful and happy results of the watchfulness or the intolerance of Massachusetts; its legislation may be reproved for its jealousy, yet not for its cruelty; and Williams and Wheelwright suffered not much more from their sentence, than some of the best men of the colony encountered from choice. For rumor had spread not wholly extravagant accounts of the fertility of the alluvial land along the borders of the Connecticut; and the banks of that river were already adorned with the villages of the puritans, planted just in season to anticipate the rival designs of the Dutch.

1630. The valley of the Connecticut had early become an object of desire and of competition. The Earl of Warwick was the first proprietary of the soil under a grant from the council for New-England; and it
1631.
Mar.
19.
was next held by Lord Say and Seal, Lord Brooke and others as his assigns.[2] Before any colony could be established with their sanction, the people of
1633.
Oct.
New-Plymouth had built a trading-house at Windsor, and conducted with the natives a profitable commerce in furs. At the same time "Dutch Intruders" from Manhattan, ascending the river, raised at Hartford the house "of Good Hope," and strug-
1635. gled to secure the territory to themselves. The

[1] Farmer's Belknap, p. 20, and 432, from Exeter town Records.
[2] Trumbull's Hist. of Connecticut, v. i. App. No. i.

younger Winthrop, the future benefactor of Connecticut, one of those men in whom the elements of human excellence are mingled in the happiest union, returned from England with a commission from the proprietaries of that region, to erect a fort at the mouth of the stream; a purpose, which was accomplished. Yet before his arrival in Massachusetts Bay, settlements had been commenced by emigrants from the environs of Boston at Hartford, and Windsor, and Wethersfield; and in the last days of the pleasantest of the autumnal months a company of sixty pilgrims, women and children being of the number, began their march to the west. Never before had the forests of America witnessed such a scene. But the journey was begun too late in the season; the winter was so unusually early and severe, that provisions could not arrive by way of the river.; imperfect shelter had been provided; cattle perished in great numbers; and the men suffered such privations, that many of them in the depth of winter abandoned their newly-chosen habitations, and waded through the snows to the sea-board.

CHAP. IX.

1635. July 7.

Oct. 8.

Oct. 15. O.S.

Nov. 15.

Yet in the opening of the next year a government was organized, and civil order established; and the budding of the trees and the springing of the grass were signals for a greater emigration to the Connecticut. Some smaller parties had already made their way to the new Hesperia of puritanism. In June the principal caravan began its march, led by Thomas Hooker, "the light of the Western Churches." There were of the company about one hun-

1636. April 26.

May.

dred souls; many of them, persons accustomed to affluence and the ease of European life. They drove before them numerous herds of cattle; and thus they traversed on foot the pathless forests of Massachusetts; advancing hardly ten miles a day through the tangled woods, across the swamps and numerous streams, and over the highlands that separated the several intervening vallies; subsisting, as they slowly wandered along, on the milk of the kine, which browsed on the fresh leaves and early shoots; having no guide through the nearly untrodden wilderness, but the compass, and no pillow for their nightly rest but heaps of stones. What hardships did they endure in crossing the hills of Worcester county? What dangers in following the windings of the Chickapee, and fording with their cattle its rapid current? How did the hills echo with the unwonted lowing of the herds! How were the forests enlivened by the loud and fervent piety of Hooker![1] Never again was there such a pilgrimage from the seaside "to the delightful banks" of the Connecticut. The emigrants had been gathered from among the most valued citizens, the earliest settlers and the oldest churches of the Bay. John Haynes had for one year been the governor of Massachusetts; and Hooker had no rival in public estimation but Cotton, whom he surpassed in force of character, in boldness of spirit, and in honorable clemency. Historians, investigating the causes of events, have endeavored to find the motives of this settlement in the jealous

---

[1] Hooker was "a Son of Thunder." See Morton, p. 239, and 240.

ambition of the minister of Hartford. Such inge- CHAP.
nuity is gratuitous. The Connecticut was at that IX.
time supposed to be the best channel for a great internal traffic in furs; and its meadows, already proverbial for the richness of their soil, had acquired the same celebrity as in a later day the banks of the Genesee, or the bottom lands of the Miami.

The new settlement that seemed so far towards the West, was environed by perils. The Dutch still indulged a hope of dispossessing the English, and the natives of the country beheld the approach of Europeans with malignant hatred. No part of New-England was more thickly covered with aboriginal inhabitants than Connecticut. The Pequods, who were settled round the Thames, could muster at least seven hundred warriors; the whole number of the effective men of the emigrants was much less than two hundred. The danger from the savages was incessant; and while the settlers, with hardly a plough or a yoke of oxen, turned the wild fertility of nature into productiveness, they were at the same time exposed to the incursions of a savage enemy, whose delight was carnage.

For the Pequods had already shown a hostile spirit. 1633.
Several years had elapsed, since they had murdered the crew of a small trading vessel in Connecticut river. With some appearance of justice they pleaded the necessity of self-defence; and sent messen- 1634.
gers to Boston to desire the alliance of the white men. Nov.
The government of Massachusetts accepted the excuse, and immediately conferred the benefit, which

CHAP. was due from civilization to the ignorant and pas-
IX. sionate tribes; it reconciled the Pequods with their
hereditary enemies, the Narragansetts. No longer
at variance with a powerful neighbor, the Pequods
1636. again displayed their bitter and emboldened hostility
July. to the English by murdering Oldham, near Block-
Island. The outrage was punished by a sanguinary
but ineffectual expedition. The warlike tribe was
not overawed; but rather courted the alliance of its
neighbors, the Narragansetts and the Mohegans, that
a union and a general rising of the natives might
sweep the hated intruders from the ancient hunting
grounds of the Indian race. The design could be
frustrated by none but Roger Williams; and the
exile, who had been the first to communicate to the
governor of Massachusetts the news of the impending conspiracy, encountered the extremity of peril
with magnanimous heroism. Having received letters
from Vane and the council of Massachusetts, re-
questing his utmost and speediest endeavors to prevent the league, neither storms of wind nor high
seas could detain the adventurous envoy. Shipping
himself alone in a poor canoe, every moment at the
hazard of his life, he hastened to the house of the
sachem of the Narragansetts. The Pequod ambas-
sadors, reeking with blood, were already there;
and for three days and nights the business compelled
him to lodge and mix with them; having cause every
night to expect their knives at his throat. The
Narragansetts were wavering; but Roger Williams
succeeded in dissolving the formidable conspiracy.

It was the most intrepid and most successful achievement in the whole Pequod war; an action, as perilous in its execution, as it was fortunate in its issue. When the Pequods were to contend single-handed against the common interests of all the English settlements, it was their ignorance only, which left them confidence.

The honor of military success belongs almost exclusively to Connecticut. The court of the three infant towns, decreed a war; ninety men, one half of the colony, were levied for actual service; and the continued depredations and murders, committed by the Pequods, demanded immediate action. Massachusetts and Plymouth both desired to send assistance; but the brave men of Connecticut, under the command of John Mason, resolved on immediate action. Uncas, the Sachem of the Mohegans, was their ally. They descended the river; and had designed to sail for the mouth of the Thames. It was deemed better to proceed to Narragansett Bay, and, by crossing the country, to effect a surprise. The tribes of Miantonomoh watched the progress of the expedition with doubtful friendship; and all the Indians, but Uncas and the Mohegans, deserted the enterprise, which to them seemed desperate. But there was no room for apprehension. Never was the superiority of Europeans more signally manifested; never was the feebleness of the natives more plainly displayed.

The unhappy Pequods were as yet so little familiar with the English, that they had not learned to

CHAP. distrust their own strength. Their hundreds of war-
IX. riors were confident of their own courage; their bows
1637. and arrows still seemed to them formidable weapons; ignorant of European fortresses, they viewed the rush-work palisades of their forts with complacency; and as the English boats sailed by the places, where the rude works of the natives frowned defiance, it was rumored through the tribe, that its enemies had vanished through fear. Exultation followed; and hundreds of the Pequods spent much of the last night of their lives in revelry, at a time when the sentinels of the English were within hearing of
May their songs. Two hours before day the soldiers of
26. Connecticut put themselves in motion towards the enemy, and as the light of morning began to dawn, they made their attack on the principal fort, which stood in a strong position at the summit of a hill. The colonists felt that they were fighting for the security of their homes; that, if defeated, the war-whoop would immediately resound near their cottages, and their wives and children be abandoned to the scalping knife and the tomahawk. They ascend to the attack; a watch-dog bays an alarm at their approach; the Indians awake, rally, and resist, as well as bows and arrows can resist weapons of steel. The superiority of number was with them; and fighting closely, hand to hand, though the massacre spread from wigwam to wigwam, victory was tardy. "We must burn them," shouted Mason, and cast a firebrand to the windward among the light mats of the Indian cabins. Hardly could the English with-

draw to encompass the place, before the whole encampment was in a blaze. Did the helpless natives climb the palisades? the flames assisted the marksmen to take good aim at the unprotected men; did they attempt a sally?—they were cut down by the English broad swords. The carnage was complete; about six hundred Indians, men, women and children, perished; most of them met death in the hideous conflagration. In about an hour the whole work of destruction was finished, and two only of the English had fallen in the battle. The sun, as it rose serenely in the east, was the witness of the victory.

With the light of morning three hundred or more Pequod warriors were descried, as they proudly approached from their second fort. They had anticipated success; what was their horror as they beheld the smoking ruins, strown with the half-consumed flesh of so many hundreds of their race! They stamped on the ground and tore their hair; but it was in vain to attempt revenge; then and always to the close of the war, the feeble manners of the natives hardly deserved, says Mason, the name of fighting; their defeat was certain and unattended with much loss to the English. The aborigines were never formidable in battle, till they became supplied with the weapons of European invention.

A portion of the troops hastened homewards to protect the settlements from any sudden attack; while Mason with about twenty men marched across the country from the vicinity of New-London to the

English fort at Saybrook. He reached the river at sunset; but Gardner, who commanded the fort, observed his approach; and never did the heart of a Roman consul, returning in triumph, swell more than the pride of Mason and his friends, when they found themselves received as victors, and "nobly entertained with many great guns."

In a few days the troops from Massachusetts arrived, attended by Wilson; for the ministers always shared every hardship and every danger. The remnants of the Pequods were pursued into their hiding-places; every wigwam was burned, every settlement was broken up, every cornfield was laid waste. Sassacus their Sachem, was murdered by the Mohawks, to whom he had fled for protection, and who, yielding to a base instinct of human nature, sought security for themselves by sacrificing the life of the refugee. The few who remained alive, about two hundred, surrendered in despair, and were enslaved by the English, or incorporated among the Mohegans and the Narragansetts. There remained not a sannup nor a squaw, not a warrior nor a child, of the Pequod name. A nation had disappeared from the family of man.[1]

1638. The vigor and courage displayed by the settlers on the Connecticut in this first Indian war in New-England, struck terror into the savages; and secured a long succession of years of peace. The infant was

[1] On the Pequod war, I have before me the special contemporary accounts of Mason, Underhill, and Vincent; besides the later narratives of I. Mather, Hubbard, Trumbull, Dwight, Thatcher, Drake, &c. &c.

safe in its cradle; the laborer in the fields; the solitary traveller during the night-watches in the forest. The houses needed no bolts; the settlements no palisades. Under the benignant auspices of peace, the citizens of the western colony resolved to perfect its political institutions, and to form a body politic by a voluntary association. The constitution which was thus framed, was of unexampled liberality. The elective franchise belonged to all the members of the towns, who had taken the oath of allegiance to the commonwealth; the magistrates and legislature were chosen annually; and the representatives were appointed among the towns according to their population.[1] Nearly two centuries have elapsed; the world has been made wiser by the most various experience; political institutions have become the theme, on which the most powerful and cultivated minds have been employed, and the most various experiments attempted; dynasties of kings have been dethroned, recalled, and dethroned again; pretenders have formed a numerous and little regarded body in the crowd of ambitious aspirants; and so many constitutions have been framed, or reformed, stifled, or subverted, that memory may despair of a complete catalogue; but the people of Connecticut have found no reason to deviate essentially from the frame of government, established by their fathers. No jurisdiction of the English monarch was recognized; the laws of honest justice were the basis of their commonwealth; and therefore its foundations were last-

[1] Trumbull, App. No. iii.

ing. These humble emigrants succeeded in inventing an admirable system; for they were near to nature, listened willingly to her voice, and easily copied her forms. No ancient usages, no hereditary differences of rank, no established interests, impeded the application of the principles of justice. Liberty springs spontaneously into life; the artificial distinctions of society require centuries to ripen. History has ever celebrated the commanders of the armies on which victory has been entailed, — the heroes who have won laurels in scenes of carnage and rapine. Has it no place for the founders of states; the wise legislators, who struck the rock in the wilderness, so that the waters of liberty gushed forth in copious and perennial fountains? They who judge of men by their influence on public happiness and by the services which they render to the human race, will never cease to honor the memory of Hooker and of Haynes.

1638. In equal independence a puritan colony sprung up at New-Haven under the guidance of John Davenport as its pastor, and of Theophilus Eaton, whose integrity and virtues are asserted by the unanimous consent of the early historians, and by his annual election to the office of governor till his death, a period of twenty years. What though the form of this new society was a little more austere? The spirit of humanity had sheltered itself under the rough exterior.[1] The emigrants held their lands of

---

[1] A nearly perfect copy of their code of laws, from the Boston Atheneum, has been examined. It was printed in 1656, and is to the bibliographer, one of the rarest books. I cannot too strongly acknowledge the liberality, with which the Atheneum is managed.

the Indians and rested their frame of government on a common compact. Thus the vehement intolerance of England kindled the lights of religion and liberty in the remote wilderness; the pleasant villages which grew up on the Connecticut, and spread along the Sound, and on the opposite shore of Long-Island, were happy in the enjoyment of tranquillity, the exercise of frugal industry, the practice of temperance and of courage.

CHAPTER X.

THE UNITED COLONIES OF NEW-ENGLAND.

CHAP. X.

1630.
Nov.
24.

THE English government was not indifferent to the progress of the colonies of New-England. The fate of the first emigrants had been watched by all parties with benevolent curiosity; nor was there any inducement to oppress the few sufferers, whom the hardships of their condition were so fast wasting away. The adventurers were encouraged by a proclamation,[1] which, with a view to their safety, prohibited the sale of fire-arms to the savages.

The stern discipline, exercised by the government at Salem, produced an early harvest of enemies; resentment long rankled in the minds of some, whom Endicott had perhaps too passionately punished, and when they returned to England, Mason and Gorges, the rivals of the Massachusetts company, willingly echoed their vindictive complaints. A petition even reached King Charles, complaining of distraction and disorder in the plantations, but the issue was unexpected. Massachusetts was ably defended by Sal-

[1] Hazard, v. i. p. 311, 312.

tonstall, Humphrey and Cradock, its friends in England; and the committee of the privy council reported in favor of the adventurers; who were ordered to continue their undertakings cheerfully, for the king did not design to impose on the people of Massachusetts the ceremonies, which they had emigrated to avoid. The country, it was believed, would in time be very beneficial to England.[1]

Revenge did not slumber,[2] because it had been once defeated; and the triumphant success of the puritans in America disposed the leaders of the high-church party to listen to the clamors of the malignant. Proof was produced of marriages celebrated by civil magistrates; and of the system of colonial church discipline; proceedings which were wholly at variance with the laws of England. "The departure of so many of the best," such "numbers of faithful and free-born Englishmen and good Christians," a more ill-boding sign to the nation, than the portentous blaze of comets and the impressions in the air, at which astrologers are dismayed,[3] began to be regarded by the archbishops as an affair of state; and ships bound with passengers for New-England, were detained in the Thames by an order of the council. But greater apprehensions were raised by a requisition, which commanded the letters patent of the company to be produced in

---

[1] Winthrop and Savage, v. i. p. 54—57, and 101—103. Prince, p. 430, 431. Hutch. Coll. p. 52—54. Hubbard, p. 150—154. Chalmers, p. 154, 155. Hazard, v. i. p. 234, 235.

[2] Winthrop, v. ii. p. 190, 191. or Hazard, v. i. p. 242, 243. Hubbard, p. 428—430.

[3] Milton pleads for the puritans.

England;[1] a requisition, to which the emigrants returned no reply.

1634. April 10. Still more menacing was the appointment of an arbitrary special commission for the colonies. The archbishop of Canterbury and those who were associated with him, received full power over the American plantations, to establish the government and dictate the laws; to regulate the church; to inflict even the heaviest punishments; and to revoke any charter which had been surreptitiously obtained, or which conceded liberties, prejudicial to the royal prerogative.[2]

Sept. 18. The news of this commission soon reached Boston; and it was at the same time rumored, that a general governor was on his way. The intelligence awakened the most lively interest in the whole colony, and led to the boldest measures. Poor as the new settlements were, six hundred pounds were raised towards fortifications; "the assistants and the deputies discovered their minds to one another," and the fortifications were hastened. All the ministers assembled at Boston; it marks the age, that their opinions were consulted; it marks the age still more, that they unanimously declared against the reception of a general governor. "We ought," said the fathers in Israel, "to defend our lawful possessions, if we are able; if not, to avoid and protract."[3]

1635. Jan. 19.

---

[1] Winthrop, v. i. p. 135. 137. Hubbard, p. 153. Hazard, v. i. p. 341, 342.
[2] Hazard, v. i. p. 344—347. Hubbard, p. 264—268. Hutchinson, v. i. App. No. iv. Winthrop, v. i. p. 143. Chalmers mistakes a year.
[3] Winthrop, v. i. p. 154.

It is not strange that Laud and his associates should have esteemed the inhabitants of Massachusetts to be men of refractory humors; complaints resounded of sects and schisms; of parties, consenting in nothing but hostility to the church of England; of designs to shake off the royal jurisdiction.[1] Restraints were, therefore, placed upon emigration; no one above the rank of a serving man, might remove to the colony without the special leave of the commissioners; and persons of inferior order were required to take the oaths of supremacy and allegiance.[2]

1634. Dec.

Willingly as these acts were performed by religious bigotry, they were prompted by another cause. The members of the Grand Council of Plymouth, long reduced to a state of inactivity, prevented by the spirit of the English merchants from oppressing the people, and having already made grants of all the lands from the Penobscot to Long-Island, determined to resign their charter, which was no longer possessed of any value. Several of the company desired as individuals to become the proprietaries of extensive territories, even at the dishonor of invalidating all their grants as a corporation. The hope of acquiring principalities subverted the sense of justice. A meeting of the lords was duly convened, and the whole coast from Acadia to beyond the Hudson, being divided into shares, was distributed, in part at least, by lots. Whole provinces gained

1635.

[1] Gorges, c. xxvi.   [2] Hazard, v. i. p. 247—348.

CHAP. an owner by the rattling of dice, the drawing of a
X. lottery, the decisions of chance.¹

1635. Thus far all went smoothly; it was a more difficult matter to gain possession of the prizes; the independent and inflexible colony of Massachusetts formed too serious an obstacle. The grant for Massachusetts, it was argued, was surreptitiously obtained; the lands belonged to Robert Gorges by a prior deed; the intruders had "made themselves a free
June. people." The general patent for New-England was surrendered to the king; to obtain of him a confirmation of their respective grants, and to invoke the whole force of English power against the charter of Massachusetts, were, at the same time, the objects of the members of the Plymouth company, distinctly avowed in their public acts.²

Now was the season of greatest peril to the rising liberties of New-England. The king and council already feared the consequences, that might come from the unbridled spirits of the Americans; his dislike was notorious;³ and at the Trinity term in the court of king's bench a *quo warranto* was brought against the company of the Massachusetts Bay. At the ensuing Michaelmas several of its members who resided in England, made their appearance, and judgment was pronounced against them individually; the rest of the patentees stood outlawed, but no judgment was entered up against them.⁴ The un-
Dec. expected death of Mason, who, as the proprietary of

---

¹ Gorges, b. ii. c. ii. Hubbard, p. 226—229. Hazard, v. i. p. 383.
² Hazard, v. i. p. 382. 390—394.
³ Gorges, b. ii. c. i. p. 43.
⁴ Hazard, v. i. p. 423—425. Hutchinson's Coll. p. 101—104.

New-Hampshire, had been the chief mover of all the aggressions on the rights of the adjoining colony, suspended the hostile movements,[1] which Gorges had too much honesty and too little intrigue to renew.[2]

The severe censures in the Star Chamber, the greatness of the fines which avarice rivalled bigotry in imposing, the rigorous proceedings with regard to ceremonies, the suspending and silencing of multitudes of ministers, still continued; and men were "enforced by heaps to desert their native country. Nothing but the wide ocean, and the savage deserts of America, could hide and shelter them from the fury of the bishops."[3] The pillory had become the bloody scene of human agony and mutilation, as an ordinary punishment; and the friends of Laud jested on the sufferings which were to cure the obduracy of fanatics. "The very genius of that nation of people," said Wentworth, "leads them always to oppose, both civilly and ecclesiastically, all that ever authority ordains for them." They were provoked to the indiscretion of a complaint, and then involved in a persecution. They were imprisoned and scourged; their noses were slit; their ears were cut off; their cheeks were marked with a red-hot brand. But the lash, and the shears, and the glowing iron, could not destroy principles, which were rooted in the soul, and which danger made it glorious to profess. The

---

[1] Winthrop, v. i. p. 187.
[2] Winthrop, v. ii. p. 12. Hazard, v. i. p. 403.
[3] Rushworth, v. ii. p. 410. Hazard, v. i. p. 420. Neal's Puritan's. Nugent's Hamden. The words are from Milton, the puritan poet; the greatest poet of our language.

injured party even learned to despise the mercy of their oppressors. "The mutilated defenders of liberty again defied the vengeance of the Star Chamber; came back with undiminished resolution to the place of their honorable infamy, and manfully presented the stumps of their ears to be grubbed out by the hangman's knife." Rising superior to fear, they derided the power, which, vainly desirous of producing passive obedience, only displayed its own feebleness by inflicting punishments without attaining its end. The dungeon, the pillory, and the scaffold, were but stages in the progress of civil liberty towards its triumph.

Yet there was a period, when the ministry of Charles hoped for success. No considerable resistance was threatened within the limits of England; and not even America could long be safe against the designs of despotism. A proclamation was issued to prevent the emigration of puritans;[1] the king refused his dissenting subjects the security of the wilderness.

It was probably a foreboding of these dangers, which induced the legislation of Massachusetts to exaggerate the necessity of domestic union.[2] In England the proclamation was but little regarded. The puritans, hemmed in by dangers on every side, and at that time having no prospect of ultimate success, desired at any rate to escape from their native country. The privy council interfered to stay a

---

[1] Hazard, v. i. p. 421. p. 73. iii. Mass. Hist. Coll. v. iii.
[2] Colony Laws, edition of 1660, p. 398.

squadron of eight ships, which were in the Thames, preparing to embark for New-England.[1] It has been said that Hamden and Cromwell were on board this fleet.[2] The English ministry of that day might willingly have exiled Hamden; no original authors, except royalists writing on hearsay, allude to the design imputed to him; in America there exists no evidence of his expected arrival; the remark of Hutchinson[3] refers to the well-known schemes of Lord Say and Seal and Lord Brooke; there are no circumstances in the lives of Hamden and Cromwell, corroborating the story, but many to establish its improbability; there came over during this summer, twenty ships and at least three thousand persons;[4] and had Hamden designed to emigrate, he whose maxim[5] in life forbad retreat, and whose resolution was as fixed as it was calm, possessed energy enough to have accomplished his purpose. He undoubtedly had watched with deep interest the progress of Massachusetts; and "the Conclusions" had early attracted his attention.[6] It has been conjectured,[7] asserted,[8] and even circumstantially related,[9] that he passed a winter with the colony of New-Plymouth. A person who bore the same or nearly the same name,[10]

[1] Rushworth, v. ii. p. 409. Hazard, v. i. p. 422.
[2] Bates and Dugdale in Neal's Puritans, v. ii. p. 349. C. Mather, b. i. c. v. 8. 7. Neal's N. E. v. i. p. 168. Chalmers, p. 160, 161. Robertson, b. x. Hume, c. liii. Belknap, v. ii. p. 229. Grahame's U. S. v. i. p. 299. Lord Nugent in his Hamden, v. i. p. 254, should not have repeated the error. Edinburg Review, No. 108.
[3] Hutchinson, v. i. p. 44.
[4] Winthrop, v. i. p. 268.
[5] Nulla vestigia retrorsum.
[6] Nugent, v. i. p. 173, 174.
[7] Belknap's Biog. v. ii. p. 229.
[8] N. Amer. Review, v. vi. p. 28.
[9] Fr. Baylies, Memoir, p. i. p. 110, takes fire at the thought.
[10] ii. Mass. Hist. Coll. v. viii. p. 258. More probably John Hamblin; a very common name in the old colony.

was undoubtedly there; but the greatest patriot-statesman of his times, the man, whom Charles I. would gladly have seen drawn and quartered, whom Clarendon paints as possessing beyond all his contemporaries, "a head to contrive, a tongue to persuade, and a hand to execute," and whom the fervent Baxter revered as able, by his presence and conversation, to give a new charm to the rest of the Saints in Heaven, was never in America.[1] Nor did he ever embark for America; the fleet, in which he is said to have taken his passage, was delayed but a few days; on petition of the owners and passengers, King Charles removed the restraint;[2] the ships proceeded on their intended voyage; and the whole company, as it seems, without diminution, arrived safely in the Bay of Massachusetts.[3] Had Hamden and Cromwell been of the party, they too would have reached New-England.

A few weeks before this attempt to stay emigration, the lords of the council had written to Winthrop, recalling to mind the former proceedings by a quo warranto; and demanding the return of the patent. In case of refusal, it was added, the king would assume into his own hands the entire management of the plantation.[4]

The colonists did not allow their courage to sink on the reception of an order, which menaced the destruction of their liberties. They demanded a

[1] Folsom's note in Norton and Folsom's Select Journal, No. i. p. 46.
[2] Rushworth, vol. ii. page 409. Aikin's Charles I. v. i. p. 471—473.
[3] Winthrop, v. i. p. 266, is decisive.
[4] Hubbard, p. 268, 269. Hazard, v. i. p. 432, 433. Hutchinson's Coll. p. 105, 106.

trial before condemnation. They urged that the recall of the patent would be a manifest breach of faith, pregnant with evils to themselves and their neighbors; that it would strengthen the plantations of the French and the Dutch; that it would discourage all future attempts at colonial enterprize; and finally, "if the patent be taken from us," such was their cautious but energetic remonstrance, "the common people will conceive that his majesty hath cast them off, and that hereby they are freed from their allegiance and subjection; and therefore will be ready to confederate themselves under a new government for their necessary safety and subsistence, which will be of dangerous example unto other plantations, and perilous to ourselves, of incurring his majesty's displeasure."[1] They therefore subjoin the petition, that they may be suffered to live in the wilderness, and obtain from the royal clemency the favor of neglect.

But before their supplication could find its way to the throne, the monarch was himself already involved in disasters. Anticipating success in his tyranny in England, he had resolved to practice no forbearance; with headlong indiscretion, he insisted on introducing a liturgy into Scotland; and compelling the uncompromising disciples of Knox to listen to prayers, translated from the Roman missal. The first attempt at reading the new service in the cathedral of Edinburgh was the signal for that series of momentous events, which promised to restore liberty to

[1] Hubbard, p. 269—271. Hutch. v. i. App. No. v. Hazard, v. i. p. 434. 436.

England, and give peace to the colonies. The movement began as great revolutions almost always do, from the ranks of the people. "What ye villain," shouted the old women at the dean, as he read the liturgy, "will ye say mass in my lug?"—"A pape, a pape," resounded the multitude, incensed against the bishop; "stane him, stane him." The churchmen narrowly escaped martyrdom. The tumult spreads; the nobles of Scotland take advantage of the excitement of the people to advance their ambition. The national covenant is published, and is signed by the Scottish nation, almost without distinction of rank, or sex; the defences of despotism are broken down; the flood washes away every vestige of ecclesiastical oppression. Scotland rises in arms for a holy war; and enlists religious enthusiasm under its banner in its contest against a despot, who has neither a regular treasury, nor an army, nor the confidence of his people. The wisest of his subjects esteem the insurgents as their friends and allies. There is now no time to oppress New-England; the throne itself totters;—there is no need to forbid emigration; England is at once become the theatre of wonderful events, and many fiery spirits who had fled for a refuge to the colonies, rush back to share in the open struggle for liberty. In the following years few passengers came over; the reformation of church and state, the attainder of Strafford, the impeachment of Laud, the great enemy of Massachusetts, caused all men to stay in England in expectation of a new world.[1]

[1] Winthrop, v. ii. p. 7. 31. 74.

CONDITION OF NEW-ENGLAND.

Yet a nation was already planted in New-England; a commonwealth was matured; the contests in which the unfortunate Charles became engaged, and the republican revolution that followed, left the colonists for the space of twenty years nearly unmolested in the enjoyment of the benefits of virtual independence. The change which their industry had wrought in the wilderness was the admiration of their times; the wonder of the world.[1] Plenty prevailed throughout the settlements. The wigwams and hovels in which the English had at first found shelter, were replaced by well-built houses. The number of emigrants, who had arrived in New-England before the assembling of the Long Parliament, are esteemed to have been twenty-one thousand two hundred.[2] One[3] hundred and ninety-eight ships had borne them across the Atlantic; and the whole cost of the plantations had been almost a million of dollars. A great expenditure and a great emigration for that age; yet two years ago more than fifty thousand persons arrived at the single port of Quebec in one summer; bringing with them a capital of more than three millions of dollars. In a little more than ten years, fifty towns and villages had been planted; between thirty and forty churches built; and

---

[1] Lechford, p. 47. Johnson, b. ii. c. xxi.
[2] Johnson, b. i. c. xiv. Josselyn's N. E. p. 258. Dummer's Defense of N. E. Charters. Hutchinson, v. i. p. 91. Davis, in ii. Mass. H. Coll. v. i. p. xxiii. Neal's N. E. v. i. p. 213, and Douglass' Summary, v. i. p. 381, are in error. Mather, b. i. c. viii. S. 7.

[3] I have no doubt, 198 and not 298. Compare Savage and Winthrop, v. ii. p. 331, and v. ii. p. 91, where there is another example of a mistake in printing from the Arabic numerals of Johnson. The accounts preserved of the arrivals in America, will not admit the larger statement.

CHAP. strangers, as they gazed, could not but acknowledge
X.
God's blessing on the endeavors of the planters.[1]
Affluence was already beginning to follow in the
train of industry. The natural exports of the country were furs and lumber; grain was carried to the
West-Indies; fish also was a staple. The business
of ship-building, in which so great excellence has
been attained, was early introduced; vessels of four
hundred tuns were constructed before 1643. So long
as the ports were filled with new comers, the domestic consumption had required nearly all the produce
of the colony. But now, says Winthrop,[2] and in
the history of American industry, the fact is worth
1643. preserving, "our supplies from England failing much,
men began to look about them, and fell to a manufacture of cotton, whereof we had store from Barbadoes."

1641. The Long Parliament contained among its members many sincere favorers of the puritan plantations;
yet the English in America, with wise circumspection, did not for a moment forget the dangers of a
foreign jurisdiction. "Upon the great liberty which
the king had left the parliament in England, some
of our friends there wrote to us advice to solicit for
us in the parliament, giving us hope that we might
obtain much. But consulting about it, we declined
the motion for this consideration, that if we should
put ourselves under the protection of the parliament,
we must then be subject to all such laws as they

[1] New England's First Fruits, in i. Mass. Hist. Coll. v. i. p. 247.
[2] v. ii. p. 119.

should make, or at least, such as they might impose upon us. It might prove very prejudicial to us."¹ The love of political independence declined even benefits.

When letters arrived, inviting the colonial churches to send their deputies to the Westminster assembly of divines, the same sagacity led them to neglect the invitation. Especially Hooker of Hartford, whom historians have so often taunted with jealous ambition, and who was remarkable for avoiding notoriety, "liked not the business," and deemed it his duty rather to stay in quiet and obscurity with his people in Connecticut, than to turn propagandist and plead for independency in England.²

Yet such commercial advantages as might be obtained without a surrender of their chartered rights, were objects of desire.; Hugh Peter and two others had been despatched as agents for the colonies; and their mission was favorably received. The house of commons publicly acknowledged, that "the plantations in New-England had by the blessing of the Almighty had good and prosperous success, without any public charge to the parent state;" and their imports and exports were freed from all taxation, "until the house of commons should take order to the contrary."³ The general court of Massachusetts received the ordinance hardly as a boon from a sovereign, but rather as a courtesy and a benefit from a friendly state, and while they entered it on their records as a

---

¹ Winthrop, v. ii. p. 25. i. Hist. Coll. v. vi. p. 156.
² Winthrop, v. ii. p. 76.
³ Hazard, v. i. p. 114. Winthrop, v. ii. p. 98. Hutchinson, v. i. p. 110. Chalmers, p. 174.

CHAP. X.

1641.

memorial for posterity, they sought to requite the kindness by reciprocity of legislation.

Still more important for New-England were the benefits of a secure domestic legislation. Among the first fruits may be esteemed the general declaration of the principles of liberty; the promulgation of a bill of rights.[1] Universal suffrage was not established; but every man, whether inhabitant or foreigner, freeman or not freeman, received the right of introducing any business into any public meeting and of taking part in its deliberations.[2] The colony moreover offered a free welcome and aid at the public cost, to Christians of every nation, who might fly beyond the Atlantic " to escape from wars or famine, or the tyranny and oppression of their persecutors."[3] The nation by a special statute made the fugitive and the persecuted the guests of the commonwealth. Its hospitality was as wide as misfortune.

The same liberality dictated the terms, on which the jurisdiction of Massachusetts was extended over New-Hampshire; and the strict interpretation of the charter offered an excuse for claiming the territory. Maryland suffered for almost twenty years the evils of a disputed jurisdiction, before its citizens asserted their claims to self-government; the people of New-Hampshire, dreading the perils of anarchy, provided a remedy by the immediate exercise of their natural rights; and by their own voluntary act they were annexed to their powerful neighbor; not as a prov-

April 14.

[1] See the Laws of 1641, in the ed. of 1660, p. 1. 26, 27, 28 and 50. Winthrop, v. ii. p. 55.
[2] Laws, ed. 1660, p. 50.
[3] Laws, ed. 1660, p. 73.

ince, but on equal terms, as an integral portion of CHAP. the state. The change was effected with great deliberation. The banks of the Piscataqua had not 1641. been peopled by puritans; and the system of Massachusetts could not properly be applied to the new acquisitions. The general court adopted the measure which justice recommended; neither the freemen nor the deputies of New-Hampshire were required to be church members. Thus political harmony was established; though the settlements long retained marks of the difference of their origin.¹

1642.
Sept.
8.

The attempt to gain possession of the territory on Narragansett Bay was less deserving of success. Massachusetts proceeded with the decision of an independent state. One Gorton, a wild enthusiast, whose opinions on religion were probably not clear to himself, and certainly remained obscure to others, had created disturbances in the district of Warwick. A minority of the inhabitants, wearied with harass- 1641. ing disputes, requested the interference of the magistrates of Massachusetts,² and two sachems, near Providence, surrendered the soil to the jurisdiction of that state.³ Gorton and his partisans did not disguise their scorn for the colonial clergy; they were advocates for liberty of conscience, and, at the same time, enemies to colonial independence; they denied the authority of the magistrates of Massachusetts, not only on the soil of Warwick but every where;

¹ Belknap, c. ii. Adams, p. 30. 2—4. Winthrop, v. ii. p. 59. Hubbard, p. 371, 372. Compare Hubbard, p. 406. Winthrop, v. ii. p. 28 and 93. ³ Winthrop, v. ii. p. 120—123.
² iii. Mass. Hist. Coll. v. i. p.

CHAP. X.
1643.

in as much as it was tainted by a want of true allegiance. Such opinions if carried into effect, would have destroyed the ecclesiastical system of Massachusetts and subverted its liberties; and were therefore thought worthy of death; but the public opinion of the time as expressed by a small majority of the deputies, was more merciful; and Gorton and his associates were imprisoned. It is the nature of a popular state to cherish peace; the people murmured at the severity of their rulers, and the imprisoned men were soon set at liberty; but the claim to the territory was not immediately abandoned.[1]

The enlargement of the territory of Massachusetts was in part a result of the virtual independence, which the commotions in the mother country had secured to the colonies. The establishment of a UNION among the puritan states of New-England was a still more important measure.

1637.

Immediately after the victories over the Pequods, at a time, when the earliest synod had gathered in Boston the leading magistrates and elders of Connecticut, the design of a confederacy was proposed. Many of the American statesmen, familiar with the character of the government of Holland, possessed

[1] On Gorton, see Winthrop, v. i. p. 91. 296, v. ii. p. 58, 59, and Eddy's note, p. 142—148. 156. 165, 166. 280. 295. 299. 317. 322. Colony Records, v. ii. Johnson, b. ii. c. xxiii. xxiv. Lechford, p. 41, 42. Gorton in ii. Mass. Hist. Coll. v. viii. p. 68—70. Morton, p. 202—206. Gorton in Hutchinson, v. i. App. xx. Hubbard, p. 343, 344. 401—407. and 500—512. Hazard, v. i. p. 546—553. C. Mather, b. vii. c. ii. 8. 12. Callender, p. 35, 38. Hopkins, in ii. Mass. Hist. Coll. v. ix. p. 199—201. Hutchinson, v. i. p. 114—118. Hutchinson's Coll. p. 237—239. Backus, v. i. p. 118 and ff. Eliot in i. Mass. Hist. Coll. v. ix. p. 35—38. Knowles, p. 182—189. Savage on Winthrop, v. ii. p. 147 —149. Baylies, N. P. v. i. c. xii.

sufficient experience and knowledge to frame the necessary plan; but time was wanting; the agents of Plymouth could not be seasonably summoned, and the subject was deferred. The next year it came again into discussion; but Connecticut, offended "because some pre-eminence was therein yielded to the Massachusetts," insisted on reserving to each state a negative on the proceedings of the confederacy. This reservation was refused; for in that case, said Massachusetts, "all would have come to nothing."

The vicinity of the Dutch, a powerful neighbor, whose claims Connecticut could not, singlehanded, defeat, led the colonists of the west to renew the negotiation; and with such success, that within a few years THE UNITED COLONIES OF NEW-ENGLAND were "made all as one."[1] Protection against the encroachments of the Dutch and the French, security against the tribes of savages, the liberties of the gospel in purity and in peace, these were the motives to the confederacy, which did, itself, continue nearly half a century, and which, even after it was cut down, left a hope, that a new and a better union would spring from its root.

The union embraced the separate governments of Massachusetts, Plymouth, Connecticut, and New-Haven; but to each its respective local jurisdiction was carefully reserved. The question of State Rights is nearly two hundred years old. The affairs

---

[1] Winthrop, v. i. p. 237. 284. 299. v. ii. p. 350. 266. Hubbard, p. 466. Johnson, b. ii. c. xxiii.

of the confederacy were entrusted to commissioners, consisting of two from each colony. Church membership was the only qualification, required for the office. The commissioners might deliberate on all things, which are "the proper concomitants or consequents of a confederation;" they were to assemble annually, or oftener, if exigences demanded. The affairs of peace and war, and especially Indian affairs, exclusively belonged to them; they too were the guardians, to see speedy justice assured to all the confederates in every jurisdiction, equally as in their respective states. The common expenses were to be assessed according to population.

Thus remarkable for unmixed simplicity was the form of the first confederated government[1] in America. It was a directory, apparently without any check; there was no president, except as a moderator of its meetings; and the larger state, Massachusetts, superior to all the rest in territory, wealth and population, had no greater number of votes than New-Haven. But the commissioners were, in reality, little more than a deliberative body; they possessed no executive power, and while they could decree a war and a levy of troops, it remained for the states to carry their votes into effect.

Provision was made for the reception of new members into the league; but the provision was wholly without results. The people beyond the

---

[1] On the Confederacy. The Records in Hazard, v. ii. Winthrop, v. ii. 101—106. Morton, p. 229. Hubbard, c. lii. Hutchinson; Neal; Belknap's N. H.; Baylies, part ii. p. 116 and ff. very fully. Pitkin's United States, v. i. p. 50, 51.

Piscataqua were not admitted, because "they ran a different course" from the puritans "both in their ministry, and in their civil administration;" the plantations of Providence also desired in vain to participate in the benefits of the union;[1] and the request of the island of Rhode-Island was equally rejected, because it would not consent to form a part of the jurisdiction of Plymouth.[2] Yet this early confederacy survived the jealousies of the Long Parliament; met with favor from the protector; and remained safe from censure on the restoration of the Stuarts.

Its chief office was the security of the settlements against the natives, whose power was growing more formidable, in proportion as they became acquainted with the arts of civilized life. But they were at the same time weakened by dissensions among themselves. Now that the Pequod nation was extinct, the more quiet Narragansetts could hardly remain at peace with the less numerous Mohegans. Anger and revenge brooded in the mind of Miantonomoh; he hated the Mohegans, for they were the allies of the English, by whom he had been arraigned as a criminal. He had suffered indignities at Boston, alike wounding to his pride as a chieftain and his honor as a man; his savage wrath was kindled against Uncas, his accuser, whom he detested as doubly his enemy; once, as the sachem of a hostile tribe, and again as a traitor to the whole

[1] Mass. Mss. State Papers, Case i. File i. No. 17.   [2] Hazard, v. ii. p. 99—100.

Indian race, the cringing sycophant of the white men. Gathering his men suddenly together, in defiance of a treaty to which the English were parties,[1] Miantonomoh, accompanied by a thousand warriors, fell upon the Mohegans. But his movements were as rash, as his spirit was impetuous; he was defeated and taken prisoner by those, whom he had doomed as a certain prey to his vengeance. By the laws of Indian warfare the fate of the captive was death. Yet Gorton and his friends, who held their lands by a grant from Miantonomoh, interceded for their benefactor. The unhappy chief was conducted to Hartford; and the wavering Uncas, who had the strongest claims to the gratitude and protection of the English,[2] asked the advice of the commissioners of the United Colonies. Murder had ever been severely punished by the puritans; they had at Plymouth, with the advice of Massachusetts, executed three of their own men for the murder of one Indian; and the elders, to whom the case of Miantonomoh was referred, finding, that he had, deliberately and in time of quiet, murdered a servant in the service of the Mohegan chief, that he had fomented discontents against the English, and that, in contempt of a league, he had plunged into a useless and bloody war, could not perceive in his career any claims to mercy. He seemed to merit death; yet not at the hands of the settlers. Uncas received his captive, and conveying the helpless victim beyond

[1] Hubbard's Indian Wars, p. 42.   [2] ii. M. H. C. v. viii. p. 137. 141.

the limits of the jurisdiction of Connecticut, put him to death.¹

The tribe of Miantonomoh burned to avenge the execution of their chief; but they feared a conflict with the English, whose alliance they vainly solicited, and who persevered in protecting the Mohegans. The Narragansetts were at last compelled to submit in sullenness to a peace, of which the terms were alike hateful to their independence, their prosperity and their love of revenge.²

While the commissioners, thus unreservedly and without appeal, controlled the relation of the native tribes, the spirit of independence was still further displayed by a direct negotiation and a solemn treaty of peace with the governor of Acadia.³

Content with the security which the confederacy afforded, the people of Connecticut desired no guarantee for their independence from the government of England; taking care only by a regular purchase to obtain a title to the soil from the assigns of the Earl of Warwick.⁴ The people of Rhode-Island, excluded from the colonial union, would never have maintained their existence as a separate state, had they not sought the interference and protection of the mother country; and the founder of the colony was chosen to conduct the important mission.

1644.
1646.

1643.

---

¹ Records in Hazard, v. ii. p. 7—13. I. Mather's Ind. Troubles, p. 56, 57. Morton, p. 234. Winthrop, v. ii. p. 130. 134. Hubbard's Indian Wars, p. 42—45. Johnson, b. ii. c. xxiii. Trumbull, v. i. p. 129—135. Drake, b. ii. p. 67. Relation in iii. Mass. Hist. Soc. v. iii. p. 161 and ff. See the opinions and arguments of Hopkins and Savage, of Davis and Holmes.

² Hazard, v. ii. p. 40—50. Winthrop, v. ii. p. 198. 246. 380.

³ Winthrop, v. ii. p. 197. Hazard, v. i. p. 536 and 537, and v. ii. p. 50. 54.

⁴ Trumbull, v. i. App. No. v. and vi.

CHAP. X.

Embarking at Manhattan, he arrived in England not long after the death of Hamden. The parliament had placed the affairs of the American colonies under the control of Warwick, as governor-in-chief, assisted by a council of five peers and twelve commoners.[1] Among these commoners was Henry Vane, a man who was ever as true in his affections, as he was undeviating in his principles, and who now welcomed the American envoy as an ancient friend. The favor of parliament was won by his incomparable "printed Indian labors,[2] the like whereof was not extant from any part of America;" and his merits as a missionary induced "both houses of parliament to grant unto him and friends with him, a free and absolute charter[3] of civil government for those parts of his abode."[4] Thus were the places of refuge for "soul-liberty" on the Narragansett Bay incorporated "with full power and authority to rule themselves." To the Long Parliament, and especially to Sir Henry Vane, Rhode-Island owes its existence as a political state.

1644. Mar. 14.

A double triumph awaited Williams on his return to New-England; he arrived at Boston, and letters from the parliament ensured him a safe reception from those who had decreed his banishment. But what honors awaited the successful negotiator, on his return to the province which he had founded! As he reached Seekonk, he found the water covered

[1] Hazard, v. i. p. 533. 535.
[2] Rhode-Island Hist. Coll. v. i.
[3] ii. Mass. Hist. Coll. v. ix. p. 185.
[4] Winthrop, vol. ii. page 193.
Knowles, p. 200. See also Callender and Backus; both very good authorities, because both followed original documents.

with a fleet of canoes; all Providence had come forth to welcome the return of its benefactor. Placed in the centre of his fellow-citizens, the group of boats started for the opposite shore; and, as they paddled across the stream, Roger Williams, placed in the centre of his grateful fellow-citizens, and glowing with the purest joy, "was elevated and transported out of himself."[1]

And now came the experiment of the efficacy of popular sovereignty. The value of a moral principle may be tried on a small community as well as a large one; the experiment on magnetism, made with a child's toy, gives as sure a result, as when the agency of that subtle power is watched in its influence on the globe. There were already several towns in the new state; filled with the strangest and most incongruous elements; anabaptists and antinomians; fanatics, as its enemies asserted, and infidels; so that if a man had lost his religious opinions, he might have been sure to find them again in some village of Rhode-Island. All men were equal; all might meet and debate in the public assemblies; all might aspire to office; every public law required confirmation in the primary assemblies. And so it came to pass, that the little democracy was famous for its "headiness and tumults;" its stormy town-meetings, and the angry feuds of its herdsmen; but true as the needle to the pole, the popular will instinctively pursued the popular interest; amidst all the jarring quarrels of the rival statesmen in the

[1] Knowles, p. 202. The work of Knowles is of high value.

CHAP. X.

1647.
May 19.

1651.
April 3.

Nov.

1652.
Oct. 2.

plantations, good men were chosen to administer the government; and the spirit of mercy, of liberality and wisdom was impressed on its legislation.[1]

Yet danger still menaced. The executive council of state in England had granted to Coddington a commission for governing the islands; and such a dismemberment of the territory of the narrow state must have terminated in the division of the remaining soil between the adjacent governments. Williams was again compelled to return to England; and with John Clarke, his colleague in the mission, was again successful. The dangerous commission was vacated, and the charter and separate existence of Rhode-Island confirmed. The general assembly in its gratitude desired that Williams might himself obtain from the sovereign authority in England an appointment as governor for a year over the whole colony; but if gratitude blinded the province, ambition did not blind its benevolent author. Williams refused to sanction a measure, which would have furnished a dangerous precedent; and was content with the honor of doing good. His entire success with the executive council was due to the powerful intercession of Sir Henry Vane. "Under God the sheet-anchor of Rhode-Island was Sir Henry."[2] But for him, Rhode-Island would perhaps have been divided among its neighbors. "From the first beginning of the Providence colony," thus did the people in town-meeting address Sir Henry Vane, "you have been a noble and true friend to an outcast and des-

[1] ii. Mass. Hist. Coll. v. vii. p. 78, &c. [2] Backus, v. i. p. 286.

pised people; we have ever reaped the sweet fruits of your constant loving-kindness and favor. We have long been free from the iron yoke of wolvish bishops; we have sitten dry from the streams of blood, spilt by the wars in our native country. We have not felt the new chains of the presbyterian tyrants, nor in this colony have we been consumed by the over-zealous fire of the (so called) godly Christian magistrates. We have not known what an excise means; we have almost forgotten what tythes are. We have long drunk of the cup of as great liberties as any people, that we can hear of, under the whole heaven. When we are gone, our posterity and children after us shall read in our town-records your loving-kindness to us, and our real endeavor after peace and righteousness."[1]

Far different were the early destinies of the Province of Maine. A general court was held at Saco, under the auspices of the Lord Proprietary, who had drawn upon paper a stately scheme of government, with deputies and councillors, a marshal and a treasurer of the public revenue, chancellors, and a master of the ordnance, and every thing that the worthy old man deemed essential to his greatness. Sir Ferdinand had "travailed in the cause above forty years" and expended many thousand pounds; yet all the regalia which Thomas Gorges, his trusty and well beloved cousin and deputy could find in the principality, were but "one old kettle,

[1] Letter from the Town of Providence, to Sir Henry Vane, August 27, 1654.

CHAP. a pair of tongs, and a couple of cob-irons." Ag-
X.
amenticus soon became a chartered borough, though
1641. it was in truth but "a poor village;"[1] like another Romulus, the veteran soldier resolved to per-
1642. petuate his name, and under the name of Gorge-
Mar.
1. ana, the land round York became as good a city as
seals and parchment, a nominal mayor and aldermen,
a chancery court and a court-leet, sergeants and white
rods, can make of a town of less than three hundred
inhabitants and its petty officers. Yet the nature of
Gorges was generous, and his piety sincere. He
sought pleasure in doing good; fame, by advancing
Christianity among the heathen; a durable monument, by erecting houses, villages and towns. The
contemporary and friend of Raleigh, he adhered to his
schemes in America, for almost half a century; and,
long after he became convinced of their unproduc-
tiveness, was still bent on plans of colonization, at
an age, when other men are but preparing to die
with decorum. Firmly attached to the monarchy,
he never disobeyed his king, except that as a church-
man and a protestant, he refused to serve against the
Huguenots; when the wars in England broke out,
the septuagenarian royalist buckled on his armor,
and giving the last strength of his gray hairs to the
defence of the unfortunate Charles, probably found
death in the bootless service. In America his fortunes had met with a succession of untoward events.
1643. The patent for Lygonia had been purchased by
April
7. Rigby, a republican member of the Long Parliament,

[1] Winthrop, v. ii. p. 100.

and a dispute ensued between the deputies of the respective proprietaries. In vain did Cleaves, the agent of Rigby, solicit the assistance of Massachusetts; the colony warily refused to take part in the strife. It marks the confidence of all men in the justice of the puritans, that both aspirants now appealed to the Bay magistrates and solicited them to act as umpires. The cause was learnedly argued in Boston, and the decree of the court was oracular. Neither party was allowed to have a clear right; and both were enjoined to live in peace. But how could Vines and Cleaves assert their authority? On the death of Gorges, the people repeatedly wrote to his heirs. No answer was received; and such commissioners as had authority from Europe, gradually withdrew. There was no relief for the colonists but in themselves; and the inhabitants of Piscataqua, Gorgeana and Wells, following the American precedent, with free and unanimous consent[1] formed themselves into a body politic for the purposes of self-government. Massachusetts readily offered its protection. The great charter of the Bay company was unrolled before the general court in Boston, and "upon perusal of the instrument it was voted, that this jurisdiction extends from the northernmost part of the river Merrimack, and three miles more, north, be it one hundred miles, more or lesse, from the sea; and then upon a straight line east and west to each sea."[2] The words were precise; nothing remained

---

[1] i. Mass. Hist. Coll. v. i. p. 103. Nos. 17. 44, 45, 46, 47. File x.
[2] Mass. State Papers, Case i. No. 88.
File vii. Nos. 4. 20. 58. File viii.

but to find the latitude of a point three miles to the north of the remotest spring of the Merrimack, and to claim all the territory of Maine which lies south of that parallel; for the grant to Massachusetts was prior to the patents, under which Rigby and the heirs of Gorges had been disputing. Nor did Massachusetts make an idle boast of the territorial extent of its chartered rights; commissioners were promptly despatched to the eastward to settle the government; one town after another gave in its adhesion and its promise of allegiance. The greatest care was observed to guard the rights of property; every man was confirmed in his possessions; the religious liberty of the episcopalians was left unharmed; the privileges of citizenship were extended to all the inhabitants; and the whole eastern country was so pleased with the result, that when the claims of the proprietaries in England were urged before Cromwell, the towns of York, Kittery, Wells, Saco, and Cape Porpoise, remonstrated against any change, on the ground of their own former experience. They besought the protector for permission to remain with Massachusetts; to sever them from that colony would be to them "the subverting of all civil order."[1]

Thus did Massachusetts, following the most favorable interpretation of its charter, extend its frontier to the islands in Casco Bay. It was equally successful in maintaining its independence of the Long Parliament; though the circumstances of the

[1] Mass. State Papers, Case i. File xii. No. 64, a very valuable document. I have also compared Hubbard, Williamson, and Folsom.

contest were ultimately fatal to the immediate assertion of the liberty of conscience.

With the increase of English freedom, the dangers which had menaced Massachusetts, appeared to pass away; its government began to adventure on a more lenient policy; the sentence of exile against Wheelwright was rescinded; a proposition was made to extend the franchises of the company to those, who were not church members; provided "a civil agreement among all the English could be formed" for asserting the common liberty. For this purpose letters were written to the confederated states; but the want of concert defeated the plan. The law which, nearly at the same time, threatened obstinate anabaptists with exile, was not designed to be enforced. "Anabaptism," says Jeremy Taylor[1] in his famous argument for liberty, "is as much to be rooted out as any thing, that is the greatest pest and nuisance to the public interest." The fathers of Massachusetts reasoned more mildly; the dangers, apprehended from some wild and turbulent spirits, "whose conscience and religion seemed only to sett forth themselves and raise contentions in the country, did provoke us," such was their language at the time, "to provide for our safety by a law, that all such should take notice, how unwelcome they should be unto us, either comeing or staying. But for such as differ from us only in judgment and live peaceably amongst us, such have no cause to complain; for it hath never beene as yet putt in execution against

[1] Works, v. viii. p. 213, Heber's ed.

any of them, although such are known to live amongst us."[1] Even two of the presidents of Harvard college were anabaptists.

While dissenters were thus treated with an equivocal toleration, no concessions were made towards the government in England. It was the creed of even the most loyal deputy, that "if the king, or any party from him, should attempt any thing against this commonwealth," it was the common duty "to spend estate, and life, and all, without scruple in its defence;" that "if the parliament itself should hereafter be of a malignant spirit, then if the colony have strength sufficient, it may withstand any authority from thence to its hurt."[2] Massachusetts called itself "a perfect republic;"[3] nor was the expression a vain boast; the commonwealth, by force of arms, preserved in its harbors a neutrality between the ships of the opposing English factions; and the law which placed death as the penalty on any "attempt at the alteration of the frame of polity fundamentally,"[4] was well understood to be aimed at those, who should assert the unqualified supremacy of the English parliament.

Whilst the public mind was agitated with discussions on liberty of conscience and independence of English jurisdiction, the community, in this infancy of popular government, was disturbed with a third topic of the deepest interest. "The great question about the authority of the magistrates and the li-

---

[1] Hutchinson's Coll. p. 216.
[2] Winthrop, v. ii. p. 176. 183.
[3] Respublica perfecta.
[4] Colony Laws.

berty of the people troubled the country;[1] and the youthful state was divided into political parties, in favor and against a strong executive.

The democratic party had for many years been acquiring a control of public opinion. The oldest dispute in the colony related to the grounds and limits of the authority of the governor. In Boston, on occasion of dividing the town lands, "men of the inferior sort were chosen." Eliot, the apostle of the Indians, maintained, that treaties should not be made without consulting the commons.[2] The doctrine of rotation in office was asserted even to the neglect of Winthrop, "lest there should be a governor for life." When one of the elders proposed that the office of governor should be held for life, the deputies immediately resolved, that no magistrate of any kind should be elected for more than a year. The governor and magistrates once assembling in a sort of aristocratic caucus, nominated several persons for office, and the people took care to reject every one of the candidates thus proposed; and, on the other hand, when one of the ministers attempted to dissuade the people from choosing the same officers twice in succession, they disliked the interference of the adviser more than they loved the doctrine of frequent change, and re-elected the old magistrates almost without exception. The condition of a new colony, which discarded the legislation of the mother country, necessarily left many things to the opinions of the executive; the people were loud in demanding

[1] Winthrop, v. ii. p. 228. [2] Plebe inconsulto.

a government of law and not of discretion. No sooner had the benevolent Winthrop pleaded against the establishment of an exact penalty for every offence, because justice, not less than mercy, imposed the duty of regulating the punishment by the circumstances of the case, than the cry of arbitrary power was raised; and the people refused the hope of clemency, when it was to be obtained from the accidental compassion and the capricious judgments of a magistrate. The authority, exercised by the assistants during the intervals between the sessions, became a subject of apprehension. The popular party, having a majority of the deputies, proposed to substitute a joint commission; the proposition being declined as inconsistent with the patent, they then desired to reserve the question for further deliberation. When to this it was answered, that in the mean time the assistants would act according to the power and trust committed to them by the charter, the deputies immediately rejoined by their speaker, Hawthorne, "You will not be obeyed." The same spirit occasioned the strenuous, though unsuccessful efforts to deprive the magistrates of their negative on the doings of the house; the negative power was feared as a bulwark of fixed authority, one obstacle in the way of the free enforcement of the popular will.[1]

Such had been the progress of public opinion, when the popular party felt a consciousness of so

[1] Winthrop, v. i. p. 82, 83. 151, 152. 299, 300, 301, 302—v. ii. p. 167. 169. 172. 204. 210. 307. 343.

great strength, as to desire an occasion for testing its power in a struggle with its opponents. The opportunity could not long be wanting. The executive magistrates, accustomed to a tutelary vigilance over the welfare of the towns, had set aside a military election in Hingham. There had been, perhaps, in the proceedings sufficient irregularity to warrant the interference. The affair came before the general court. "Two of the magistrates and a small majority of the deputies were of opinion, that the magistrates exercised too much power, and that the people's liberty was thereby in danger; while nearly half the deputies and all the rest of the magistrates judged, that authority was overmuch slighted, which, if not remedied, would endanger the commonwealth and introduce a mere democracy." The two branches being thus at variance, a reference to the arbitration of the elders was proposed; but "to this the deputies would by no means consent; for they knew that many of the elders were more careful to uphold the honor and power of the magistrates, than themselves well liked of." The angry conferences of a long session followed; but the magistrates, sustained by the ministers, excelled the popular party in firmness and in self-possession; the latter lost ground by joining issue on a question, where its own interest eventually required its defeat.

For the root of the disturbance at Hingham existed in "a presbyterial spirit," which opposed the government of the colonial commonwealth. Some of those, who pleaded the laws of England against the charter and the administration in Massachusetts, had been committed by Winthrop for contempt of the established authority. It was now proposed to procure their release by his impeachment. The measure was the most beneficial that could have been proposed. Hitherto the enemies of the state had united with the popular party; and both had assailed the charter, as the basis of magisterial power; the former, with the view of invoking the interposition of England, the latter, in the hope of increasing popular liberty. But the true-hearted citizens could not be induced, even in the excitement of political divisions, to wrong the purest of their leaders; and the factious elements were rendered harmless by decomposition. Winthrop appeared at the bar, only to triumph in his integrity. "Civil liberty," said the noble-minded man in "a little speech" on the occasion, "is the proper end and object of authority, and cannot subsist without it. It is a liberty to that only, which is good, just and honest. This liberty you are to stand for, with the hazard not only of your goods, but, if need be, of your lives. Whatsoever crosseth this, is not authority, but a distemper thereof."

It now became possible to adjust the long-continued difference by a compromise. The power of the magistrates over the militia was diminished by law;[1] but though the magistrates themselves were by some declared to be but public servants, holding "a ministerial office;" and though it became a favor-

[1] Winthrop, v. ii. p. 246.

ite idea, that all authority resides essentially with the people in their body representative, yet the Hingham disturbers were punished by heavy fines; while Winthrop and his friends retained, what they deserved, the affectionate confidence of the colony. The opposition of Bellingham was due to his jealousy of Winthrop and Dudley, the chief officers of the state, whom he would willingly have supplanted.

The court of Massachusetts was ready to concede the enjoyment of religious worship under the presbyterian forms;[1] yet its enemies, defeated in their hope of a union with the popular party, were resolutely discontented, and now determined to rally on the question of liberty of conscience. The attempt was exceedingly artful; for the doctrine had been rapidly making progress. Many books had come from England in defence of toleration; many of the court were well inclined to suspend the laws against anabaptists, and the order subjecting strangers to the supervision of the magistrates; and Winthrop thought, that "the rule of hospitality required more moderation and indulgence." In Boston a powerful liberal party already openly existed. But now the apparent purpose of advancing religious freedom was made to disguise measures of the deadliest hostility to the frame of civil government. The nationality of New-England was in danger. The existence of Poland was sacrificed in the last century by means of the Polish Dissidents, who, appealing to the Russian cabinet to interfere in behalf of liberty of con-

CHAP. X.

1645.

[1] Winslow, p. 28.

science, opened the doors of their country to the enemy of its independence. The Roman Catholic bigots were there the impassioned guardians of Polish nationality; the Calvinists of New-England were of a cooler temperament; but with equal inflexibility they anchored their liberties on unmixed puritanism. "To eat out the power of godliness," became an expression, nearly synonymous with an attempt to acknowledge the direct supremacy of parliament. William Vassal of Scituate, was the chief of the "busy and factious spirits, always opposite to the civil governments of the country and the way of its churches;" and at the same time, through his brother, a member of the Long Parliament and of the commissioners for the colonies, he possessed influence in England. The movement began in Plymouth by a proposition "for a full and free tolerance of religion to all men, without exception against Turk, Jew, Papist, Arian, Socinian, Familist, or any other." The deputies, not perceiving any political purpose, were ready to adopt the motion. "You would have admired," wrote Winslow to Winthrop, "to have seen how sweet this carrion relished to the palate of most of them."[1] The plan was defeated by delay; and Massachusetts became the theatre of action.

The new party desired to subvert the charter government and introduce a general governor from England. They endeavored to acquire strength by rallying all the materials of opposition. The friends of pres-

---

[1] Hutch. Coll. p. 154.

byterianism were soothed by hopes of a triumph; the democratic party was assured that the government should be more popular; while the penurious were provoked by complaints of unwise expenditures and intolerable taxations.[1] But the people refused to be deceived; and when a petition for redress of grievances was presented to the general court, it was evidently designed for English ears. It had with difficulty obtained the signatures of seven men, and of these, some were sojourners in the colony, who desired only an excuse for appealing to England. The document was written in a spirit of wanton insult;[2] it introduced every topic, that had been made the theme of party discussion; and asserted what Lord Holt and Lord Treby would have confirmed, but what the colonists were not willing to concede, that there existed in the country no settled form of government according to the laws of England. An entire revolution was demanded; "if not," add the remonstrants, "we shall be necessitated to apply our humble desires to both houses of parliament;" and there was reason to fear, that they would obtain a favorable hearing before the body, whose authority they labored to enlarge.

For Gorton had carried his complaints to the mother country; and though unaided by personal influence or by powerful friends, had succeeded in all his wishes. At this very juncture an order respecting his claims arrived in Boston; and was

[1] Johnson, ii. Mass. Hist. Coll. v. viii. p. 6.
[2] Compare Hutch. Coll. p. 189, 212, 213.

CHAP. X.
1646.

couched in terms, which involved an assertion of the right of parliament to reverse the decisions and control the government of Massachusetts. The danger was imminent; it struck at the very life and foundation of the rising commonwealth. Had the Long Parliament succeeded in revoking the patent of Massachusetts, the Stuarts, on their restoration, would have found not one chartered government in the colonies; and the tenor of American history would have been changed. The people rallied with great unanimity in support of their magistrates. A law had been drawn up and was ready to pass, conferring on all residents equal power in town affairs, and enlarging the constituency of the state. It was deemed safe to defer the important enactment, till the present controversy should be settled; the order against anabaptists was likewise left unrepealed; and notwithstanding strong opposition from the friends of toleration in Boston, it was resolved to convene a synod for the permanent settlement of the ecclesiastical polity.

Nov. 4.

At length the general court assembled for the discussion of the usurpations of parliament and the dangers from domestic treachery. The elders did not fail to attend in the gloomy season. One faithless deputy was desired to withdraw; and then with closed doors, that the consultation might remain in the breast of the court, the nature of the relation with England was made the subject of debate. After much deliberation it was agreed, that Massachusetts owed to England the same allegiance as the free Hanse-Towns had rendered to the empire; as Normandy, when its dukes were kings of England, had paid to the monarchs of France. It was also resolved not to accept a new charter from the parliament; for that would imply a surrender of the old. Besides; parliament granted none but by way of ordinance, which the king might one day refuse to confirm; and always made for itself an express reservation of "a supreme power in all things." The elders, after a day's consultation, confirmed the decisions. "If parliament should be less inclinable to us, we must wait upon Providence for the preservation of our just liberties."

The colony then proceeded to exercise the independence which it claimed. The general court replied to the petition in a state-paper, written with great moderation; and the disturbers of the public security were summoned into its presence. Robert Childe and his companions appealed to the commissioners in England. The appeal was not admitted. "The charter," he urged, "does but create a corporation within the realm, subject to English laws." —"Plantations," replied the court, "are above the rank of an ordinary corporation; they have been esteemed other than towns, yea, than many cities. Colonies are the foundations of great commonwealths. It is the fruit of pride and folly to despise the day of small things."

To the parliament of England the legislature remonstrated with the noblest frankness against any assertion of the paramount authority of that body.

"An order from England," say they, "is prejudicial to our chartered liberties and to our well-being in this remote part of the world. Times may be changed; for all things here below are subject to vanity, and other princes or parliaments may arise. Let not succeeding generations have cause to lament and say, England sent our fathers forth with happy liberties, which they enjoyed many years, notwithstanding all the enmity and opposition of the prelacy, and other potent adversaries, and yet these liberties were lost in the season, when England itself recovered its own. We rode out the dangers of the sea; shall we perish in port? We have not admitted appeals to your authority, being assured they cannot stand with the liberty and power granted us by our charter, and would be destructive to all government. These considerations are not new to the high court of parliament; the records whereof bear witness of the wisdom and faithfulness of our ancestors in that great council, who, in those times of darkness, when they acknowledged a supremacy in the Roman bishops, in all causes ecclesiastical, yet would not allow appeals to Rome.

The wisdom and experience of that great council, the English parliament, are more able to prescribe rules of government and judge causes, than such poor rustics, as a wilderness can breed up; yet the vast distance between England and these parts, abates the virtue of the strongest influences. Your councils and judgments can neither be so well grounded nor so seasonably applied, as might either be useful to us, or safe for yourselves, in your discharge, in the great day of account. If any miscarriage shall befall us, when we have the government in our own hands, the state of England shall not answer for it.

Continue your favorable aspect to these infant plantations, that we may still rejoice and bless our God under your shadow, and be there still nourished with the warmth and dews of heaven. Confirm our liberties; discountenance our enemies, the disturbers of our peace under pretence of our injustice. A gracious testimony of your wonted favor will oblige us and our posterity."

In the same spirit, Edward Winslow, the agent for Massachusetts in England, publicly denied that the jurisdiction of parliament extended to America. "If the parliament of England should impose laws upon us, having no burgesses in the house of commons, nor capable of a summons by reason of the vast distance, we should lose the liberties and freedom of English indeed."[1] Massachusetts was not without steadfast friends in the legislature of England; yet it marks an honest love of liberty and of justice in the Long Parliament, that the doctrines of colonial equality should have been received with favor. "Sir Henry Vane, though he might have taken occasion against the colony for some dishonor, which he apprehended to have been unjustly put upon him there, yet showed himself a true friend to New-England, and a man of a noble and generous

[1] Winslow's New-England's Salamander, p. 24.

CHAP. X.
1647.

mind."[1] After ample deliberation the committee of parliament magnanimously replied, "We encourage no appeals from your justice. We leave you with all the freedom and latitude, that may, in any respect, be duly claimed by you."[2]

Such were the arts by which Massachusetts preserved its liberties. The people sustained their magistrates with great unanimity; hardly five and twenty persons could be found in the whole jurisdiction to join in a complaint against the strictness of the government; and when the discontented introduced the dispute into the elections, their candidates were defeated by an overwhelming majority.[3]

The harmony of the people had been confirmed by the courage of the elders, who gave fervor to the enthusiasm of patriotism. "It had been as unnatural for a right New-England man to live without an able ministry, as for a smith to work his iron without a fire." The union between the elders and the state could not, therefore, but become more intimate than ever; and religion was venerated and cherished as the security against political subserviency. When the synod met by adjournment, it was by the common consent of all the puritan colonies, that a system of church government was established for the

---

[1] Winthrop, v. ii. p. 248 and 317.
[2] Hutchinson, v. i. 136—140, is confused and inaccurate. Was it from ignorance? His errors are repeated by Chalmers and Grahame. The inquirer must go to the original authorities—Colony Records. Hutchinson's Collection, p.188—218. Winthrop, v. ii. 278—301, and 317—322. N. E.'s Jonas, cast up at London, in ii. Mass. H. C. v. iv. p. 107, &c. E. Winslow's N. E.'s Salamander Discovered, in iii. M. H. C. v. ii. p. 110, &c. See also Johnson, b. iii. c. iii. Hubbard, c. lv. Hazard, v. i. p. 544, &c.
[3] Winthrop, v. ii. p. 307.

congregations.[1] The platform retained authority for more than a century, and has not yet lost its influence. It effectually excluded the presbyterian modes of discipline from New-England.

The jealousy of independence was preserved in its wakefulness. The Long Parliament asserted its power over the royalist colonies in general terms, which seemed alike to threaten the plantations of the north; and now that royalty was abolished, it invited Massachusetts to receive a new patent and to hold courts and issue warrants in its name. But the colonial commonwealth was too wary to hazard its rights, by merging them in the acts of a government, of which the decline seemed approaching. It has been usual to say, that the people of Massachusetts foiled the Long Parliament. In a public state-paper they openly refused to submit to its requisitions, and yet, with extreme caution, they never carried their remonstrance beyond the point, which their charter appeared to them to warrant.[2]

After the successes of Cromwell in Ireland, he voluntarily expressed his interest in New-England, by offering its inhabitants estates and a settlement in the beautiful island, which his arms had subdued. His offers were declined; for the emigrants already loved their land of refuge, where their own courage and toils had established "the liberties of the gospel in its purity," and created the peaceful abundance of thriving republics.

[1] Result of a Synod, &c. See also Winthrop and Hubbard. Cotton Mather is diffuse on the subject.
[2] Hutchinson, v. i. App. viii.

CHAP. X.

1651. to 1654.

The war between England and Holland hardly disturbed the tranquillity of the colonies. The western settlements, which would have suffered extreme misery from a combined attack of the Indians and the Dutch, were earnest for attempting to reduce New-Amsterdam; but Massachusetts could deliberate more coolly, and its elders wisely answered, that the wars of Europe ought not to destroy the happiness of America, that "it was safest for the colonies to forbear the use of the sword, but to be in a posture of defence;" and the largest state in the confederacy refused to become a passive instrument for the execution of injustice at the bidding of its neighbors. The nature of the reserved powers of the members of the union now became the subject of animated discussion; but a peaceful intercourse with Manhattan continued.[1]

1654. The European republics had composed their strife, before the fleet, which was designed to take possession of the settlements on the Hudson, reached the shores of America. It was a season of peace between England and France; and yet the English forces, turning to the north, made the easy conquest of Acadia; an acquisition, which no remonstrances or complaints could induce the protector to restore.[2]

The possession was perhaps considered a benefit to New-England, of which the inhabitants enjoyed

[1] Hazard, v. ii. has all the documents on this subject. Trumbull, v. i. p. 202—214, gives a wrong coloring to the affair. He is followed by Marshall. The heart of Irving is always right; in relating the incident, his delightful humor yields to the serious eulogy of benevolence.
[2] Haliburton, v. i. p. 61.

the confidence of Cromwell throughout all the period CHAP.
of his success. They were fully satisfied that the X.
battles which he had fought, were the battles of the
Lord; and "the spirits of the brethren were carried
forth in faithful and affectionate prayers in his behalf;" but at the same time they charged him to rule
his spirit, rather than to storm cities. Cromwell, in
return, was moved by the sincerity of their regard;
he seems to have found relief in pouring out his heart
to them freely; he confessed that the battle of Dunbar, where "some, who were godly," were fought
into their graves, was of all the acts of his life, that,
on which his mind had the least quiet; and he declared himself "truly ready to serve the brethren
and the churches" in America. The declaration was
sincere. The people of New-England were ever
sure, that Cromwell would listen to their requests,
and would take an interest in all the little details of
their condition. He left them independence; perhaps
he gave them advantageous contracts; he favored
their trade. When his arms had made the conquest
of Jamaica, he offered to them the island, with the 1655.
promise of all the wealth which the tropical clime
pours prodigally into the lap of industry; and though
they frequently thwarted his views, his magnanimity
preserved for them his regard. English history must
judge of Cromwell by his influence on the institutions
of England; the American colonies remember the
years of his power as the period, when British sovereignty was for them free from rapacity, intolerance
and oppression. He may be called the benefactor of

the English in America; for he left them to enjoy unshackled the liberal benevolence of Providence, the freedom of industry, of commerce and of government.[1]

Yet the puritans of New-England perceived that their security rested on the personal character of the protector, and that other revolutions were ripening; they, therefore, never allowed their vigilance to be lulled. The influence of the elders was confirmed; the civil and the religious institutions had become intimately connected. While the spirit of independence was thus assured, the evils ensued, that are in some measure inseparable from a religious establishment; a distinct interest grew up under the system; the severity of the laws was sharpened against infidelity on the one hand, and sectarianism on the other; nor can it be denied, nor should it be concealed, that the elders, especially Wilson and Norton, instigated and sustained the government in its worst cruelties.

Where the mind is left free, religion can never have dangerous enemies. No class has then an interest or a motive, to attempt its subversion; while the interests of society demand a foundation for the principles of justice and benevolence. Atheism is a folly of the metaphysician, not the folly of human nature. Of savage life, Roger Williams declared, that he had never found one native American, who denied the existence of a God; in civilized life, when it was said of the court of Frederic, that the

---

[1] Hutchinson's Coll. p. 233 and Mass. State Papers, Case i. File ff. Hutch. Hist. App. No's. ix, x. vii. No. 34. File x. No. 77.

place of king's atheist was vacant, the gibe was felt as the most biting sarcasm. Men revolt against the oppressions of superstition, the exactions of ecclesiastical tyranny; but never against religion itself. When an ecclesiastical establishment, under the heaviest penalties, requires universal conformity, the diversity of human opinion necessarily involves the consequence, that some consciences are oppressed and wronged. In such cases, if the wrong is excessive, intellectual servitude is followed by consequences, analagous to those, which ensue on the civil slavery of the people; the mind, as it bursts its fetters, is clouded by a sense of injury; the judgment is confused; and in the zeal to resist a tyranny, passion attempts to sweep away every form of religion. Bigotry commits the correlative error, when it attempts to control opinion by positive statutes, to substitute the terrors of law for convincing argument. It is a crime, to attack truth under pretence of resisting injurious power; it is equally a crime, to enslave the human mind, under the pretence of protecting religion. The reckless mind, rashly hurrying to the attack of superstition, has often, though by mistake, attacked intelligence itself; but religion, of itself alone, never had an enemy; except indeed as there have been theorists, whose harmless ingenuity has denied the existence between right and wrong, between justice and its opposite. Positive enactments against irreligion, like positive enactments against fanaticism, provoke the evil, which they were designed to prevent. Danger is inviting.

CHAP. X.
1650.

If left to himself, he that vilifies the foundations of morals and happiness, does but publish his own unworthiness; and the law which punished the offence by branding, was right in its spirit; it was wrong only in making the magistrate the instrument. The blasphemer brands himself. A public prosecution is a mantle to cover his shame; for to suffer for opinion's sake is courageous; and courage is always an honorable quality. Public opinion, when freely exercised, can give life to institutions and mould the forms of society; and there are some kinds of crime which it alone can punish, and which it punishes with terrific energy. When public opinion, deliberately, and without passion, pronounces the sentence of ignominy, it sticks like the fabled garment, which could not be taken off but with the flesh itself. In such a case, the punishment is always around the culprit, and he can no more escape from it, than from the atmosphere.

The conscientious austerity of the colonists, invigorated by the love of power, led to a course of legislation, which, if it was followed by the melancholy result of bloodshed, was also followed among the cool and reflecting freemen of the new world by complete emancipation from bigotry, achieved by the friends of religion, without any of the excesses of intolerant infidelity. The inefficiency of fanatic laws was made plain by the fearless resistance of a still more stubborn fanaticism.

Saltonstall wrote from Europe, that, but for their severities, the people of Massachusetts would have been "the eyes of God's people in England." The consistent Sir Henry Vane had urged, that "the oppugners of the congregational way should not from its own principles and practice, be taught to root it out." "It were better," he added, "not to censure any persons for matters of a religious concernment." The elder Winthrop had, I believe, relented before his death, and, it is said, had become weary of banishing heretics; the soul of the younger Winthrop was incapable of harboring a thought of intolerant cruelty; but the rugged Dudley was not mellowed by old age. "God forbid," said he, "our love for the truth should be grown so cold, that we should tolerate errors.—I die no libertine."—"Better tolerate hypocrites and tares than thorns and briars," affirmed Cotton. "Polypiety," echoed Ward, "is the greatest impiety in the world. To say that men ought to have liberty of conscience is impious ignorance."—"Religion," said Norton from the pulpit, "admits of no eccentric motions." But the people did not entirely respond to these extravagant views, into which personal interest, combined with honest bigotry, had betrayed the elders, and the love of unity, so favorable to independence, had betrayed the leading men. The public mind was awakened to inquiry; the topic of the power of the civil magistrate in religious affairs, was become the theme of perpetual discussion; and it needed all the force of established authority to sustain the doctrine of persecution. Massachusetts was already in the state of transition, and it was just before expiring, that

CHAP. X.

1651.

July 20.

bigotry, with convulsive energy, exhibited its worst aspect.

Anabaptism was to the establishment a dangerous rival. When Clarke, the pure and tolerant baptist of Rhode Island, one of the happy few who succeed in acquiring an estate of beneficence, and connecting the glory of their name with the liberty and happiness of a commonwealth, began to preach to a small audience in Lynn, he was seized by the civil officers. Being compelled to attend with the congregation, he expressed his aversion by a harmless indecorum, which would yet have been without excuse, had his presence been voluntary. He and his companions were tried and condemned to pay a fine of twenty or thirty pounds; and Holmes, who refused to pay his fine, was whipped unmercifully.

Since a particular form of worship had become a part of the civil establishment, irreligion was now to be punished as a civil offence. The state was a model of Christ's kingdom on earth; treason against the civil government was treason against Christ; and reciprocally, as the gospel had the right paramount, blasphemy, or what a jury should call blasphemy, was the highest offence in the catalogue of crimes. To deny any book of the old or new testament to be the written and infallible word of God, was punishable by fine or by stripes, and, in case of obstinacy, by exile or death. Absence from "the ministry of the word" was punished by a fine.

1653. By degrees the spirit of the establishment began to subvert the fundamental principles of Indepen-

LAWS AGAINST IRRELIGION AND SECTARIANISM.

dency. The liberty of prophesying was refused, except the approbation of four elders, or of a county court, had been obtained. Remonstrance[1] was useless. The union of church and state was fast corrupting both; it mingled base ambition with the former; it gave a false direction to the legislation of the latter. And at last the general court claimed for itself, for the council, and for any two organic churches, the right of silencing any person who was not as yet ordained. Thus rapidly did human nature display its power! The creation of a national, uncompromising church led the congregationalists of Massachusetts to the display of the very passions, which had disgraced their English persecutors; and Laud was justified by the men whom he had wronged.

CHAP.
X.

1658.

But if the baptists were feared, as professing doctrines tending to disorganize society, how much more reason was there to dread such emissaries of the quakers, as appeared in Massachusetts! The first and most noisy advocates of any popular sect, are apt to be men of little consideration. They who have the least to risk, are most clamorous for novelties; and the early advocates of the quakers in New-England displayed little of the mild philosophy, the statesman-like benevolence, of Penn and his disciples; though they possessed the virtue of passive resistance in perfection. Left to themselves, they appeared like a motley tribe of persons, half fanatic, half insane; without consideration, and without

[1] See Felt's Salem, p. 188 and 533. iii. Mass. Hist. Coll. v. i. p. 40.

CHAP. definite purposes. Persecution called them forth to
X. show, what intensity of will can dwell in the depths
of the human heart. They were like those weeds,
which are unsightly to the eye, and which only
when trampled, give out precious perfumes.

The rise of "the people called quakers," was one
of the most remarkable results of the protestant
revolution. It was a consequence of the moral warfare against corruption; the aspiration of the human mind after a perfect emancipation from the long reign of bigotry and superstition. It grew up with men, who were impatient at the slow progress of the reformation, the tardy advances of intellectual liberty. A better opportunity will offer for explaining its influence on American institutions. It was
1656. in the month of July, 1656, that two of its mem-
July. bers, Mary Fisher and Ann Austin, arrived in the road before Boston.[1] There was as yet no statute respecting quakers, but on the general law against heresy, their trunks were searched, and their books burnt by the hangman; they themselves, after being kept for five weeks in close custody, and examined, as if to discover signs of witchcraft, were thrust out of the jurisdiction. Eight others were, during the year, sent back to England. The rebuke enlarged the ambition of Mary Fisher; she repaired alone to Adrianople, and delivered a message to the Grand

[1] I compose the narrative from comparing the quaker accounts, by Gould and Sewell, full of documents, with those of the colonial historians. There is no essential difference. Every leading work has something on the subject.—The apologies of the colonists, especially Norton's book, The Heart of N. E. Rent, still exist, and are before me.

Sultan. The Turks thought her crazed, and she passed through their army "without hurt or scoff."

Yet the next year, although a special law now prohibited the introduction of quakers, Mary Dyer, an Antinomian exile, and Ann Burden, came into the colony: the former was claimed by her husband, and taken to Rhode Island; the latter was sent to England. A woman who had come all the way from London, to warn the magistrates against persecution, was whipped with twenty stripes. Some who had been banished, came a second time; they were imprisoned, whipped, and once more sent away, under penalty of further punishment, if they returned again. A fine was imposed on such as should entertain any "of the accursed sect;" and a quaker, after the first conviction, was to lose one ear, after the second another, after the third to have the tongue bored with a red-hot iron. It was but for a very short time, that the menace of these enormities found place in the statute book. The colony was so ashamed of the order for mutilation, that it was soon repealed, and was never printed. But this legislation was fruitful of results. Quakers swarmed, where they were feared. They came expressly because they were not welcome; and threats were construed as invitations. A penalty of ten shillings was now imposed on every person for being present at a quaker meeting, and of five pounds for speaking at such meeting. In the execution of the laws, the pride of consistency involved the magistrates in acts of extreme cruelty.

CHAP. X.

The extravagances of the early itinerant quakers had created universal apprehension; even in Rhode-Island, though that colony would "have no law, whereby to punish any for only declaring by words their minds concerning the things of God." But the Dutch of New-Holland joined in the attack; and "if no execution took place in Virginia," says the tolerant Jefferson, "it was not owing to the moderation of the church or spirit of the legislature."

The government of Massachusetts at length resolved to follow the advice of the commissioners for the united colonies; from which the younger Winthrop alone had dissented. Willing that the quakers should live in peace in any other part of the wide world, yet desiring to deter them effectually from coming within its jurisdiction, the general court, after much resistance and by a majority of but a single vote, banished them on pain of death. The object of severity was not to persecute, but to exclude them. "For the security of the flock," said Norton, "we pen up the wolf; but a door is purposely left open, whereby he may depart at his pleasure." Vain legislation! and frivolous apology! The soul, by its freedom and immortality, preserves its convictions or its frenzies even amidst the threat of death.

It has been attempted to excuse the atrocity of the law, because the quakers avowed principles, that seemed subversive of social order. Any government might on the same grounds find in its unreasonable fears an excuse for its cruelties. The argument justifies the expulsion of the Moors from

Spain, of the Huguenots from France; and it forms a complete apology for Laud, who was honest in his bigotry, persecuting the puritans with the same good faith, with which he recorded his dreams. The fears of one class of men are not the measure of the rights of another.

It is said, that the quakers themselves rushed upon the sword, and so were suicides. If it were so, the men who held the sword, were accessaries to the crime.

It is true, that some of the quakers were extravagant and foolish; they cried out from the windows at the magistrates and ministers, that passed by; and mocked the civil and religious institutions of the country. They riotously interrupted public worship; and women, forgetting the decorum of their sex, smeared their faces and even went naked through the streets. Indecency, however, is best punished by slight chastisements. The house of Folly has perpetual succession; yet numerous as is the progeny, each individual of the family is exceedingly short-lived, and dies the sooner, where its extravagance is excessive. A fault against manners may not be punished by a crime against nature.

The act itself admits of no defence; the actors can plead no other justification than delusion. Prohibiting the arrival of quakers was not persecution; and banishment is a term, hardly to be used of one who has not acquired a home. When a pauper is sent to his native town, he is not called an exile. A ship from abroad, which should enter the harbor of

Marseilles against the order of the health-officer, would be sunk by the guns of the fort. The government of Massachusetts applied similar quarantine rules to the morals of the colony, and would as little tolerate what seemed a ruinous heresy, as the French would tolerate the plague. I do not plead the analogy; the cases are as widely different, as this world and the next; I desire only to relate facts with precision. The ship, suspected of infection, might sail for another port; and the quaker, if he came once, was sent away; if he came again, was sentenced to death, and then might still quit the jurisdiction on a promise of returning no more. Servetus did but desire leave to continue his journey. The inquisition hearkened to secret whispers for grounds of accusation; the magistrates of Massachusetts left all in peace but the noisy brawlers, and left to them the opportunity of escape. For four centuries Europe had maintained the monstrous doctrine, that heresy should be punished by death. In Spain more persons have been burned for their opinions, than Massachusetts then contained inhabitants. Under Charles V., in the Netherlands alone, the number of those who were hanged, beheaded, buried alive, or burned, for religious opinion, was fifty thousand, says father Paul; the whole carnage amounted, says Grotius,[1] to not less than one hundred thousand. America was guilty of the death of four individuals; and they

---

[1] Sarpi, Istoria del Concil. Trid. L. v. Opere, v. ii. p. 33. E con tutto, che il numero ne' Paesi Bassi tra impiccati, decapitati, sepolti vivi, ed abbruciati aggiugnesse a cinquantamila. Annales, p. 12, ed. 1678. Carnificata hominum non minus centum millia.

fell victims rather to the contest of will, than to the opinion, that quakerism was a capital crime.

Of four persons, ordered to depart the jurisdiction on pain of death, Mary Dyar, an Antinomian exile, and Nicholas Davis, obeyed. Marmaduke Stephenson and William Robinson had come on purpose to offer their lives; instead of departing, they went from place to place "to build up their friends in the faith." In October, Mary Dyar returned. Thus there were three persons, who were arraigned on the sanguinary law. Robinson pleaded in his defence the special message and command of God. "Blessed be God who calls me to testify against wicked and unjust men." Stephenson refused to speak, till sentence had been pronounced; and then he imprecated a curse on his judges. Mary Dyar exclaimed, "The will of the Lord be done," and returned to the prison "full of joy." From the jail she wrote a remonstrance. "Were ever such laws heard of among a people, that profess Christ come in the flesh? Have you no other weapons but such laws to fight against spiritual wickedness withal, as you call it? Woe is me for you. Ye are disobedient and deceived. Let my request be as Esther's to Ahasuerus. You will not repent that you were kept from shedding blood, though it was by a woman." The three were led forth to execution. "I die for Christ," said Robinson: "We suffer not as evil doers, but for conscience' sake," were the last words of his companion. Mary Dyar was reprieved. "Let me suffer as my brethren," she exclaimed, "unless you will annul your wicked law." She was conveyed out of the colony; but soon returning, she also perished on the gallows. "We desired their lives absent, rather than their deaths present," was the miserable apology offered for these proceedings.

These cruelties excited great discontent. Yet William Leddra was put upon trial for the same causes. While the trial was proceeding, Wenlock Christison, already banished on pain of death, entered the court, and struck dismay into the judges, who found their severities ineffectual. Leddra was desired to accept his life, on condition of promising to come no more within the jurisdiction. He refused, and was hanged.

Christison met his persecutors with undaunted courage. By what law, he demanded, will ye put me to death?—We have a law, it was answered, and by it you are to die.—So said the Jews to Christ. But who empowered you to make that law?—We have a patent, and may make our own laws.—Can you make laws repugnant to those of England?— No.—Then you are gone beyond your bounds. Your heart is as rotten towards the king as towards God. I demand to be tried by the laws of England, and there is no law there to hang quakers.—The English banish Jesuits on pain of death; and with equal justice we may banish quakers.—The jury returned a verdict of guilty. Wenlock replied, "I deny all guilt; my conscience is clear before God." The magistrates were divided in pronouncing sentence; the vote was put a second time, and there appeared a majority for the doom of death. "What do you gain," cried Christison, "by taking quakers' lives? For the last man that ye put to death, here are five come in his room. If ye have power to take my life, God can raise up ten of his servants in my stead."

The voice of the people had always been averse to bloodshed; the magistrates, infatuated for a season, became convinced of their error; Wenlock, with twenty-seven of his friends, was discharged from prison; and the doctrine of toleration, with the pledges of peace, hovered like the dove at the window of the ark, waiting to be received into its rightful refuge.

The victims of intolerance met death bravely; they would be entitled to perpetual honor as martyrs, were it not that their own extravagances occasioned the foul enactment, to repeal which they laid down their lives. Far from introducing religious charity, their conduct irritated the government to pass the laws, of which they were the victims. But for them the country had been guiltless of blood; and causes were already in action, which were fast substituting the firmness and the charity of intelligence for the severity of religious bigotry. It was ever the custom, and it soon became the law in puritan New-England, that "none of the brethren shall suffer so much barbarism in their families, as not to teach their children and apprentices so much learning, as may enable them perfectly to read the English tongue."

"To the end that learning may not be buried in the graves of our forefathers," it was ordered, "that every township, after the Lord hath increased them to the number of fifty householders, shall appoint one to teach all children to write and read; and where any town shall increase to the number of one hundred families, they shall set up a grammar school; the masters thereof being able to instruct youth so far as they may be fitted for the university."[1] The press began its work in 1639. "When New-England was poor, and they were but few in number, there was a spirit to encourage learning." Six years after the arrival of Winthrop, the general court voted a sum, equal to a year's rate of the whole colony, towards the erection of a college. In 1638, John Harvard, who arrived in the Bay, only to fall a victim to the most wasting disease of the climate, desiring to connect himself imperishably with the happiness of his adopted country, bequeathed to the college one half of his estate and all his library. The infant institution was a favorite; Connecticut, and Plymouth, and the towns in the East,[2] often contributed little offerings to promote its success; the gift of the rent of a ferry was a proof of the care of the state; and once at least every family in each of the colonies gave to the college at Cambridge twelve pence, or a peck of corn, or its value in genuine, unadulterated wampumpeag;[3] while the magistrates and wealthier men

[1] Col. Laws, 74, 186.
[2] Folsom's Saco and Biddeford, p. 108.
[3] Pierce's History of H. C. Winthrop, v. ii. p. 214, 216. Everett's Yale Address, p. 3.

were profuse in their liberality. The college, in return, exerted a powerful influence in forming the early character of the country. In this, at least, it can never have a rival. In these measures, especially in the laws establishing common schools, lies the secret of the success and character of New-England. Every child, as it was born into the world, was lifted from the earth by the genius of the country, and, in the statutes of the land, received, as its birthright, a pledge of care for its morals and its mind.

There are some who love to enumerate the singularities of the early puritans. They were opposed to wigs; they could preach against veils; they denounced long hair; they disliked the cross in the banner, as much as the people of Paris disliked the lilies of the Bourbons; and for analogous reasons. They would not allow Christmas day to be kept sacred; they called neither months, nor days, nor seasons, nor churches, nor inns, by the names common in England. The grave Romans legislated on the costume of men, and their senate could even stoop to interfere with the triumphs of those, to whom civic honors are denied; the fathers of New-England prohibited frivolous fashions in their own dress; and their austerity, checking extravagance even in woman, frowned on her hoods of silk and her scarfs of tiffany, extended the length of her sleeve to the wrist, and limited its greatest width to half an ell. The puritans were formal and precise in their manners; singular in the forms of their legislation; rigid in the observance of their principles.

The courts of Massachusetts respected in practice the code of Moses; the island of Rhode-Island enacted for a year or two a Jewish masquerade; in New-Haven the constituent committee were called the seven pillars, hewn out for the house of wisdom. But these are only the outward forms, which gave to the new sect its marked exterior. If from the outside peculiarities, which so easily excite the sneer of the superficial observer, we look to the genius of the sect itself, Puritanism was Religion struggling for the People. "Its absurdities," says its enemy, "were the shelter for the noble principles of liberty." It was its office to engraft the new institutions of popular energy upon the old European system of a feudal aristocracy and popular servitude; the good was permanent; the outward emblems which were the signs of the party, were of transient duration; like the clay and ligaments, with which the graft is held in its place, and which are brushed away, as soon as the scion is firmly united.

The principles of puritanism proclaimed the civil magistrate subordinate to the authority of religion; and its haughtiness, in this respect, has been compared to "the infatuated arrogance" of a Roman Pontiff. In the firmness with which the principle was asserted, the puritans did not yield to the Catholics; and, if the will of God is the criterion of justice, both were in one sense in the right. The question arises, who shall be the interpreter of that will? In the Roman Catholic church the office was claimed by the infallible Pontiff. Puritanism conceded no such power to its clergy; the church existed, independent of its pastor; the will of the majority was its law; and each one of the brethren possessed equal rights with the elders. Puritanism exalted the laity. Every individual who had experienced the raptures of devotion, every believer, who, in his moments of ecstasy, had felt the assurance of the favor of God, was in his own eyes a consecrated person. For him the wonderful counsels of the Almighty had chosen a Saviour; for him the laws of nature had been suspended and controlled, the heavens had opened, the earth had quaked, the sun had veiled his face, and Christ had died and had risen again; for him prophets and apostles had revealed to the world the oracles and the will of God. Viewing himself as an object of the divine favor, and in this connection denying to himself all merit, he prostrated himself in the dust before heaven; looking out upon mankind, how could he but respect himself, whom God had chosen and redeemed? He cherished hope; he possessed faith; as he walked the earth, his heart was in the skies. Angels hovered round his path, charged to minister to his soul; spirits of darkness leagued together to tempt him from his allegiance. His burning piety could use no liturgy; his penitence could reveal his transgressions to no confessor. He knew no superior in sanctity. He could as little become the slave of a priestcraft, as of a despot. He was himself a judge of the orthodoxy of the elders; and if he feared the invisible powers of the air, of darkness, and of hell, he feared nothing on earth. Puritanism constituted, not the Christian clergy, but the Christian people, the interpreter of the divine will. The voice of the majority was the voice of God; and the issue of puritanism was therefore popular sovereignty.

The effects of puritanism display its true character still more distinctly. Ecclesiastical tyranny is of all kinds the worst; its fruits are cowardice, idleness, ignorance and poverty; puritanism was a life-giving spirit; activity, thrift, intelligence followed in its train; and as for courage, a coward and a puritan never went together.

It was in self-defence, that puritanism in America began those transient persecutions, of which the excesses shall find in me no apologist; and which yet were no more than a train of mists, hovering, of an autumn morning, over the channel of a fine river, that diffused freshness and fertility wherever it wound. The people did not attempt to convert others, but to protect themselves; they never punished opinion as such; they never attempted to torture or terrify men into orthodoxy. The history of religious persecution in New-England is simply this; the puritans established a government in America such as the laws of natural justice warranted, and such as the statutes of England did not warrant; and that was done by men, who still acknowledged the duty of a limited allegiance to the parent state. The episcopalians had declared themselves the enemies of the party, and waged against it a war of extermination; puritanism excluded them from its asylum.

Roger Williams, the apostle of "soul-liberty," weakened the cause of civil independence, by impairing its unity, and he was expelled, even though Massachusetts always bore good testimony to his spotless virtues.[1] Wheelwright and his friends, in their zeal for strict Calvinism, forgot their duty as citizens; and they also were exiled. The anabaptist, who could not be relied upon as an ally, was guarded as a foe. The quakers denounced the worship of New-England as an abomination, and its government as treason; and therefore they were excluded on pain of death. The fanatic for Calvinism was a fanatic for liberty; and he defended his creed, for, in the moral warfare for freedom, his creed was a part of his army, and his most faithful ally in the battle.

For "New-England was a religious plantation, not a plantation for trade. The profession of the purity of doctrine, worship, and discipline was written on her forehead." "We all," says the confederacy in the oldest of American written constitutions, "came into these parts of America to enjoy the liberties of the gospel in purity and peace." "He that made religion as twelve and the world as thirteen, had not the spirit of a true New-England man." Religion was the object of the emigrants; it was also their consolation. With this the wounds of the outcast were healed, and the tears of exile sweetened.[2]

Of all contemporary sects, the puritans were the

[1] Backus, v. i. p. 155. Winthrop, v. ii. p. 193. Norton's choice sermons, p. 15. Higginson's Cause of God, p. 11.
[2] Norton's Heart, &c. p. 58. Articles of Confederacy.

most free from credulity; and in their zeal for reform pushed their regulations to what some would consider a sceptical extreme. So many superstitions had been bundled up with every venerable institution of Europe, that ages have not yet dislodged them all. The puritans at once emancipated themselves from a crowd of observances. They established a worship purely spiritual. To them the elements remained but wine and bread; they invoked no saints; they adored no crucifix; they kissed no book; they asked no absolution; they paid no tithes; they saw in the priest nothing more than a man; the church, as a place of worship, was to them but a meeting-house; they dug no graves in consecrated earth; unlike their posterity, they married without a minister, and buried the dead without a prayer. Witchcraft had not been made the subject of sceptical consideration; and in the years in which Scotland sacrificed hecatombs to the delusion, there were three victims in New-England. Dark crimes, that seemed without a motive, may have been pursued under that name; I find one record of a trial for witchcraft, where the prisoner was proved a murderess.

On every subject but religion, the mildness of puritan legislation corresponded to the popular character of puritan doctrines. Hardly a nation of Europe has as yet made its criminal law so humane, as that of early New-England. A crowd of offences was at one sweep brushed from the catalogue of capital crimes. The idea was never received, that the forfeiture of life may be demanded for the protection of property; the punishment for theft, for burglary, and highway robbery, was far more mild than the penalties imposed even by modern American legislation. Of divorce I have found no example; yet a clause in one of the statutes recognizes the possibility of such an event. Divorce from bed and board, the separate maintenance without the dissolution of the marriage contract, an anomaly in protestant legislation, that punishes the innocent more than the guilty, was utterly abhorrent from their principles. The care for posterity was every where visible. Since the sanctity of the marriage bed is the safeguard of families, and can alone interest the father in the welfare and instruction of his offspring, the purity of the wife was protected by the penalty of death; a penalty, which was inexorably enforced. If, in this respect, the laws were more severe, in another they were more lenient, than modern manners approve. The girl, whom youth and affection betrayed into weakness, was censured, pitied, and forgiven; the law compelled the seducer of innocence to marry the person, over whose heart he had obtained such power. The law implies an extremely pure community; in no other would it find a place in the statute-book; in no other would public opinion tolerate the rule. Yet it need not have surprised the countrymen of Raleigh, or the subjects of the grand-children of Clarendon.

The benevolence of the early puritans appears from other examples. Domestic discipline was highly valued; but if the law was severe against the undutiful child, it was also severe against a faithless parent.—Even the brute creation was not forgotten; and cruelty towards animals was a civil offence.— The sympathies of the colonists were wide; a regard for protestant Germany is as old as emigration; and during the thirty years' war, the whole people of New-England held fasts and offered prayers for the success of their Saxon brethren.

The first years of the residence of puritans in America, were years of great hardship and affliction; it is an error to suppose that this short season of distress was not promptly followed by abundance and happiness. The people were full of affections; and the objects of love were around them. They struck root in the soil immediately. They enjoyed religion. They were from the first, industrious, and enterprising, and frugal; and affluence followed of course. When persecution ceased in England, there were already in New-England "thousands who would not change their place for any other in the world;" and they were tempted in vain with invitations to the Bahama Isles, to Ireland, to Jamaica, to Trinidad. The purity of morals completes the picture of colonial felicity. "As Ireland will not brook venomous beasts, so will not that land vile livers." One might dwell there "from year to year and not see a drunkard, or hear an oath, or meet a beggar."[1] The consequence was universal health; one of the chief elements of public happiness. The average duration of life in New-England, compared with Europe, was

---

[1] New-England's First Fruits, printed 1643, p. 23, 26.

doubled; and the human race was so vigorous, that of all who were born into the world, more than two in ten, full four in nineteen, attained the age of seventy. Of those who lived beyond ninety, the proportion, as compared with European tables of longevity, was still more remarkable.

I have dwelt the longer on the character of the early puritans of New-England, for they are the parents of one-third the whole white population of the United States. In the first ten or twelve years, and there was never afterwards any increase from England, we have seen, that there came over twenty one thousand two hundred, or four thousand families. Their descendants are now not far from four millions. Each family has multiplied on the average to one thousand souls. To New-York and Ohio, where they constitute half the population, they have carried the puritan system of free schools; and their example is spreading it through the civilized world.

Historians have loved to eulogize the manners and virtues, the glory and the benefits, of chivalry. Puritanism accomplished for mankind far more. If it had the sectarian crime of intolerance, chivalry had the vices of dissoluteness. The knights were brave from gallantry of spirit; the puritans from the fear of God. The knights were proud of loyalty; the puritans, of liberty. The knights did homage to monarchs, in whose smile they beheld honor, whose rebuke was the wound of disgrace; the puritans, disdaining ceremony, would not bend the knee to the King of kings. The former valued courtesy; the

CHAP. X.

latter, justice. The former adorned society by graceful refinements; the latter founded national grandeur on universal education. The institutions of chivalry were subverted by the gradually increasing weight, and knowledge, and opulence, of the industrious classes; the puritans, rallying upon those classes, planted in their hearts the undying principles of democratic liberty.

1660. The golden age of puritanism was passing away. Time was silently softening its asperities, and the revolutions of England prepared an era in its fortunes. Massachusetts never acknowledged Richard Cromwell; it read clearly in the aspect of parties, the impending restoration. The protector had left the benefits of self-government and the freedom of commerce to New-England and to Virginia; and Maryland, by the act of her inhabitants, was just beginning to share in the same advantages. Would the dynasty of the Stuarts deal benevolently with the colonies? Would it imitate the magnanimity of Cromwell, and suffer the staple of the south still to seek its market freely throughout the world? Could the returning monarch forgive the friends of the puritans in England? Would he show favor to the institutions, that the outcasts had reared beyond the Atlantic?

END OF VOL. I.